x

For Peter, Michael, Andrew, Robert,
all my lovely chaps

By the same author
Country Walks in Clavering (1987, out of print)
Discover Clavering (1990, out of print)
Discover Walden (1996)
History Walks in Clavering (forthcoming)

© Jacqueline Cooper, 2000

ISBN 1 873669 06 2

Published by Cooper Publications, 24 Pelham Road, Clavering, Saffron Walden, Essex, CB11 4PQ.

Origination by The Local History Press Ltd, 3 Devonshire Promenade, Nottingham, NG7 2DS. Printed by The Russell Press, Russell House, Bulwell Lane, Basford, Nottingham NG6 0BT.

Contents

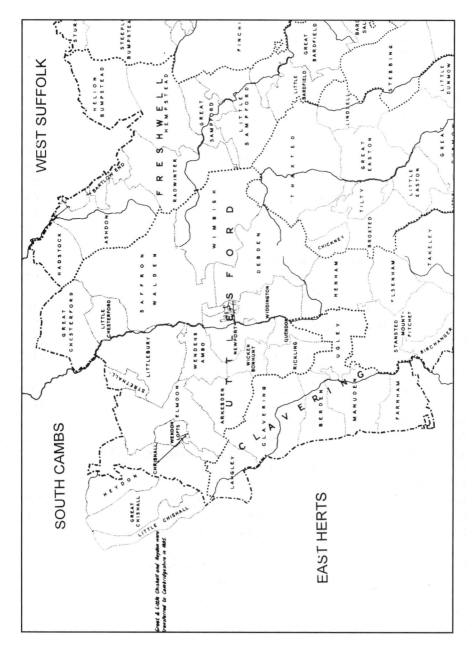

Map 1: North-west Essex (courtesy of Essex Record Office)

4

List of illustrations, tables & maps

§ Town Archive
† Museum
¶ ERO
* John Ryland Museum Manchester

Acknowledgements for help with photographs to John Clayden (cover picture), Sean Brady and Malcolm White. Photographs as follows by courtesy of: § Saffron Walden Town Council; ‡ Saffron Walden Museum; † Saffron Walden Town Library; ¶ Essex Record Office; *John Rylands Library, Manchester.

Acknowledgements

The core of this book began as an MA thesis, *Philanthropy and Social Control in Saffron Walden*, for the course in Local & Regional History at the University of Essex, but its origins ripple out in all directions and I owe a great debt to many people who have helped along the way. They include Eileen Ludgate whose Clavering & Langley Local History Group first inspired a passion for history; Tom Williamson who enthused an understanding of the wider landscape; Ruth Finnegan, Michael Drake and others whose pioneering Open University course, *Family & Community History* opened up a whole new world, and Susan Oosthuizen who tutored it so brilliantly; while Arthur Brown's books and lectures have been most influential in the themes of this book.

Closer to home, Martyn Everett at the Town Library and his wife Zofia at the Essex Record Office Archive Access Point, both in Saffron Walden, have given to me, as they do to so many researchers, unstinting moral and practical support. Access to archives has also been greatly facilitated by the excellent co-operation of Malcolm White of Saffron Walden Town Council; Julia Bazley and the other staff of Saffron Walden Museum; and other archivists in the Essex Record Office and various repositories.

A number of people have generously given time to read, comment or offer advice on sections of the book: they include John Archer (allotments), Gillian Collins (education), Rev. David Monkton (religion), Maureen Scollan (police), Kate Thompson (poor laws) and Dan Weinbren (friendly societies). Early drafts of the chapters on allotments, crime and protest were also discussed with D.A. Stacey. There has been additional help from Fiona Bengsten, Sean Brady, Barry Dackombe, Mrs M. Day, Sarah Kirkpatrick, Olive Newman, J.E. Maddams, Margaret Richardson, Malcolm White and Rev. Harry Wood. Martyn Everett, Imogen Mollet and Angela Archer have kindly read and commented on the whole text, with numerous useful suggestions.

My greatest debt, however, is undoubtedly to fellow delver into the town archives, Laurie Barker, who has left no stone unturned to read every chapter in detail and offered criticism, encouragement, additions, examples and explanations, freely sharing the fruits of his own family history research. The book could not have been completed without his input. I would also like to thank my family, friends and employers for their patience and understanding, and Susan Griffiths of Local History Press who never failed to answer myriad queries, and took great care in designing this volume. Not least, the other historians, whose works are referenced here, and who left us such a rich legacy on which to build. In the course of researching *The Well-Ordered Town* and the earlier book, *Discover Walden*, I have learned to love the town, and feel proud to give back to its people this distillation of seven years of study, in gratitude for so much they have shared with me.

Jacqueline Cooper
Clavering, July 2000

Foreword

Although there are several written accounts of the history of the town, periods of Walden's history remain largely unexplored by the historian. A pity, because the town is remarkable for the large number of old buildings which survive to give testimony to the past, and for retaining a vast quantity of historical documentation.

This is particularly true for the nineteenth century. When we reflect on Saffron Walden's history we are inclined to think of the Mediaeval and Tudor periods which shaped the town, but we tend to forget that the Saffron Walden we know was forged in the nineteenth century. Many of the buildings that dominate the Market Place are nineteenth century buildings, and the cultural institutions that provide the focus for our community, such as the Library and the Museum, have their origins in the first half of the nineteenth century.

Our image of the first part of the nineteenth century has been shaped by the historical fictions of television, and by the emphasis of past local historians who have looked at the positive achievements of the period, but who have neglected to explore the darker side of the social picture. The theft of the commons by enclosure, desperate poverty, the construction of the vast and intimidating workhouse, were all part of the same social processes that gave rise to the allotment system and the Town Mission.

These social changes did not go uncontested in a town that had been shaken by Bread Riots in 1795. The countryside around the town became the focus for widespread rural unrest that made itself felt through rick-burning and poaching, as ordinary people attempted to make history and not just be its passive victims.

Jacqueline Cooper has not been content to accept traditional accounts of Walden's past but has returned to the original historical records in a painstaking attempt to reconstruct the social structure and daily life of Saffron Walden in the first half of the nineteenth century. Her research has laid bare the unequal power relations that split the community into 'haves' and 'have-nots' and explains how the often self-serving nature of social philanthropy was used as a means of reinforcing that division.

This is the real stuff of local history, which will force us to discard our 'chocolate-box' image of Saffron Walden.

Martyn Everett
Local Studies Librarian
Saffron Walden

Introduction

'We cannot but hope that an additional stimulus to the exertions of the Noble Recorder, and other friends of humanity and social order, will be given both to the allotment system which has been so benevolently established in this parish, and in devising measures by which the young may be brought up in habits of industry instead of their becoming unworthy members of the community and neighbourhood to which they belong... express a hope that the painful scenes yesterday and today will not again be witnessed in this well-ordered town.'

John Player's weighty speech, as foreman of the grand jury at the conclusion of a trial which shocked Saffron Walden in 1833, very much sums up the theme of this book, the efforts to keep order against a rising tide of poverty and petty crime among a burgeoning population. A sense of crisis first became noticeable in the 1790s. In 1792 the remarkably prescient book, *Rights of Man* by the revolutionary Tom Paine, was banned from Walden's bookshop and the seller hounded out of town. His crime was daring to make available a volume which deplored the way the poor were treated and proposed radical reforms of the class system. Three years later came the famous Walden food riots. Seventy years on, a 50,000-word journal kept by the town missionary highlighted the appalling conditions in which many of the town and parish poor still lived. Yet in between these dates, the leading lights of the town had expended huge amounts of energy on a carefully-constructed system of philanthropic, educational and religious outreach to the poor. This book is a story of this extraordinary and significant period in Saffron Walden's history.

Although the book as a whole encompasses this 70-year span, in fact each chapter has its own chronology, and can be read as a separate essay, while linked by a common theme, divided into two parts. The first part, 'Challenges', looks at the economic and social background, political and judicial problems, such as the sectarian rivalry and central government interference, which threatened to undermine attempts to present a united front to deal with pauperism, crime and protest. The so-called 'Captain Swing' riots, which erupted all over southern England in 1830, were a seminal event. The second part, 'Responses', illustrates the third arm of elite action — the others being the poor law and the criminal law — the use of philanthropy to deflect those challenges.

As a result of all this effort, if Walden worthies gazed with pride around their town in the mid-nineteenth century, they could congratulate themselves on having materially contributed to the comforts of the poor. Much of the extra provision, expanded from the 1820s onwards, was a vital lifeline, but these efforts also did little to address the fundamental inequalities which produced such dire poverty in the first place. Worthies were merely papering over the cracks, and moreover to the sound of their own applause. The first-hand evidence of Solomon Barton's journal, of which verbatim extracts appear as a postscript to the book, poses a question mark over whether an external appearance of busyness and quiescence constituted the well-ordered town of elite desire. It may emerge that much of what we enjoy today was actually built on the backs of the less well-remembered citizens, and came at a high price, the promotion of a deeply unjust social system; and that true 'respectability' could seldom be conveyed via charity, but must ultimately be linked with good housing, public health, sound education, secure employment and a living wage.

So much has been written about Walden that it is worth underlining what is new in this volume, a great deal of which has not previously been gathered together within one book. The chapter on allotments, for instance, explores material unique not only here, but in the wider studies of allotments: a clear link between Walden's scheme and the 1830 riots forms a central pivot of the argument. Likewise, the discussion on Primitive Methodism is original and offers, as do the details on friendly societies, rare glimpses into working-class self-help in this period. There are also relatively original discussions on political radicalism, anti-poorlaw protest, agricultural show prizes, workhouse schooling and many other topics. A reappraisal of central figures like John Player and the third Lord Braybrooke also seems called-for. The town history is put into its local, regional and national context, stressing cross-border influences in religion and radicalism. My own village of Clavering, the largest in the district, features among rural examples.

Many far-flung and thus under-used resources are in evidence: the regular Walden coverage in the *Essex Standard* accessed at Colchester Library, and other newspapers kept at the Colindale Newspaper Library; Charity Commission, Guardians' and Home Office correspondence at the Public Record Office; British and National School archives in London; reports in Parliamentary Papers; Methodist archives in Manchester and Primitive Methodist material only recently deposited at the Essex Record Office. The unique and invaluable Town Mission records, lost to Walden for 30 years, are here restored to prominence. The fascinating collection of John Player mss in Saffron Walden Museum have yielded numerous gems. Indeed the time is long overdue when town archives belonging to Saffron Walden Town Council, the Museum, the Library, the ERO and other repositories should be linked. For example, an education survey and its Bible Society context of 1825, its constituent sections separately housed, are here brought together; likewise an employment survey and listing of 1832. Many of the town's records, after cataloguing by the Saffron Walden Archive Society, will ultimately be available in digital form for ease of access.

Finding archives is one thing: turning them into book form something else. But historical research, to be worthwhile, needs to be shared in some accessible form, whether written, oral or digital. This is a critical and challenging study, but the aim is less to denigrate the achievements of early nineteenth century philanthropists, than to put their activities into their social context, redressing the balance somewhat from the sanitized, one-dimensional and mythical. The material has been very carefully checked both by myself and others, but a book which breaks new ground on complex issues is unlikely to have escaped some errors of interpretation or emphasis. Sometimes, authors just have to be bold, for to write only that which is utterly certain and safely anodyne would be to produce a very dull and limited book, or never to publish at all. Historians must analyse and interpret, compare and contextualize, however tentatively, otherwise history books become inward-looking, serving only to repeat what is already known and not to move our thinking forward.

The hope is that *The Well-Ordered Town* will be seen as a contribution to debate, rather than as words set in stone. This is *A Story of Saffron Walden, 1792–1862*, not the whole story or the only story. To the end that others may be inspired to pick up where I have left off, considerable space is devoted to a useful index, detailed references and a complete bibliography of primary sources and selected secondary works. There is enormous scope for further studies: on the malting industry, transport networks, slum housing, farming, enclosure, local politics, the old and new poor laws, the Quarter Sessions, labourers' unrest, charities, friendly societies, schooling, religious Dissent, the relationship between the town and Audley End, and numerous other subjects.

I lack the resources truly to rescue the nineteenth century Walden poor from what E.P. Thompson so memorably called 'the enormous condescension of posterity', but have nevertheless attempted to do so. That the poor had their story too cannot be doubted, but sadly it is not an easy one to discover, for many were illiterate and left little record of, for example, their own vibrant culture, although the existence of a 'hidden transcript' can be inferred. Most records were kept by the literate middle-classes, who put their own gloss on events. Archives often paint a negative picture, of opportunistic thieving, drunkenness and 'idleness', occasionally breaking out into rebellion, while poaching was endemic. A strongly-demarcated line was drawn between the undeserving poor and the more respectable types who eagerly embraced allotments, friendly societies, schooling and the consolations of religion. It was necessary to public order to present an image of a united, happy town, and a day of communal celebration provides a good place to begin.

Now come with me on a journey back in time… Walden's old medieval street pattern is little-altered, but the streets are dirtier and dustier, churned up by carts and carriers and coaches. The little cottages are more tumbledown and dung-heaps a common feature. The market place is recognisable, though lacking the mock-Tudor frontage on the Town Hall, or the Italianate Corn Exchange: where 'Boots' now sits in unrepentant modernism, there is the old Rose & Crown inn; where cars now vie for parking spaces, there are horses and, on market days, cattle being sold, causing just as much disruption. There are even more pubs, dozens of stores and tradesmen's workshops. In season, the pungent smell of maltings fills the air, their chimneys punctuating the skyline. The 'idle' lounge on street corners, while the industrious get up early to tend their allotments before work. Frequently skipping school to do tasks for their parents, urchins scramble everywhere. It is Saffron Walden, 1832, a summer evening in June and there is a holiday atmosphere in town. Men in tall hats and women in shawls mill around the parish churchyard in anticipation of a great event. Flags are flying in the breeze, the Walden Band is poised ready to play, a hush descends and all eyes turn upwards to the church, waiting to cheer what is happening above…

Fig.1.1 *The new £3,000 spire of St Mary's Parish Church, Saffron Walden, soon after its opening in June 1832.*

PART ONE: CHALLENGES

Chapter 1

'This Well-ordered Town'
Saffron Walden in the 1830s

'The new stone tower and spire of our beautiful church being completed on Wednesday evening… an immense concourse of people assembled in the church-yard and streets adjoining, to witness the putting on of the top stone, which dangerous undertaking was performed amidst the most enthusiastic cheering of the multitude. An elegant blue flag was previously hoisted with an oak bough upon the scaffolding above the site; and the celebrated Walden band stationed on the roof of the church, on receiving a signal from Mr Ward, one of the architects, immediately struck up with a fine slow movement, and continued playing many favourite pieces till late in the evening. This beautiful ornament to the town has been more than 12 months erecting, the expense of which is estimated at nearly £3,000.'[1]

On a midsummer evening in the year 1832, amid the cheering of the multitude and the playing of the band, an event of some symbolism took place in Saffron Walden, a small market town in north-west Essex. The townsfolk gazed up-wards, beneath the ancient Parish Church, to watch the placing of the topmost stone on architect Thomas Rickman's new 'substantial and handsome spire of stone', the cost of which far exceeded a lifetime's wages for most of those who stood below. [Fig.1.1] After the builder placed the stone, the musicians, having somehow clambered up to the roof with their instruments, set to playing and suitable tunes wafted over the town from on high. Maybe there were a few who could remember when the building had been a virtual ruin and was closed for public worship in 1790, but thousands had been spent on its repair since then, an organ and clock installed and now, with its beautiful soaring spire, the Church of the Establishment was a fitting symbol for a new age. So the people cheered and the music played. It was truly a day to remember.[2]

But there was something odd. Since Anglicans and Dissenters, Tories and Whigs, had buried their differences to work together on the spire project, why was it felt necessary to hoist 'an elegant blue flag' onto the scaffolding on this apolitical occasion? The date may offer a clue. Was it connected perhaps with the fact that, fortuitously or by design, the ceremony was fixed for Wednesday 6

June, almost simultaneously with the passing through Parliament of the Liberal Government's Great Reform Act, with its attendant threat to the old order? In the same newspaper which reported the spire ceremony, there was much contempt of Reform celebrations at the neighbouring town of Thaxted, known for its greater radicalism, where 'a motley group of about 100 persons were parading the town on Tuesday, headed by a band of music, consisting of four musicians (two clarinets, drum and triangle) making the most discordant sounds, by way of rejoicing, at the news of the Whig Bill being passed'.[3]

But in the true Blue town of Saffron Walden, any attempt at celebrating Reform could be outshone by the magnificent spire ceremony which sent an altogether different message to the populace: new-fangled ideas might be abroad, but no discordant band would play here. Instead there took place what was intended to be an impressive celebration of elite philanthropy and achievement. Whatever their differences, those in power would work together in common cause, demonstrating a solidarity which would unite them against any future interference from central authority, or internal discontent within, either of which would undermine the *status quo*. The tall spire, thrusting upwards in its fresh new stone, symbolised the ascendancy of the Establishment, its prosperity and its confidence. The worthies were in control, co-operating to build a new Walden. Solidarity had been augmented by philanthropy, and all was well. At least, that was how things appeared.[4]

Notwithstanding the lively participation of the crowd, however, these sentiments were not necessarily shared by all those who viewed the scene, although no one would deny that it was a town which seemed to look after its poorer inhabitants. In 1832, the same year the spire was unveiled, the new Almshouse for the elderly was occupied and the rebuilt cattle market opened. Out in the countryside, 'tis true, there was incendiarism and animal poisoning, poaching and petty theft, but in town, even the excitements of Reform passed off peacefully, and the impression was later given that this was a tranquil town. Whether this was so may emerge in the first half of this book. But first, what sort of place was it at this time, John Player's 'well ordered' town?

The Place

Saffron Walden, the principal town in north-west Essex, was part of a parish of about 7,400 statute acres, measuring about five miles from north to south, and three-and-a-half miles from east to west. (Map 2) Most of this was farmland or parkland, with a few scattered hamlets, notably Little Walden, Sewards End, North End and Audley End village which between them had about one-seventh of the houses. The largest, Little Walden, had grown up at the head of two tributary valleys, the Madgate and Kingsgate Slades. In the 1830s, Little Walden was surrounded by a large area of farmland, with a scattered collection of 56 farmhouses and cottages. Sewers (Sewards) End, also very rural, was smaller with 44 cottages and houses. With only a dozen households, North End, like the small settlements of Springwell and Duck Street, owed its original siting to nearby springs. Audley End village was formerly known as Brookwalden, the settlement attached to Walden Abbey, which had stood on the site of Audley End mansion, seat of the Braybrookes since the eighteenth century. The village had once been much more populated, but the first lord redeveloped it and by the 1830s there remained only 18 cottages and houses.[5]

The town itself had shifted to the area around Walden Castle, with its market developing in the Middle Ages. In the nineteenth century, Walden retained much of its medieval street layout and ancient buildings. (Map 3) The built-up part, which had most of the 990 houses, was largely gathered around the market, Parish Church and High Street areas with the largest populations in Castle Street. The town had expanded little for almost a century, and a proposal in the mid-1830s to alter the ancient borough boundaries (which were the same as those of the parish) did not meet with favour. And so Saffron Walden sat in its valley, 'embosomed by hills', a compact and attractive town, but one whose prosperous appearance belied reality for many of its citizens. Two geographical aspects are also worth noting, one its nearness to various county boundaries, for cross-border influences could matter more than county ones; the other was its position off the beaten track, a few miles from the main London to Cambridge road, which had an effect on the economy and communications of the town.[6] (Map 1)

Getting about

Nevertheless it was not too difficult for those who could afford it to travel in and out of town, transport facilities offering contact with the outside world morning, afternoon and evening. As well as the steady stream of wagons loaded with barley or malt, there were other wagons and carriers plying their trade, and a choice of transport to London, even on Sundays, to the disapproval of some: 'The Jury present ... that the practice which has of late been carried on in this town of stagecoaches and waggons travelling on the Lords Day also of shops being open for the sale of any kind of goods on that day as being a public nuisance'.[7]

1823 In 1823 there had been three coach operators: a 'New Post Coach' and the 'Independent' which left early in the morning and returned the same evening; and the 'Defiance', which ran three days a week, returning on alternate days. A decade later the thriving coach and carrier sector included almost daily stage-coaches to London and three times a week to Haverhill: the Walden coach, popularly known as 'The Fly', travelled from Holborn to Cambridge via Sparrows End and Windmill Hill, Saffron Walden (see cover picture). Transport offered employment to grooms, ostlers and horsemen, not to mention the craftsmen like collar-makers, wheelwrights and coach-makers, and of course the unemployed who were put to work keeping the roads in order.[8]

Much of this was to change in the 1840s, with the opening of the London–Cambridge railway at Wendens. As in many other places, this spelt the end of the coaching era. The London coaches were replaced with omnibuses to Wendens station, and the carrier services became more local, taxiing passengers to the railway station. Malt and other products were still sent by wagon to Bishops Stortford and thence by barge to London, for the Stort Navigation had been constructed in 1769, partly through pressure from the Saffron Walden maltsters who needed cheaper transportation. A plan by the Walden Corporation, maltsters and farmers to build a canal linking the Stort Navigation to Cambridge, had fallen by the wayside due to Lord Howard de Walden's (the first Lord Braybrooke) strong opposition: the canal would have cut across his estate and ruined the landscaped park which was his life's work. This caused long-lasting bitterness. An alternative route later on also failed to materialise, likewise another attempt in the early nineteenth century, probably because of the expense, which was then put at well over half-a-million pounds.[9]

A similar fate had befallen early attempts to bring a railway through the town: again Lord Braybrooke proved intransigent. It was the third lord's intervention which ensured that the main London–Cambridge line was built out of sight of his mansion. A further suggestion, first made in 1835 at the height of the railroad boom, of constructing a branch line to Walden particularly upset him. The leading inhabitants, led by the maltsters, keenly desired such a link, feeling it would be of great 'utility and benefit to this district'. Braybrooke, however, was convinced the Wendens station would damage Walden's economic interests, while at the same time a branch line would not be used. He told Wyatt George Gibson, one of the prime movers: 'I am strongly of opinion that any railway passing 2 miles from a town will hurt it, if any effect at all is produced; but as to any one going out of his way to Walden while travelling at the rate of 20 miles an hour such an idea is preposterous'.[10]

Letters flowed back and forth over several months until, isolated in opposition, Braybrooke eventually after much wrangling very reluctantly allowed a line to be surveyed. Further plans were drawn up, and in 1844 a petition signed by 'a large majority of the influential and respectable inhabitants of this town' was urging a station to be built near the town. Lordly opposition was still anticipated, but it was hoped that Braybrooke might agree to a route which tunnelled under his fields near Thieves' Corner (and thence through Ross Farm to Thaxted) — for these fields could be purchased — rather than through his preserves and estate (see also chapter 2). In the event, of course, the town's branch line missed the early boom and did not materialise for another 30 years.[11]

A canal or a railway would have dramatically opened up transport facilities, enabling Walden commerce and industry to expand, and offer more jobs for its under-employed poor. The best the vestry could do was to make the unemployed work on highway improvement schemes to improve road access to the town. When malting declined, it was said to be due to poor transport facilities compared to other places, yet once Walden had been the centre of malting in Essex. When the population of the town dipped in the 1850s, this was also blamed on the lack of a railway. If so, there was a high price to pay for aristocratic privilege, although costs and other factors such as the emigration boom of the mid-50s must have played a part. Other towns such as Cambridge also suffered a fall in their population during mid-century.[12]

Comings and Goings

Until then, the Walden population had been rising for some time, traceable through the ten-yearly censuses from 1801 onwards. Although a small town, Walden was quite large by Essex standards and, surprisingly, in 1831 was the fourth largest in Essex. Returns over the six decades are not always comparable, as census criteria were always altering, but the virtual doubling of numbers over the first half of the century, the post-war boom and the mid-century fall in population emerge clearly. [Table 1.1].[13]

Year	Dwellings	Being built	Uninhabited	Population	% change
1801	657	n/a	25	3,181	
1811	669	10	7	3,403	+7%
1821	850	12	18	4,154	+22%
1831	941	33	18	4,762	+15%
1841	1030	1	82	5,111	+7%
1851	1,173	20	71	5,911	+16%
1861	1,181	2	59	5,474	-7%

Table 1.1 *Saffron Walden Census, 1801–61*

The boom after the French wars ended in 1815 was a common phenomenon, as soldiers and sailors returned and sired new offspring. One who returned, for instance, was John Barker (brother of Daniel, the town pinder), who served as a driver of horse-drawn gun carriages in the Royal Artillery from the age of 20 in 1794 until 1814. Finally discharged due to disability, he received a pension for the rest of his life and settled with his family in Walden.[14]

Other effects on population included more people moving into the town, making use of relatives or job opportunities, marrying Walden spouses, rejoining families they had once left or taking positions as servants, labourers or apprentices. Many families were inter-related, sometimes with whole rows of houses containing people of the same surname. In Castle Street, where a large proportion of the working population then lived, most people were natives, and at Canes Buildings almost everyone. Among the Barker families in the 1841 census, the 13 Barkers in Castle Street and one in East Street had originated from two or three families native to the town, but there were also family connections with Hadstock, Littlebury, Wimbish and Norfolk. Service for at least a year was a favourite means of gaining settlement, although counter-balanced by young people leaving the town to be servants elsewhere (see chapter 4). This did not always work out: young Benjamin Barker, for instance, was sent in 1827 to work as a footman, but two years later suffered a removal order back to Walden from Walthamstow. But there was nothing for him here, and eventually he left for London. Skilled workmen were also drawn to towns for work opportunities, but the influx may have been controlled in some way by other traders, perhaps through a guild. Certainly the better-off were more mobile, as census statistics show: at mid-century around one-third of Walden residents were incomers, but a disproportionate number of them were the better-off or more skilled.[15]

Since many villages were also growing, were more babies surviving? A particularly noticeable rise in the Walden baptism parish registers in 1813 might have been due to the procreativity of returning soldiers and a good harvest, but the Vicar of Walden was also perhaps sweeping up the unbaptised. It is not easy to establish the size of families as some were not baptised, died in infancy, were away from home on census night or left the town before marriage, but poor families were not always over-large. The first applicants for allotments, for instance, had an average of four or five dependent children, and these were the poorest families in Castle and Church Streets. An education survey of 1825 found that three school-age children was about average in town, though twice as many in Sewards End. Detailed family history research suggests the real picture is complex. Looking at the most common surname in 1841, Barker, with 146 individuals in Walden: some of these Barker families had no children at all, while others commonly lost one or two, or even up to five, of their original brood, although survival rates were improving over time. Stillbirth was decreasing and infant mortality declining, but it was still a strong factor in family size and population. Other influences included earlier marriage, increased fertility, the spread of smallpox inoculation and improved medical care and hygiene. Accidents were frequent, particularly among children, a worrying number of whom seemed to fall in fires or drown in ponds, while young lads fell under cart wheels. But with agricultural work in decline, there may have been fewer farm-related accidents. However, years of distress, such as 1826 when burials more than doubled, could make up for it. All of these factors worked together to affect population levels so that, in 1831, at the start of the decade examined in most detail in this book, there were 1,000 families living in Saffron Walden. Whatever the reasons for the rise in population, they were less important than the effects, real or perceived.[16]

One very noticeable aspect of nineteenth century communities is the predominance of youth. Around half the parish population was aged under 20, a lot more young women than men, but many of these moved on. Males and females were more evenly matched among children and adults. At the other end of the scale, although average life expectancy remained low, with only a fifth living beyond middle-age, the increasing use of the workhouse as an old people's home for the whole district may explain why the numbers of elderly later expanded.[17]

A Place to Live

All these extra people needed somewhere to live, and Walden had its own brick-making and a flourishing building industry, with housing units almost doubling over the first half of the century, although the boom stagnated after a while, with large numbers of empty houses. At one time, this was the biggest non-agricultural source of employment, the largest firms, the Wards and Hockleys between them offering weekly-waged employment to a large proportion of the regular workers. There were opportunities for apprenticeships, and often a family tradition in the building trade: William Ward employed nine members of the Adams family from teenage to middle age, as bricklayers or labourers. Demand ranged from shabby shacks for the poor to high-class artistry at Audley End. Here, there was nothing like the abundance of work which had existed under the first Lord Braybrooke, Lord Howard de Walden in the eighteenth century, but the third lord inherited considerable repair problems in 1825 and brought in a team of two dozen or more skilled artisans, including bricklayers, sawyers, painters, carpenters, joiners and masons. Over a 20-year period, they refurbished internally and built new rooms, windows, turrets and lodges. Many of the artisans came from afar, but some were on temporary loan from Wards, the town builders who had a long association with Audley End: Richard Ward worked for 35 years on the eighteenth century renovations, and Joseph Ward oversaw the completion of the park wall. Thus the buoyancy of the building sector was owed partly to the proximity of Audley End.[18]

But there was also a boom in public buildings at this time. The new Almshouses, the church spire, the replacement cattle market, the Agricultural Hall/Museum, the Union workhouse, the British and National schools, the Gasworks, the Corn Exchange cum post office/savings bank: all these offered building work and put cash into the local economy. Out in the countryside, brick farmhouses appeared at Peaslands, Turnip Hall, Brick Kiln and Stonebridge; while in the town, the better-off citizens were erecting handsome villas for themselves, often on the warmer, southern slopes of the town, away from the smell of malt and the noise of the market. Built in red or yellow brick, they appeared in London Road, Baileys Lane (Audley Road), Chaters Hill and elsewhere. Fairycroft was one such building. During the nineteenth century, the face of old Cuckingstool End Street changed considerably. Tales of ducking-stools for scolding wives had no place in a modern, well-ordered town and the Old Pond, said to be unseemly, expensive to maintain and frequently full of dead and putrid animals, was filled in around 1818. New houses gradually replaced old and in time, to reflect a more prestigious address, the name changed to the High Street.[19]

But there was, needless to say, a downside to the picture. The less reputable builders found work too, constructing flimsy tenements and sub-dividing larger units for the burgeoning lower classes, who could not afford decent housing. Unless they were willing to live on the isolated outskirts, the poor could be accommodated only in cheap tenements on back land which, being often taken up with stables, gardens and workshops, resulted in the inner courts which can still be found behind the frontages of Castle Street. Partitioning enabled landlords to draw a larger rent from the poor. Entrepreneurs like Abel Cain, who came to Walden from Bermondsey as a wheelwright, diversified into building slum housing. In 1821–2, he built cottages in Church Street and the whole of Upper Square in Castle Street. Castle Street was positively overcrowded: somehow this one street expanded from 104 dwellings at the end of the eighteenth century to 230 by the mid-nineteenth. Much of Church Street, East Street, Gold Street and Bridge Street were also full of run-down housing for the poor.[20]

The slums of Walden tend not to be obvious, for on the face of it the occupancy rate recorded in the census does not seem excessive. But the bad state of Walden's homes for the poor was noted on several occasions. In the early years of the century, the visiting parish officers were appalled to find the poor 'generally in a lamentable situation, living much cramped for room, and families lodging together in one chamber very indecently and in a way likely to conduce to the increase of vice amongst them'. Nothing had changed half a century later: 'I found this poor woman in a cottage of two rooms, it contained a family of six persons, a man and his wife, the woman who is ill, a son 22 years of age, and a daughter 16, and two other children'. The logistics of washing, cooking and sleeping in such dirty, cramped, draughty conditions have left little record. It is unsurprising that many men preferred the warmth and conviviality of the public house or beerhouse, nor that women were so drawn to chapels which offered them something homelier and gave meaning to difficult domestic lives.[21]

The link between overcrowding and loose morals seemed to be a dominant concern, rather than lack of sanitation, although from time to time the grand jury issued dire warnings about dirty drains and dungheaps polluting the town. Many of their presentments on sanitary subjects, however, seemed to relate to the trading rather than the residential areas of the town, especially the Market Place. Maltings owner Samuel Porter's brewhouse in Butchers Row was complained about on at least three occasions over several years. But infectious epidemics were great concentrators of official minds and events like the 1831 cholera threat would see them scurrying into action, printing regulations, visiting the poor, lime-washing homes in the mistaken belief that this would stem the scourge (see chapter 4). But they were ignorant of the real cause: polluted water. What happened to the sewage and rubbish emanating from the overcrowded yards and tenements? Only occasionally do we find out: 'the bad state of the Foundry Lane occasioned by the filth being thrown into it and running into it from certain cottages in the said Lane in the occupation of Banks and others belonging to Mr. Leverett and also from certain cottages in the said lane in the tenure of Housden and others'.[22]

After 1835, there was a new Town Council which was a little more active in public health, and from complaints in the minutes can be gleaned the fact that, at Hockley's Yard in Rosse (Roos) Lane, a dozen families were sharing two privies, and in Bridge Street four families were sharing one. Not surprisingly, these were causing a nuisance. The latter was owned by no less a personage than Ald. Thomas Smith. Lacking a proper sewage system, internal sanitary arrangements would also seem to be most unwise, yet the trustees of the General Baptist Church decided to provide their minister with just such an indoor facility in the cellar of his manse at Hill Street. This soon led to complaints from the Rev. Squiers who thought the old privy perfectly clean and comfortable but the new one obnoxious, smelly, unsavoury, damp and disagreeable. Eventually builder William Ward was employed to move the privy out of the cellar and back into the garden again. Out in the countryside, the 'bumby' (whereby household waste was in a sense composted for ultimate garden use) was a common receptacle well into the twentieth century, but difficult to replicate in town tenements and yards without gardens.[23]

Fig.1.2 *Pastoral scenes like these, produced by an engraver before the new spire was built in 1832, are responsible for much of our 'rural-idyll' illusions about the lives of the rural poor in the nineteenth century.*

But the rural poor did not, any more than their urban cousins, reside in pretty, picturesque cottages with roses round the door. The bucolic rural scenes so beloved of engravers of the period seldom betray reality. [Fig. 1.2] A reporter from a national newspaper, who toured this part of Essex in mid-century, described the living conditions of many: 'there is almost a continuous succession of bad cottages... great numbers are situated in low and damp situations and their heavy and grass covered thatches appear as if they had almost crushed the buildings down into the earth. Little or no light can ever find its way into the wretched little windows, many of which are half stopped up with rags and pieces of paper'.[24]

Work on the Land

Notwithstanding the poverty of those who toiled in it, agriculture was pre-eminent in the local economy, as could be judged from the generous subscriptions amounting to £1,300 readily given for the building of a new cattle market in Hill Street in 1832. It was claimed that this would increase trade and therefore furnish 'additional occupation to the labouring classes'. The facility was a visible statement of the importance of the farming interest, just as was the new Corn Exchange, built in the Market Place in 1848.[25] [Fig. 1.3]

This was all part and parcel of the 'agricultural revolution' which had begun in the eighteenth century and was still going on through the first half of the

Fig.1.3 *A remarkably early piece of photography, this picture of Saffron Walden market was one of a number taken in mid-century. The building site which became the Corn Exchange dates the picture to 1848. The lamp-post in the centre was later replaced by the drinking fountain. The trestle-table market stalls, horse-and-cart and dress of the figures posing for the camera conjure up another age.*

nineteenth. In this same spirit of modernisation, it had been seen as inevitable that the old farming system should give way to the new, in order that agricultural improvements could raise yields. North-west Essex, unlike most of the county, was an area where open-field agriculture still persisted even at the end of the eighteenth century. This was the medieval system, whereby large unhedged fields were divided into long narrow strips, cultivated by different owners. This was seen by landowners as most inefficient, even though it meant that ordinary smallholders had some land of their own and did not have to rely totally on waged labour for others. Parliamentary enclosure of some Walden land had taken place as early as 1764, and in 1812 the process of enclosing the remaining areas of open field in Saffron Walden was set in train with a Parliamentary Act, although it did not actually materialise until the 1820s. Much of Walden parish was ancient and the best land had already been enclosed piecemeal over the centuries, so only certain parts were affected. By then, the remaining areas of open field were mostly on less accessible, poorer or heavier soils. The main areas affected were around Little Walden, off the Sewards End road, to the west of Westley Farm, on the southern edge near Claypits, near Springwell and a few other places. Scattered strips were exchanged, property sold and woodland planted.[26]

The effect on the Walden poor is hard to gauge. In many areas, enclosure was heavily blamed as one cause of worsening distress among farm-workers, and it certainly cannot have helped anyone other than the rich, although some land exchanges were to the advantage of the Almshouse charity. The second Lord Braybrooke benefited, and two of the four new farms which appeared were set up on his consolidated lands. Martin Nockolds, the commissioner who carried out the administration, had links with the Braybrookes. The other principal participants in the enclosure process were the Vicar of Walden, the Rev. Nicholas Bull, the banker, James Searle and the brewer, A.F. Gibson.[27]

Farming, of course, was by this time very much changed in other ways. The old custom of young farm servants living in the master's household, said to have led to greater friendliness among the classes, was largely a thing of the past in Essex, although it had once been common around Saffron Walden. There were far fewer jobs on the land, wage levels were pitiful and much farmwork was organised on a daily basis, with no guarantee of employment in bad weather. The lot of the agricultural labourer was therefore a very precarious one indeed. Many blamed this on rising population, but opportunities had fallen in real terms anyway. There was nothing unusual in this in the Walden area: it was thus throughout the cereal-growing lands of East Anglia. In Essex by 1831 there were over 38,000 men trying to survive with farm-work, and unemployment in the county could reach horrendous levels in years of distress. In Walden, if the census summary reports are reliable and comparable, the numbers employed in agriculture fell considerably, a trend which was to have direct effects on the poor laws, crime and philanthropy (see later chapters).[28]

The contribution of farmwork to the local economy was explored in two surveys carried out by John Player in 1829 and 1832, for consideration by an employment committee set up by the parish officers to deal with distress. Apart from Lord Braybrooke, there was a handful of larger employers who offered most of the farmwork, plus a scattering of smaller holdings with fewer men, and some employing none at all. By 1851 there were about 48 farmers or farm bailiffs. The largest farms did not necessarily offer the most jobs: although in 1851 they each farmed about 500 acres, the Kitcheners at Little Walden Park employed only a dozen labourers, whereas the Clarkes at Roos Farm employed 32; farms of 300 acres could need 26 labourers or only half this number. Thus work prospects were variable. No doubt farmers' sons made a big difference, and women's, children's and other casual labour is impossible to quantify.[29]

Player's 1832 survey highlighted particular concern about the young, so often those involved in misdemeanours. There were then 46 Walden boys and lads aged 12 to 20 who were frequently unemployed. The committee wanted to know whether they were willing to work, what work they had already done, and whether they could read and write. There was a recognition that young men on highways unemployment schemes may not have had the opportunity to acquire farming skills so there was a need to 'train up young men in industrious habits and teach them skills'. A proposal to establish a parish farm for this purpose, however, never materialised.[30]

Even for those in work, financial rewards were low for, with surplus labour, there was no incentive to pay more. Rural north-west Essex was one of the worst-paid parts of the county. While the 1833 Poor Law Report claimed local wages were ten shillings, more local evidence suggests they could be as low as six or seven shillings in villages, even in the 1840s. This dire situation dated back to the late eighteenth century, when wages and prices began to get out of line, but increasing distress should have brought a hike in wages particularly since, as was seldom admitted, many farmers had done very well for themselves during the higher prices of the French wars. But there was little sharing of this bounty with those who did the work.[31]

There were two completely opposing views. On the one hand the landowning fraternity would blame the perfectly understandable 'necessity imposed on farmers to reduce the number of their labourers in consequence of the diminution of their capital, owing to a succession of bad crops and the general depression of agriculture'. On the other hand, they were unlikely to have read a critical, contemporary comment in a working-class newspaper, the *Poor Man's Guardian*:

> 'The fall of prices, consequent on the cessation of war, while it enormously increased the wealth and luxuries of the non-productive classes in towns, inflicted a corresponding ruin on the producers in both town and country... Every tradesman or merchant that saved money during the war, as well as every fundholder or other annuitant, has had his income at least doubled by the fall in prices; while the producers, out of whose toil the whole is drained, have their burdens, of course increased in the same degree.' [32]

An analysis of farm-workers' wages on the Audley End estate, by far the largest, bears out this comment. Increased cultivation of waste land, enclosure, innovations such as hollow draining, crop rotation and improved stock breeding upped profits, while tenant farm rents doubled during the French wars. In the 1820s — years of increasing distress for the burgeoning poor — while a fortune was spent on indulging aesthetic tastes in mansion and park, Audley End estate labourers found their wages, pushed up by the unusual circumstances of the French wars, soon fell quite sharply afterwards in a situation of labour surplus, and after that consistently did not keep up with the cost of living until the eve of the New Poor Law. The latter, of course, brought its own problems (see chapter 4).[33]

The security of reasonably regular employment at Audley End would have compensated to some extent. There is a tendency to lump 'the poor' together, and to use the term 'agricultural labourer' as a catch-all. But labourers could possess a wide variety of skills, and there were many different layers among the poorer classes. Greatly to be desired was to become part of a small nucleus of respectable men with regular employment, perhaps also with tied cottages, and for the select few, skilled and trusted, this could be a job for life. Kinship networks were always advantageous. An example was the Marshall family, generations of whom worked for the Clarkes at Roos Farm, an unusual survival in these changed times. In 1829 ten members of the family helped with harvest, and later in 1841 James Marshall, father of nine, was commended for spending

33 years with the same master, similar to the accolade his father William received seven years earlier for bringing up 12 children without any poor relief (see chapter 10). Similarly, Turner Clarke also employed five members of the Scott family.[34]

At Audley End, the same surnames could be found over time in the farm accounts: various Barkers, for instance, were a fixture. Robert Barker, perhaps aided by his father John's war record, worked for Braybrookes all his married life; there was also Richard Barker (unrelated), expert mole-catcher, much prized on the estate lawns; Richard was the son of the thatcher, William 'Rags' Barker who worked for the Braybrookes for 20 years. When William was killed falling from a haystack at Duck Street farm (part of the estate), the town's prestigious surgeon was called (arriving within 20 minutes), Braybrooke gave a pound to William's widow, and paid a woman to lay out the corpse and two guineas for an elm coffin. There were also a James and John Barker (not necessarily related) who did jobs around the farm. Other names occurring three or more times on the Braybrooke pay-roll included Browne, Clayden, Parish, Pledger, Richardson, Tinworth and Travis. Not all lived on the estate, however. Braybrooke also employed various bailiffs, woodwards, warreners, gamekeepers and others in the hamlets to work in his woods and farms.[35]

But for many in the rural outposts of Walden, there was little security. The scattered farming settlements north of the town, turned in on themselves to form a tight, inter-related community with each other, were somewhat forgotten by those in town. To the east, Sewards End was a particularly poverty-stricken hamlet. Occasionally, when visitors sought out these remote cottages, they found quite another world from the bustling, well-ordered town: 'I visited various families on Ashdon Road, near the Boundary of the parish of Walden, known by the name of Red Gate. These houses stand straggling in the fields, I found ten families in that neighbourhood, I visited eight, the others were from home. They all seemed very pleased I had called, as scarcely any one ever visited them, here in such an out of the way place and the roads being so bad in bad weather.'[36]

Surveys of Employment

John Player's surveys covered only the more fortunate workers, those on regular weekly wages. He reported to the 1829 committee, based on 'hastily obtained' figures of 571, that there were 241 men and boys employed by the farming interest, an additional 62 by Lord Braybrooke and the rest in the town, alongwith 88 on the roads. Leaving aside the Braybrooke men, therefore, farming still occupied about half of those listed. In 1832 he listed about 750 regular workers' names. Unless Player under-recorded numbers in his earlier 1829 survey, the regular workforce seemed to be expanding, perhaps through the building boom. Most were labourers, not all in agriculture, and a third were 'mechanics', the largest numbers working as carpenters, maltsters, grooms and bricklayers. The various trades, crafts and shops offered (apart from labouring jobs) regular work for only a small percentage of the total, and similarly in a multitude of other occupations.[37]

The employment opportunities offered by the Audley End estate were of major importance, but a comparison of the 1829 and 1832 surveys can be misleading: for instance Braybrooke claimed 106 employees in 1832, up from 62 in 1829, but 16 were only temporary and 22 were boys or lads, who were cheaper to employ. A lot of the Audley End workers named by Player were not named in the farm accounts, which casts some doubt on the validity of this otherwise unique survey: were these actually *regular* men?[38]

With a quarter of the regular workforce from elsewhere, the employment committee criticised the habit of local employers in taking on non-native workers, but this was inevitable, and most outsiders had not come far. Braybrooke chaired the committee, but many of his own workers were not local. Large estates commonly employed from afar. The household servants, the gardeners who tended the grounds and those who staffed the game preserves inhabited a different world: the hatred felt towards gamekeepers, for instance, would make it an untenable job for a local man.[39]

What is clear is that the economy of market towns like Walden was still intimately linked to agriculture. The cloth trade, never as large here as elsewhere but quite sizeable at one time, had by the 1830s long receded from its heyday in the 1770s. At that time the Walden textile workers produced corduroys, moleskins, cotton checks, bolting-cloths and sacks, the industry supporting several hundred weavers, woolcombers and spinners in the town and nearby villages. A particularly sad entry among the coroner's records notes how a man called Edward Francis cut his throat while depressed, after losing his occupation with woolcomber, George Archer. As late as 1823, a Church street weaver J.D. Archer was still producing worsteds but, like the short-lived silk-weaving boom, it all faded in the face of competition elsewhere. The change can be traced in the apprenticeships arranged by the town charities, indentures for which survive in the town archives from the seventeenth to the nineteenth centuries. Apart from shoemaking and tailoring, weaving had at one time been a large source of apprenticeships for young lads, but there were none now. The change also had a serious effect on women's employment prospects, for once home spinning had been a useful supplement to family income, with a knock-on effect on poverty. The 1851 census shows there was work for 65 dressmakers, often poor women. Most of the breadwinners were men.[40]

Malting

Saffron Walden was most famous for its busy malting industry, which had existed for 400 years, and was itself a stimulus to cereal-growing in the adjacent countryside. It was said to be the leading malting centre in Essex. Malting was seen as *the* success story of the Walden economy at this time. The pungent smell of malting barley, in wood-fired kilns, pervaded the town, and horse-drawn wagons brought in barley and took away loads of malt by road. The number of maltings increased to over 30 by 1831, over half of them at one time on one side of the High Street. Other clusters included Ross Lane (now Debden Road) and

Gold Street. The ownership of this highly valuable industry was in the hands of a few men, of whom the Gibsons were the leaders, acquiring large tracts of land specifically to grow the high-quality barleys suited to local soils.

Through their business empire, the Gibsons controlled the product from beginning to end: the barley fields, the maltings, the brewery and a large chain of public houses. They grew it, they made it and they sold it, and their ales were very popular. Numbers of drinking establishments in Walden increased over time, with as many as 21 listed in 1832. Until they leased out their pub interests in 1838, the Gibsons' 71-strong public house empire reached into four counties, stretching from Cambridge in the north to Sawbridgeworth in the south, from Castle Hedingham in the east to Buntingford in the west. In town they owned a dozen pubs including the *White Horse*, *Eight Bells*, *Cross Keys*, *Kings Arms*, *Sun Inn* and *The Hoops*.[41]

While malting was big business for some, this was not so for the workforce. The growing industry had not absorbed the same number of people who once found employment in the old Walden trades. Player's 1832 survey identified 100 or so regulars in the maltings, a third of them in the Gibson operations. Malting was not labour-intensive and the job opportunities it offered were therefore not in proportion to its importance: 'The manufacture of malt for which the town is well known, requires, although so valuable a portion of our domestic trade, but a few hands', as John Player put it. Brewing mostly took place elsewhere as there were few breweries in Walden. The malting process required experience, to arrest the process of germination at just the right time, so that the malted barley became in just the right condition for brewing. The work was skilled but seasonal between October and May and, while this sequence was proceeding, employees had to work long hours. Out of season there would be much under-employment. One of the more sympathetic maltsters, Charles Porter tried to explain this to John Player: 'you are under a great mistake as to Maltsters earning, men in their work require much more than a Man that goes to regular day work, Maltsters are up 3 hours sooner in a Morning and often 2 hours later at night, as such they cannot lay but very little by'.[42]

Notwithstanding Porter's apparent solicitude for his workers, he was one of at least ten malting-owners in the town and elsewhere who suffered malt and barley thefts in the early 1830s, in a scam of long-term and wide-ranging proportions. The eventual trial of the so-called 'gang', its revelations profoundly shocking town elites, showed how easy it was for this valuable commodity to be stolen by trusted workers. As will become clear later, perks and pilfering from employers were a common means of supplementing income (see chapter 6).[43]

Other Trades

There were numerous other trades, crafts, commercial premises and shops in Walden, in addition to the market. In earlier times tradesmen had been regulated by a guild system and by associations, such as the late eighteenth century society of cordwainers which united against 'persons who have no right to trade'.

But a growing economy needed freedom from such restrictions and Walden business, in companion with its population, expanded rapidly in the first half of the nineteenth century. The 1841 census lists almost 150 different occupations, ranging from bellhanger to bird-stuffer, from wagoner to wine merchant. Many of these were not high-income trades. Dressmaking might be the only option for a widow with children to support, and small-scale shoemakers were frequently almost as poor as labourers. There was value in diversity, for overcrowded trades such as tailoring (38 tailors in 1841, 55 in 1851), dressmaking (20, later 65), baking (18, later 21) and grocery (20, later 29) must have suffered from strong competition, even though the town attracted customers from dozens of villages over a wide rural area, travelling in by carrier's cart. Charles Baron's large bootmaking business no doubt did well, for harvest earnings commonly went on new footwear. By the 1830s in Walden you could buy not only the staples like bread, meat, fish, groceries, drapery and hardware, but a wide range of goods including jewellery, clocks, umbrellas, patent medicines, musical instruments, toys, books and fine wines.[44]

Trade directories of the period are not wholly reliable sources, but in broad terms a comparison over time suggests that, while there were well over a hundred trades and crafts in town, some were perhaps beginning their long decline, and others were diversifying. The number of shops was increasing, and there was an influx of professional services, such as bankers, accountants, attorneys, auctioneers, insurance agents, surgeons and even a professor of music.[45]

How did people gain a foothold in town business? Many migrated from elsewhere of course, but the manor court land transactions also reflect the rise of the middling sort, often by inheritance, marriage or personal upward-mobility. Frances Player, who married 'Gentleman' John Player, brought a useful inheritance from her father, Samuel Cole. John Emson, who built up one of Walden's leading grocery/drapery businesses in the Market Place (later Emson Tanners), seems to have begun his rise soon after the French wars. Another draper, James Humphreys inherited property from a relative who brought him up.[46]

Rich and Poor

At mid-century, the 1851 census offers for the first time a quite comprehensive picture of the local economy, and a most enterprising, busy and successful one it seems, albeit that the malting industry had passed its peak. Notwithstanding its transport problems and lack of manufacturing industries, Saffron Walden was a compact and tightly-knit community, a busy, working town, overlain by the smell of malt and the sound of new building, its traditional town centre gatherings of farmers in the market place, alongside a burgeoning 'white-collar' sector in their commercial premises. Self-sufficient in virtually everything, the assumption would be that here was a town full of opportunity for the working class to gain skills and become 'respectable', even perhaps upwardly mobile. Whether this was so, and if not why not, may emerge in later chapters. What is not explained, of course, is the process whereby some people had a chance of decent jobs and others lost the opportunity of being absorbed into the town's prosperity. Was it really due to 'idleness', or were they deliberately being kept as lumpen? A chapter on the town economy, however brief, should not ignore the deep contrasts between rich and poor.

The 1825 crash of Searle's Bank was an event which underlined the very different world inhabited by the richer elite of the town. Until the collapse, the Searles, who were leading members of Abbey Lane Independents, were long-established and esteemed members of the business and philanthropic community. They had been busy acquiring land and property for a long period, but perhaps this was where they overstretched their resources for when trouble struck, they went under, whereas the Gibsons, who ran the other bank, survived. But it was part of a widespread crisis and something very similar happened in many other towns such as Chelmsford, where Sparrow's Bank picked up most of the business of Crickitt's Bank, when the latter crashed on 17 December 1825. There were then 500 banks, issuing too much currency and this, together with a tightening fiscal policy, unwise speculations and agricultural depression, set off a panic and crisis reigned from 11–28 December 1825. There was a run on Searle's Bank, which suspended payments and collapsed, taking the Cambridge Town & County Bank, with which it was linked, down with it. On 27 December, Searle & Co were suspended.[47]

One wonders if James Searle senior had seen the crisis coming, but he had died of typhus shortly before, leaving his partners James Searle jnr and Samuel Brown Searle to deal with the aftermath. Initially mourned at Abbey Lane as an 'excellent and invaluable' man, the respect turned to dismay a few weeks later when the pastor reported 'the church has been convulsed by the lamentable failure of his bank — and affairs are yet unknown which have occasioned the catastrophe'. The crash left a trail of debt, sending ripples far and wide. The upset to the town's businesses can be gauged from a letter to one of the town drapers, James Humphreys, whose correspondent told him: 'I think you are fortunate in getting the rents considering the shock your town has received'. The Searles fell from grace socially as well as financially. One angry worthy wrote of the Searles' link with the Bible Society: 'It is anticipated by men of serious principles, that there will be a great falling off, owing to the conduct of the Searles, who under a mask of piety, have acted so deceptively'.[48]

This 'catastrophe' had two important effects on the town. A rival, the Saffron Walden & North Essex Bank, had been founded in Walden in 1824, run by the Gibsons initially in partnership with the Catlins. With the business acumen typical of many Quakers, the Gibsons managed to weather the storm. The Gibson & Catlin Bank picked up the losses and consolidated their position as the town's premier bank, which gave them even more clout than they already possessed. Secondly, since the Searles' assets had to be sold to pay off debts, it offered opportunities for land and property acquisition.[49]

These and other land transactions over the years are reflected in the 1842 Saffron Walden Tithe Award, an accurate and detailed snapshot of land and property, owners, tenants, acreage and usage, consequent on the 1836 Tithe Act. It confirmed that Lord Braybrooke, as well as his large holdings elsewhere, was far and away the biggest landowner in Walden, with over half of the parish land, 3,945 out of almost 7,400 acres plus cottages. The Gibsons, who also owned land outside the parish, had about 340 acres in Walden, most of it in the name of Francis Gibson.[50]

Personal wealth is much harder to quantify, for men were rated on land and buildings, not on money in the bank. A partial snapshot of employers' wealth was included by John Player in his 1832 survey of employment. Easily the highest rated were Lord Braybrooke and Messrs Gibson at £766 and £680 respectively. Eight others were rated at £200–£500, a dozen between £100–£200, 17 from £50– £100, and 18 people, including John Player himself, under £50. Thus about 60 ratepayers paid the largest proportions of rates to run a town of a thousand families.[51]

Living only a stone's throw away were the multitudes of the unenfranchised, non-ratepaying poor, whose lives could not have been more different, their situation varying by degrees from 'respectable' to utterly destitute. There were winners and losers, but too many of the latter, considering the apparent prosperity Walden was exuding. Poverty, as ever, varied in intensity and duration, depending on background, stage of life, health, the vicissitudes of the weather and of farming, and of that elusive quality, 'respectability', in the eyes of potential employers. It is impossible to quantify this, except by inference from examples. Poverty affected at least three-quarters of the population, judging by the list of poor people invited to the free dinner at Victoria's coronation. The list of those assessed for rates in the mid-1830s shows that over two-thirds of households in the parish were too poor to pay. In some parts of town, like Copthall Buildings, East Street and outlying hamlets like Sewards End, most people were poor, while others, though of low income, had compensations: if lucky enough to live at Audley End village or in the Almshouses, for instance, they enjoyed perks little known to those in the buildings and courts of Castle Street, and even less in the remoter rural outposts of the parish.[52]

There were thus two faces of Saffron Walden in the nineteenth century, the one more prosperous than ever, the other getting by through a mixture of strategies: work when available, casual labour from children, help from kin and neighbours, loans and credit from shopkeepers and others, charity handouts, outdoor relief and in some cases, no doubt, the ill-gotten gains of petty pilfering and poaching. In the rural parts of the parish, gleaning rights after harvest, a common feature of Essex villages right up to twentieth century times, could help see a family through the winter. But for the hundreds of deeply impoverished folk, who officially subsisted on a few shillings a week, the £3,000 spent on restoring the church tower, roof and spire would have been a sum beyond imagining. Yet they were expected at all times to 'bear their misfortunes quietly' in order to deserve the minimal help available from poor rates, charities and carefully-targeted philanthropy.[53]

The relationship between the poor and the middling sort will form much of the discussion in later chapters, but first the world of the elites must be explored. Who were these Walden worthies, what did they do and what motivated them? Any such discussion must begin with the man at the top of the hierarchy, Lord Braybrooke of Audley End.

Chapter 2

'All the Beauty, Wealth and Intelligence of the Town'
The Walden Worthies

'The company which consisted of all the beauty, wealth and intelligence of the town and neighbourhood presented one of the most imposing sights imaginable. They formed a circle of considerable extent around the platform on which his Lordship stood and it might be truly said as the noble Lord energetically expressed himself, this was one of the proudest days ever witnessed in Walden.'[1]

The feelings of paternal pride, which swelled in the hearts of the third Lord and Lady Braybrooke on that memorable day in October 1834, can readily be imagined. All around and below them stood 6,000 people — far more than the town population — all come to this highly popular event, the Saffron Walden Agricultural Society annual show, which Braybrooke himself had set in train. [Fig.2.1] Gazing up at him were not only 'all the beauty, wealth and intelligence' of the upper classes, the rich maltsters, bankers and gentlemen, local and county gentry and their decorative wives, but also the many layers of the middle classes: yeomen farmers, town shopkeepers, tradesmen and professionals – and the ranks of the working classes, of whom the most 'respectable' were dressed in their Sunday best, about to receive prizes for their industry and long service. It seems likely that most of the poor normally took little interest in the other-worldly doings of the gentry and aristocracy, for their lives revolved around more immediate matters: fairs, entertainments, celebrations, gossip at market, on street corners and at the beerhouse, who was in trouble with the law, hatches and dispatches, making ends meet. But on this annual red-letter day, it seemed otherwise. Here was a microcosm of nineteenth century rural society, all gathered at his behest and the resident aristocrat, Lord Braybrooke was delighted: 'No occurrence in his rather long life,' he later said, 'gratified him more than the success of this society'.[2]

The 1st and 2nd Lords Braybrooke

But the relationship between the owners of Audley End and the townsmen was not always as trouble-free as it seemed on that day. The first holder of the title,

Main Gate Entrance 27 Oct 1866 (5th Baron)

Fig.2.1 *This celebratory scene at Audley End was* <u>*sketched much later*</u>*, but captures the atmosphere and colour of the gathering of all classes, the air of excitement and the centrality of the Braybrookes, which typified the early years of the Saffron Walden Agricultural Society shows.* — the return to Audley End of Ld B (5th Baron) on 27 Oct 1866 having arrived at A.E Station. – see account 'Est Gen Info'

otherwise John Griffin Griffin or Lord Howard de Walden (1719–97), tried to get on with his neighbours, but the interests of landowners did not always coincide with those of the parish. Although he spent vast sums employing craftsmen on his estate renovations, made generous donations to church repairs, intervened to subsidise corn for the poor during dearth, and left a valuable bequest to the poor, yet Lord Howard as an old man to his great distress found himself jeered at by the townsfolk. The reason was his opposition in the 1780s to a proposed canal which would have revolutionised the economy of the town, but ruined his landscape park at Audley End. The inhabitants of Walden subscribed the enormous sum of £9,000 as a fighting fund, proclaiming defiantly 'we do not hold ourselves as any part of his property, nor are we dependants on his will'. But Lord Howard, faced with the ruination of his life's work, blatantly used aristocratic privilege in Parliament to defeat the project, a memory which rankled for many a year.[3]

Although his successor, Richard Aldworth Neville (1750–1825) was more open-minded about the canal idea, somehow it never took off after this early setback. The first lord had expended hundreds of thousands on his entire estate in the eighteenth century. The second lord benefited considerably from his predecessor's work, inheriting over half the parish acreage, his own farm at Audley End alone covering 1,100 acres. The heirs of Lord Howard had been exhorted always to put their own house in order before all else, to act 'as I have myself

X S.W Agric Society formed in or by 1833 – see page 177

32

done for the benefit of the estate itself and its possessors'. Accordingly, the second lord went on acquiring land, benefiting from wartime conditions, and from the enclosure of the Chesterfords. By the time he passed on the title in 1825, the entire holding (both inside and outside Walden) had expanded to something like 6,000 acres and its land value increased sevenfold. Admired as Lord Lieutenant, organising the county militia, as a man of charm, an innovative farmer, and for his enlightened encouragement of education for the poor, he seems to have suffered less of the controversies of either his predecessor or successor, and to have been generally well-liked. But the life of ease and plenty enjoyed by the aristocracy was increasingly out of joint with the times, and in any case the second lord's heart lay not at Audley End but in Berkshire.[4]

Richard, 3rd Lord Braybrooke

Not so his son and heir, the Hon. Richard Neville (1783–1858), who had learned to love Audley End as a child and, unlike many aristocrats of his time, enjoyed living on his large estate and getting involved in local life: allotments, schools, provident and agricultural societies all benefited from his patronage, and he was lauded for his 'urbanity and good feeling'. [Fig.2.2] Likewise his lady performed her traditional role of benefactress to the poor, as leading light of various charities, praised for 'the daily advantage derived by her poorer neighbours from her residence among them, for in her the fatherless and the widow find a ready friend. By her the hungry are fed, and the naked clothed.' Such comments were made every year at the agricultural show, which may be one reason why the Braybrookes enjoyed it so much. The canal dispute was long past and those who devoted themselves to the maintenance of a well-ordered town appreciated the value of a resident landlord.[5]

Fig.2.2 *Richard, 3rd Lord Braybrooke of Audley End.*

The recipient of all this praise was indeed a man of considerable talents and prestigious pursuits, far beyond the local sphere, as MP, president of learned societies, writer, historian, antiquarian and breeder of prize-winning racehorses, very much a rich man's hobby. Like his father, a pragmatic agriculturist, he was also of course, like the first lord, an even more energetic renovator of Audley

End, being responsible for much of the internal decoration so much admired today. But then the third lord was even richer than his predecessors, taking care to marry well, bringing further goodly fortune into the family. Even before acceding to the title in 1825, he possessed an income of £3,500 a year, and now controlled the tenancies of most of the parish farms, lands and many properties, and also the livings of the clergy. Beneficiary of the earlier expansionist and consolidationist achievements of the first and second lords, the third Lord Braybrooke was thus an extremely wealthy man, a fact which is relevant at various points in this book.[6]

Not surprisingly this wealth and power over-awed some townsmen who fawned: when attacked by an aggressive manorial swan, while walking through the estate, one gentleman would not dream of complaining that his arm had been almost broken, but wrote instead a cringing apology for trespass: 'I should hesitate to deface wantonly the humblest wild flower that blushes on your lordships beautiful grounds'. Was such obsequiousness genuine? At any rate, town/ lord relationships were not always of undiluted amity, though the privileges of land-ownership tended to prevail. The dimming of the third lord's lustre became noticeable in the mid-30s during the disagreements over rail-roads across the Audley End estate. This Braybrooke could have tolerated a canal, but his *bête noire* was the nineteenth century mania for rail-roads, and he fought vigorously against any such modern intrusion across his land. When Walden businessmen started campaigning for a branch line, Braybrooke found himself isolated in opposition, complaining 'I have been deserted by every land owner of the line, the whole odium and responsibility of the opposition resting upon me exclusively'. After much correspondence, he reluctantly, though still disliking the whole idea, favoured one suggested route rather than others, gloomily concluding: 'I must be prepared for the worst, nor will it make any difference that I should be allowed to take care of my own interests & try by all the means in my power to palliate the coming evil if come it must'. A public meeting tried to amend relationships, but asked for permission to survey the line. In spite of all the campaigning, however, the Walden branch line did not materialise in the third lord's time, and the town remained in its backwater until the 1860s.[7]

The main line to Cambridge *was* constructed in the 1840s but Lord Braybrooke remained unhappy: he still preferred hearing 'partridges rather than steam engines and railroad whistles'. Loathing the rail-road, not least because it imported hundreds of disreputable navvies to the area, threatening the morals of his people, he put on his paternalistic lord-of-the-manor hat and took decisive action:

'from fear that the railroad population would demoralise my cottagers, I gave them all notice to quit, with an intimation that if they did not displease me by taking lodgers I had no wish to interfere with them, but that as I wished to see their sons and daughters respectably brought up, I felt it my duty to protect them from so fruitful a cause of demoralisation'.[8]

There would be little temptation to take in navvies who knocked on their doors, for this was no empty threat. The 'cottagers' were of course tied tenants, for whom such loss of home would also have meant loss of livelihood and much sought-after 'respectability'. But in return for good behaviour, the lord's tied cottagers could be among the most privileged of the Walden working classes, with a job for life, extra work for wife and children, better charity handouts, help with childbirth, schooling for their children, a chaplain for services, a home for old age and burial expenses. They lived rather separate lives from the general mass, a world within a world, a symbiotic one where, on the one side, there was an expectation of deference, obedience and good behaviour, and in return a show of stern but kindly paternalism. This was by the nineteenth century an outdated concept, but lingering on in watered-down form at Audley End.

From one point of view this Lord Braybrooke was, therefore, a man of consistent sentiments: the Jacobean interiors, the academic books, the learned societies all reflect a man of letters and antiquarian interests with a passion for the past, in which scenario the distrust of new-fangled rail-roads and the paternalistic concern for his flock, were all of a piece. Here, it seems, was a man who loved the old ways and was prepared to speak out for them. Not for him, the then common 'abdication of the governors'. This was a resident landlord who seemed to care. In reality those aristocrats like the third Lord Braybrooke were not really being truthful with themselves or with others, for proclamations of old-style paternalism could not be sustained alongside self-interest in a land of entrepreneurial capitalism. There were occasions on which the third lord revealed a less salubrious side of his character for, though old-fashioned in his sentiments, he was hard-headed enough when it suited. His true character was known, it seems. At the time of the 1836 Tithe Commutation Act, a trustee of the Saffron Walden General Baptist Chapel, George Smallfield made an outspoken comment:

> 'I should be unwilling to abet him in any of his avaricious projects; but as far as I can understand the Act, it appears that the Tithe payers would be much better off by availing themselves of the provisions of the Act than in continuing to be at all subject to **his** avarice or exactions. Perhaps I view this matter in a light too unfavourable to his Lordship; but I confess that I feel no respect for his character.'[9]

It was of course not unusual for tithes to arouse indignation, particularly among Dissenters, but the comment on Braybrooke's avarice might have found a silent echo among his labourers whose wages remained out of line with farm profits (see chapter 1); with the bricklayers whose wages for the Audley End park wall construction were slashed by a third, when moved to piece-work; with the townsfolk whose ancient Audley End Fair was moved to relieve the third lord of a 'positive nuisance'. Even the hated rail-road was turned to advantage, for it enabled the barter of a footpath diversion in return for land required for widening the Wendens road. There were prolonged rating disputes, which cost the town dearly (see chapter 5). If Braybrooke lent money for local projects, it was seldom interest-free. Even the allotment land, which he could well have afforded to give away, brought him a good rent from the pockets of the poor (see chapter 8). This kind of thing was perhaps what Smallfield had in mind, in reference to a man of huge inherited wealth whose every gift seemed calculated for effect. In spite of appearances — for a man of such power was bound to be deferred to in face-to-face society — the uneasy relationship which had occurred in the first lord's time could and did recur.[10]

In fairness, just as the somewhat sanitised portrait hitherto painted does not do justice to the man, nor does a concentration on his allegedly 'avaricious projects': the chapters which follow feature Lord Braybrooke's other activities, which were many and varied, and always energetically pursued, whatever their dilution with elements of self-interest. One overriding concern was to promote surface harmony and peace on his patch, as a well-ordered town. His 'weighty communication' to the Prime Minister to save the town's Quarter Sessions, noble expositions as Recorder at various prominent trials and discreet letters to the Home Office warning of potential trouble can all be explained thus (see chapters 6–7). Like previous Braybrookes dealing with unrest in 1795 and 1800, the third lord mixed decisive action with discretion and humanitarianism when the 1830 riots erupted in the local countryside. Moreover, when it came to philanthropic works, Braybrooke could be pro-active and visionary at times. Fired by zeal for allotments, he would personally visit existing schemes to see for himself. In a desire to promote emigration, a labour rate or parish farm, as solutions to unemployment, he would come armed with considerable market research. When the parish officers were discussing highways improvements, it seems to have been Braybrooke who produced information about McAdam's new method of road repairs. Promoting self-help, he would pay the entrance money for his men to join provident societies, and make sure they received prizes for doing so. His promotion of the New Poor Law and early chairmanship of the Board of Guardians were all of a piece with other interests, although dropped when the duties became irksome and his own influence to no avail (see chapters 4, 5, 7,10).

A shrewd operator, not averse to economy with the truth if wider aims prevailed, he was certainly a complex and interesting character. There was, at any rate, far more to the third Lord Braybrooke than the three achievements always remembered: publication of a pioneering edition of Pepys' Diary, writing the history of Audley End, and refashioning of the mansion's interiors: remembering that he once said that the Agricultural Society was the one he himself treasured the most. After a long and busy life, his end in 1858 was a sad one, the last years overshadowed by the loss of many relations, including to his great grief two sons in the Crimea.

'Gentleman' John Player

If the annual agricultural show was Braybrooke's finest hour, Queen Victoria's Coronation festivities of 1838 should have been a similar red-letter day for 'Gentleman' John Player (1786–1846), another key figure in this period of Walden's history. Nothing quite like it had occurred since almost a quarter of a century earlier when, to mark the end of the French wars, there was a huge public dinner on the Common. As an organiser *par excellence*, Player was a natural choice to run another such massive event, which involved feeding 3,760 people, most of them in a sit-down open-air banquet. The day began at 4 a.m. with a fife and drum, cannon fire and church bells. The shops closed, laden vehicles poured in from the surrounding villages, there were flags on Town Hall and Castle, and patriotic ribbons worn. Brewers' drays carrying the best old stout made their way to the Common, where the Walden Band played. A triumphal arch adorned with flowers and boughs led to the dining area where 80 tables were laid out, each seating up to 50 people. At the top sat the mayor, with councillors and aldermen to left and right, proposing toasts, but most other respectable inhabitants waited on the lesser souls at table, 'and appeared much gratified in having the opportunity of supplying their poorer neighbours with a good treat of plum-pudding and beef', after which there was a plentiful supply of pipes and tobacco and ale. After three hours of jollity, the mayor and council processed behind the band to the Town Hall. An inflated balloon and two hours of fireworks ended a memorable day. Player was thanked for his 'great exertions and able conduct in the various arrangements requisite in the preparation and completion of the festivities of the day'.[11]

Naturally it was hoped that all who shared the bounty would be grateful to their benefactors, but there were some clouds. Those not invited to the feast almost spoiled things by invading the dining area and pinching puddings. Some of the unofficial counter-attractions also made the official committee rather cross because the rustic sports, which had been advertised but for which permission had most decidedly *not* been granted, led to disagreement and fisticuffs. [Fig.2.3] Although the second day of the celebrations, a Friday, was full of jolly tea-drinking and dancing parties in most of the streets, music and singing all afternoon and evening, and rustic youths carried a pretend queen through the town, again there were more sports, the 'noisy loyalists of Castle-street' continuing to frolic right through Saturday and into Sunday. This was a time when leisure pursuits were supposedly being turned away from the rowdy to the rational, yet popular culture would keep re-surfacing. The 'well-ordered town' was still a bit rough round the edges.[12]

Fig.2.3 *Although advertised with posters around the town, the 1838 Coronation 'Rustic Sports' had not been approved by John Player and the official committee, whose fears appeared justified when high spirits spilled over into drunkenness and fisticuffs. Even so, they sound like great fun!*

Nevertheless it was a good day for John Player. Only a decade or so earlier, as a Dissenter and Whig, he was still struggling to make his mark in the town, but a lot had happened in that time. John Player was not a local man, having been born at Deptford in London, but he was sent as a child to Saffron Walden, his grandfather's town, to recuperate from illness. Towards the end of his life, he recalled those happy childhood days with sentimental nostalgia. Joining the Navy civil service as a clerk at the age of 15, Player progressed to an important post, victualling officer at the Admiralty, on a large salary of £400 a year. After one or two early amours, at the age of 28 Player found a happy match in Frances, second daughter of Samuel Cole, of a long-resident Walden family. She brought him further goodly fortune to add to his own, but sadly their only two children were stillborn.[13]

Player's health deteriorated again and, after 23 years in the Navy, he retired on a generous pension, earning an accolade: 'When I was ill, and was compelled to leave the service it was the greatest pleasure to be told by the Admiral that I had done my duty'. Player was only in his late thirties when he and his wife settled in Walden in 1823, first at a High Street house, which he renovated, moving later to the Market Place area. Their way was smoothed through a letter of recommendation from their former chapel to Abbey Lane Independents, which they joined at once. Although born a Londoner, Saffron Walden was his spiritual home, as recorded in a volume of poems, 'Home' written during these early years. Player had begun, as a young man, a lifelong habit of recording everyday impressions, opinions, letters, hymns and poems and 'from the age of 18... troubled the periodicals of the day with occasional offerings', as he put it. To our modern taste, poetry was not one of Player's best talents, but he himself thought he was rather good at it: 'Poetry has been a favourite study with me', he once wrote, 'I may fairly class myself among the minor Poets of the Day'. More importantly, Player's civil service training made him an excellent recorder and organiser. Now, as a man of independent means with infinite leisure, he embarked on a new career of community service in the town he had loved since childhood.[14]

But things were not easy at first. His health was poor and various dreadful remedies perpetrated on his insides by Dr Thomas Spurgin, the town's Dissenter surgeon he consulted, nearly killed him. The 'cures', for what turned out to be a non-existent condition, included a damaging internal operation, 12 applications of 'Bongies' and lots of castor oil and other purgatives. But he got over it: 'I came to Essex, and the air of the country restored my health, and I hope that health has been used for good'. One of Player's first stabs at public activity, however, met with disappointment. Taking his 'highest delight in intellectual order', in 1827 he tried to start a Philosophical Society with discussions, lectures and public readings. Such institutions existed elsewhere and he felt that Walden should not be the last place to have one. To Player the need for such lofty pursuits was self-evident for 'philosophical institutions cannot fail to extend our satisfactions, and to enlarge our capacities for usefulness in society'.[15]

Player tried to gather support by writing letters to potential supporters. However, perhaps because he was a leading light of the Independent chapel and politically a Whig, this did not go down very well with the stodgy Establishment in Saffron Walden, and led to some unpleasant rumours which hurt him deeply. From his letter to the vicar, it is clear that churchmen suspected the meetings would be used for proselytising, but Player insisted that all he was doing was seeking 'for one denomination of Christians a mental advantage which would benefit all'. The vicar, Rev. Nicholas Bull, denied there was any objection, but there must have been some, for a few days later Player was complaining to another prominent churchman about the increasing detraction and falsehood and 'littleness on the part of some from whom I expected better things'. Again the recipient, a former mayor, denied that there was any truth in what he called Player's 'flippant' allusions, commenting that possibly some people had misunderstood its purpose. To another friend, Player again despaired of the 'want of kindly feeling and cordial co-operation' he was encountering and, in spite of her encouraging reply, gloomily told her he was 'no longer sanguine as to the practicality of establishing one under existing circumstances'. It was not, he realised, going to be easy spreading culture among the middle class audience required to make such ideas work. Many years later he wrote: '...no matter discomposes me so severely as an act of unmerited obloquy, & overbearing injustice'.[16]

Player had under-estimated the inbuilt inertia of the establishment, and in particular the suspicion with which Dissenter activism was viewed. Yet a start had been made, since the town had been enjoying well-attended lectures for two or three years, and indeed there had been some kind of Book Society in the town earlier. Perhaps it was just a little too soon for bolder ideas. Five years later, in a brave new world of electoral Reform and Nonconformist rights, the cultural barriers were also falling, and Player became the first president of the Literary & Scientific Institution for 'the promotion and diffusion of useful and scientific knowledge', an aim which was little different from the failed plan for a Philosophy Society. Hobbies were shared and enthusiasms conveyed: Player himself on moral philosophy, Spurgin the surgeon on electro-magnetism, Mr Youngman on printing, Francis Gibson on architecture, his brother Jabez on gold and silver, Rev. Josiah Wilkinson on language, James Humphreys on disposing of the dead (an early reference to cremation?), William Thurgood on popular education, his father on the poor laws and another speaker with ideas on ameliorating the condition of the poorer classes of society. Thus the poor were sometimes thought of. On occasion, even ladies attended.[17]

The organisers were very careful to exclude religious subjects so as not to upset the Establishment, although there was still a certain amount of 'destruction and opposition'. But at long last Player and his cerebral friends (mostly Dissenters) were free to cultivate their mental powers in serious mode, circulating books and periodicals amongst themselves, reciting poetry and reading out their essays to each other. The correspondence surrounding the earlier disappointment therefore suggests that, while the support of the Gibson brothers and others was vital to the viability of the Institution, the drive which brought into being what is now a much-revered part of the town fabric, the Town Library, was very much tied in with John Player's earlier frustrated dreams.

This shaky start, real or imagined, did not permanently dent John Player's public career, and probably taught him some valuable lessons in diplomacy. The rise of the Institution paralleled that of the Museum, and again Player was one of the prime movers. As a religious man, a great thinker, fond of history and natural history, language, poetry and travelling, it was natural for him to be part of a group of like-minded men who became known as 'The Philosophers' — others including Joseph and Joshua Clarke, Jabez and Francis Gibson and Thomas Spurgin — believing passionately in mental improvement as the way forward to a better world. He amused himself collecting minerals and seashells and would 'unite with others in occasional bursts of pleasure while I inspect my acquisitions'. Such items included some he must have gleaned from his Admiralty days: a lock of Napoleon's hair, and a piece of willow which shaded his tomb on St. Helena. From such early gatherings, at the home of Jabez Gibson in Hill Street, a collection emerged which formed the basis of what became the town's museum.[18]

There are differing views as to whether Lord Braybrooke played any large part in this, but it was in the 'newly erected house' on Castle Hill that the Museum found a permanent home. Men from both sides of the religious/ political divide worked together from 1832 in the Natural History Society, sharing their talents: carpenter William Ward made cases for specimens, surgeon Thomas Spurgin took charge of entomology, former clerk John Player was later secretary. Opening on 12 May 1835, the result was a museum where 'the privileged classes mingle with the community at large in order to aid the dissemination of useful and practical knowledge'. In fact, like the Institution, it was rather more exclusive than that.[19]

John Player's other great interest was the spade husbandry allotments scheme, to which he devoted enormous energy (see chapter 8). It was Lord Braybrooke who instigated the scheme but, as a busy man whose public and personal duties often took him out of the area, he needed 'an active and efficient superintendent' to deal with the mundane details, and 'Gentleman' John Player was his man. They were almost contemporaries in age, both being in their forties when they worked together on the allotments idea. Following this early success, 'Gentleman' John Player became the busiest of busy worthies, an indispensable organiser in a score of cultural, philanthropic, religious, educational, legal and statutory organisations. In a public life largely concentrated in the 20 years, 1825–45, he was deacon and treasurer of Abbey Lane and Independent Chapel, a leading light of the Agricultural, Allotments, Benevolent, Bible, Books, Clothing, Horticultural, Mental Improvement, Missionary, Natural History, Religious Tracts and Clothing societies, was trustee of various charities, served on one-off efforts like the Cholera Committee and the Cattle Market appeal, supported other causes like the British & Foreign School Society, and various Dissenter causes (see later chapters). It would be easier to list the local organisations which did not include him.

He also held public office, as circumstances permitted, although sometimes with less enthusiasm, for instance as a reluctant vice-chairman of the Guardians and before that a pro-active parish officer (see chapters 4–5). As a Dissenter who, for most of his life, had been banned from the bench and Corporation, he relished the prestigious roles of judicial and political power. As magistrate, presiding over the transgressions of the largely poor law-breakers of the town, he was described as able and fair, although the diary of cases he kept in the early 1840s sometimes gives a different impression (see chapter 6).[20]

John Player held particularly strong views about the discrimination against Dissenters like himself, and strongly criticised the exclusivity of the Corporation: 'no self elected Body therefore should make laws and regulations for many who have not a reasonable interest or voice in their nomination'. It was a moment of triumph to find himself elected the first Dissenter mayor of the reformed council, a choice which suggests that both parties saw him, in this difficult time of transition, as a peace-maker who could bridge the gap between the old-guard Tories, who had run the town for generations, and the much-distrusted, reforming Liberals (see chapter 3). Becoming mayor also put him at the centre of the coveted bench and in his first Quarter Sessions, when there was only one prisoner, Player gloried in the novelty of it all, 'perhaps the first time for nearly 300 years that a Dissenter presided as chief magistrate in this town'.[21]

His finest hour came after leading a deputation to the Home Office, to return amid much rejoicing, having saved the town's Quarter Sessions (see chapter 6). Although joking to a friend about the 'weight of duties pressing on my poor faculties', Player in mid-office reflected: 'Happily things go on tolerably calmly; and in another year I fancy the mountain of duty for the mayor to perform will be an amusing pastime, while there will be fewer opportunities for the exhibition of that ire, and the display of those sarcastic powers which some are so gratified to indulge whether or not it commends to others their good sense, their justice or their good manners'.[22]

Player thus admitted that his triumphal mayoral year was not without its share of controversy. And indeed throughout his year of office, the pro-Tory *Essex Standard* kept up a tirade of abuse, although Player himself ignored it: 'happily I have not seen a single impression of the Standard, so that I know not if the Editor lend himself to the dispensation of home wrought stuff for the benefit of little minds of idle folk'. On Player's appointment, they had published a disparaging comment about the irony of the splendid ancient mace inscribed *Reluctantibus phanaticis*, translating as 'the fanatics struggling against it', being consigned to the hands of a Dissenter. When his year of office ended and the borough accounts were posted in public, an anonymous critic, presumably one of the lesser ratepayers who objected to paying for civic largesse, scrawled angry comments such as 'forged papers' on the poster, and queried the mayor's expenses. Later on Player was hurt to be passed over for aldermanic honours, but the Tory who won them, Nat Catlin, suddenly stood down in favour of his 'moderate Whig' colleague, so that Player 'scarcely believing his senses thus suddenly converted into an alderman'.[23]

Perhaps Catlin sensed that his old friend would not remain much longer in public life, for Player's health was again in decline: 'The state of my health so frequently prevents my taking an active part in various societies in which I formerly had peculiar delight', he wrote with sadness. In 1841, after an operation and further illness, he carried on as magistrate for another four years but then resigned from various other posts, some of them to fulsome tributes to the 'ability which he brought to bear upon its formation, the zeal and perseverance with which he carried out all its details'.[24]

Now John Player took up his pen again to produce his finest work, a much-acclaimed series of topographical *Sketches* of Saffron Walden published first in the Essex press, later reprinted as a book, and still today one of great charm and local interest. From a historian's point of view, his prolific outpouring of letters and articles for newspapers and periodicals, reports and notes, essays and speeches are a gift, his clerical skills and voluminous output telling us so much about the Walden of his day. After his death, at the age of 60 in January 1846, his widow Frances burned 20 volumes of his autobiography because, she said, they contained references to their neighbours: how invaluable they would have been! Was Frances perhaps a shy woman, who did not share her husband's love of the limelight? Her name seldom appears among the worthy ladies on committees.[25]

Player once consulted a phrenologist at a time when this pseudo-science was fashionable, and was flattered by the report which spoke of his 'powerful faculties so highly useful in society', his 'strong and manly determinations', his passion for benevolence and justice, sound argument, reasoning and facts. To modern sensibilities, however, Player often comes across in his speeches and writings as somewhat pompous, often employing a turn of phrase unlikely to endear him to the common folk: 'the uninformed and the too often depraved offspring of the unemployed poor', was perhaps one of his more unfortunate pronouncements. He was, like many of his class and his age, absolutely convinced of the hierarchical nature of God's world, that birth, property and education conferred superiority, and poverty was the natural order of things for the rest. The 'Nonconformist conscience' required a commitment to helping the industrious poor man 'to find for himself some fruits to sweeten the routine of the toil which he is doomed to experience'; but rising above their station in life was not the idea: 'we would utterly abrogate the preposterous idea that the labourers can by this system become independent – because Society is formed of consecutive and dependent links'.[26]

It was difficult for such as he, who never lacked for anything, truly to empathise with the poor, and this world-view, hidebound by the Malthusian caveat that indiscriminate charity only made poverty worse, formed a void which people like himself, ostentatiously carrying out good works, could not cross. Praised by friends for a 'spirit of cheerfulness and right feeling', there is yet an indefinable impression that, like many interfering busy-bodies, he was not generally liked among the poorer classes. The recipients of his tireless charity did not give him the thanks he deserved: the poor, when they were benefited, were 'not very ready to acknowledge it'. Was it really 'an ill-timed joke' when someone once threatened to burn his house, and was it just a prank to receive a threatening letter during his period as surveyor of highways? (see chapter 7) Such incidents left a disturbing after-taste. Player always remembered his failures and occasionally there are hints that underneath he retained some of the heightened sensitivity of the Philosophical Society débâcle, remembering that 'some painful associations bring over the mind an impression which no length of time can ever efface'.[27]

Yet Player wore himself out in good works, and places like Walden benefited greatly from the idealism, energy and Evangelical drive of this type of Dissenter/Whig activist so often found in English towns at this time. Who knows, if John Player had never moved to Walden, whether the vision required to bring into being the allotment scheme, the new cattle market, the Institution, the Museum, the Clothing Bank, the Provident Society, and various other initiatives, would have come from anyone else?

The Gibsons

One of the odd things about John Player's life is that there appears to be no account of his death, not even in the *Essex Herald* which had recently published his celebrated *Sketches*. This man who spent his life recording everything had nobody to write about him when he had gone. This was in contrast to the effusive obituaries about his younger friend Jabez Gibson, which filled the columns of several Essex newspapers in 1838. Jabez, an 'amiable and excellent man', was said to have been without enemies, and a true friend of the poor. As the youngest brother, Francis is credited with leaving the legacy of Bridge End Gardens; and the oldest Wyatt George with building the British School; so Jabez is remembered for the very practical enterprises of pioneering, with Player and others, the provision of gas and water supplies, the latter through thousand-feet boreholes in his Hill Street garden.[28]

Wyatt George Gibson, the one featured in this book, comes across as bluff and uncompromising, pragmatic and principled: the traditional dress and retention of the already-outdated Quaker habit of using 'thee' and 'thou' in conversation; the offer of £300 to demolish the old church spire because, as a Quaker, he was not allowed to contribute to the new one; an admonition of a fellow worthy who criticised the provision of music teaching he was encouraging in the British School (see chapter 11). When Mr Gibson gave warning that he would resign unless workhouse inmates were allowed freedom of worship, this was no empty threat. As it was, his views prevailed, and he chaired weekly meetings of the Guardians throughout the final third of his life, a depressing and dutiful task at the best of times, although it offered considerable power: one suspects that the long battle to retain discretion over outdoor relief had Gibson stamped all over it (see chapter 5). Wyatt George served for 30 years on the council, built the British School and did much else besides, praised as able, excellent, greatly esteemed for the 'high public and private character maintained by him during the whole of his long and valuable life'. His death in 1862, leaving a valuable legacy to found the hospital, was not the end of an era, as his popular, personable son, George Stacey Gibson, came to the fore.[29]

If the psyche of this multi-faceted family is explainable at all, it lies in their Quaker background. From childhood, they were brought up in a loving atmosphere and trained up in godly conversation, plainness of speech, behaviour and apparel, to avoid flippant diversions like gaming, discourage all tale bearing, and be just in their dealings, punctual in fulfilling their engagements and to carefully inspect their own affairs once a year; they were also bound to provide for the poor and help educate their offspring. These subjects were on the list of queries at every quarterly Friends' meeting and, as with so many successful Quaker entrepreneurs, for the Gibsons kin and religious duties were successfully spliced with a strong practicality, adapting old-fashioned values to the requirements of business and public life. Having a family firm helped. It was grandfather, George Gibson, a Maldon businessman, opening a shop in Market Square, Walden in 1763, who founded the empire. He consolidated his successful milling/malting business through a clever marital alliance into the Wyatts, a rich brewing family. Atkinson Francis, his son, continued acquiring parcels of land all over the parish both during the French wars and afterwards. A.F. Gibson then passed on to his three sons land and properties of considerable value, as well as the family business. The brothers carried on in the same vein in the 1820s, being involved in at least 27 of the land and property transactions going through the manor court over an eight-year period. This was a concerted effort to complement their business interests with land ownership. The commercial acumen, the hard work and integrity were all Quaker characteristics.[30]

When the Gibsons decided to expand into banking, it could scarcely fail. The story of how they came to run the premier town bank is well-known (see chapter 1). Indirectly the Searle's bank crash, disastrous at the time, proved eventually to be to Saffron Walden's advantage, for the Gibsons got richer and richer but, as Quakers, felt bound to plough back large portions of their wealth into the town for many decades to come.

And yet, philanthropy was one thing, taxes were another. On several occasions, it seems surprising to discover, Messrs Gibsons appealed against their poor rate assessment, including 1822, but were over-ruled. It seems that they, like other rich men, preferred to give money away voluntarily rather than be forced to do so. The Quakers' refusal to pay church rates and tithes was of course based on strong religious principles, but this awkwardness about contributing to the poor rate seems out of place in lives which appear, at least on the surface, to have been exemplary. It may have related to their exclusion at this time, as Dissenters, from political and judicial power. Wyatt George Gibson felt strongly that the views of those who paid most rates should not be ignored. (see chapter 12). Their gifts to the town were not merely monetary, of course. The family gave generously of time and energy to charitable causes and there was special help both for their own workers and retired employees, and for poorer members of the Society of Friends.[31]

Other Tory Worthies

With the Gibson name on banknotes, beer and beneficence, they, like Player and Braybrooke, tend to appear as the only men of any significance, but this is far from so. Notably, there was the relatively tight clique of families who had run the local and legal government of the town for decades: up until 1835, these were of course all Anglicans and Conservatives, mostly wealthy, with wide kin and business networks. Four names in particular recur frequently: the Archers, Catlins, Fiskes and Smiths, one or other of whom, over a 70-year-period up to 1835, held the mayoralty over 40 times.[32]

The first Archer mayor took office in the early eighteenth century and the surname appears on the mayoral list over a score of times over the next hundred years, including 1795 when the hapless Henry Archer found himself in the thick of the famous Walden food riots. The Archers were rich maltsters, corn factors and property owners, owning a lot of land round the town, philanthropic in church, education and charity work. They were linked by marriage to the Catlins, who were also wealthy corn merchants, maltsters and landowners. Nat Catlin, like his close friend John Player, was busy in politics and philanthropy, while his older brother, Thomas Archer Catlin, had a particular interest in the young, serving on the Broomfield charity for apprentices, the Charity School and above all the National School, in whose promotion he exhibited 'unwearied diligence'. The luckiest person to enjoy T.A. Catlin's patronage was his young clerk, Edward Stokes who inherited his malting business and a bequest of £1,000.[33]

Then there were the surgeon brothers, Charles and Samuel Fiske who grew wealthy enough to build themselves a mansion each: one at Fairycroft, the other along the road at Farmadine. Charles Fiske's favourite cause was the revived but under-funded Grammar School which benefited from a generous bequest when he died, earning a warm tribute from remaining trustees for his munificence. The Fiskes were another of those distinguished old families who had supplied Walden mayors for decades, the first in 1773. Their uncle was a long-serving town clerk, who dealt with the administrative problems of the Walden food riots. Their grandfather, Rev. Robert Fiske, had been Vicar of Wendens Ambo for 42 years, and there were other family connections with Wilkes, lord of the manor at Elmdon. Less of a dynasty but no less a fixture of the well-ordered town was Thomas Smith, another wealthy businessman, owner of a flourishing tannery, several times mayor, and holding the most prized charity position in town, that of Master of the Abbey Lane Almshouses, and was also prominent on vestry, Guardians, bench, Corporation, charities and societies. Nearby lived Charles Barns Wilkins, currier, leather cutter and something of a crime-busting mayor in his time: there was a by-now rare use of the stocks during one of his periods of mayoralty.[34]

Other Tory notables included Stephen Robinson who, like John Player, enjoyed the status of 'gentleman', by trade a maltster and corn-factor, and was co-brother at the Almshouses. Market Place chemist and druggist, Henry Burrows was deeply involved in political life, as was leading local attorney, Charles Teissier Master, who one year contrived to be both mayor and town clerk at the same time, overcoming doubts expressed about the legality of this arrangement. Later he combined the clerk's job with that of coroner and Clerk of the Peace, earning a goodly sum. It is of course difficult to prove that jobbery and other 'perks' were a common feature in the running of well-ordered towns, but there is no reason to suppose that Walden differed from the norm. Possibly we misunderstand the way gentlemen did things in those days.[35]

The opportunism of John Emson is a case in point. By the 1830s, Emson had been building up his Market Place grocery/drapery business for some time. His name became noticeable after he successfully campaigned to move the cattle market from outside his premises. Having seen the Liberals defeated in Essex, he resigned his leadership of the Walden group, calling himself a 'Nondescript' because he disliked Radicalism. In no time at all, Emson seemed to rise to prominence and several things changed in his favour: he obtained a long lease on the old Corporation malt mill; and then found himself co-opted onto the Corporation as alderman and equally rapidly elevated to mayor. A change of political colour may have been irrelevant to all this, but cannot have been a hindrance (see chapter 3).[36]

The 'New Men'

At least John Emson was able to penetrate the self-elected oligarchy of the old families, one subject of complaint by 'the new men' who were coming to the fore by the 1830s (see chapter 3). But apart from their politics, were the Whig/Liberal worthies much different in terms of their own ambitions? Certainly the attitudes of some Whigs/Liberals towards the poor, and to the maintenance of public order were, if anything, more severe. One name which constantly recurs is that of Robert Driver Thurgood, professionally a conveyancer and auctioneer, but a man of many parts. Everywhere in the 1830s–50s town, Thurgood seemed to be in the thick of things. As vestry clerk, he played a vital role in the application of the old poor law. With the increasing importance and scope of the population census, Thurgood got the job of surveying the households of the parish. With the Radicals gaining a foothold, it was Thurgood who was secretary of the local recruiting drive. As Dissenters were for the first time allowed into local government, there was Thurgood taking a seat on the new town council. When the Board of Guardians came into being, he slipped into the well-paid role of clerk, and did much to minimise the potential controversies of the early years (see chapter 5). With the advent of civil registration, who but Thurgood should become the first superintendent registrar. After Rowland Hill proposed his radical idea for pre-paid universal penny postage, it was Thurgood who, as stamp distributor, moved a town council petition in favour of the controversial scheme. Once again it was Thurgood stirring up the campaign against church rates. And when incendiarism broke out during his mayoralty, there he was, urging the ratepayers to finance a town constabulary. Here was a pragmatic, outspoken person of Radical principles increasingly acquiring power behind the scenes. Seldom now remembered, he was probably the most under-estimated figure in the maintenance of the well-ordered town (see chapter 3).[37]

Many other interesting personalities in Walden at this period were part of the new wave of Whig/Liberal councillors, the so-called 'Yellow' party, nearly always leading lights of the dissenting congregations too. Charles Porter, son of Samuel who had been jailed after the 1795 Walden bread riots, was one such, though now a respectable maltster. So was John Clark, a leading light of the Horticultural Society. Then there was the memorably-named Hannibal Dunn, who was married to a daughter of the Lord Mayor of London: Dunn's business interests encompassed being ironmonger, agent for agricultural implements, cabinet maker, upholsterer, auctioneer, appraiser and insurance agent. Charles Baron, member of an old Walden family and proprietor of a large firm of Market Street bootmakers, was another, equally known as a plant breeder: he bred the originals on which Chater's hollyhocks were based.[38]

Many of the town's shopkeepers were 'new men': people like ironmonger, Robert Paul, whose moment of glory as mayor ended in sudden death in office. Draper, James Humphreys, leading light of the Hill Street Baptists for 42 years, was another; as were grocers, John Robson and William Wiseman, Henry Hart the printer, Thomas Spurgin the surgeon. Others were just beginning their career in public life in this period, such as a man who became an outstanding botanist, Joshua Clarke, who joined the Town Council in 1841 and served continuously until his death in 1890, during which period he was mayor ten times. One of the richest maltsters in Essex, Joshua Clarke was involved in numerous causes, notably the Museum.[39]

It is hard to assess the impact of those who owned land and property in the town, but lived at a distance, such as the Marquess of Bristol; and of others who had once been more prominent, such as the Maynards, who had been recorders of Saffron Walden in the mid-eighteenth century and made a large contribution to the original Town Hall. They still owned substantial chunks of Ashdon, as well as estates in other parts of the country such as Walthamstow, retaining links to the town. This may explain the job opportunities which arose, particularly in service, in Walthamstow. William Tuke Robinson, who was a JP in Walthamstow, became the owner of land and property in Walden, including Hall Farm and all the smallholdings and cottages in Little Walden formerly owned by James Searle.[40]

Among those who featured prominently in public life, many were lowly rated, including 'Gentleman' John Player. This suggests that people were 'worthies' not necessarily for reasons of property, but through their involvement in public life, philanthropy and often politics. Many were Dissenters, and were typical of the middling sort increasingly making their mark in towns and cities all over England. In many cases, it is hard to equate the Dissenter/Whig men with the 'firebrand' label accorded by the Tory press. A 'league table' of their contributions to Walden life would show widespread involvement in good works and leisure pursuits, with John Player, virtually a full-time do-gooder, at the top. It is only fair to say that probably many others among them felt no great involvement in the well-ordered town. Not all men of wealth and influence chose to sit on committees and stand for elections. Among those who potentially might have got involved in public life, only a proportion did so, of whom most belonged to only one or two organisations, with a very small core of the active elite. Perhaps as few as one or two percent of the townsfolk were involved at committee or trustee level, with an even tinier proportion in positions of leadership. This chapter and the next one are therefore reflecting the activities of only a small minority of the town population.

47

A New Walden

Nevertheless it was a pro-active minority, for there was beginning a time of tremendous energy in public life, of a kind we might envy today. People seemed to have a sense of vision about what the town could become. From our more jaded perspective, there seemed then to be a 'can do' philosophy which, backed by the largesse of the richer elites, made men like John Player, Robert Driver Thurgood and the Gibson brothers — all very different types of men — feel that they were building a new world, a new Walden. What they had in common was, in the end, more enduring than any sectarian divide. Men of all parties and religions intermingled in kinship, business, committees and social circles. The Barons were related through marriage to the Clarkes; the Catlins were one-time bankers with the Gibsons; the Searles, Archers and Robinsons were partners in a brewery; some chapel men helped raise funds to rebuild the church spire; some church men sat on the Dissenters' British School committee; all worked together on the ecumenical Town Mission. Together they raised subscriptions for worthy causes like a new cattle market, campaigned for allotments, knocked on doors doing social surveys, sat on juries, drank together at the *Rose & Crown*. Working together in all sorts of ways, they helped forge a new middle-class identity.[41]

At least this was true most of the time, but not always. The 1830s were a time of great change which put enormous strain on society. In the intimacy of this small market town, where everyone knew everyone else's business, middle-class relationships were not following their normal smooth path. For a few fraught years, sectarian divisions threatened to undermine the goodwill between the various factions, so much so that it was suggested that the 'unchristian-like' arguments should not take place in the old council chamber in church. By 1836, divisions were seemingly irreparable: 'It is impossible for any one not intimately connected with this our once peaceful town, to conceive the change which one short year has made in our comfort and respectability'. With accusations of 'exclusive dealing' and 'incalculable' mischief done to society in Walden, the well-ordered town appeared to be under dire threat. What was happening in Saffron Walden to occasion such an outburst of feeling?[42]

Chapter 3

'The Formidable Clique of Gamboogers'
Small Town Politics

'No small portion of the inhabitants (particularly of the lower class) have, through the insinuations and calumnies of mock patriots and designing knaves, been led to believe that they have been most unjustly deprived of their rights and privileges, and that for many years past transactions have been carried on little short of robbery... The Corporate Body has completely floored the formidable clique of gamboogers; and the dupes of the latter are biting their lips with anger, on finding how and by whom they have been cajoled.'[1]

The 'formidable clique of gamboogers', in immortal phrase, were the rising Radical element among the Saffron Walden Liberals who, as in other towns in the 1830s, were upsetting the old guard who had run things in a cosy little clique for as long as anyone could remember. The colourful account quoted above was typical of a stream of similar invective emanating from one of the more reactionary local Tories, who was Walden correspondent of the *Essex Standard* throughout this decade. Such extremism found a ready home, however, in the *Standard* which had been founded in 1831 by the Colchester Corporation and others specifically to oppose electoral Reform, and its wide circulation included Saffron Walden. John Player once claimed that even the Tories in Walden disliked the *Standard*: 'I am aware that many may read it who are utterly incapable of participating in such food; and these I know will condemn what is unfair & dishonourable'. However, reports by the anonymous Walden correspondent, though deeply partisan, have the value of reflecting an era of change and tension, when party politics in towns like Walden became a less gentlemanly affair; for a while, indeed, it seemed that political and sectarian divisions threatened to weaken the essential middle-class unity required in the face of growing poverty and unrest. These divisions and other aspects of the 1830s political scene in Walden are the subject of this chapter.[2]

Radicalism in Walden

The tradition of political Radicalism in England goes back at least as far as the Peasants' Revolt, and later to the remarkable Levellers during the Civil War,

centuries ahead of their time in seeking equal rights for all. These early movements had echoes in Saffron Walden, and Radicalism came to the fore again in
the early 1790s when there were constant worries about a French-type revolution occurring on this side of the Channel. This was a worry which turned to
alarm when Tom Paine published in two parts his remarkably prescient best-
seller, *Rights of Man*. In the sleepy little town of Saffron Walden, it was possible
for a brief period in 1792 to buy this outspoken work full of extraordinary ideas:
income tax, family allowances, free education, old-age pensions, maternity/
marriage and funeral assistance: in fact many of the democratic ideas now commonplace but then seen as dangerously revolutionary in this country, particularly the attack on inherited wealth. It appealed to the self-made man and a
sixpenny edition sold 200,000 copies all over the country.[3]

Part two, which carried all these radical ideas, could be purchased at
Christopher Payn's book shop in the Market Place, at least until the authorities
woke up. The government organised a royal proclamation against seditious
writings, and alarmed townsmen took advantage and called a public meeting
with Lord Howard de Walden in the chair, to set up an Association for Suppressing Sedition. A copy of their resolutions was deposited at the *Rose & Crown*,
and over six days was signed by 87 people, all opposed to 'the dangerous tendency of certain seditious and libellous publications'. Tradition has it that local
Radicals read the book in the public houses and, recognising that such meeting-
places could be centres of plotting, the Association told publicans not to allow
any defamatory conversation and to stop people circulating treasonable pamphlets, otherwise they would lose their licences. Similar associations appeared
in many places as an antidote to Radicalism. Draft presentments were drawn
up to prosecute Christopher Payn, 'a wicked, malicious, seditious and ill disposed person', but he left the town rapidly and emigrated to America, the land
of the free, as did Tom Paine himself.[4]

With the outbreak of war with France in 1793, patriotism was the order of the
day, although the label 'Jacobin' continued to be used for anyone thought to
hold Radical opinions. Discontent was always likely to resurface when times
were hard, as during the 1795 food riots in Walden (see chapter 7). But generally
the war was a time to emphasise the established order, as evidenced in the formation of two companies of Saffron Walden Volunteers, in common with similar corps all over the country, numbering up to half-a-million men nationally.
Under the major, Thomas Hall (presumably the Corporation clerk), each Walden
company had about 75 privates, as well as sergeants, corporals and drummers.
Among the names are those of Daniel Hockley the builder, Thomas Smith the
tanner and Jacob Nockolds. On one occasion in 1805 a company was on permanent duty in Epping, having marched the 27 miles there in one day.[5]

Although Radicalism lay quiescent, Paine's questioning of the *status quo* was
not forgotten, and the 1830 'Captain Swing' wage riots sent ripples of fear, as
did any kind of insubordination by the lower classes (see chapter 7). To Conservative men of property, such opposition, whether moderate Whig, politically
Radical or through socialistic combinations, was all the same, equated with the
type of peoples' insurrection all too common across the Channel. However, it

was impossible to ignore the clamour for change among the thrusting middle-classes in most towns, and Saffron Walden was no exception. After Catholic emancipation, electoral Reform became the issue of the day.[6]

Elections and Reform

On the occasion of the Saffron Walden Tory dinner in 1831, one man spoke for all: 'I cannot help but feel great anxiety at the measures which are now going on in the country'. But, he added, at least in Saffron Walden 'we are not afflicted with that mania for Revolution lately so prevalent through the country'. This was not strictly true as there was a growing group of Reformers in the town and surrounding countryside, although it is difficult to discover much about them. One supporter must have been Robert Driver Thurgood who, as secretary of the 'Reformers' Registration Club', later worked to gather Liberal votes in the town and 34 surrounding villages. Supporters came together in 1831 in the town for a 'Friends of Reform in Walden' dinner. Among the 'agricultural and commercial gentlemen' present was Vicesimus Knox Esquire, later to be Saffron Walden Recorder, an Essex barrister of repute, who commented that three-quarters of the English Bar supported Reform. Although there were 90 people at the dinner, the *Standard* claimed only 20 were gentlemen, the rest being shop-boys and 'a hodge-podge of apprentices and little people, specially treated for the occasion, and assuming the rank and title of "freeholders".' Knox, although a Whig-Radical, found himself defending the Tory Corporation from criticism, and the baronet in the chair, Sir Francis Vincent of Debden Hall, was described as 'one of your modern Whigs, a convert in politics as well as in religion'.[7]

Although most of the town's Tories were said to be against Reform, there were only two Walden signatories sent in with an Essex 'Declaration against the Reform Bill' on the grounds of too sudden and violent change: Francis Hall and Samuel Fiske. The Tories' dinner, soon afterwards, attracted an attendance of 130, among them the Catlins, John Archer, Henry Burrows, C.T. Master, Waite Spicer and William Ward: 'Although the town is celebrated for its saffron, all was blue on this occasion... there is only one True Blue feeling prevalent in the Corporation, and an ardent attachment to our glorious Constitution in Church and State'. They remained confident that their anti-Reform candidate, Col. J.T. Tyrell would be elected next time.[8]

Both political dinners took place in between the reading of the first and second parliamentary bills for electoral Reform, which were defeated. When the news reached Walden that the House of Lords had thrown out the second Reform bill, it was market day and the intelligence was 'to the no small gratification of the numerous and respectable agriculturalists who attend there and of a large majority of the most influential inhabitants'. This reaction was far from universal and there were protests all over the country, some of them violent, culminating in riots, incendiarism and fury at the bishops in the Lords who had defeated the bill. As a result there were great tensions at the seat of power, amendments to a third bill, resignations and new governments formed and finally, after extraordinary political machinations, Earl Grey's Great Reform Act — the beginning of so much future change — duly came into being in June 1832. Among those who voted for it was Lord Braybrooke, presumably following Lord Grey's thinking that the interests of the aristocracy were not incompatible with moderate reform.[9]

The rejoicing in Essex towns like Thaxted was not reported from Walden and, according to an ex-Radical who wrote to the *Standard*, this was because there was not enough support: 'An illumination was proposed immediately after the passing of the Grey Bill, but... not one in twenty of their neighbours chose to make such fools of themselves'. As noted earlier, the timing of the new spire ceremony may well have been a deliberate move to wrongfoot any such celebrations in the town. Eventually, three months later the Radicals held another event, which naturally drew forth heavy sarcasm from the same paper, who mocked the 'cheap dinner at one of our public houses' attended by only 23 people, not all electors; that the meal was badly cooked, many people drunk and, as a result, several more respectable types 'went home completely disgusted with reform and its quackeries'.[10]

The actual extension of the new franchise seems quite modest: the right to vote was extended in boroughs like Walden to adult males owning or occupying freehold property worth at least £10 a year. The vast majority remained voteless for many years to come, and the right to vote was lost if the man had received any parish relief during the previous year. It was the middle classes who benefited: farmers, shopkeepers and manufacturers, many of whom were also religious Dissenters. Whig/Dissenter John Player was in no doubt of its importance: 'the passing of the Reform Bill was an event pregnant with advantages of no common order. The projection of it evidently looked to the removal of dilapidations, rather than to the substitution of new theories in Government... The Reform Bill has in the representation of the people obviated a ludicrous anomaly.' Although caught up at the time in the excitement of the Reform cause, for the mass of Walden poor, Reform made little difference to their lives, for neither party sought to address the fundamental inequalities of society.[11]

The 1832 Election

The first election after the Reform Act, in December 1832, was expected to be a lively one. Up until the new law, parliamentary representation had been limited to a handful of county families, and elections often fixed. Bribery and corruption were commonplace. Now there was scope for ten Essex MPs to represent a county of over 317,000 people, separated into north and south divisions. Among those standing in the northern division, which stretched right across to Harwich and Colchester as well as Saffron Walden, was Charles C. Western, who had been an MP for over 40 years, but lost support when he came out for Reform, albeit pleasing his Dissenter supporters. The local polling place was to be either Saffron Walden or Thaxted, but those in charge of keeping order were worried by the latter's bad reputation. In the event the choice fell on Walden, which pleased the town's publicans particularly. If Thaxted had been chosen, it was said that 'very few of the respectable electors, blue or yellow, would have allowed themselves to be carried there, owing to the rough treatment heretofore experienced by many of them from the populace, when passing through that town to Chelmsford'.[12]

In order to minimise trouble, polling was now limited to two days but, aware that Parliamentary elections in Essex had always been excitable affairs, there was a worry that the large crowds attracted to Walden could stir things up. Permission was sought from the Home Office for up to 140 special constables, fearing that 'tumult or riot may reasonably be apprehended in the said town during the said election'. Other polling towns were taking similar precautions. Western's handbills doing the rounds of the Walden pubs were allegedly 'laughed at by farmers, tradesmen and others in the most unceremonious manner', and his 'mob orators' criticised.[13]

Elections then were colourful affairs: when Western and the other candidate, Thomas Brand visited the town in the autumn, they were met by the local committee at Audley End and escorted into town with the Walden Band playing and flags flying. At this time grocer/draper John Emson, who later left the party, must have been still a Whig supporter, for it was from the balcony of his Market Place house that Western addressed the crowds gathered below, speaking of the slavery and Corn Laws issues, but above all of electoral Reform. In his election address, he poked fun at the Walden oligarchy, describing it as 'a little blue egg inscribed "Corporation of Walden" in most tiny and insignificant characters'.[14]

However, things were not going the Whigs' way in Essex. As election day neared, they were said to be in a 'ticklish situation' in the northern division. In those days, the ballot was far from secret and supporters were able to lobby voters directly. Hence when the Tory candidate, Col. Tyrell, accompanied by the inevitable band and banners, visited Walden with his fellow candidate for the first poll, the opposition shouted down speakers and used 'the most desperate tricks and manoeuvres to catch a few votes to prop up their tottering cause… No person wearing a blue riband could proceed to the booths, but on instant a dozen gambooge fellows surrounded him and thrust into his hands yellow cards, bellowing in his ears to vote for Western and Brand.' It was all hugely entertaining and attracted immense crowds, but the 'specials' had little to do, and the elections were virtually trouble-free everywhere. However, the county did not follow the national trend, which was overwhelmingly in favour of the Whigs. Although the result was close, the Tory victory in Essex was interpreted as showing that there was no local support for Reform.[15]

Triumphantly the *Standard* commentator enjoyed the disappointment and 'intolerable gloom' of those in Walden he called the 'chop-fallen and humbled supporters of Whiggery'. When the unseating of Western became known at 9 o'clock on Saturday evening, the reaction among the Tories was ecstatic:

'Numerous parties of Blues were waiting at the different inns to hear the result of the contest, and on the glorious tidings being made known, the most deafening shouts were heard from one street to another, and in a few minutes it spread like wildfire through the whole town. After this, not a Yellow was to be seen — their houses and shops closed - and all were silent as death - many of them, we are told, were carried to bed very ill, and some of the leaders cannot be prevailed upon yet to appear in public.'[16]

The Bench and the Corporation

Notwithstanding the disappointments of the 1832 Reform election in Essex, things were changing rapidly elsewhere. The Radical element in Walden does not seem to have been as vociferous as those in Parliament and in some other Essex towns, even though the Tory press used labels like 'Whig firebrands' and 'Jacobins'. A truly Radical programme would have embraced unconditional suffrage, a secret ballot, annual elections, even the abolition of the monarchy and hereditary peers, an unlikely scenario at this time. In reality, as noted earlier, those who can be identified as 'the Yellow Party', variously described as Whigs/Liberals/Radicals, were mostly tradesmen and professionals, running shops and small businesses within the town, who wanted a greater voice in public life. Perhaps they were lower down the pecking order, Tory supporters including corn merchants, maltsters, surgeons, currier, tanner and druggist, whereas the leading Whigs were grocers and drapers, a bootmaker, auctioneers and some of the smaller maltsters. The major difference, however, was not necessarily economic, but religious: most Tories (with the notable exception of the Gibsons) were Anglicans, whereas many Dissenters were Whigs and thus excluded from participation in corporate local government and the magistracy (although they now took part in vestry and other activities). As this 'middling sort' came to prominence in so many towns at this time, defence of the *status quo* explains much of the contempt expressed in the Tory press.

Exclusion from the bench rankled greatly, for magistrates were important people. They dealt not only with crime, but also many quasi-judicial matters, such as oaths, covenants, land transactions, debts, sacrament certificates, master-servant disputes, fees for the Militia, swearing in constables and licensing alehouses. They were also a vital part of the machinery of the old poor law: sorting out settlements, bastardy payments, whipping beggars on their way. Via the system of grand jury presentments, public nuisances among the burgeoning population were addressed, setting in train urgent work needed on road and bridge repairs, dirty drains and dungheaps. In the last throes of an outmoded paternalist tradition, they retained for a time the old functions of regulating the market and enforcing weights and measures requirements, the kind of work once central to the Sessions and to keeping the populace happy, to prevent a recurrence of the eighteenth century food riots.[17]

During the period 1831–5, whereas the justices met about 250 times to cover a vast range of duties, the Corporation met only 20 times with just 18 agenda items. As in many towns, much of the Corporation income was spent in keeping order but it appeared, based on their surviving records (admittedly not very extensive), to be otherwise virtually moribund by the 1830s, largely civic and ceremonial and of far less practical importance in day-to-day administration than the vestry and the bench. Their meetings were irregular events, arranged *ad hoc* a few times a year, held in different venues, mostly with just one or two agenda items, after which they would all adjourn to feast at the premier inn, the *Rose & Crown* which, one suspects, was the real attraction of the event. They never took any initiative over new utilities so vital to a growing population — such as cleaner water, sewage disposal and gas supplies — probably because, as larger ratepayers, they would have had to pay for such modern improvements. If these innovations did arrive, it was often through private enterprise. After the ructions of earlier centuries, the Corporation had settled down from the late seventeenth century charter, with its complement of mayor, recorder, deputy recorder, aldermen, town clerk and coroner, all controlled by a tiny oligarchy of self-elected, privileged families, who saw no need for change.[18]

Although many activities took place under other umbrellas, in a rapidly-changing society, the old corporations were said to have outlived their useful-ness, and the new standards required to deal with problems in the industrial towns had a knock-on effect on smaller market towns too. Once the parliamen-tary franchise was widened, the old municipal system appeared even more of an anomaly. At the very least, the sands had run out on their religious and po-litical exclusiveness and reluctance for local improvements.

The Municipal Commission

In the wake of the 1832 Reform Act, the Government was determined to abolish the 178 ancient Corporations and evidence was gathered, as with the Poor Law and charity reforms, by travelling commissioners (see chapters 4 & 9). The Mu-nicipal Commission was formed, said John Player, 'to strengthen those energies in the domestic economy… to ascertain delapidations & to estimate the need of repair… It is performing its task impartially and well.' It was questionable whether it was any longer legal for Dissenters to be excluded from office, after the repeal in 1828 of the seventeenth century Test & Corporation Acts, which had up to then disqualified Dissenters from political office. Municipal reform was long overdue for important Dissenter businessmen like the Gibsons, wealthy gentle-men like John Player and the other men who supported the local economy.[19]

In January 1834 the Saffron Walden Corporation was suddenly stirred into action, for their very existence was under threat, from the imminent visit of the Municipal Commission. Critics seized the opportunity to bring up long-stand-ing grievances against the Tory Corporation, and the latter reacted with abso-lute fury, attacking the Commission as 'illegal and unconstitutional'. Their dull minutes and infrequent meetings suddenly came to life, as they declared them-selves 'unconscious of having either in a corporate or magisterial capacity done any act calculated to prejudice the interests of the town or to bring discredit on themselves as a body'. The Saffron Walden Recorder, Lord Braybrooke, care-fully distanced himself from the whole messy business, by remaining neutral, but this was accepted as he was a peer of the realm and above such things. At first the then mayor, Lewis Archer ignored the Commissioner's request for a meeting, but then, on being ordered to do so and stating they had nothing to hide, allowed the Town Clerk to give full co-operation.[20]

Player made extensive notes about anomalies in the selection of officers, according to the terms of the town charter, the method of appointing Almshouse trustees and the non-existence of the Grammar School (see chapters 9 & 11). A strong critic of the old system, he wrote to the press of 'the perverseness with which the privilege of self elected Bodies are to be tenaciously maintained in opposition to the general weal'. While carefully avoiding personal insults, he was particularly worried about the lack of democracy:

> 'Without casting the slightest intentional reflection on the members of the Corporation as now constituted, it is held to be liable to abuse if vacancies are ever to be filled up as at present – one inseparable consequence arising out of the natural partialities of kindred in the having of several members of one family in the Body Corporate, which might without caution giving an undue preponderance where favours are to be bestowed: with the present number of aldermen, two families can command a majority'.[21]

The Commissioner who came to Walden in March 1834, Thomas Jefferson Hogg, spent three full days in the town, meticulously combing through properties and privileges, boundaries and titles, and examining every detail of the various town charters and expenditures. Commissioner Hogg was the same one who a few months later in a rowdy enquiry was aggressively castigating the corrupt Colchester Corporation for evasion and inefficiency. Yet in Walden he was full of praise for the way the accounts were kept, money was spent, business conducted and property like the Almshouses cared for. Jabez Gibson, one of the Dissenters likely to benefit from municipal reform, moved a unanimous vote of thanks to all concerned, including the Commissioner 'for the impartial manner in which he had conducted the inquiry, and the patience he had evinced during the tedious investigation'. In the words of one report, 'the greatest good humour prevailed during the investigation', which exonerated the Walden Corporation. According to a somewhat more colourful version, the enquiry had 'been the means of opening the eyes of the credulous, and dispelling the long-standing and erroneous impressions under which so many of our townsmen have laboured; and showing, in their true light, the real views and intentions of those popularity-hunting THINGS who have misguided them'.[22]

Commissioner Hogg was no government toady. He agreed that the corporations should be reformed, but found little evidence to justify their abolition, a view which brought him into serious conflict with his superiors. After Walden, he went on to visit other towns, working every day for seven months, and did not finish writing his report on Saffron Walden until June 1835. However, he had not been allowed to see the government's general report before it was published, and afterwards protested at length about its bias and inaccuracy. Nevertheless, the bill was passed before his work could be published. He then engaged in a long dispute about under-payment of his monthly 100-guinea salary, the implication being that dissent from the views of his colleagues had cost him

Fig.3.1 *A somewhat unflattering bust on the exterior of Eaden Lilley's, Market Hill, said to be that of John Emson, founder of Emson's grocery and drapery shop in the early nineteenth century.*

dear. It is now known that the commissioners were expected to select evidence to justify a new statute already decided upon, and hence the highly partisan published report included many exaggerated comments on some of the 300 towns visited, and excluded the findings on towns like Walden which presumably offered little damning evidence, whereas Dunmow, Harwich and Maldon were among those included.[23]

The Walden Corporation decided not to go to the expense of sending a deputation to London to oppose the bill, but did send a petition to the House of Lords, 'this body having undergone the fullest examination by the Municipal Commissioner appointed for that purpose and there being in no instance any violation of the trusts committed to their charge'. In the absence of more detailed records of just how the Corporation operated at this time, the conclusion has to be that Saffron Walden Corporation were indeed innocent of charges levied by the Radicals of inefficiency and corruption. But of course the rot could be more endemic. Men of property who had been in power for too long could abuse the trappings of office in perfectly legal ways, through idleness, nepotism, privilege, monopoly and patronage of the favoured few.[24]

No meetings of the Corporation are recorded for three months after Hogg's visit, but then the old Corporation exemplified these tendencies in rushing through various measures before the axe fell on their privileges. Several items on the agenda concerned Market Place grocer/draper, John Emson, who had switched political allegiance, allegedly in reaction to extreme anti-Establishment tendencies among the Radicals, and now called himself a 'Nondescript' (see chapter 2). His elevation to alderman and then rapidly to mayor, without having to serve a trial period, particularly upset his former political colleagues: 'the acceptance of the gown by the former gentleman has given great offence to the liberal party'.[25] [Fig.3.1]

The Municipal Corporations Act

In September 1835 the 178 old closed corporations were abolished and replaced with elected town councils, meeting more regularly and with one third of their members facing re-election every year in rotation. Having previously had ten self-elected aldermen, there were now to be only four, but also twelve democratically-elected councillors. Householders with a certain income and paying poor rates had a vote in borough elections. The new bodies could levy rates and form watch committees and, if they wished, establish borough police forces and take over local improvement commissions. Hitherto private meetings now had to be held in public.[26]

The big change was that the new councils were open for the first time to Dissenters who now felt the chance had come to promote their vision for the town. The council elections were held in two stages and of the 180 entitled to vote, 168 votes were cast. There were 42 candidates for just 16 seats, and among those who failed to get elected were some of the stalwarts of the old Walden Corporation. It was obviously a hard pill for an Archer to swallow, if he failed to get elected after his family had been aldermen and mayors for generations. Several Whigs also failed to win a seat but in most cases got onto the council in later years. After the second election, the result was a new council split almost equally, though the Tories retained a small majority. More significantly, in religious affiliation, the Dissenters — Independents, Baptists and Quakers — for the moment had a much stronger voice, having been totally excluded before. Indeed the high number of votes (148) cast for Quaker, Jabez Gibson, a Dissenter hitherto banned from office, was remarkable. Joining the old guard and a few newer Tory councillors were the 'new men', including two Gibsons and Player, R.D. Thurgood, Robert Paul, John Clark and, at a second later election, Hannibal Dunn and James Humphreys. Between the two parties, they now represented a cross-section of the middle-class and many of its commercial interests. Repeated in towns all over the land, it must have seemed like an enormous political revolution.[27]

Needless to say the result brought forth a shower of rhetoric from the *Standard* correspondent, who managed to ignore the remarkable Dissenter presence and instead highlight the fact that it had not been a total Whig take-over. He accused the 'Yellow Committee' of employing 'the lowest jackall' at two shillings a day to perform their dirty work in secretly canvassing for votes, undermining fair play by 'propagating iniquitous falsehoods'. No parliamentary election, he exclaimed, 'ever produced a twentieth part of the angry feelings which at present distract the town'. Feelings ran even higher and there was 'another pretty broil, a few degrees hotter than the first', when all four aldermanic honours were given out to Tories before the second election took place. This enabled the Whigs to get more members onto the council again, but allegedly by underhand means, squeezing out a respected Tory by a majority of only one vote. In both elections 'renegade churchmen have been made the tools of the church-haters', who would soon find out their mistake.[28]

The unhappy atmosphere was mentioned by Lord Braybrooke when he wrote to the Home Office that, since the Municipal Bill, there was far more evidence of party spirit in the town, 'the Dissenters being almost as numerous as the Church men and opposing each other upon all occasions, whereas before there was no bone of contention'. Lord Braybrooke thus confirmed the validity of the reports which appeared regularly in the *Essex Standard* during the 1830s of which the 'formidable clique of gamboogers' quoted in the chapter title was but a mild example. On one occasion, the newspaper's editor commented that it would be preferable to hold meetings at the Town Hall instead of the Church, 'as the latter place is not quite calculated for the fierce and unchristian-like ebullitions of certain spouting democrats'. The Municipal Corporations Act was indeed to prove the beginning of a period of several years of party political disputes, which for a time threatened to undermine the show of unity felt essential when dealing with the poorer classes.[29]

More efficient watching and lighting of the parish became a priority under the new council, as well as improvements in policing (see chapter 6). Although there were already some oil lamps, a sixpenny rate was raised in order to pay for 60 gas lamps and a lamp lighter in parts of the town, noticeably where the richer houses were situated. Every year there were also repairs to pay for, as the lamps were frequently vandalised. From now on, the council was elected by the ratepayers, with a third of the members retiring each autumn and therefore subject to a greater degree of public scrutiny of what they had achieved. A notable feature of the new council was that it continued to resist central government control of its activities. In many ways, however, after this initial flurry of activity, the council was really not much more dynamic than its predecessor. There was little municipal progress until the 1870s and most of the improvements which occurred in this period — gas, water, the Corn Exchange, the Institution, the Museum — were the result of private enterprise. Whereas in Colchester there was a very effective Commission set up for municipal improvements, no such body appeared in Walden. When there was urgency, things could happen, as in 1831 when the cholera scare forced the temporary appearance of a very active Board of Health (see chapter 4).[30]

The most immediate and best-known effect of the MCA was that it put 'moderate' Whig John Player, hitherto a Dissenter barred from office, into the mayoral chair, even though Whigs had not quite pulled off the clean sweep they hoped for. [Fig.3.2] This was a triumphant achievement for Player, but his mayoral year was far from smooth. The refusal of smaller ratepayers to pay for improvements demanded by the rich hampered progress. When the borough accounts were, for the first time, published at the end of his year, a disgruntled ratepayer scribbled comments on one copy, complaining of over-spending, prosecution expenses as 'forged

Fig.3.2 *'Gentleman' John Player, first Dissenter Mayor of Saffron Walden. The painting was done in 1842, four years before his death at the age of 60.*

Fig.3.3 *Borough accounts, 1837: note the marginal scribbles by a disgruntled ratepayer, complaining of 'monstrous' expenses, 'forged papers' and other queries.*

papers', money wasted on a common seal, writing out lists of burgesses and mayoral entertainment expenses. [Fig.3.3] Player later had to defend the 'unusual items of expenditure' which appeared in the first year of the new council and would not recur, items like copying charters and buying a deed chest, as well as a rise in expensive criminal prosecutions and fighting the campaign to keep the Quarter Sessions, which most ratepayers had supported: 'I am sorry that the opposition should resolve it a question of pounds shillings and pence', he commented (see chapter 6).[31]

When a report on his mayoral dinner found its way to the offices of the *Essex Standard*, the editor refused to print it and said some people had walked out of the dinner because a Baptist minister had proposed the health of the members of the old Corporation, causing something of a stir. Towards the end of Player's term of office, the *Standard* correspondent was in a permanent state of fury, describing a state of open warfare between the two parties and calling on the 'respectable portion of townsmen' to fight back. In more than one report he launched a veritable tirade against the Yellow party, accusing them of 'perfidy… personal hostility… paltry and base upstarts… contemptible measures… barefaced and most unblushing impudence… low minded faction and ignorant brutality…

vulgar ambition… unbounded insolence… ceaseless hate…'. This was strong stuff, and one wonders how representative the *Standard* was of Walden opinion. The Liberal press preferred to claim that the town was now being run on democratic principles. On the other hand, the MCA did cause just such a deep rift in many towns during this time of transition, when the *status quo* had been thoroughly upset. Bitterness deepened, with further political and religious controversies, and the investigations of the Charity Commission (see chapters 9 & 12).[32]

The conflicts simmered for several years to come, rising to the surface whenever occasion presented itself, as with the periodic municipal and aldermanic elections. The *Essex Standard* continued to criticise the 'rancorous party spirit' in Walden, while the *Essex & Herts Mercury*, a Radical paper, allegedly supported by many Dissenting ministers and deacons, denied there was any such feeling. After the highly popular Jabez Gibson died in 1838, there was an outburst of bitter hostility over who should take his place, and a similar row the following year after the death in mayoral office of Liberal Robert Paul, with Tory accusations of a return to the old, condemned practice of self-election.[33]

Party politics was not the only divide. There was also considerable ill-feeling at times between the different layers of wealth. In particular, the poorer ratepayers always objected to paying for municipal improvements — such as policing and gas lighting — demanded by the richer businessmen. As noted above, gas lighting was one of the first improvements carried out by the fledgling council, but the power of the burgesses was demonstrated in 1839 when they defeated an attempt to impose an extra threepenny rate on top of the existing sixpence to further improve the town lighting. Large numbers of the opposition came to a public meeting called by the Mayor, Samuel Fiske in the town hall. The opposition speakers said that lighting improvements should be paid for by subscription and 'those persons whose property required so much protection, should liberally head the list'. So those who wanted the lighting left on all night had to raise a private subscription to meet the deficiency, while grumbling that some boroughs managed a one shilling rate for lighting.[34] The lesser ratepayers won the day, unswayed by the arguments of gas company shareholders who included John Player:

> 'One and all resisted the imposition of any further rate, and preferred "walking in darkness" rather than be at any additional expense about it; some of the little tradesmen and mechanics stating that they believed if all were rated who ought to be, and some of the salaries reduced or got rid of, the deficiency might be made up… The inspectors, contractors, clerks, deputy clerks, assistant deputies, etc. etc. etc. appeared to be completely stunned or, as the mechanics termed it, floored, and the meeting ended in nothing'.[35]

Obviously the municipal reforms were not quite the undiluted success they seemed to be, for wider powers and more bureaucracy equalled greater expenditure and the 'new men' found, as reformers always do, that to the common man ideology matters less than economics. Such divisions created a tension in the balance of power which aided democracy and was certainly an improvement on the complacency and lack of public accountability of earlier times. But the slow progress may have been the reason why, after the euphoria of the early years, political excitement waned and electoral apathy set in. The change could be seen in the declining numbers interested in becoming councillors, falling from 42 candidates in 1835 to 17 in 1840 and 11 a decade later. There were still occasional highlights, notably the annual mayor-making ceremonies, when 'church bells rang merrily and the band paraded the principal streets in the evening'. But when a somewhat low-key attempt was made to celebrate Victoria and Albert's wedding in 1840, even the Walden Band failed to stir feelings. Members of both parties sat uneasily together at a ten-shillings celebratory dinner with the council at the *Sun Inn*, allegedly a dull affair, for most people were simply 'not at all in a humour for holiday-making'. Naturally the *Standard* correspondent blamed all this apathy on the 'ruinous proceedings' of the Government and those who had brought in municipal changes which put the rates up.[36]

Soon afterwards the Town Council were in trouble again, this time accused of financial incompetence by the auditors, who objected to 'unnecessary or extravagantly charged' items in the annual accounts. But the council overruled their own auditors. Meanwhile, Conservatives, both electors and elected, seemed to be losing interest. It was becoming harder to replace the true blue stalwarts, for other Tories would not 'in the present crazy state of the Corporation vessel, venture to embark for a three years voyage'. This was perhaps a reference to the local authority's expenditure which had been criticised before, but which the Whigs continued to maintain was above reproach.[37]

When banker, Francis Gibson, a Conservative, came onto the council in 1840, some Dissenter Radicals had 'sad misgivings', for Francis was the nominee of other wealthy Conservatives. But another commented that having a banker on the council would improve accountancy: 'let the Borough accounts be passed, printed and published, without the farce of Auditors and leave the management of the fund to wiser heads, who whilst protecting their own interests will hardly neglect those of their poorer townsmen', he wrote, with an aside which jokingly suggested that, in addition to the new 'Bastille' gaol being built, the town should also construct a debtors' prison. The interchange was typical of party political relationships, but the brief period of deeper conflict seemed to be drawing to a close.[38]

It was also at this time that John Player retired from politics, his health in decline. Although a 'moderate' Whig, the departure of Player coincided with the beginning of the end of the era of bitter party politics. During the 1840s Town Council meetings gradually became more muted affairs, hostilities breaking out largely during elections to various bodies, such as the Board of Surveyors. This had worked well in its first year, carrying out road improvements, buying water carts and pumps and other tasks; but when targeted by 'a few cunning Radicals' the existing members refused to work with them, and the Board ended up at an impasse. Particular personalities could still stir up controversy, as happened to Robert Driver Thurgood when he tried to get his son, Richard, into the town clerk vacancy in 1848. [Fig.3.4] Since his other son, solicitor William, was already Clerk to the Justices and Thurgood senior was Clerk to

Fig.3.4 (above) *Silhouette of Robert Driver Thurgood, Clerk to the Guardians, Borough councillor and one-time Mayor of Saffron Walden, leading member of Saffron Walden Liberals and man of many other parts.*

Fig.3.5 (right) *Broadsheet published by 'A Burgess', criticising Thurgood for trying to put his family in charge of key posts in the town.*

TO THE

BURGESSES

OF THE BOROUGH OF

Saffron Walden.

GENTLEMEN,

Let me call your attention from an Imaginary "DIALOGUE" to a statement of FACTS:

Are you aware that MR. THURGOOD, who is now disturbing the peace of the Borough, himself took time to consider whether he would become the purchaser of MR. MASTER's Business before the introduction of "THE STRANGER!" If not it seems fitting this fact should be made known to you.

And are your so blinded to the motives and actions of the former Gentleman now, as not to see that *Self*, or rather Family aggrandizement lies at the bottom of all this ferment? *Public Grounds* are alleged for his opposition, and the COUNCIL are threatened with perpetual strife, because in the discharge of their duty, they have not thought proper to concur with him in dividing the Offices held by MR. MASTER,—proved to be worth at the most, but little beyond a single Appointment held by his eldest Son,—that of the Clerkship to the Borough Justices. I would ask, does this come well from a Man who himself holds another Office,—the Clerkship to the Board of Guardians, more than double the value of those held by MR. MASTER? Ought not he and his Family rather to be content with what they have, without seeking to disturb the quiet of the TOWN, for a *pretended* principle, in which it is manifest he does not himself concur,—or why should he be so very anxious to secure the Town Clerkship for another Son, and thus centre Three Offices in one Family, against which he now so much inveighs?

Do you not, Gentlemen, see the drift of all this? And are you content to have the Town bound in the trammels of one Family, —to be tied hand and foot to one Man! If not, ASSERT MANFULLY, your opinion at the POLL to DAY!!

A BURGESS.

Saffron Walden, Nov. 1st, 1848.   YOUNGMAN, WALDEN.

the Guardians, this would have put the same family in control of local government, criminal law and poor law, naturally causing some disquiet. The poster put up around the town by an anonymous critic seems remarkably outspoken, but not untypical of political broadsheets at the time.[39] [Fig.3.5]

On the whole, however, public life was resuming its old gentlemanly ways, and even when the balance of power shifted in favour of the Tories again, 'good feeling among the parties prevailed'. Similar shifts occurred in many towns, as the petty squabbles inevitable at a time of radical change, gradually settled into a way of life and local politicians, who increasingly found themselves working together in philanthropic and business concerns, buried many of their differences which, in any case, assumed less importance in the face of outside threats: the growing depression, poverty and unrest of 'the hungry Forties'.[40]

Conclusion

The general impression is that, although there was some political excitement in Walden in these years, the more extreme forms of Radicalism achieved little prominence here. The moderate Whigs, socialistic Radicals and other more authoritarian members of the Liberal party were a mixed bunch in Parliament, and even more so in a small market town. Any reforming movement needs leaders, and Walden seems to have lacked such: Player was critical, but not outspoken: he liked to get on with everybody and largely fits his description as a 'moderate' Whig. Those members of the gentry, clergy and legal profession who supported the Reform cause, were unlikely to precipitate any other type of revolution. A few middle-class townsmen like Thurgood were more active but, one suspects, partly for their own advancement.

There were no obvious signs of the renewed Radicalism called Chartism which emerged elsewhere in the country, particularly in the industrial areas, with its People's Charter. Out of 39 of the largest towns in Essex and Suffolk, 28 had a Chartist presence, but not Walden, Thaxted or Dunmow. It was really too small and old-fashioned a town, still dominated by agriculture, to sustain any real challenge for long. In larger towns shoemakers, tailors, watchmakers and builders commonly supported the cause, but Chartism could only flourish if the literate middle classes supported it. The well-being of the 'new men' was just as much dependent on the local economy as those of the older establishment, in fact more so, for their shoemaking, drapery, grocery, ironmongery and other businesses relied on constant replenishment, whereas the Tory ranks included many men of inherited wealth. A man who would risk his livelihood to pursue an ideology was rare indeed. The 1830s Radicals might have been 1840s Chartists too, but the word itself did not break the surface. Elites were aware of Chartism elsewhere, and such knowledge informed their actions, hence it was not without influence. Meanwhile those who worried about the inequalities of society could find self-expression, mutual support and social conscience in other less risky ways: in provident societies, in allotments and other philanthropic works, educational and religious outreach. These were means of practical, humanitarian and spiritual activism in an increasingly difficult world.[41]

And difficult it was, particularly in the 1840s. The poor had no part to play in most of the events described in this chapter. They might enjoy the heady atmosphere of election campaigns and mayor-making jollifications, but neither the reform of the franchise nor of the corporations achieved much for them: indeed they paved the way for the reform of the poor laws, an enactment which blighted generations. As a contrast to the world of the worthies, that of the poor, as expressed through the records of pauperism, crime and protest, was very different.

Chapter 4

'A Most Unthankful Duty'
The Old Poor Law

'At best it is a most unthankful duty to fill a parochial office; and whether by care the parishioners be saved their money or by want of it, their money be spent, the result is the same'.[1]

Thus did John Player express a common woe, that the overseer's lot was not a happy one: he was criticised by the poor if things went one way, and equally blamed by the better-off if they veered towards the other. The context of this particular comment was Player's reply to a complaint from maltings owner, Charles Porter that one of his men, who had never before applied for poor relief, had been refused parish road-work: 'the Rates, I am paying for the relief of the poor, my men ought to share in it... men that are willing to work and try to keep away from the parish in my opinion ought to be encouraged', he felt. Player denied the accusation, insisting that parish business was carefully conducted without any bias. Come to the Friday vestries, he invited Porter, and get some 'insight into the real state of the poor', then people would support the parish officers more. Faced with criticism, a typical defensiveness arose, so that it seemed that the problems of the overseers outweighed those of the poor themselves. This chapter is an examination of how the town was run under the old poor laws which prevailed up to 1835, for nothing was more essential to the maintenance of a well-ordered town than their efficient operation.[2]

The Old Poor Law in Walden

At one time a hotch-potch of abbeys, churches, guilds, benefactors and charities had tackled the problem piecemeal, and Walden had all these agencies. Poverty was looked on then as a natural state, often a life-cycle experience, descending in sickness and old age or a seasonal problem, caused by poor harvests. Kin and neighbours helped each other, while the parish dealt with temporary crises, which could normally be handled so long as population remained low. But when population rose dramatically, the poor law came under great strain. While the various forms of voluntary poor relief continued, a statutory provision was emerging and one which was to dominate the lives of the poor for more than two centuries, evolving in different ways to suit the local historic, geographical and economic conditions of each parish. The 43rd statute of Elizabeth of 1601 was the important one, basically remaining in force until the nineteenth century, although tinkered with at intervals, most significantly with the 1662 settlement regulations. The 1601 statute brought together existing officers and created new ones, as well as fixing a basic method of regular poor rate funding and who should benefit from relief. All this put considerable power and responsibility into the hands of the parish officers, for the rates had to be collected, relief distributed, settlement established and proper accounts kept. Distinguishing between the impotent, deserving and undeserving poor became a central dilemma. The impotent had certain rights and there was discretion to help the deserving, but those deemed undeserving could be removed from the parish or compelled to work. In Walden, this evolved into a multi-faceted system of considerable sophistication.[3]

Saffron Walden was a parish with a town embedded within it, so that their administration ran side by side. To describe this system is to become buried in complexity, but an attempt must be made, for it demonstrates how power was devolved in a variety of interlocked ways, so that the inactivity of the Corporation is put into context. At one time the Guild of Holy Trinity was of great importance in Walden government, but an absence of later records obscures its subsequent role. The Walden Corporation evolved from a charter of 1514, and the vestry meeting gradually assumed an importance beyond the ecclesiastical, while the quarter and petty Sessions also had various administrative functions. The Chipping Walden and Brookwalden Manor Courts, once of far greater importance, by the nineteenth century dealt largely with the administration of land. They had their own officers, who worked in conjunction with market officials and town constables, but manor court constables were able to police the wider parish beyond the town, and could then bring cases before the Sessions. The manor courts, until 1835, also appointed pinders (officials who gathered and impounded stray animals), a role usually filled by the lower classes but, if suitable, often the same men were elected year after year. For instance, Daniel Barker served Walden as pinder for a quarter of a century.[4]

The origins of the constable's office were lost in the mists of history, perhaps even pre-dating the manor. Constables, probably nominated by the corporation, were paid by the vestry and sworn in yearly by the magistrates. They also assisted the overseers with poor law duties, such as fetching in the fathers of illegitimate children. In addition, the Corporation nominated a beadle, appointed by the Justices, and his powers included the judicial, such as prosecuting those who begged for alms or played games of chance on the highway. Through the grand jury presentments, the Sessions could influence the work of the other bodies: for instance in 1824 they recommended the employment of street keepers.[5]

The town charter required other officers to be appointed by the Saffron Walden Corporation (as well as mayor and aldermen): recorder, deputy recorder, town clerk, coroner, sergeants-at-mace and clerk of the market (there was also a town crier). The clerk of the market had the power to instantly put on trial market traders who contravened weights and measures: at one time they might be summonsed to the market court still covered in dust from the streets, hence the old expression, 'Court of Pie Powder'. A Court of Record appointed the market jury, and the ale-tasters and flesh-searchers of earlier times. Trespass and distraining of beasts and chattels were also mentioned here (although the pinder came under the manor court). But in the 1830s, much of the business of this Court of Record (also known as the Three Weeks Court) concerned unpaid debt. In 1833, a particularly busy year, it met 18 times, mostly to pursue small sums. In an age when borrowing and buying on tick was the norm, this was how shopkeepers and tradesmen got their money back. A typical small claim was Nathaniel Jeffery complaining of William Barker the elder in a plea of 5s.3d. But there were larger debts: for instance Lord Braybrooke complained of Robert Eldred, who had been discharged from prison, and had to pay off in instalments a debt of over £11. In 1836 grocer/draper, John Emson summonsed a large collection of people for small sums.[6]

While the manor court met twice a year, the bench quarterly (apart from summary justice whenever there were cases to hear), the Court of Record once or twice a month and the Corporation only intermittently, the vestry met every week, for they had most to do. This body, originally a church meeting, had evolved from the secular provisions of the 1601 statute, and now in Saffron Walden developed into an institution of men of status and influence, with a keen interest in law and order. Although many corporate towns had a somewhat narrower elitist body known as a select vestry, there is no record of such an institution in Walden. Instead major resolutions were taken by 'a meeting of the inhabitants' (meaning the principal ones, that is excluding the majority of the population, who thus had no say in how the parish was governed), and special committees to tackle particular tasks such as unemployment crises. Leading Dissenters, so long as they had not refused to pay rates, by the 1820s could take part alongside Anglicans in vestry business.[7]

And so, Saffron Walden was a self-contained and self-governing entity, day-to-day decisions falling on a mixture of paid and unpaid officers, who thereby shared among themselves much of the responsibility for keeping the town well-ordered and who were able, through this personal contact, to see poverty at first hand. This collection of various bodies is best delineated by actual example. Looking at 1832, admittedly an exceptionally busy year, the Corporation held one of its infrequent meetings and set up a committee to look into the nuisance of the cattle market. This was to be paid for by public subscription as well as Corporation monies. Then the necessary land transaction went through Chipping Walden Manor Court. Since it was the Quarter Sessions which had earlier received complaints about the old cattle market, it was to the bench that John Player, 'an indefatigable promoter of every improvement', addressed a speech about the new one. Meanwhile the Sessions also dealt with expenditure on the new jury room, the subject of heated exchanges between the vestry and the Corporation as to who should pay for it. The vestry raised a church rate and borrowed money to pay for the new spire. The £5,000 almshouse opened in March 1832, the £3,000 spire in June, the £1,300 cattle market in July. Although often similar collections of people sat on all these committees and dipped into their pockets for multifarious subscriptions and appeals, and their lives interweaved in many areas, the various projects were each dealt with under different arrangements.[8]

Of all the parish officers, those of surveyors of the highways and overseers of the poor were the most onerous. It was a challenging time for these men, who were all property-owners and led busy lives aside from their public duties. The potential for discontent among the masses, if there were maladministration of this essential safety net, ensured that dutiful types would generally be found to undertake the work, albeit that they often felt, as John Player, that it was a thankless task. On the other hand, the status element could mean that if a gentleman were passed over for office, this also caused offence, as in 1831 when the parish officers complained that one of their chosen successors, Thomas Smith, had not been given the job by the magistrates for some reason. The sensitivity of this period, immediately after the 'Swing' riots (see chapter 7), may have been a consideration.

Overseers were the busiest of all, and indeed this became such a demanding job that, from at least 1794, the vestry decided that to collect the rates, the parish needed a salaried vestry clerk, also referred to as the deputy overseer, who seemed to have powers to give incidental relief in addition to that organised by the unpaid overseers. Notwithstanding the paid help, the list of overseers' potential responsibilities was quite staggering, albeit that not all the tasks occurred during any one term of office: prepare valuation lists, levy rates, register electors, send in parliamentary returns, perambulate parish boundaries, take the population census (from 1801), draw up jury lists, arrange transport of witnesses to trials, lend out spinning wheels, arrange apprenticeships, find homes for orphans, deal with bastardy cases, vagrants and settlement examinations, organise the fire, medical and police services, as well as the essential organisation of poor relief, pursuing absent fathers and prosecuting those who tried to fiddle their claims. Careful accounts were required, to avoid criticism from ratepayers. These reflect the wide range of work but throw up some anomalies: why, for instance, were fines for assault, poaching, drunkenness and malicious injury sometimes coming into this account? Presumably the fines related to those in receipt of poor relief or living in the workhouse. Overseers were particularly stretched after poor harvests and during hard winters, which would be a cue to lay in a stock of fuel for the poor to buy cheaply, the carriage being paid for by local benefactors. During periodic crises, like the 1795 bread riots, the mayor, magistrates and parish officers were in the front-line. The principal parts of the overseers' role involved rates, settlement, relief and the town workhouse. These will be examined in turn.[9]

The Poor Rates

The idea of rates, a form of local tax, in some form could be traced back to the fourteenth century in places, and the method was universal by 1700. Under the 1601 statute, the method of funding was by raising a poor rate from among the better-off inhabitants. The poor rate was assessed and collected at so much per pound of rateable value on their property, and so was not a tax on personal wealth, but only in its tangible form of land and buildings. Imposition of such a tax on the better-off was one of the central achievements of the poor law and from this all else followed. Rate levels went up and down, but of course were unpopular. The largest payers, the Braybrookes and the Gibsons, notwithstanding their wealth, were among those who objected, at various times, to their rate assessments. Soon after the French wars, Atkinson Francis Gibson (father of Wyatt George) objected to the rating of his property and asked for it to be surveyed again. Another Gibson appeal some years later went to the Essex Quarter Sessions, on the grounds that their brewhouse and premises were over-rated by comparison with four other prominent men in the town.[10]

Settlement

Poor relief and assistance were only available to those who had a right to legal settlement in the parish, the 1662 Act of Settlement having decreed that strangers must prove their right to remain and must carry a certificate from the parish responsible for them. Enforcing this meant that parish officers needed detailed local knowledge about the inhabitants, and had to investigate their place of origin and qualifications to settle in Walden. There were several categories of qualification, and if one could not be proved, the strangers could be removed on the carrier's cart back to where they came from. The poor had tried all sorts of ways to get around these iniquitous laws, as they needed the freedom to move around to find work. From 1795, people could not be removed until they actually became a drain on the rates, but nevertheless the settlement laws remained a litigious minefield. The system became a cul-de-sac and caused much hardship, as hapless, harassed paupers were transferred at considerable expense from one place to another. The children must have suffered greatly.[11]

Saffron Walden has a large collection of settlement, removal and examination documents which illuminate this sad and difficult business. Surviving records relate to 684 documents dealt with by the Saffron Walden overseers between the 1690s and 1850, and cases were rising by a quarter or more each half-century, the busiest decade being the 1820s. Some were very vexing matters to resolve, such as the settlement rights of the 12 children of Edward Deadman, six of whom belonged to Walden and the other six to Waltham Abbey. Another extreme case was the Church family. James Church, his wife and seven children returned to Walden from London in July 1831, presumably because they were destitute, but were given 50 shillings by the overseers to go back again. In 1834 they were removed from Hackney back to Walden, but later returned to London again. In 1837, James died, leaving his widow Ann, now burdened with eight children aged from 17 down to nine months, none with legal settlement and some too ill with scarlet fever to be removed. She once again appealed to the Walden overseers for help.[12]

Obviously this type of assistance, giving relief to Walden people living elsewhere, was kept to a minimum. One such list of those 'allowed to live at a grate distance from Walden and payd by overseers' contained only seven names, living in Waltham

Abbey, Halsted, Coggeshall, Warley, Ongar, Royston and Huntingdonshire. They hoped, by offering temporary help, such large families might earn settlement elsewhere. By the 1820s most Essex towns operated similar arrangements, and the county has a rich store of letters sent by such out-of-town paupers, who could become adept at exploiting the system. From Walden, the overseers sent relief to a man living in Suffolk, John Willis, 'a poor fellow, a great invalid and totally incapable of doing any work', and after his death, his widow thanked 'the gentlemen of Saffron Walden for their kind liberality to her deceased husband', a piece of humility which earned her 30 shillings towards his funeral and a continued weekly allowance.[13]

Settlement certificates, dating back to legislation of 1696/98, became the most precious of documents, and those lacking such had to go through the humiliating ritual of an examination to prove their right to settlement and obtain relief. These examinations could involve endless trouble and expense for parishes at either end. The 'trial' on Samuel Nichols' claim for settlement in 1825 entailed travel to four different places to gather evidence, and an appeal over the removal of James Smith and his family from Hackney in 1829 cost the town a sum much in excess of what the Smiths would have needed. Nevertheless, these potential claimants had to be treated with suspicion, otherwise the town would be overrun with mendicants, it was felt. It cannot have been easy to sort out for, while some were frauds, others simply lacked the documents for various reasons.[14]

The category of gaining settlement through being 'hired for service', proved particularly hard to interpret, until abolished under the New Poor Law. The parish officers had to sit in judgement, for instance, on 29-year-old Maria Saveall who had once worked as housemaid in a Walden household, earning £9 a year for four years; on George Savill who, before becoming a journeyman, had been apprenticed to a Walden blacksmith 18 years earlier; and on Benjamin Rider who 12 years earlier had worked at Clophams (or Cloptons) farm in Little Walden for £7 a year, but then with various masters. He tried to gain settlement as a horse-keeper on a Cambridgeshire farm, paying for his own board and lodging, but fell out with his master. All of these had earlier associations with the town and were using this as the basis of their claims, for normally apprenticeship would gain a full-term settlement. Parish officers utilised the settlement laws to regulate and monitor immigration into their parish. In this sense any poor person, and not just the under-employed, out-of-work or destitute, could be under scrutiny.[15]

Outdoor Relief

Providing settlement was established, people in distress could apply for outdoor relief, which could be regular or occasional. In a typical period, for example, overseer John Clarke handed out half-a-crown to Thomas Onions whose children were in distress, eight shillings to John Brooks in distress, two shillings to James Smith who was ill, six shillings to John Cornell whose wife was ill and three shillings to William Jeffery whose children were ill. For the regular poor,

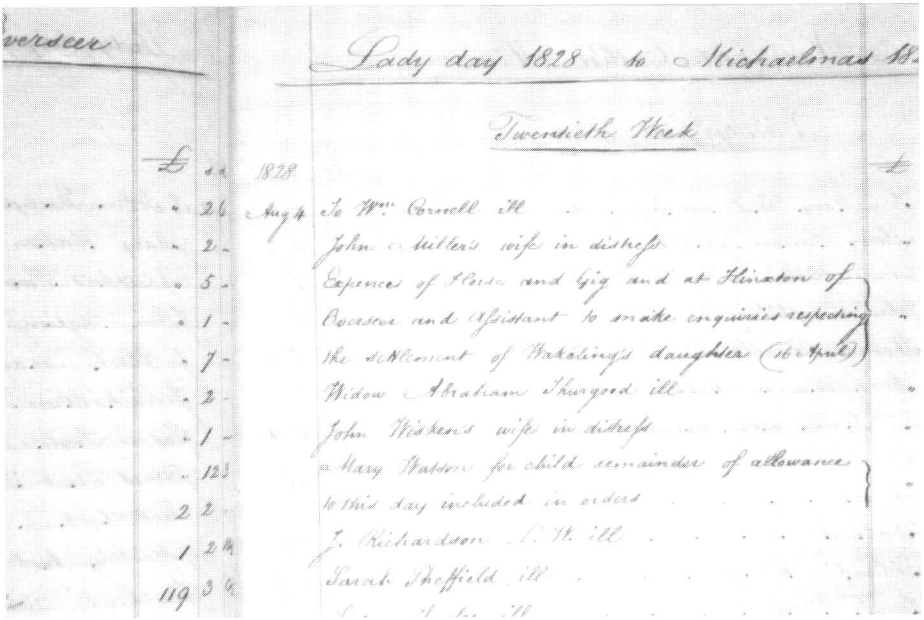

Fig.4.1 *A page from the overseers' accounts, showing a variety of payments in 1828 for illness, distress, child allowance and settlement enquiries.*

there were small weekly doles, which were available to various classes of pauper: the elderly, the infirm and disabled, young widows and deserted wives with children, orphans being fostered and of course the illegitimate young. In addition there were increasingly large numbers of weekly payments, goods and assistance on a temporary or occasional basis (although some people stayed on the list for some time). These covered a multitude of needs, from the cradle to the grave, for all manner of crises for reasons of ill health, accident, unemployment or other causes of poverty. [Fig.4.1] The overseers would most often write 'illness' or 'distress', sometimes 'wife confined', 'child dead' or occasionally 'deranged'. A pair of shoes here, a peck of bread there, a few shillings to help families through the week: this was the day-to-day work of the overseer, who also seemed to have discretion to make extra payments when required, which causes some confusion in the records.[16]

A controversial aspect of outdoor relief was 'the scale', said to have spread everywhere after originating in Speenhamland, Berkshire during a particularly distressed period in 1795 (although similar schemes operated elsewhere). The 'Speenhamland' scheme was a method of supplementing low wages with relief, using a scale based on the price of bread and the size of families. Something similar operated in Walden early in the nineteenth century, whereby the widow's allowance went up in tandem with the price of bread. But outdoor relief had to be more flexible than this, and was adjusted up or down as people's circumstances changed. For example, an elderly Barker couple started off with

2s. per week in 1797, rising for a brief period, but generally around the same level up to 1806 when it was reduced from 2s.3d to 1s.6d, the year before the man died.[17]

Another example was unmarried mother Mary Barker, who fell pregnant with her first daughter aged 18, and had a second illegitimate daughter seven years on. Four years later, in 1783, she went for the first time on regular relief totalling 2s. per week, but this was halved when her first child, Ann came of age in 1793. From 1794 she was living at Audley End and a few years later her relief began to rise to as much as 2s.6d, until the second child, Mary junior reached 21, when relief payments began to go down again. Mary junior also received relief for a few years: she was ill for a time and died in 1809. A year later her mother's allowance began to rise considerably and by 1813, the year before her death at the age of 60, she was receiving 5s. Some historians have seen the old poor law as a kind of mini welfare state, very comprehensive given its period, and such detailed case histories suggest that a reasonable kind of safety net did operate for the needy in Walden, albeit that the sums given out were the minimum necessary.[18]

Numbers on occasional relief noticeably dropped in 1820, which may have been connected with the brief boom in the silk-weaving industry, which for a time offered home-based work for women. But in answer to a parliamentary enquiry in 1824, Walden replied that the numbers seeking help had risen in recent years, and they were giving help only during illness, the relief 'according to the wants and the number of the family'. The two assistant Poor Law commissioners, Ashurst Majendie and Alfred Power, who visited Walden in turn in the early 1830s, gave somewhat opposite reports on whether scaled allowances were still in use here, and there were also differing views on whether relief in money or kind was best. Noticeably, in 1834, presumably in anticipation of the New Poor Law, the overseers' list was severely pruned. If a specified amount of help extended to the genuinely needy, it was a different matter with the 'idle' and even more so anyone who tried to defraud the parish. With the increasing cost of poor relief, attitudes from the 1820s had hardened towards such fraudsters. One offender in 1822, John Barker, was given a public whipping in the Market Place and then discharged, while Robert Barker senior was put in the house of correction for a month in 1829.[19]

Walden Workhouse

The third arm of the old poor law, besides settlement and outdoor relief, was relieving the most destitute in the workhouse. Although not specifically ordered under the Elizabethan Poor Law, such buildings did begin to appear in towns in the early eighteenth century, particularly after 1723, when parishes were enabled to buy or rent buildings and contract out the maintenance and employment of the poor. Many villages had their own poor-houses: in Clavering what was referred to as a 'new little house for poor people' was converted from the former guildhall by the church gate as early as 1760, while the Ashdon poorhouse was also a former guildhall, converted in 1775. The Walden workhouse was one of at least 170 which appeared in Essex in the course of the eighteenth century. Formerly the *White Hart*, it was bought in 1734 and the site extended into an adjoining cottage in 1798, partly to build a bridewell. The Walden workhouse stood at the top of the High Street, then called Cuckingstool End Street, its locality known as Workhouse Hill. Set in over an acre of ground, it was quite a substantial set of buildings, with men's and women's rooms, keeping room, hall, kitchen, meal house with 36 benches, dairy, wash-house, cellars, hospital, linen room, garret, yard and gardens.[20]

Proceeds from workhouse tasks helped offset the running costs. In the early days this largely consisted of spinning but references to spinning wheels fade from the records in the early nineteenth century. Sack-making had also been introduced by the late eighteenth century, making as much as 50% profit. The sacks could be sold through shops in town, and this evolved into quite a little manufactory for sacks, ropes and twine, in which not only the fitter adults but also the children in the house could be employed and paid customary wages. Taking some of the children into the workhouse was an occasional expedient, to enable the rest of the family to survive. In 1804, for instance, the four children of Thomas Baker from North End went into the workhouse, while he contributed weekly payments towards their maintenance. A 'double Necessary' was built in the yard for the use of the workers. The business turned in a good income, and as the old poor law ended, as much as £120 in one year could be received from sack sales. Other work including grinding barley and later on the tedious task of picking oakum, pulling tarred rope apart with fingers or spikes.[21]

By comparison with its successor, the huge, grim, prison-like Union workhouse, the old town workhouse *appeared* a pleasanter place to live, albeit that there were petty rules, for everyone except the sick had to 'come to their meals at the ringing of the bell and be all seated before any begins to eat meals and no one is to rise from table without leave'. There are records of a hog being killed for the paupers' Christmas dinner, and after complaints about food, the overseers decided to regulate the meals. The diet table, with meat three times a week, compares favourably with the normal fare of poor families, and with the more bland and boring diet later offered in the Union Workhouse: for breakfast there was milk porridge and for supper bread and cheese, while the main meal changed every day, from boiled beef and vegetables, to suet dumplings, to seed cake, to pork and vegetables, to peas soup, to bullock's cheek, and to Hasty Pudding. In the bridewell, next door to the workhouse, the prisoners received 1½ pounds of bread per day.[22]

Looked at from a modern perspective, this institution aimed to offer in rudimentary form many of the functions which we now call social services: an old peoples' home, a maternity unit, a mental refuge, a general hospital, a children's home, a boarding school, a hostel for the homeless. It was there for the unfortunates of society: the sick, insane, elderly, homeless, orphans, illegitimate, widowed and others with no one to look after them. There is some evidence that Walden Workhouse was well-kept, but nevertheless entering the workhouse meant losing much dignity and submitting to a regime based on economy and expediency. The building of a bridewell in the yard is a sign of potential miscreants needing containment, and the insurance cover on the building suggests a fear of arson. Through its doors trudged a succession of the saddest of Walden citizens, the destitute and desperate and demented: 'Shepherd admitted on account of lowness of mind and attempt to destroy himself', recorded one overseer; 'Ann Rice died having fallen into the fire in a fit' was another report, and ten-year-old Mary Ann Cornell was another who was accidentally burnt to death in the workhouse. One old man, Thomas Coe, who had lived there some time, told companions he was ashamed of his life and made a rope out of stocking and neckerchiefs, tied his hands to the buttonhole of his coat, and hung himself from a beam in the bridewell, where he had been confined. All in all, the old poor law workhouse, the only resort for those *in extremis*, cannot have been greatly loved.[23]

Assistance with burials, marriages and births was another aspect of the old poor law, with schooling, service, employment travelling expenses, payments to carriers and tradesmen and other items. Ratepayers naturally looked for economies and penny-pinching explains the pro-active nature of many apparently altruistic arrangements such as migration schemes, paternity payments and apprenticeships, for all were drains on the rates. A poor lad fixed up with an apprenticeship was one less pauper draining the rates, particularly if he could gain a settlement out of town, but opportunities were declining. There might be clothes for a girl going into service, or a youngster fixed up to learn a trade, such as Stephen Adams who went as apprentice carpenter to builder William Ward. Pauper children did not always have the background to make a success of such opportunities: in 1831 when Isaac Thurgood was sent from the workhouse to labour at Pounce Hall farm for two shillings per week, he was returned for ill-conduct three months later and another boy sent in his place.[24]

Until the mid-nineteenth century, what we now term 'the emergency services', such as policing and fire-fighting were also organised and paid for at parish level, both making use of workhouse facilities. The town fire engines were housed in former spinning rooms. The trouble was that no one wanted to pay for these expensive services. For many years, there were disputes about who should maintain them, and they were transferred from the poor rate to the highway rate and, when that was declared illegal, to the church rate. Only much later did the town council agree to take over the fire service. Arguments about paying for gaol facilities were also an issue with the Guardians in its early years, and with the county police in the 1840s/50s (see chapters 5 and 6).[25]

Medical Services

Likewise medical services were a huge drain on the rates, and this also included paying for pauper funerals, laying out the dead and providing coffins. For laying out and arranging William Dubry's funeral, the cost was 5s.6d. During 1826, for instance, the parish provided a total of eight coffins for the poor, including one for an unknown child, and another for a lodger at the *Castle Inn*. Genuine needy cases living far away could also appeal to the Walden overseers, a poignant case occurring in 1829 when the widow of Thomas Pluck, who had died in

Bethnal Green, was destitute and, since her neighbours were as poor as she, there was no one to help pay for the funeral, and she begged the Walden overseers' assistance in burying him.[26]

The incident of the pauper's pall is a meaningful one. The parish loaned out a pall for internments of 'the lowest classes of the poor', although many spent precious pennies hiring one instead, 'so obnoxious was this unseemly vestment'. When workhouse pauper, Jane Hills, died in 1831, the vicar, Rev. Nicholas Bull was so disgusted by it that he buried the pall in the grave with her, saying 'the poor, as well as the rich and great, were entitled to a decent funeral'. The parish officers were apparently unaware of the condition of the pall otherwise, it was quickly said, they would have provided a better one.[27]

It became more common for surgeons to be paid a fee by the parish officers to tend the poor, and in Walden this system was in place by at least 1794 (probably much earlier), when the overseers agreed to spend £22 a year to include attending smallpox cases and casualties. By 1825 the town surgeons were earning twice as much for 'attending the sick smallpox, delivering of such poor women as shall be thought fit objects by the overseers, attending poor persons out of the parish who are legal inhabitants and living in the adjoining parishes and all other casualties'. Regular sick payments were made for temporary needs, and help given to mothers lying-in, with nursing help at home, for instance the seven shillings paid to a nurse for 'sitting up with Stocks boy'. Insane paupers, if unmanageable, were taken off to St Luke's Hospital in London. After the opening of Addenbrookes Hospital, from at least 1833, some seriously ill paupers went to Cambridge for free treatment, a service for which the parish subscribed two guineas a year, an arrangement which was 'a positive benefit to the parish as the paupers are maintained at the Hospital without any additional expense'. There was also an arrangement with an Ophthalmic Infirmary. To nurse the ordinary sick poor, a room was erected at the workhouse in 1819, to be used for poor people 'afflicted with the prevailing fever'.[28]

Infectious epidemics were one of the greatest fears, and dealing with such threats also fell on parish officers. To avoid the cost of an epidemic sweeping through the poor streets, in 1744 the parish had been bequeathed a pesthouse on waste ground, with a 100-year lease from the lord of the manor at a nominal rent. This comprised a keeping room, a wash house, a bed chamber, two other chambers and a garret. It was well used, 'the inhabitants having on many occasions experienced the very great utility of such a building at distance from the town for the reception of persons suffering from the small pox'. Isolation made economic sense too: after the lease ran out and the pesthouse fell into disrepair, a smallpox victim had to be nursed in town instead. As a result, the disease spread 'to a most alarming extent and many persons died' and, worse still, it cost the parish over £100.[29]

The technique of inoculation with live material had been known by the late eighteenth century, and as early as 1772 Newport had a smallpox inoculation scheme in place. Edward Jenner's cowpox vaccine was in use by the early nineteenth century. In 1820 a meeting of the Walden inhabitants decided that a vaccination programme was the best way to prevent the spread of smallpox. As happened with many other such problems, the method was to set up a large committee, with gentlemen going forth in pairs to knock on the doors of the poor and check whether they had been vaccinated. By this means they quickly covered the parish, including the rural outposts of North End, Audley End, Sewards End and Little Walden. The town surgeons were given 1s.6d for each person vaccinated, with the parish paying for the poor. Every name on a list of 80 persons in this category was ticked, so presumably the campaign was successful. Constant vigilance was required, as smallpox continued to flare up at intervals, and undisclosed smallpox was declared 'a nuisance subject to indictment'.[30]

Even more frightening, because it affected the middle classes too, was the cholera scare of 1831 which galvanised the Government to set up a Board of Health, issuing regulations for implementation by 1200 local boards, of which Saffron Walden was one. This was packed with worthies, magistrates and medical men, with over 50 inhabitants asked to help visit the poor and enforce regulations on lime-washing, cleanliness and decay, which were wrongly identified as the cause of spreading infection (in fact it was polluted water and poor drainage). Posters were erected and the campaign lasted several months, but generally there were few cases overall, mostly affecting children. They reported on various offensive corners, stagnant pools, bad drains and dungheaps. As the threat receded, the central board was dissolved at the end of 1832 and local boards faded away.[31]

Social Control

Another way of drawing attention to public health problems was via a grand jury presentment at the Quarter Sessions, although it is not clear how effective this was. If cleanliness was seen as next to godliness, the opposite was also perceived, and when it fell to parish officers to make value judgements on the characters of those who asked for help, degenerate living conditions could betoken a lifestyle to match. In the early years of the century, a change of tone is noticeable in the overseers' records, with complaints that some of the poor were living and bringing up their children in ways which 'tend very much to the encouraging of vice & immorality which is apparent in the Idleness Dishonesty & Prostitution of many of them'. As on other occasions, the favoured response was to set up a large committee to go knocking on doors and visiting the poor to see for themselves what was going on, and 'adopt measures for gradual promotion of industry and virtue amongst them'. This, they felt, would help both the poor and the rest of the community, and eventually save expense. One decision was to buy three acres of wood, stack it and offer it for sale to the poor in order to stop them stealing fuel, 'it appearing that the poor cannot buy wood for their money at this time, & therefore plead some excuse for their depredations of hedges'. Another was highways work paid out of poor rates.[32]

Two months later the visiting committee came back with some terrible reports, finding the poor 'generally in a lamentable situation, living much cramped for room, and families lodging together in one chamber very indecently and in a way likely to conduce to the increase of vice amongst them... it is evident that the children of some of them are brought up to idleness and dishonesty; and they have no doubt but there are several instances of young people cohabiting together'. It was felt that the children would be better off working in the sack manufactory, but there is no direct evidence of action being taken to tackle the housing problems blamed for vice, prostitution and, implicitly, incest. This directly concerned parish officers, for of course bastard children became chargeable to the parish they were born in. One would have expected this to be a common problem among the poor, but a later report suggested that bastardy was much below average in Essex. Abortion and infanticide might be implicated, but these remain a grey area of history.[33]

Walden parish officers chose to persecute some unmarried mothers and pursue absent fathers and the penalties could be harsh: in 1816, Hannah Goodwin was put in the house of correction for one year after having a bastard child, and the father ordered to pay 12 shillings plus 2 shillings weekly, after complaints from the overseer. Five years later, Lydia Augur was similarly committed for a year. It was not unknown for the parish officers to force the parties to marry, a process once known as 'knobstick' weddings. In 1795 William Dubarry was told he must either marry Elizabeth Barker or promise to pay for the child's maintenance. This was still happening well into the nineteenth century, with two cases in 1825: in August the constable was paid to bring down Henry Gladwen on a charge of bastardy, and a fortnight later the parish paid his marriage fees. The following October they paid for Thomas Clark to marry Mary Flack, bought the ring and, to make sure he turned up to the wedding, kept him in custody the night before. It was worth the total cost to the parish of £1.17s.6d.[34]

But such forced nuptials were perhaps more at risk than normal of break-ups, and if this happened once again the parish officers had to pursue reluctant fathers to do their family duty, people like William Esland of Castle Street whose five children, aged one to eleven, were taken into the workhouse, and his meagre household inventoried by the overseers, presumably so that the goods could be sold to help repay all the poor rates being spent on the family. Three years later a William Esland, was up before the magistrates, and put in the house of correction for three months, as a rogue and vagabond, again leaving his family chargeable to the parish, and two years on, there was a similar case. People like Esland would be well-known to the parish officers, much of whose workload, they felt, was complicated by the fecklessness of such as he.[35]

The poor law, probably using intelligence supplied by visitors, was always a useful lever to inculcate good behaviour among the disorderly poor, if only at the most mundane level: 'stop William Augar's allowance till the dog is got rid of', ordered the overseers on one occasion, thinking no doubt that Augar used the dog to hunt game. All in all, the overseers' role was a fraught one, as one holder of the office, Godfrey Burdett, must have felt when his conduct was publicly criticised for problems which occurred during his term of office in 1827. Apparently, he complained about irregularities in the accounts from 1820–27 during R.D. Thurgood's period as vestry clerk. The words 'extravagant and illegal' were bandied about, but the affair ended with Burdett himself suffering ignominy, as 23 ratepayers signed a petition criticising his conduct after the accounts were found to be 'perfectly correct'. Possibly it was a case of inexperience in an arduous role. Even seasoned organiser, John Player found the job 'a most unthankful duty'.[36]

The 1829 Committee

It happened that Player's term of office as overseer, from 1829–30, coincided with one of the worst seasons. At the workhouse, numbers almost doubled, and payments of outdoor relief and unemployment pay also rose considerably, the list of those 'in distress' visibly lengthening. Walden sought to be pro-active. As often happened in harsh winters, the overseers ordered 3,000 bushels of coals to be purchased and sold cheaply to the poor, with subscribers covering the transport; later on Messrs Gibsons offered to supply fuel wood to the poor at one shilling a hundredweight. A special employment committee was formed to tackle able-bodied pauperism, meeting five times followed by a public meeting. Their most important initiative, allotments, was not the only idea discussed (see chapter 8). There were also tickets, spade husbandry and highways work schemes.[37]

Saffron Walden was said to be the first vestry to introduce a ticket system, to check improper applications from men leaving employment. Something of the spirit of this measure must have already existed, since the parish committee had long insisted that no one could do parish highways work unless they applied via the committee. The ticket system perhaps formalised this process, so that able-bodied applicants to the vestry for work or relief had to provide documentary proof that they had genuinely tried every possibility. Potential employers

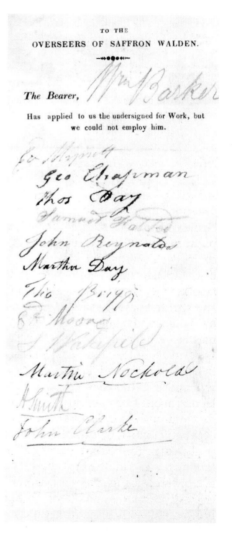

TO THE
OVERSEERS OF SAFFRON WALDEN.

The Bearer,

Has applied to us the undersigned for Work, but we could not employ him.

Fig.4.2 *A surviving example of an employment ticket belonging to William Barker, who asked a dozen farmers to testify that there was no work available, so that he could apply to the overseers for relief.*

must each sign the printed ticket, showing name, dates, reason for discharge (illness, want of employment, neglect) and amount of pay. Thus William Barker had to obtain the signatures of 12 employers to certify they had no work for him. [Fig.4.2] Another ticket authorised Edward Augar to be employed on the roads, but only 'at piece work so that he may be industrious'. Although regarded in official circles as rather dubious, the system remained in use in Walden for over 20 years, and from here spread to other parts of Essex, Suffolk, Norfolk, Cambridgeshire, Hertfordshire and Bedfordshire, recorded in 21 Poor Law Union areas by 1844. When later criticised by Poor Law assistant commissioners as illegal, Walden Guardians insisted labourers were not victimised: it was 'unlikely to wound the feelings of any one… no respectable poor man looks upon it as a piece of severity but rather a confirmation that he truly requires the relief he seeks, while only those who are of a different character dislike it'. Thus was legitimised a system which gave the overseers, and later the Guardians (many of whom were farmers) considerable power over the able-bodied under-employed. The whole business of tickets was tedious, humiliating and wasteful on shoe-leather, and could delay relief for a week or more, possibly even avoid giving it altogether, if there were not enough signatures.[38]

Spade Husbandry and Highways Work

A specific way of employing the fittest and most reliable of the able-bodied poor, used in several areas, was by offering them work digging fields by spade. Some farmers liked this method since it cost no more than ploughing, yet the land was particularly well-cultivated and produced better yields, because the soil was less compacted, and manure was added. Ratepayers liked it, since the landowners paid the otherwise under-employed labourers and thus saved rates. The more energetic labourers liked it because they could earn much more than from highways work, and slightly more than from ordinary farmwork. A comparison of amounts earned by six labourers, James Atkinson, William Banks, Peter Barker, John Harvey, Thomas Housden and Thomas Wright, who took part showed that over six days of back-breaking toil — or 'persevering labour' as it was called — they each earned the princely sum of 12s.9d, as compared to eight shillings or less on the roads. This was enough, said John Player for a man to support his family through his own labour, 'instead of wasting his energies upon unprofitable work, and of engaging in demoralising associations with the Men of idle habits who are of necessity sent for occupation into the public Roads'.[39]

The scheme, covering up to 20 acres, was at first limited to men with large families who had 'the best characters for industry and general conduct' and the largest families to maintain. Experiments took place to see how much a man could dig in a day. A total of 52 acres were dug for 16 landowners, who paid between twopence and fourpence a rod, depending on the difficulty of the land. When labourers' unrest started building up in December 1830, the committee were anxious to ensure some of the single men were offered such work, and that all received the same remuneration. No doubt in response to the 'Swing' troubles even then spreading into the area, several more landowners offered a few

79

acres each so that the under-employed could dig land in winter (see chapter 7). Similar winter arrangements recurred at intervals, but such work was always limited. For the remainder, by far the majority, it was back to the old standby, work on the highways.[40]

With highways the only communication with the outside world, their state of repair was a vital aspect of the economy. The appalling roads around Walden so impressed one early benefactor, that he left provision in his will 'to amend the foul highways of Sewers End'. The impact of such charitable bequests was very limited, however, and in general highway repairs, ever since the sixteenth century, had fallen on parishes, via unpaid surveyors of highways. They had no choice but to accept this unpopular task, and were supposed to make sure that qualifying parishioners gave statute labour for several days a year, to keep roads in repair. In spite of the use of highway rates and transferring this statute labour the country roads were neglected and got worse and worse. As distress grew, from the early nineteenth century, the Walden surveyors' work became inextricably bound up with that of the overseers, since highways repairs were then used as a way of putting the under-employed, able-bodied labourers to work.[41]

There was thus nothing new about the idea of making the poor work on the roads, but again Walden had its own variation on the theme. In Walden, the surveyors tried to acquire something useful out of this system, by making the poor lower the difficult stretches like Sparrows End Hill and Windmill Hill, to encourage the coaching trade. [Fig.4.3] The surveyors had a paid assistant to keep an eye on absentees and shirkers. The work proceeded from at least the mid-1820s but, as distress worsened, the numbers grew, reaching 130 in 1829, while costs rocketed. The extra income from allotments was claimed to be behind a temporary reduction in expenditure, but it soon began creeping up again. Poor law officials, visiting the town in the 1830s, regarded the practice as corrupt: 'Hills have been lowered and roads much improved, but the works have been carried on, not from choice, but to employ the people'.[42]

As well as the cost, there was also the moral aspect. The commissioner echoed a common view that road men were idle layabouts: 'The general improvidence of the artisans who waste their summer earnings, throws many on the parish in the winter'. Those who had to oversee the workers could suffer abuse: on at least one occasion, a labourer, William Barker, was jailed for assaulting the overlooker, Mr Flack. Men who absented themselves or refused to accept the work could be prosecuted. Although socially useful, road repairs, stone-breaking and other such parish work was not given any status and was deliberately underpaid, so it is not surprising if some fitted John Player's description of 'men of idle habits'. Player felt the roadwork system was pernicious, mixing the 'deserving' and 'undeserving' poor, spreading stigma to all: 'What is parish employment in general', he asked, 'but a painful system that tends both to criminalise the populace and to cue their minds against every worthy and upright feeling'. But Player must have known that not all those 'on the roads' fitted this image. According to a listing made in 1831, over three-quarters were married men, probably because single men were discouraged by earning less, sometimes not much more than half. The median age was 32, with almost half under 30. Almost a third were aged over 60, including two in their

Fig.4.3 *Windmill Hill, showing the cutting which resulted from roadwork schemes for the unemployed. One of the town's allotment sites was (and still is) over the roadside hedge to the left.*

80s or 90s, who could scarcely be called 'idle' if still doing such physical work at that advanced age, albeit for a pittance.[43]

Through the road work system, the ratepayers were in a way subsidising employers, particularly farmers who were never blamed for the high levels of unemployment which forced them to 'reduce the number of their labourers in consequence of the diminution of their capital, owing to a succession of bad crops and the general depression of agriculture'. Later in his life, however, Player actually praised the achievements of the road gangs in improving the forbiddingly steep hills which led into town, so it seems a pity that this useful work was not classed as a legitimate use of local rates and paid accordingly, which would have removed the stigma and perhaps given men some pride in their work. In the winter of 1831–2, some attempt was made to improve the system by using piece work: classifying the workers according to skill and productivity so that those working together could earn the same rate; and allotting a mile of road specifically to the men employed at the gravel pits. Unemployed road labour officially died with the coming of the New Poor Law, according to a reference in 1836 to 'the ancient corrupt and by-gone practice' of giving pauper wages to the able-bodied to do parish work, but it seems likely that it survived in some form.[44]

The 1832 Committee

In 1832, with highways expenditure rising again, the vestry set up the employment committee again, chaired by Lord Braybrooke, once again holding one of their brain-storming sessions, investigating a wide range of ideas for employing the poor. By now there were 159 allotments in the parish, but they were not solving all the problems (see chapter 8), and they were concerned to maintain 'the order and harmony which has distinguished this parish up to the present period'. This suggests that the 'Swing' riots two winters before were still exerting an effect (see chapter 7). Lord Braybrooke investigated the idea of a labour rate, whereby employers could be excused rates if they took on a worker at an agreed wage. As the largest ratepayer and a considerable employer, this could have reduced his rate bills, but it does not seem to have materialised. Likewise, the committee rejected as unsuitable his offer of at least 26, going up to 52, acres of land for a parish farm, to teach skills to young farming apprentices.[45]

A simpler idea was simply to 'name and shame' the able-bodied on casual relief by posting a list of them all in a public place, which notice would 'tend to awaken a better spirit in some of the poor', and persuade others to tell tales on their fraudulent neighbours. There was also an employment survey carried out by John Player (see chapter 1), after which the committee exhorted employers to 'abstain in future from hiring servants… belonging to other parishes, it having been ascertained that if this rule had been acted upon some years ago every person in the parish would have been at this time actually employed'. Since Lord Braybrooke chaired the committee, this was an ironic statement as the survey showed that about a fifth of his own employees were outsiders.[46]

Another idea on which Braybrooke was keen, but Player was not, was that of encouraging the poor to emigrate: 'A great country like England ought to be able to tackle the employment problem without recourse to emigration', Player once wrote. Little seems to have happened in 1832, but two years later, with Parliamentary backing, Walden set up a committee to act as general agents for emigration, offering up to £100 to would-be emigrants. The fare to Canada was only £6 or so, half price for children, and if they stayed away, large sums of poor relief or road wages might be saved. Once again Braybrooke personally gathered evidence from contacts in London, and young Walden émigrés, William Perrin and John Mumford, who had already gone to Canada. These contain many details which underline the good things across the Atlantic lacking in nineteenth century England: the greater equality of society, availability of well-paid work, opportunity to acquire land. This was what the poor cared about, and such advantages would offset the warning: 'We have no poor laws in this country therefore they must not expect any parish assistance here'.[47]

The scheme was most popular in eastern England, but the big, bold move of emigration tended to attract the sturdier, skilled, independent types, who had been more useful to the local economy anyway. Braybrooke helped some from Littlebury and elsewhere to go. Many hundreds went from this area during the nineteenth century, although enthusiasm to help them cooled. The types of paupers the parish would prefer to get rid of were the large, impoverished families needing constant support from the ratepayers.

End of the Old Poor Law

The old poor laws, while they had great faults, had worked surprisingly well for nearly three centuries, given all the potential tensions involved. But out in the Walden hinterland, poverty was far worse than in town. The parochial basis of the old system did not permit the better-off town to help out the poorer villages and north-west Essex was one of the most deprived areas of the county. Only scaled allowances kept people going: without them in Clavering, for instance, it was reported that 'all the larger families would be thrown upon the parish, which is already too much the case'. Relief and wages were intimately spliced together. Since farmers could not 'be persuaded to relinquish the detestable plan of giving low wages and making it up to those who have families out of the poor rates', thoughts turned to drastic reform. Rate levels were felt to be intolerable, while minds had been hardened by the impact in 1830 of the 'Swing' riots, which convinced many that the poor were ungrateful.[48]

And so, even as Walden tossed ideas around in 1832, the new Whig Government was setting in train the biggest shake-up ever known in the history of local government, the New Poor Law, preceded by the appointment of a Poor Law Commission. Accordingly assistant commissioners toured the country, visiting 3,000 places including Walden, to collect evidence towards radical reform. The first such visitor, Ashurst Majendie seemed rather pleased with the Walden vestry, commenting 'the business of the parish seems to be conducted with great regularity and economy'. The following year, however, assistant commissioner, Alfred Power was much more critical of what he called the 'undefined character' of outdoor allowances in Walden, which resulted in too much relief being given: 'The whole evidence shows the danger of such an attempt. It appears that such endeavours to constitute the distributors of relief into a tribunal for the reward of merit, out of the property of others, have not only failed in effecting the benevolent intentions of their promoters, but have become sources of fraud on the part of the distributors, and of discontent and violence on the part of the claimants'. By inference, it appears that the Walden parish officers were being accused, at governmental level, of committing fraud and the poor of violent reaction. No local evidence has come to light to support this charge, and it may be a question of perception: the commissioners, charged with finding evidence to suit a policy already decided on, chose to ignore the balancing act of maintaining a well-ordered town in hard times, for the old poor law was not an isolated part of the parish fabric, but interwoven with other relationships.[49]

John Player had written in 1830: 'If the poor laws be enacted for the relief of the poor, it is also equally true that they were made for the satisfaction of the rich'. But the rich were no longer satisfied by the old system. It had begun as a safety net for comparatively small numbers, but was now regarded not as an extra but as a right among many people, whether 'deserving' or otherwise. The commissioners blamed 'the scale', but this is now known to have been the reverse of the truth, for increased relief at this time related to rising unemployment, and increasing population, whether or not parishes used the scale. The scale was not the cause of poverty, but rather the unavoidable consequence. In fact in per capita terms poor relief in Essex was actually costing less in the early 1830s than it had a decade earlier. The final Poor Law report, however, ignored this. It has long been seen as a biased document, relying on anecdotal evidence to substantiate a myth that the old poor law increased poverty and encouraged idleness and dependency, but at the time it seemed to make sense, particularly the attack on able-bodied pauperism, the target of much of the complex panoply of the new statute.[50]

Although figures were higher in the rural area, in Walden only about a quarter of paupers were able-bodied, most of them on the roads: of the 100 engaged, 15 were elderly. On the eve of change, there were 123 old, infirm people and 75 children receiving outdoor allowances, plus 14 adults and 25 children in the workhouse. Thus before the advent of the new law (and afterwards), most of those needing help were aged and infirm, orphans or bastards, widows with young children, temporarily infirm, 'idiots' and other 'deserving' poor. Together with help from neighbours and relatives, those few shillings a week enabled them to keep going. In future, they too were planned to be sucked up into the new system.[51]

The district statistics were worrying, for the new Saffron Walden Union had more people out of work than, for instance, Dunmow Union which was very poor, or Chelmsford Union, which had a higher population. Over the whole Union of 24 parishes, out of a total population of almost 18,000, surveys suggested that up to one-sixth of the people could need help at any one time. Thus the legacy inherited in 1835 by the new Saffron Walden Board of Guardians.[52]

Chapter 5

'Some Plums in the Pudding'
Early Years of The New Poor Law

'On Monday evening about half of 7 an alarm of fire was raised at the Old Workhouse and a small portion of the most dilapidated part was in a short time con-
sumed but the respectable inhabitants mechanics and others gave active assistance, so that the flames were confined to the place in which it broke out... all the
inmates 50 or more in number slept in the house after the fire with the exception
of 2 or 3 who were allowed to go to their houses for the night. There being reason
to suppose that the fire could not have been the result of accident a reward of
£100 has been offered by the County Fire Office (where the property was insured) for the discovery of the incendiary.'[1]

This account of the Saffron Walden workhouse fire just before Christmas 1835 dif-
fers somewhat from the oft-quoted newspaper report which describes how 'most
of the lower classes' demonstratively enjoyed watching the hated building burn
and refused to help put it out. The reason is that the report quoted above was the
Guardians' official press release, and therefore represented a desire to play down
an event which thoroughly shook the town establishment. Afterwards, the Guardians decided to celebrate Christmas in the workhouse in a suitably festive fashion:
'Ordered that the inmates in the workhouse be allowed on Christmas day each one
pint of beer and some plums in the pudding and that the men working in the Mill
shall be allowed to leave on Thursday evening and return to their work on Monday
morning and be paid their full week's wages'.[2]

However the season of excessive goodwill soon passed, for at their next
meeting the punishments for bad behaviour were laid down. The reaction of
onlookers to the fire at Saffron Walden's old workhouse — like similar incidents
elsewhere — represented a dramatic comment, not on the old poor law, but on
the new one which was, as its authors intended, deeply and bitterly loathed.
The realisation was just beginning to sink in that the old system was being replaced by something altogether much more fearsome and thus the old town
workhouse, once a lifeline, was now become the symbol of a harsh regime which
promised to tighten the screw on their already difficult lives. But for one rare
moment, the supposedly peaceful town of Saffron Walden was lit up by a dramatic gesture, widely supposed at the time (though never proven) to be
incendiarist. The blaze may have caused little damage, but the event left its
mark. This chapter will attempt to reflect how the early work of the early Guardians was interwoven with attempts to prevent this kind of protest recurring.[3]

The coming of the Saffron Walden Board of Guardians in 1834–5 was a seminal moment, for it marked the end of a concentration on purely local concerns. Whereas sectarian bickering and the tensions of the old poor law were largely matters of internal import to the 'well-ordered town', the New Poor Law was something else. As with crime and protest, the welfare and orderliness of the surrounding district became the direct concern of an organisation based in the town. The advent of the large, rather remote Board of Guardians meant that the old parish vestries, for centuries a contact point between the poor and the other classes, were reduced in functions and status. This was planned to be a shake-up of major proportions in the lives of the poor, aimed at transferring labour and reducing rates, by means of the workhouse test and settlement enforcement.

Saffron Walden Union Board of Guardians

The Poor Law Commission was set up in February 1832, and its report came out exactly two years later. With its promise of reducing escalating rate bills for the gentry, it was rushed through Parliament, giving little time for organised opposition to build up, becoming law in August 1834. The old system, apart from settlement laws, was abolished and parishes united into unions under central control. Seven months later, on 25 March 1835, the Saffron Walden Union Board of Guardians came into being to administer a large and extremely deprived area consisting of Walden and 23 rural parishes with about 18,000 residents, most of them poor. There were 6 ex-officio and 32 elected Guardians who met every Friday, firstly from April at the *Rose & Crown* in the Market Place, and later at the workhouse. The first clerk to the board was the former vestry clerk, Robert Driver Thurgood, whose son William followed in father's footsteps, keeping the job in the family for half-a-century. Lord Braybrooke, also a strong supporter of the new law, was the first chairman of the Saffron Walden Board. His deputy was Wyatt George Gibson, soon to take over as chairman, a post he held until his death 24 years later. The remainder were mostly farmers elected by the parishes, a pattern common to most rural Boards of Guardians and one which was to make the underlying objectives of the new law difficult to implement for farmer-guardians had a vested interest in maintaining the *status quo* of low wages and a large casual workforce, the very system which the New Poor Law was designed to undermine.[4]

Poverty was re-defined by the new Act, with a deepening of the distinction between the genuinely impotent and the able-bodied pauper. But the 38 special constables appointed to deal with any trouble were not needed, and the first few months under the new system went quietly enough, the Guardians busying themselves in coming to grips with their huge new responsibilities. Fortunately the season was fair and employment reasonable, so the new approach was helped on its way: 'the Walden Union promises extremely well', reported the assistant commissioner in the spring of 1835, claiming that the virtual extinction of able-bodied pauperism in the first season of the New Poor Law was not due purely

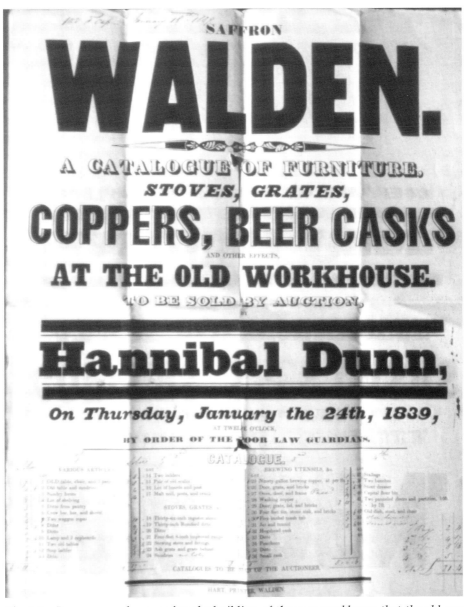

Fig.5.1 *It was several years after the building of the new workhouse that the old one and its contents were sold off. This poster, advertising the 1839 sale of workhouse property by auctioneer Hannibal Dunn, includes pencilled notes showing the amount paid for each item.*

to the good weather. Within three months of the new statute, the town overseers, then Francis Gibson and Cornell Spicer were seeking advice about what to do with the old workhouse (this was before the fire). A priority for the new Board was to build a big new workhouse to replace both the Walden one and those in the villages. As the new law took effect, the old High Street building contained only the most destitute of the Walden poor, 14 adults and 25 children. At a squeeze, up to 100 could be accommodated, but the old building was not suited to the classification of paupers required by the Poor Law Commission. By the autumn of 1835 the new building was under way, although the old one and its contents were not finally sold off until several years later.[5] [Fig.5.1]

There was an unexplained false start in obtaining land for the new work-house. Initially three acres in White Street Field were to be purchased from Lewis Archer, but this proved unsuitable, so Lord Braybrooke leased some land to the Union instead, and the Guardians ended up paying compensation to Archer. The change also apparently upset Isaac Norris, Braybrooke's tenant at Pounce Hall, who presumably farmed on the land chosen. But at last things started moving, Braybrooke commenting to W.G. Gibson: 'I am glad to hear the new Workhouse is about to be commenced in earnest, & that the Guardians labours seemed to be diminishing'.[6]

Protest at the Workhouse

Braybrooke spoke too soon. This was September 1835, and three months later came the workhouse fire. If this was arson, any one of a number of factors could have sparked off a protest against the new regime, which was being introduced in the same building which had hitherto operated under the old system. By December, the old Walden workhouse had been receiving paupers under the new system for several months, and the mistress, the third one that year, Ann Burkmyre was an unpleasant woman (see chapter 11). There was to be much stricter discipline with no leave of absence allowed, no doubt to avoid any temp-tation to cohabit, visit beershops or other immoral behaviour. There were many other irksome regulations: the new dietary regime was dull and meagre com-pared to the old one; compulsory workhouse uniforms consisted of institutional grey calico suits for men, women and children; shoemaker paupers were to be forced to make the shoes for the inmates (samples of workhouse shoes were all muddled up in the fire).[7]

A few months earlier a large sum was spent on fire insurance for the workhouse buildings, and only a month before the fire, the Guardians feared that plans to revise the lists of paupers would 'probably create much dissatisfaction'. Outdoor relief was the lifeline of the poor and elsewhere it was found that sudden attempts to end this were the catalyst for arson. At nearby Dunmow, for instance, special constables appointed to deal with poor law unrest failed to prevent protests against the ending of outdoor relief, threats to those implementing the new law and dam-age to their property. Soon afterwards, the workhouse at Bishops Stortford was fired. When incendiarism occurred in the same period at Suffolk workhouses, Col. Wade — the assistant poor law commissioner who later worked with Walden Un-ion — insisted categorically 'that the fires were not connected with the New Poor Law', thereby rather suggesting that they were.[8]

The Walden Guardians called a meeting on 22 December, the day after the fire, instructing Thurgood, the clerk, quickly to send the official press release quoted above. In an accompanying letter to Edwin Chadwick at the Poor Law Board in London, the sensitivity of the incident is apparent: 'I understand that you have heard of the fire through the medium of Lord Braybrooke and I have by this night post sent a copy of the above to all the local papers to prevent an unfair statement getting abroad — perhaps you might think that the above should appear in the London papers'. The Guardians then must have been none too pleased when 'an unfair statement' did get abroad and the *Essex Standard*, while retaining the emphasis on the 'respectable' classes helping to put out the fire, also included some more colourful details, such as the hour and a half it took to put it out. Most annoying for the Guardians, the reporter found out that 'the alarm was much increased in consequence of most of the lower classes refusing to render any assistance, but who on the contrary evidently enjoyed the scene, shouting most hideously 'Let it burn, it cannot be at a better place', 'No poor laws', 'Put it out yourselves' etc. It is generally believed that the fire was not accidental but perpetrated by some of the inmates.'[9]

Further evidence of the seriousness of the incident was the employment of a Bow Street police officer to investigate the case but without success. Nor did a massive £100 reward persuade anyone to come forward: surely a lack of response every bit as significant as the attitude of the crowd on the night, for this sum was equivalent to at least four years' labouring wages. But it was not politically acceptable to admit that the new law might cause the disorder it had been aimed at preventing. Thurgood recorded only: 'Confusion at workhouse because of fire on Monday evening last. Strictly to enforce regulations against tobacco pipe smoking', thereby inferring, without actually saying so, that someone had caused the blaze by having an illicit smoke. No further reference occurs in the minutes until over 18 months later, when it was noted that holding religious services in the workhouse had been found to be 'highly beneficial in suppressing a spirit of insubordination especially about the time when a part of the workhouse was burned. This it must be remarked is not theoretical evidence but practical fact'. The Guardians maintained discretion, claiming only six months after the fire that the new law had 'excited but little attention in this vicinity'.[10]

Protest on the Common

While the workhouse fire has been often described, it is less well known that it was not the only anti-poorlaw protest to take place in Walden. Six months later, a Cambridgeshire curate, the Rev. W.H. Maberly of Bourn brought his widespread anti-poor law campaign to the town, choosing Walden no doubt as fertile ground for whipping up opposition, because of the earlier fire. One of eight such meetings he organised, the one he called on the Common for Saturday 16 July 1836 occasioned a flurry of alarmed activity, for he was seen as the worst sort of cleric, 'an itinerant agitator' trying to 'sow the seeds of discontent among the poor of Essex'. Maberly's visit to Walden occurred during John Player's mayoral year. Player — who had once worried that 'were the poor laws abrogated, we should be pained by overwhelming mendacity' — was at this time a supporter of the New Poor Law which was 'productive of great good in this and other Unions, and must lead to improve the condition and elevate the character of the labouring poor throughout the kingdom'. He did not anticipate any breach of the peace but nevertheless tried to hinder the delivery of Maberly's handbills around the town. The Home Office told Player that Maberly's conduct had been brought to the attention of Lord John Russell, since similar complaints were coming from his activities in Ely and Bury. The handbills, which appear quite mild in tone, asked those in opposition 'to meet me on Saffron Walden common at 12 o'clock in the forenoon to petition against the abominable poor law bill. Come in thousands, but come peaceably. Your peaceable deportment is sure and certain victory. Our enemies are watching for this'.[11]

The meeting went ahead and like others elsewhere, apparently passed off without incident, with Player commenting with some satisfaction, in a letter to his friend Jabez Gibson:

'Mr. Maberly came and went away again. The source and substance of his and Mr. Clark's convictions appeared to be to abuse the Whig Ministry. Your two valuable brothers very kindly gave me their presence and offers of assistance, but happily for all parties there was no positive breach of the peace, and I saw no wisdom making one. The special constables were here in readiness in the Town Hall — had their assistance been needed there is every reason to imagine as true Walden men they would have exhibited all needy spirit.'[12]

Of Maberly's politics, he added: 'I fear he is too far gone in his madness to observe reason where opposite conduct promotes a party purpose'. Player was pleased that the *Essex Herald* criticised Maberly for his Walden campaign, 'labouring to stir up feelings amongst those who without possessing influence, to obtain a modification of its provision, are likely to express their feelings in riotous outbreaks, if not in crimes at which we are certain he would shudder… why should the Rev. Maberly endeavour to irritate the poor of Essex who with a few exceptions have shown a laudable disposition to second the exertions which we are making to ensure their independence?' The troublesome priest continued campaigning, touring the Eastern counties to whip up opposition, but it only led to losing his curacy. When arrested in Cambridge in 1837, supporters rescued him by rushing on the police station.[13]

First Year of New Poor Law

It would of course have been a foolish labourer who allowed magistrates and constables to notice them joining in Maberly's diatribe. In any case, his protest meeting was badly timed, for the rates were going down, the harvest was good, the weather fair and the labourers occupied, allegedly because of the disciplinary effects of the New Poor Law. This, at any rate, was what the chairman of the Guardians, Lord Braybrooke claimed: 'There is not at this time, nor has there been for some weeks past, a single able bodied pauper in the Union receiving relief. At the commencement of the hay season, the number of able bodied paupers in the Union workhouse was eight, and they were discharged by order of the Board, it being considered that by exertion they might obtain employment, which they unquestionably did, as they have not since required assistance.' Braybrooke, constantly pained by the size of his rate demand, was even more delighted at the reduction in rates, which seemed to fully justify the change in the law. In some parishes the costs had almost halved, in Walden they were down by almost a third and over the whole 24 parishes of the Union by even more, compared to the previous average. Nationally, poor relief expenditure fell considerably, partly due to slightly more favourable economic conditions in the later 1830s.[14]

As well as this come-uppance for the able-bodied idlers, coupled with exciting financial news, there was the bonus of a salutary effect on behaviour: 'The habits of the poor are decidedly improved, and their manners become more respectful', reported Lord Braybrooke. 'They have also been rendered generally more industrious since they have been thrown upon their own resources, which fact is admitted throughout the Union; and in many instances labourers have gladly accepted work which they had refused, so long as they found they could obtain parochial relief without due exertions'. The conclusion was that the new law was undoubtedly continuing 'to work exceedingly well, and has produced results which the most sanguine advocate of the new system could have anticipated'.[15]

But not everywhere was as apparently 'well-ordered' as Walden. Only a few miles away down the Thaxted road, the poor in that town were suffering considerable anguish, according to contemporaneous comments by the man who had been their vicar for 30 years. In a series of letters, the Rev. Thomas Jee tried to arouse Lord Braybrooke's compassion over the suffering which the new law was causing among his poor parishioners: 'some of the aged poor in this parish have been treated with great harshness and neglect', later repeating that the new law 'has been severely felt in this neighbourhood… on account of the low rate of wages, which for a long time past have been only seven shillings a week'. Warning of great discontent and organised thieving, he added that because the overseers would not pay the sexton to bury the poor, the latter refused to dig any more graves: 'these are grievances of a very serious nature'. In the autumn of 1836 he reported that well-armed characters were pillaging by day and night and Thaxted was 'almost a lawless state', listing crimes and names including some he called 'idle and dissolute poachers… so notoriously bad that no farm would employ them'.

The Walden poor may not have been quite so badly off as the Thaxted poor, but the contrast in the two accounts is certainly striking. The official account on the Walden Union was presenting a generalised, sanitised, selective account of a situation which was far more complex than anyone dared to admit. The assistant commissioners, who kept an eye on things, dismissed the increase of crime in neighbouring Dunmow Union as an isolated and temporary effect. The official line was that, in spite of some teething troubles, the workhouse system very soon brought able-bodied pauperism perfectly under control.[16]

Fig.5.2 *The frontage of the new Union in Radwinter Road, showing the clock which, along with the workhouse bell, strictly regulated the lives of its inmates, and informed vagrants when they could enter the casual ward for the night. The photograph was taken when the old building was disused, prior to its conversion in 1999 to luxury flats.*

The New Union Workhouse

During that allegedly halcyon summer, a frightening new structure was going up in fields by the Radwinter road. [Fig.5.2] By August 1836 the three-storey, cruciform structure was finished, designed for surveillance and classification both internally and externally, with eight staircases, making vertical connections for various categories of inmates, and a central building overlooking all four external exercise yards. It had 300 beds, later expanded to 400, with separate areas based on age, gender and marital status, and rooms for the sick, insane, fever cases, lying-in, aged paupers and a nursery. Assistant commissioner Alfred Power felt that a poor area like Walden needed a large building, the reason being that they should have a workhouse large enough 'to be always one third empty in order to keep up its prospective terrors'. Inculcating this fear of the workhouse was thus unashamedly part of the grand plan.[17]

And fear there was. The Union – or the 'Spike' as it was nicknamed after the implement used to pick oakum — became a hated institution from the beginning, albeit that many sojourned there only temporarily. The feelings of the poor, and of those who might through life's misfortunes one day become paupers, as they watched this huge, prison-like structure rise on the outskirts of the town, can only be imagined. No wonder that Wyatt George Gibson, even though a dedicated Guardian, stated categorically that the Quaker poor were 'especially provided for in their own society and would never be found within the walls of a workhouse'(see chapter 12).[18]

The Union was ready for its first unhappy occupants in the autumn of 1836: 'The new workhouse being now occupied… ordered that the paupers in the workhouse at Clavering be forthwith removed to the union workhouse and that the Governor do provide the means of their conveyance'. Many village workhouses were sordid establishments, but the move from familiar surroundings to the clock-regulated rigour of the huge new Unions must have been a wrench. Something of the confused and despairing feelings of old people literally carted away from their native villages can be recaptured from an eye-witness account of what happened in Clavering. The pathetic scene was remembered 80 years later by a very old lady, Eliza Button who, as a little girl in the 1830s had peeked through a hole in the poorhouse door (next to the churchyard) and saw how well-fed the inmates were: 'They had suet pudding, fine and brown, and had 'taties with a slice of meat on 'em…' But, recalled Eliza, 'when Walden Workhouse was finished, the pore things was taken off there in waggons; the Mistress stood at the door. They cried "Good-bye Missis", 'twas pitiful to hear 'em.' Down the ages, the pathos of the scene carries a timeless echo. A different kind of welcome awaited them at Walden where the mistress, Mrs. Burkmyre was a 'comical violent woman' (see chapter 11).[19]

Clavering's old poorhouse continued to be controversial, its sale causing a rift between parish ratepayers and the incumbent, Rev. George Brookes who tried and failed to get compensation for the loss of schoolrooms in the old building. The parish wanted all the money to offset their own rate contribution to the new workhouse, whereas the vicar wanted just £26 to help him open a new school, but he had no legal agreement and no premises for another six years. A similar situation occurred in Walden, where the Town Council unsuccessfully claimed £240 to replace the gaol which had been housed at the old workhouse. Other village properties, including Radwinter, Rickling, Wimbish, Hempstead, Ashdon, Chrishall and elsewhere, were also sold off one by one and the money contributed to the new Union building. The new workhouse was very expensive. Initially costed at £5,880, the final bill was £7,300, much of which had to be borrowed. Problems with loans, legal matters and structural defects rumbled on for years. The architect had won a £10 prize for the workhouse design but, only a few months after opening, the concrete floors started cracking and needed boarding.[20]

The Work of the Guardians

Financial, legal and structural problems were not the only headaches for the new Board of Guardians. To make this huge new edifice of responsibility work, the weekly meetings dealt with multifarious matters, many inherited from the old poor law, but applied over a wider area and with an edge of authority lacking in some of their constituent parishes. The volume of work may be judged from the clerk's complaint about the payments for his 'arduous duties', so that his annual £100 salary was later raised to £120, which he felt was still inadequate, as he had to delegate much of the work: 'if I performed all the duties myself it would employ my whole time'. The Board was involved in jobs, wages, housing, settlement, charity, education, politics, diet, uniforms, medical care, migration, emigration, schooling, discipline, religious services and other matters, as well as organising the Union staff, its ten surgeons, village relieving officers and clerical administration. It was a huge set-up, of which only a small part can be explored here.[21]

The New Poor Law initially aimed, somewhat ingenuously, to redistribute the workforce to areas where there was more work. Two full-time agents were appointed in Manchester and Leeds, and the Walden Board made enquiries about sending their out-of-work paupers. One of the Guardians, Matthew Winder of Wimbish, reported that there were jobs only for well-behaved labourers with children aged at least 12. Six months later a batch of families went off to Manchester from Ashdon, Hempstead and other villages. Later on, when news of a thousand labouring vacancies in Leeds was announced, the Board reacted with typical pragmatism: would tools be needed? how would the migrants travel? would their wages later contribute to the Guardians' costs? But the migration scheme did not last long and made little impact overall in this area, moving only about 134 migrants from Essex altogether, although it was much more widely used in Suffolk, so the Board's hopes of ridding itself of large expensive pauper families were largely unfulfilled. In any case such help was not intended to be a blank cheque. When George Matthews' family, who had moved from Clavering to Manchester, needed medical aid to nurse them over smallpox, their medical bills totalling £12.15s.5d were afterwards deducted at the rate of five shillings per week from the family's wages which, even though they totalled 40 shillings a week, must have taken over a year to repay. Many of the pauper migrants similarly faced huge problems when they moved.[22]

The Guardians also occasionally advanced repayable loans for families wanting to emigrate to Canada, South Africa and even Australia, no longer only the preserve of convicts, with young workhouse inmates actually asking to be sent there, knowing there was no future for them in England. Village vestries might find it cost-effective to help them on their way or make repayable loans, as when Langley ratepayers raised £20 to emigrate John Wilson, his wife and seven children, 'a sober and good labourer' but one whose family had cost this small village £4.13s.4d in relief in the past year. This was the reality of the poverty in the very poor villages in this area, but emigration could make little impact on the problem: every poor migrant was replaced by dozens more. In any case, when assisted emigration became too popular, the bounty allowing free passage was discontinued.[23]

Workhouse Food

The migration and emigration schemes were thus short-lived activities, compared to the never-ending organisation of more mundane matters. Of these, diet was an important aspect of keeping order in the workhouse. The coming of the Union provided lucrative business for many local traders, who received bulk orders for basics. In October 1839, for instance, John Emson's grocery business sold 700 bushels of potatoes at 11d. a bushel to the workhouse. The Guardians spent a few pence per pauper per day on food, and quantity and quality were supposed to be strictly controlled. In 1840 when the diet tables were amended, men were to receive precisely 218½ ounces of food per week, plus broth or gruel and soup, while women got 205½ ounces. Meals were rather bland. Typically there would be bread and broth for breakfast, meat or soup for dinner usually with potatoes, and bread and cheese, broth or gruel for supper.[24]

Although the diet was probably better than that enjoyed by many village poor, there was contemporary criticism elsewhere that convicts were better fed than paupers. Paupers were not allowed to bring their own supplies into the workhouse, and special treats frowned upon by the assistant commissioners: the insertion of plums in the paupers' pudding the Christmas after the fire was not supposed to become a precedent, apparently, for after allowing extra fare at Christmas for some years, the Board were later rapped over the knuckles by the auditor for the extra expense and told not to do it again, although this was apparently overruled. The inmates 'wanted more': when in 1843 a London gentleman and former guardian visited the Walden Union, he wrote in some concern to the Board that 'a great many able-bodied labourers got about me complaining they had not enough to eat and they did not look well'. They needed, he felt, more hot dinners, not cold food. The Guardians did not agree.[25]

They had earlier had considerable problems over the children's diet which was a focus of concern: when the workhouse children became ill with fever one year, there were rumours that the workhouse was built on an unhealthy site, but the visiting surgeon, Thomas Spurgin decided to tackle the problem by changing the meals to make them less heavy and greasy. Many years later, complaints were still being made about the 'unwholesome' siting of the workhouse near the Slade. There was also a great scandal over food, when the mistress of the workhouse, Mrs. Burkmyre, was found to be short-weighting the children's rations in order to feed her chickens. The scandal, though covered up by the usual minuted euphemisms in order not to provoke unrest, was followed by an almost complete change of staff, and an insistence that food be weighed in front of the paupers in future (see chapter 11).[26]

Work and Welfare

The workhouse was intended to live up to its name, but most of the available tasks were deliberately degrading and pointless, to increase the deterrent value of the institution. Even before the new building was ready, the new Guardians were investigating work possibilities, and ordered the miller to keep the mill at work during mealtimes so as to employ as many paupers as possible. Worsted and knitting needles also were to be provided. But there was never much on offer and it was poorly paid. Options included sack making, stone breaking, pumping water or other domestic tasks, while others spent hours 'picking oakum', a common workhouse task of singular tedium. When a filling was needed for mattresses and pillows, the Guardians enquired about having the paupers do the work of detaching the fibre from the cocoa nut. In 1847 the visiting assistant commissioner noted that the able-bodied were 'well kept to work in the workhouse'.[27]

The welfare of the paupers was in the hands of visiting medical officers and a resident nurse, the latter sometimes of dubious quality: at least one was dismissed for 'want of sobriety'. In 1847 facilities improved with new separate sick and infection wards and other facilities. As in the old workhouse, there were sometimes appalling 'accidents', but the Guardians perhaps took them more seriously. When an old man, Joseph Freeman died of 'inflammation of the lungs', it was stressed that his death 'was in no way connected with the bruises he had formerly received', and the clerk minuted an order for bed guards to stop old people falling out of bed. On another occasion, the press gave a false account of a pauper who cut his throat, but the Board swiftly complained that this story was printed 'evidently for the purpose of bringing the operation of the new Poor Law Act into disrepute', pointing out the man was an ex-prisoner and a 'bad character', just trying to draw attention to himself.[28]

Such incidents, normally glossed over in the official records, were perhaps a reflection on poor-quality staff, a common situation in workhouses, due to penny-pinching and the dispiriting nature of such posts. The Board's medical officers had to take great care not to cast the New Poor Law in a bad light by neglecting the paupers in their areas. In Hempstead, surgeon Alexander Brown was reprimanded for neglecting the sick and told 'to exercise more caution in future to the paupers entrusted to his care'. In Walden, the Board rejected an accusation by the Essex coroner that Thomas Spurgin had left paupers 'entirely to the tender mercies of his assistant'. The latter attended a sick man, Thomas Deller of Debden, 'in a most slovenly manner', and he subsequently died. But they remained vigilant about malpractice: it was the Guardians who first alerted the authorities to the 'very peculiar circumstances' surrounding the death of Richard Chesham in Clavering, ultimately leading to the execution of his wife, Sarah.[29]

All sorts of medical problems transferred from the overseers to the Guardians, including lime-washing contaminated homes, removing sick paupers to the workhouse, occasional serious cases to Addenbrookes, the insane to the asylum and infectious persons to the pesthouse. The pesthouse was expanded urgently in 1837 when the clerk reported 'the small pox has been brought into this town and is raging among the paupers'. But just as under the old poor law, surgeons still had a difficult time persuading suspicious folk to allow themselves to be vaccinated, and there were complaints about lack of co-operation, for people distrusted injections. The poor law surgeons in Walden itself, Samuel Fiske and Thomas Spurgin, received 1s.6d for each person vaccinated and surgeons who neglected this essential work were reprimanded. On another occasion, three able-bodied labourers, Alfred Eldred, Adam Adams and William Clayden were given three shillings and four loaves of bread each, receiving the food at the entrance to Mill Field where they lived, and where the disease was raging, in return for staying away from town, to stop the disease spreading. The Poor Law authorities agreed to this somewhat unusual suggestion.[30]

Change on the Board

With so much tedious and difficult business to get through, it seems surprising that anyone wanted to be a Guardian. Members of the Board were subject to annual re-election and, once the novelty wore off, many Unions found the village posts hard to fill. Being a Guardian made you unpopular, but some found the motivation to continue, whether financial, ideological, political and, it must not be forgotten, humanitarian. In the 1837 Walden Guardian elections, however, some lost their seats because of their alleged 'too ready acquiescence in the views of the Whig Commissioners, relative to the enforcement of certain regulations considered by them to be necessary for the proper management of the inmates, but which the generality of the inhabitants considered harsh and nec-

essary'. Tory, Charles Barns Wilkins was off and Liberal, John Clark came on the Board. The criticism referred to the classification of inmates and separation of married couples. Another early loss to the Board was its chairman, Lord Braybrooke who, like many gentry in other areas, rapidly grew bored with the business. He was worn out by 'the number of hours I have spent in the service of the Union', its 'arduous' duties and 'long and anxious sittings'. In 1837 he appeared at only a quarter of the meetings, and scarcely any in 1838 before his resignation in April. The Board seemed deeply disappointed, feeling that a high-status chairman was essential to make the New Poor Law work, but his replacement, Wyatt George Gibson, was made of stronger stuff and remained *in situ* throughout the rest of his life. [Fig. 5.3] [31]

Fig.5.3 *The authoritative figure of Wyatt George Gibson, Walden banker and noted Quaker, who was chairman of the Saffron Walden Guardians from 1838 until his death in 1862.*

Why had Braybrooke grown jaded with the role so soon after his triumphalist report on the outstanding success of the New Poor Law? There may have been other factors beyond an understandable weariness in a role so lacking in glamour. Braybrooke was in dispute over his rate assessment, much of which was of course spent on the poor. The appeals concerned four of his tenant farms as well as Audley End itself. On one occasion, in a barefaced display of power, the third lord 'declined to allow the valuers of the parish to go over his residence for the purpose of enabling them to assess the same'. It was a complicated legal battle, with appeals to the Chelmsford Sessions, angry ratepayers' meetings, the appointment and disbandment of a special committee and, because of the delay in making the parochial assessment, further interest to pay on borrowed money. Even after the council, maintaining their initial assessment was perfectly valid, gave in 'to preserve peace in the parish and prevent expense', there were still arguments about who should pay legal fees, and various bills for lawyers and valuers. The action, which cost the town a great deal, must have seriously strained relationships.[32]

According to the Tory press, the other four Walden Guardians were no longer in harmony either, because of arguments on the Town Council (see chapters 2–3). This may be why John Player tried to escape from the Board, going so far as to publish a notice requesting people not to elect him, because of poor health and the long walk to the Union for meetings every week. However someone must have prevailed upon Player to do his duty, since he not only remained on the Board but agreed, apparently with reluctance, to be joint vice-chairman.[33]

Workhouse Discipline

All this internal upset was unhelpful, too, in presenting a front of unanimity for applying a new statute which had the potential to cause great unrest. Saffron Walden, the well-ordered town, had on its outskirts this large institution full of unhappy people. Workhouses were commonly disorderly, but records of internal problems in the early years are patchy. Those who rebelled in Walden Union were treated with standardised severity. Regulations were drawn up soon after the workhouse fire, when there was a 'spirit of insubordination' in the workhouse. The disorderly were put in the refractory ward with bread and water for up to 24 hours, and if they still misbehaved or made a noise, would find themselves up before a magistrate. Soon after, four inmates were summonsed and punished for an unidentified 'misdemeanour'. Occasionally inmates were prosecuted for minor infringements like wandering off wearing the Union clothing. Two men were also punished for 'returning in a state of intoxication from the funeral of William Prior late one of the inmates having been intrusted with the corpse to Elmdon'. So too was a Sampford pauper who 'misbehaved himself by tearing a piece off one of the blankets and knocking a hole in the wall of the refractory room'. Later on there was hard labour for two men who abused the workhouse schoolmaster, kicked the governor, damaged a wall and behaved improperly before divine service. Another was jailed after going out and ending up drunk in a ditch, and others imprisoned for making a hole in the wall of the mill house and smashing windows.[34]

Men who ran away, dumping their families on the rates, were pursued, sometimes with 'wanted' handbills and rewards, and prosecuted, although the Guardians regularly complained of the unfair cost of such court cases. This got worse: a quarter of the Union inmates in 1839, and over 40% in 1840 were wives and children of paupers who had deserted their families. Over a four-year period, 38 absconders were pursued, most of them outdoor paupers, of whom ten were caught, and a further 15 went back to their families without being apprehended. The Guardians also tracked down, as had the old vestry, the fathers of illegitimate children to pay weekly allowances for their offspring. A Walden man, John Whitehead was forced to reimburse the Union for maintenance of Susan Start's illegitimate child of which he was the father, and another town resident, labourer George Bacon similarly to pay for the child of Mary Ann Miller. Another record concerned proceedings against Edward Kent of Walden, 'reputed father of Mercy Archer's bastard child who with its mother is now in the workhouse'.[35]

These were of course age-old problems, very familiar from the days of the old poor laws. What did seem to be worse under the new one was the incidence of vagrancy, for the workhouse offered temporary bed and board for the itinerant homeless, much to the annoyance of the Guardians. Tramps had to be medically certified, washed and fed, although four hours work was demanded in exchange. The Board demanded more stringent regulations for this 'crying evil', saying that vagrants just obtained breakfast at one workhouse, then walked to the next one for supper, and all the cost had to be born by Walden ratepayers, rather than the Union as a whole. On one occasion six young vagrants all destroyed their clothing during the night and most escaped with the old garments supplied as replacements. Similar complaints went on for years and after numbers peaked in 1848, the rules were revised and vagrant callers at Walden Union diminished dramatically.[36]

Able-bodied Outdoor Relief

Perhaps the greatest challenge, however, was the issue of outdoor relief for the able-bodied. The Guardians were anxious to avoid scandal locally, but they needed to show the Commission they were following the rules. Bearing in mind the earlier protests, they sought to promote the New Poor Law 'as expeditiously as prudence would allow… not just preventing ratepayers being imposed on by idle and dissolute but also protecting virtuous though indigent poor against oppression'. And so there was, as in other Unions, a prolonged struggle to retain local autonomy, and this was the crux: the Guardians wanted discretion to help occasional cases of genuine need; the Commissioners insisted on the letter of the law. Originally the edict forbidding able-bodied outdoor relief had been due to be implemented *en bloc* under the new law but protests such as the workhouse fires, had persuaded the Poor Law Commission to introduce the change more gradually, in order to dilute any further rebellion.[37]

To start with Saffron Walden Guardians had 'a very strong desire to adhere scrupulously to the very letter of the regulations', and Braybrooke's triumphant first-year report seemed to bear out such an approach. In August 1837 a general circular allowed out-relief only for certain cases like emergencies, sickness and widows. But the assistant commissioner for the area, by now Col. Wade, was a hard-liner. He was adamant that topping up low wages with relief was 'one of the crying evils of the old system', and he would not tolerate special cases being put forward on allegedly humanitarian grounds, accusing the Saffron Walden Guardians of 'clinging with equal pertinacity and professions of kind and human feelings towards the poor, and far be it from me to assert that many are not actuated by such feelings… it was precisely practices of this description that I was desirous of extinguishing by the resolutions in question and which it is evident will never be voluntarily relinquished by the Guardians'.[38]

Wade may have had Walden in mind when, in November 1837, he warned that in Essex the boards *were* increasing out-relief to the able-bodied. In spite of this official discouragement, the Guardians went on trying to slip in what they called 'slight deviations', wanting to blend benevolence with duty. And so there might be a destitute pauper given just 'a trifling allowance in kind' rather than having his family broken up; then another 'trifling sum' of seven or ten shillings for young girls from large families going out to service; and, for the sake of 'policy humanity and justice', support for widows with young children, so the latter would not lose employment and education opportunities. They wanted, they said, to exercise discretion in order to benefit the community and promote good feeling towards the new system. They felt particularly strongly that destitute widows should not be forced into the workhouse, but sadly women had no autonomy under the new law. Nothing in the Guardians' long, detailed appeal made the slightest impression on Col. Wade: 'this kind of relief must necessarily cease' and people must be warned of the change, he insisted.[39]

A report in the Essex press at this time also claimed that Walden Board were being too lenient towards the able-bodied poor, quoting a complaint from the Poor Law authorities that the Guardians were using discretion, carrying the workhouse system beyond the rules, whereas the official view was that wages could only be raised by applying the full rigour of the system. As the correspondence continued and annual guardian elections loomed, Wade privately condemned what he called 'the last dying speck of the expiring Board or the first of the new one', and refused to discuss it further. However, after another round of guardians' elections, the Board persisted in submitting names of those they wanted to help outside the workhouse. The type of cases for which they pleaded special needs included small allowances for men whose wives were either dead or crippled and who could not manage their children without aid. Wade maintained his stance. Among his Guardians' notes, John Player scribbled that from June 1838 no relief was to be given to the able bodied except in sudden or urgent necessity, and from 7 December that year there was to be strict adherence to the workhouse system. The Poor Law Commission had already recommended Guardians to encourage people to join medical clubs, and the tightening up in 1838 influenced the appearance that year of two new provident societies for the poor (see chapter 10).[40]

Nevertheless as winter deepened, the Guardians kept trying. They put forward a deserving case typical of many throughout the Union area: Joseph Chipperfield, able-bodied, hard-working bricklayers' labourer, who was walking eight miles from Clavering every day to his work, but only earning eight shillings a week. Even with his son contributing an additional 1s.9d, this was not enough to keep his wife and seven children. It meant they each had only half the food allowance of a workhouse pauper. This was an emergency as they were in great distress and, said the Guardians, 'relief in some way *must* be afforded'. There were many other similar cases. It made economic sense to give such a respectable family a couple of shillings a week to enable them to stay together outside the workhouse, rather than segregated and expensively housed, clothed, fed, bathed and employed within it. But it was unavailing. Wade impatiently expressed his 'great regret that at a moment when the exceedingly high price of farming produce will certainly enable the farmer to raise the wages of the labourers … there are still able bodied men in the parishes of Clavering and Ashdon in receipt only of 7s and 8s per week… not to be wondered at they are in distress so needed relief, but allowance system must not recur. Employers could afford to pay higher wages and must do so.'[41]

Soon after this, in a published report, Col. Wade recommended stronger regulations to prevent Guardians from evading the outdoor relief order. They were commonly giving relief without asking for proof of the cause, simply relying on an unsupported statement by the relieving officer. Another abuse was relieving the whole family, just because the wife or one of the children was ill. He recommended proper medical books, not just scraps of paper, to be produced at weekly guardians meetings. Although this did not mention Walden Guardians by name, it was soon after this report in early 1839 that the lengthy correspondence petered out, suggesting that the central authority had, for the moment anyway, won the ideological battle against the local institution.[42]

As was clear from several of his letters, the assistant commissioner truly believed that strict application of the workhouse test would force wages up, and prevent farmers relying on the old system of relief top-ups. In this sense, the new law was a massive experiment in social engineering, but it is very hard to see how such an ambitious plan could conceivably work in an area as poor as north-west Essex where there was an over-supply of labourers and no alternative employment. Although stricter and stricter regulations came in, this particular aim was never achieved. It seems astonishing that the Poor Law Commission ever believed they could force higher agricultural wages by the back door, particularly when rural Boards of Guardians were packed with farmers with a vested interest in maintaining things as they were. The continued illegal use of the ticket system (described in chapter 4) is demonstration of the power of the farmer-Guardians to influence policy.

The 'Hungry Forties'

Poverty really kicked in again in the early 1840s, when conditions worsened. Not every year in the 'hungry Forties' was bad, but increasing distress led to widespread rural incendiarism (see chapter 7). Various statistics suggest a period of crisis. In 1841 there were more burials than usual at the Parish Church. The abolition of able-bodied outdoor relief was, to say the least, unhelpful at such times. Fortunately assistance from neighbours and kin, and charity were still softening some of the edges of the new law, otherwise its true harshness would have been even more apparent. With 'fever' prevalent in 1841, for instance the under-funded Benevolent Society experienced a large leap in demand to 200 persons relieved (compared to 143 the year before and 100 the following year). Numbers in the workhouse had always varied week by week, but from the early winter of 1842 they rose sharply. Looking purely at the Walden inmates, whereas there was an average of 20–40 in the workhouse in the late 1830s, figures suggest that this rose to an average 250 in 1842–3, and 450 in 1844, afterwards declining. The peak was 541 over late spring that year. They cannot possibly all have been there at once, as the workhouse only accommodated 300 at this time, but even if turnover was rapid, it is a measure of the depth of distress that so large a proportion of the population might need temporary refuge at times.[43]

Generally, however, the policy seemed to be to keep the workhouse population low to save expense. This could only happen if there was some other way of helping people. Over the whole Union area of 24 parishes, the numbers on outdoor relief went up considerably from the 1840s. Names of outdoor relief recipients suddenly began to be minuted regularly at the Guardians' weekly meetings, and the long lists of ailments sound genuine enough. Typically, at one meeting, they listed 37 people in 15 parishes, needing help for complaints including pleurisy, broken leg, fever, rheumatism, inflamed lungs, scrofula, sore face, giddiness, sores, sprains, influenza and rheumatic fever.[44]

These sound like the impotent, but in 1844 all able-bodied outdoor relief was forbidden by Act of Parliament, except in cases of urgent necessity or other exceptional circumstances. What was happening to those who were not sick but still in desperate need? One compromise, favoured by assistant commissioners, was to take some children into the workhouse, leaving poor families with fewer children to feed. The feelings of the children about this arrangement are not recorded. In 1843 Saffron Walden Guardians, still suffering from the old angst, put forward 32-year-old widower William Savill who had only eight shillings a week to feed his five children, three shillings of which was needed for an infant's care. The Guardians wanted to give him another two shillings but the assistant commissioner persuaded them to take two of the children into the workhouse instead. They agreed that Savill's earnings were small but commented 'I do not like a money relief in these cases to enable a labourer to pay for a housekeeper out of the rates'.[45]

And what of the others in distress? The revolutionary statute had been brought into being to tackle able-bodied pauperism, so the question of whether the edict was actually adhered to is a central one, but historians have come to no agreed conclusion. There is a strong suspicion that in many places, Guardians circumvented the regulations by using the euphemism of sickness. One wide-ranging study included Saffron Walden in an analysis of all the Unions throughout the six counties of Essex, Suffolk, Norfolk, Cambridgeshire, Hertfordshire and Bedfordshire, over the years 1842–6. This study concluded that Saffron Walden was indeed among those evading the 1834 Act by listing a minor ailment so that a poor family could be given outdoor relief. Looking at the period 1842–6, maybe two-thirds of the adult able-bodied paupers receiving outdoor relief in this area were listed in terms of sickness or accident, whereas throughout England and Wales, the figure was less than half.[46]

By the late 1840s, the Walden Board seemed to be on better terms with the assistant commissioner, but needy cases continued to cause dilemmas, particularly in years of high prices and great distress like 1847. In that year of exceptional distress, the proprietor of the *Chelmsford Chronicle* sent a confidential letter to the Poor Law Commission, criticising the resolution of the Walden Guardians to seek unlimited power to relieve the able-bodied until the next harvest.

The writer objected that this would shake the foundations of the poor law, and it would be much preferable to take children into the House. Yet it really was impossible to apply the full rigour of the law in years like this, either on humanitarian, law-and-order or rates-related grounds. If this is so, it suggests a deep flaw in the rationale of the New Poor Law, for it ignored basic economic realities in agricultural areas.[47]

The Union at Mid-century

Pauperism went on increasing throughout the 1840s, even allowing for a peak in bad years like 1847. The number of outdoor paupers reached 2,000 in 1850, while the census on 12 April 1851 counted 317 workhouse inmates. Such misfortune could hit, not only labourers, but any small trader or artisan fallen on hard times. Just over half were of working age (most of the others were children), and of these about half were labourers. About a sixth were servants, and there were smaller numbers of shoemakers, blacksmiths, bricklayers, tailors and a few others such as currier, baker, woodman, cooper, farmer, painter, carman, thatcher. Many of these possessed useful skills, but were clearly unable to manage. Each would have a story if it were known: why was 45-year-old William Rand there with his two grown-up sons? Why were there so many poverty-stricken shoemakers and bricklayers?[48]

On that day in 1851, about 17% of the workhouse paupers were from Walden itself, and half of those of working age were farm labourers or field workers. New law or not, the same old social problems of the indigenous poor recurred. Over half the people inside the institution simply had nowhere else to go: deserted and orphaned children, those dependent on poor widows, unmarried mothers and their illegitimate offspring, the mentally ill (classed as 'insane', 'lunatic' or 'idiot'), the aged and infirm. This was the old peoples' home of its time, as suggested by the increased numbers of over-60s in the Walden census. A recent study of workhouses in Hertfordshire has found that there were commonly more old men than women, for the latter seemed to manage better in old age.[49]

Conclusion

By now the Saffron Walden Guardians represented a large, rural district of over 20,000 people, many of whom were very poor. The efforts of leading worthies to maintain a well-ordered town had perforce to be extended into this sprawling hinterland, which was never going to be easy to organise. At the beginning the task must have seemed Herculean. There was much contemporary criticism of the new law, and the Guardians also faced an image problem. It is difficult to escape the initial impression that once the novelty wore off, it began to look as though the Whig government, in rushing through a drastically reformed statute based on biased and inadequate research, had unleashed a monster and the boards of guardians had to somehow make it all work. The rationale of the Poor Law Amendment Act had assumed that there was work available if only men would seek it, but this was to over-estimate the willingness and ability of poor rural families to migrate long distances to the industrial areas where work was only temporarily more plentiful. In agricultural districts, the new system appeared to work in a year like 1835 when there was an exceptionally good harvest offering plenty of work, but in years of distress the thousands in genuine need could not all be accommodated in the workhouse without the rates going through the roof. The need for able-bodied relief outside the workhouse, opposed by the Commission, was still there during all-too-frequent crises.

Some would say that the Walden Board, as one would expect under a chairman with the integrity of Wyatt George Gibson, did their best to be humane, in very difficult circumstances. Others might say they also had financial, ideological and other reasons for pursuing the outdoor relief issue, and circumventing it when necessary; farmer-guardians certainly had strong vested interests in poor law policy, and the town revolved around agriculture. The Guardians very likely saw themselves as playing a pivotal role in sustaining a healthy local economy, by mediating between the all-important agricultural interest, the hard-pressed ratepayers and the labouring workforce. This attitude can be extrapolated from the wording of a petition sent in 1844 in opposition to the repeal of the Corn Laws. The Walden Board had been, they felt,

'successful in attaining the object at which the Legislature aimed although they have had to contend with numerous difficulties in the performance of their duties… the experience they have acquired. has enabled our Petitioners to ascertain with considerable accuracy the means which exist of employing the labouring population and they have also satisfied themselves of the extreme importance of extending rather than contracting those means… it would soon throw out of employment a vast body of farming labourers… could not then operate the new poor law.'[50]

And what of the poor themselves? After a brief flurry of opposition in the first year or two and in spite of various episodes of disorder in the workhouse, concerted opposition as such to the new statute was not a reality in this area. People were forced to accept a harsh new world. But whether this inculcated better behaviour among the poor, is open to different interpretations. A show of deference cost nothing, for a person's thoughts were his own. A man would probably take any job, however pitiful the wage, to keep his family out of the workhouse. In that sense the new regime was a 'success'. But splitting up families must have left its mark on the children and the price might be paid in the next generation. The apparent resignation with which the poor accepted the new system — or at any rate the lack of renewed protests — very likely also reflects that the Guardians achieved the local discretion they wanted and softened the edges somewhat, while retaining the deterrent value of the workhouse.[51]

As a counter argument, it could equally be said that protest simply went underground, for these were also years in which crime generally seemed to be getting worse and in particular arson, hitherto only sporadic, became much more prevalent, very clearly directed at farmers in many cases. A firm commitment to the rule of law was called for, and it is to this formal arm of the well-ordered town and its hinterland, the maintenance of law and order, that we must now turn.

Chapter 6

'This Town… infested with Gangs of Thieves and Poachers'

Crime in and around Walden

'On the night of Saturday 8 November some villains went to the Rosse Farm to steal Mr Turner Clark's poultry. They had killed four fowls when through the resolution of two of his sons and two lads, four fellows were taken and conveyed to prison. Two accomplices were received… Savill to hard labour at the treadmill for 12 months. Atkinson died previously in the Jail of a Brain-Fever… Wilson, Brewer and Miller conveyed to Chatham for transportation.'[1]

John Player's terse account of foul play at Roos Farm on a dark November night in 1828 is suffused with the perceptions of the age: the citizens' arrest; the labelling of half-drunk intruders as 'villains'; the trivial nature of the offence as compared to the breathtaking gravity of the sentence; the passing reference to the death in custody of one of the prisoners, as if his demise were of no consequence. The thieves were caught because, fortified with drink for their adventure, they failed to be discreet at a time when people were being extra vigilant because, during the early winter of 1828, there had been 'not a single night passing without some such despoiling'. The squawk of dying chickens soon after midnight alerted the farmer's son, Joseph Clarke who crept out to investigate, with his brother and two farm lads, armed with bludgeons. In a shed they found four dead chickens, still warm and bleeding, and beside them some inebriated, somnolent Walden labourers, whom they overpowered: 'I was asleep when he struck me — I was uncommon freshy', said one; 'I was forwarder in liquor than I ought to have been', admitted another, to support their story that they were just having a nap in the shed, having been at a beerhouse since late afternoon.[2]

The farmer and the witnesses received extraordinarily high prosecution expenses, a total of £140 from the public purse, rather in excess of the value of a few chickens. Did the bludgeons play any part in William Atkinson's death in jail from 'brain-fever'? Who cared? By death or transportation or a harsh 12 months on the treadmill, the district was well rid of a bunch of 'well-known characters of poaching celebrity' who were threatening men of property.[3]

Crime looms large in the annals of the poor, but it remains a frustratingly difficult subject to summarise and analyse, particularly at a distance of time. It is very tempting simply to write a populist account, listing one colourful crime after another, and there was no shortage of lurid press stories to feed the appetite for tales of 'desperate characters' and lawless 'gangs'. But crime statistics are notoriously difficult to interpret, since so much crime went unrecorded, or even unreported, and much unproven. The feeling of historians today is that the contemporaneous perception of what constituted 'crime', the mindset of those who enforced the law and the hidden purposes of law enforcement are of greater significance than the crimes themselves. These ideas are interwoven into the discussion which follows, illustrated by various cases, some summarised statistics and the various features of the legal system. The link between crime and distress is a focus, particularly with regard to poaching, the clearest example of a customary activity transformed over time into a criminal act.[4]

The Town & Quarter Sessions

Before discussing this most vital aspect of the well-ordered town, it is worth noting that justice was not entirely an elite-driven exercise, for the common folk had their court too. This was the Town Sessions, a third lower rung of the legal ladder, above which stood the borough Quarter Sessions and the county Assize. The Town Sessions, or unrecorded summary hearing, was where many of the town's poachers received their fines or months on the treadmill, often a few hours after being caught, and where serious offences were committed for trial. Here, sometimes sitting several days a week, the mayor in his parlour or one of the inns, with or without one other magistrate, dispensed summary judgement over an endless stream of complaints about drunkenness, swearing, riotous behaviour, bastardy, vagrancy, pick-pocketing, gambling, snaring, barking trees, taking wood and other minor matters, often dealt with by fines.[5]

But this was also the people's court, where the poorer residents could summons their fellow poor. The presence of such a local court tended to encourage litigiousness between neighbours, who probably would not have bothered if they had had to travel any distance for a hearing. As it was, a large number of the town families had dealings with the Town Sessions at some stage, either as prosecutors, witnesses or accused, although certain families made a habit of it: half of the 210 surnames mentioned from 1815–36 consisted of five names, and a third of just two, Augar (36) and Barker (34), not necessarily related of course. The Town Sessions was very much part of the fabric of people's lives, offering a redress for the poor and a safety valve for tension.

Most cases of violence, apart from the occasional altercation with gamekeepers, seemed to take place between the poor: wife-beating, assault, drunken fights and domestic disputes were commonplace, for lack of work did not prevent drinking to excess. Long before the Beerhouse Act of 1830, pubs were blamed for exacerbating many of the burdens of the labouring poor. Here it was said they wasted their summer earnings, joined useless 'box clubs', engaged in illicit liaisons and drunken brawls, heard seditious talk, passed game and other ill-gotten goods and, as in the Roos case, built up dutch courage for thieving and poaching expeditions: there were 'several houses which are places of known resort of idle characters particularly poachers', Walden replied to a later survey. Once the Beerhouse Act was passed, allowing rated householders to sell beer from their own house on payment of two guineas, the total number of beerhouses in Essex doubled in just 20 years. Although in Walden the numbers do not seem excessive, they proved hard to control: when two beersellers, William Burrows and William Archer, were summonsed for opening after midnight, it was because 'encouragement was unduly given to labourers to spend their weekly wages'. From the poor man's point of view, it was easy to see the social attraction of the 'Tom & Jerry Houses', particularly in villages where this might be the one warm, convivial meeting place, away from damp decaying cottages, domestic demands and the prying eyes of busybodies. They were particularly popular with young single men, as of course pubs are today. The other classes, notwithstanding their own jollifications in the *Rose & Crown*, saw them as 'nurseries of crime'.[6]

Whether drunkenness was a cause or a consequence of poverty, it certainly led to much suffering. Alcohol-related illness, accident and even death were cited in several inquisitions and many court cases. When a labourer with a large family, James Swan died after falling off a cart, it was said that the 'melancholy catastrophe' was caused by his drinking heavily. As today, battered wives often owed their misfortune to drink, but they could face little sympathy. Elias Harvey sold his furniture to spend the money in Westwood's beer shop, but as the magistrates jailed him for three months for hitting his wife Elizabeth, throwing a candlestick at her and threatening to kill her, she was warned by the magistrates to stop nagging when he came out.[7]

Prostitutes received short shrift too. Selling their bodies was a temptingly easy form of income for poor women, who were blamed more than men. After a violent incident in Stennets Yard (off Castle Street), when four men, George Burgess, William Cornell, Charles Augur and Isaac Barker, broke down the door of dressmaker Mary Ann Watson's home, they received less admonition than she, described as 'a girl of loose character and well known as such... lived a highly immoral life'. The court was told that she harboured bad girls, suggesting the house was a brothel.[8]

Beyond the Town Sessions, there was the Quarter Sessions, a facility of which Walden was very proud. Although said to have had a higher property crime rate than the average of Essex towns in the eighteenth century, this is not the impression gained by reading through a century of Quarter Sessions minutes from the 1750s to the 1850s: statistics suggest that the whole atmosphere of the town changed in the latter half of this period. Historians all agree that crime statistics are inadequate indicators, but they do provide a baseline. The only years for which Walden has both Quarter and Town Session records are 1816–36. [Table 6.1]. The latter is missing cases in the years 1826–9, yet it is clear from other sources that offences were occurring in that period. The presence of a crime-busting mayor in 1832–3, and the clearing-up of a large collection of crimes in 1833, dating back at least two or three years, also distorts the picture.

Nevertheless the huge rise of court cases in the early '30s is significant, matching the county and national trend. Nationally, recorded crime generally rose

Years	Charges	Convictions
1816–20	112	62
1821–5	84	48
1826–30	52	32
1831–5	372	220

Table 6.1 *Saffron Walden Quarter & Town Sessions, 1816–35: minimum recorded charges and convictions.*

sevenfold from 1805–42, at a time of huge population increase. Throughout Essex, recorded property crime in particular increased after 1815. Curiously, while at that time the Walden Sessions were busy enough with the usual assortment of minor thefts, assaults, fraudulence and paternity suits, the post-war crime wave did not seem to touch the town greatly, although the large numbers of vagrants passing through suggests that it was a difficult time. Some local men were, however, involved in a notorious gang rounded up elsewhere after a series of nocturnal forays in 1816. But offences were one thing, indictments another and guilty verdicts different again. Looking at the available evidence in Saffron Walden and elsewhere in Essex, for the 1820s, at most only half of indictments ever ended in a sentence, and some estimates put the figure far lower. Given also the amount of crime never reported at all and missing records of summary justice, it is easy to understate the level of what was then defined as crime.[9]

Policing the Town

Unfortunately simply listing one offence after another tells us very little about the circumstances, other than to emphasise how difficult it was becoming for the old amateur policing to suffice. Records of early policing in Walden are fragmentary, but law enforcement remained largely in the lap of a handful of magistrates, leading dignitaries led by the mayor, who appointed part-time constables for general policing, supplemented on occasion — such as the 1830 Swing riots and the 1832 general election — by special constables sworn in and paid by the day.

The magistrates had much more authority than the constables, and some years the mayor-magistrate took a particular interest in law enforcement. Convictions more than doubled, for instance, during the 1832–3 mayoralty of Charles Barnes Wilkins. No one could accuse this mayor of sitting on his dignity. He vigorously pursued a large 'gang' of malt-stealers discovered during his term of office and, at their trial, himself waded in physically to assist the constables in controlling the mêlée of persons trying to gain entrance to the exciting spectacle in court.

On another occasion, Wilkins personally 'with his usual energy, caused a vast number of the respectable inhabitants of the town' to join a posse in pursuit of an alleged 'daring gang of burglars', courageously arresting the two men and three women in a field, where they were lying in a drunken stupor. They were sent to the Assizes (see below).[10]

Policing was thus a far more personal, 'hands-on' business than today. The desire to retain local autonomy and keep down rates was the reason why, in spite of troubled times, worthies still clung to their own initiatives, such as circulating handbills, offering rewards and large prosecution expenses, while the poor were given every incentive to 'grass' on their fellows. In 1826 the 'Saffron Walden Association for Detection & Prosecution of Persons Guilty of Felonies & Misdemeanours' was formed, with members offering rewards varying from £1 to £10 for information leading to the identification of law-breakers. In 1840, during another period of tension, another such group (or perhaps the same one revived?) appeared, the 'Saffron Walden Association for the Speedy Apprehension and Effectual Prosecution of Felons & Thieves of every Denomination'. Although more of a social gathering, the rich men's club points up a continuing determination to keep policing local, rather than county-based.[11]

This was also an age when the threat to property, however petty, rather than to people, seemed the focus of worry. John Player, in his *Chronicles*, once noted: 'Woman named Barker, Castle St wounded by one of Braybrooke's warreners while with others gathering sticks in a grove where she had no right to be'. The 'woman named Barker', widow of Thomas Barker, was on poor relief, recently increased, so this sounds distinctly lacking in compassion for an old woman gathering kindling for her hearth. On another occasion he noted the story of 'John Woodley's boy', an apprentice butcher caught stealing by his master, James Archer of Castle Street. As punishment, Archer thrashed Woodley with a stick and hung him up, using a calves' halter, from a hook in the slaughter house. The boy was not badly hurt, and when the case went to court, it was dismissed, and the butcher merely told that his conduct was 'very injudicious'. The newspaper scoffed at the outcry over something so trivial by those labelled 'the thickly populated and not very refined residents occupying Castle Street'.[12]

A secure lock-up was essential to a well-ordered town, but this caused many problems. There were two buildings in use at various times, a bridewell in the yard of the High Street workhouse, rebuilt in 1807, with wooden bedsteads, blankets and the ministrations of the workhouse mistress; and a gaol under the court room in the Town Hall. The Town Hall gaol, with its straw bedding on the floor and stricter allowances, was the least comfortable, but was liked better, for a very good reason: 'prisoners generally prefer being confined there, on account of such donations as they casually receive from persons in the street'. This was because the gaol had direct contact through iron bars to the street. By the same token, however, there were complaints about prisoners spitting on passers-by.[13]

Therefore, in 1818 a subscription was raised and the workhouse bridewell rebuilt as a new gaol. But in time this too proved inconvenient and became insecure. The gaol was increasingly used as temporary lodging for more desperate characters, who had nothing to lose by breaking out, and its shortcomings became more evident. In the 1830s several prisoners found it easy to escape, sometimes by making holes in the walls, although the gaoler was exonerated from blame. With the coming of the New Poor Law, the town lost the workhouse accommodation, but the Poor Law Commission refused compensation, and nor would the newly-formed Essex police agree to build a gaol in Walden, telling the town to go on using Newport's more sturdy house of correction (although this was closed in 1841). Finally, a new lock up was built next to the Town Hall. [Fig.6.1] Meanwhile the building of Chelmsford's forbidding new county prison at Springfield, completed between 1825–8, was widely used for poachers and thieves given hard labour, although sending them there cost the town dearly in transport and maintenance charges.[14]

Fig.6.1 *The Town Hall, which housed the Sessions court and also the gaol, apart from a period when a building was used at the old High Street workhouse. This picture was taken before the later mock-Tudor frontage was built on.*

From 1829 a new law enforcement agency became available, through the formation of the Metropolitan Police, a body of full-time policemen, who were intended to prevent crime, as well as solve those which had already happened. These men could be hired as could Bow Street Runners and, although this remained a rare resort, it was an expense Walden magistrates and others were sometimes prepared to go to, for instance to investigate the workhouse fire in December 1835. The magistrates also employed outside police to help track down the principal villain in the 1833 malt-stealing case (see below). After 'Rusty' Housden escaped from the rather incompetent constables, they made use of publicity in the London police journal, the *Hue and Cry*, successfully in this case, thanks perhaps to the vivid description circulated:

'5 ft 8 or 9 inches high, of light complexion, brown hair, talks quick and sharp, has a rolling walk as if in-knee'd, slender legs and thighs, which are long in proportion to the body; has been employed in the malt-making business: had on a dark jacket, light coloured patent cord breeches, a dark plush waistcoat, and high shoes.'[15]

From 1836 onwards, after the formation of a new Town Council, a Saffron Walden borough force was organised by a Watch Committee, acting as the police authority. They had powers to hire and dismiss a head constable and part-time watchmen, such as John Mynott at Sewer's End and Jeremiah Stock at Audley End, equipped with handcuffs, doing regular patrols, but there were always problems finding good-quality, literate officers. Meanwhile, through the growth of arson and unrest in other areas of the country, demand grew for a professional police force. Essex was one of the first counties to take advantage of the 1839 County Police Act, and its first Chief Constable, Captain J.M.M. McHardy was appointed in February 1840.[16]

At this time there was a dry comment in the Essex press relating to Walden: 'It is rather singular that since the new police constabulary have been upon duty a great number of daring robberies have been committed in this neighbourhood than for many years past and scarcely one of the offenders has been brought to justice'. The 'neighbourhood' in question was the Walden area, where in Springwell 'desperate characters' had broken into William Wright's home while he was in church; and at Little Walden where cheeky thieves took everything of value from an elderly farmer, David Richardson, forcing a servant girl to serve them a meal first. Another farmer was threatened with a gun and the famous phrase, 'your money or your life'. This spate of rural burglaries turned out to be the work of a youthful gang, presumably the same ones captured by Wilkins' posse (see above). A young Walden woman, 17-year-old Amey Richardson was given 12 months on the treadmill and William Douce, also 17, and his older brother James, also from Walden, were among those transported.[17]

Another type of crime, particularly common in Essex during these years, was sheep-stealing, prevalent in villages near Walden. When one of the town butchers experienced the loss of one of his sheep, it followed the distinctive pattern noted elsewhere: 'a fat Southdown wether sheep, property of James Archer butcher, stolen from pasture field near Long Lane. The thieves killed on the spot, leaving skin, head etc behind them… a spirited reward offered by Mr. Archer.' Archer suffered similar thefts in later years: the Slade alongside the Common was another favoured place for butchering the meat.[18]

Such dreadful crimes dictated the need for better policing, but the Watch Committee prevaricated. The nearest branch of the county police was at Newport, from where Supt. John Clarke supervised a number of officers to cover the rural area around Walden, with constables based at Ashdon, Chrishall and else-where. Towards the end of 1840, McHardy visited Walden to hold discussions about taking over the borough police but the arrangements fell through. Some ratepayers wanted to join the Essex force but the Watch Committee wished to keep its powers, and McHardy lost patience with them. Yet crime was costing so much, anything up to £800 a year in the 1840s, much of it spent on maintaining increasing numbers of Walden prisoners in the county gaol, where it cost more to feed each prisoner than each pauper in the workhouse. In 1845, after a break-in at a town butcher, John Cowell, there was a comment in the press 'that the great increase of robberies in this town call for a more active and efficient detective force than the existing one'. After two worrying fires in the town centre, a well-attended public meeting was called to persuade the ratepayers to finance a more substantial borough force. The mayor, vicar and bigwigs like the Gibsons and Thomas Smith argued strongly for 'a more effective constabulary force… not only for the protection of property, but also in a moral point of view'.

Fig.6.2 *Thomas Duberry photographed in the later 1850s. Duberry began as a watchman, but at the time of this photograph was designated constable. In 1852, when William Redhead purchased a uniform from a Cambridge tailor, it consisted of coat and trousers, frock coat with silver collar, belt and buckles. A similar order was placed in 1853. The wearing of proper uniforms was part of a general tightening-up of discipline in the 1850s.*

But the large crowd attending were having none of it and noisily objected. The proposal appeared to fail, but by 1848, possibly earlier, there was nevertheless such a body in operation in Walden. Like most borough forces in Essex, it was of dubious efficacy.[19]

The new head constable, William Campling had a rough time. In July 1848, he was knocked down in a mêlée when he rather foolishly tried to prevent 'masses of the lowest order' from entering a show by a company of strolling players on the Common. In October 1849 he received 136 gunshot wounds in the legs, dying some days later. The murderer — although strongly suspected to be Benjamin Pettit — was never proved guilty, and the incompetence attending the investigation of the case underlined the need for better policing. Other head constables, often of poor quality, came and went. The system tightened up in the '50s, with proper uniforms. [Fig.6.2] However, the small borough force continued to be wracked with serious problems until, with the passing of the County & Borough Police Act in 1857, it was merged with the county force.[20]

Prosecution and Punishment

The gravest offences like highway robbery and horse-stealing, were still committed to the twice-yearly Assizes, but the vast majority of cases were dealt with locally, either summarily (perhaps in the mayor's parlour) or with a jury and all the ritual of the Quarter Sessions. Simply having a court which was *local* affected law enforcement. But even if anyone was caught and the victim was prepared to prosecute, the grand jury, meeting in private, could still decide there was no case. One occasion on which they did so occurred in 1828 when two 'thoughtless and profane' young men, George Goodacre and Archibald Duprey, were imprisoned after interrupting services at the Wesleyans' meeting in Castle

Street but, much to John Player's annoyance, three others, Rebecca Burling, Henry Wisbey and James King, were not indicted even though they also 'had more than once caused a disgraceful interruption at the time of divine service'. This case also gave rise to a rare item in the archives, a royal pardon signed by the king, releasing Goodacre and Duprey from prison. It was all rather wasted, for they continued on the fiddle and ended up transported.[21]

Transportation was the severest sentence available to the Walden magistrates, and an unusual one for a small town to possess. From its first usage in the late eighteenth century, it appears a punishment out of all proportion to the crime: an early record shows John Barker the younger transported seven years just for stealing a sack of chaff and oats. Despatched first to the dreaded hulks on the Thames, he would be examined by a surgeon for 'any putrid or infectious distemper', to await the next sailing. Back to the town came the chilling reply: 'Received from the custody of the mayor of Saffron Walden in the county of Essex the body of John Barker for transportation'.[22]

Transportation remained relatively rare, being inflicted only six times in the first quarter of the century, and on average, less than one person a year was transported by the Walden magistrates in 54 years, the last being in 1853 when 18-year-old Richard Webb was sent away for 15 years and Charles Warren for 10 years. After this date, penal servitude was substituted. But half of the total 42 transportations (which included seven women) took place in the 1830s, three in 1830 alone, and ten in 1833. This reflected national trends, where three-quarters of the total sent to Australia were despatched in the early 1830s. Normally reserved for habitual offenders, it was tantamount to permanent banishment, leaving wives and children on the parish. In the late 1840s, a survey found at least 7 women with a total of 17 children, whose husbands/fathers had been transported from 1820–41. But the dreams of Ann Smith, Maria Barrett, Mary Halls, Elizabeth Miller, Mary Richardson, Martha Stacey and Emma Smith to rejoin their menfolk remained unfulfilled. The rationale for transportation was given as the protection of the community for 'a few persons viciously disposed, under particular circumstances, by example and by enticement, may contaminate and corrupt great numbers. The removal of such persons from this country, if the ends of justice should call for that measure, may stop the further spread of the mischief.'[23]

A good reference could influence magistrates away from transportation, but it only worked once. Labourer/ blacksmith James Smith, spotted by a charwoman wearing a great coat taken from his master just before Christmas, in court produced four former employers to testify to his good character, and a threatened banishment became hard labour. But out of gaol only a few months, he stole a second coat, was arrested, broke out of prison, gave himself up, and the truth emerged. Now described as 'extremely bad' (underlined), he turned out to be an old offender, 'a cunning and very ingenious fellow', and was therefore despatched to a warmer clime where coats were less necessary.[24]

Since so few people were caught, it was necessary to make a strong example of those who were, to deter others. In these hard times, the courts were punishing poor people for taking bread, picking nuts, cutting underwood and pilfering odd items of no use to themselves, like a horseshoe or a surveyor's wheel, just to sell for a few pence. In earlier times, punishment was shorter and sharper, for whipping was in common usage. Almost two-thirds of property-related crime in Walden in the eighteenth century resulted in a whipping, a high proportion by Essex standards. A total of 113 such sentences are recorded on both men and women, mostly before 1835. In the nineteenth century, it was used less often, although some mayor-magistrates were whippers, Thomas Smith in 1822 passing the sentence nine times during his term of office, compared to other mayors only once or twice. Replying to a parliamentary return on vagrancy, Smith said vagrants had increased since whipping them was given up. Public whipping in the Market Place on market day did not die out until 1825, and private whipping was still possible up to the 1850s.[25]

Yet corporal punishment was perhaps less cruel than the daily grind of physically-ruinous labour on the treadmill, more freely used after the new county gaol at Springfield in Chelmsford became available. Apart from the sheer tedium, it ravaged joints, affecting the ability to do physical work afterwards and was particularly degrading for women. The magistrates had power to use discretion in sentencing, and the difference between a fine, gaol, whipping, hard labour or a combination of punishments, indeed for transportation itself, might turn on the need to set an example, previous character, evidence of contrition, personal testimony or other factors such as the position in society of the victim: some folk were more important than others. When Henry Smith, farmer of Audley End, assaulted John Low, the local coachman, he was fined sixpence, while at the same petty session a labourer was jailed for a month for absenting himself from his employment.[26]

The 1833 Case

From at least the 1820s, onwards through the following decades, there was an escalating series of petty, opportunistic depredations upon the property of shopkeepers, tradesmen, farmers and of course Lord Braybrooke, many remaining unsolved. Almost anyone could be targeted: a brickbat through grocer John Emson's drawing room window, beer from Sam Porter's cellar, lettuces out of William Chater's garden; Mr Paul's girl robbed him of clothes, Mr Catlin's boy took his wine, Mr Nicholls' lad bought goods illegally on his master's credit. One Christmas night a man was caught red-handed taking a turkey out of someone's larder. An attempted break-in at John Player's house was foiled by a door chain. The Gibson brothers, for all their famous philanthropy, did not escape, and other victims included the builder William Ward, Thomas Frye the churchwarden, farmer Henry Smith, surveyor Martin Nockolds. Most of this was simple opportunism, impulsively pocketing objects which could be exchanged for a few pence or some beer, but in spite of severe penalties, drapers, bakers, butchers, chemists, maltsters and others remained easy targets. Some such petty thefts might have been overlooked as perquisites in an earlier, more tolerant age, but it was now unforgivable for workers to take anything from their employers, always regarded as 'a great and serious offence'.[27]

This was one of many weighty comments made in 1833, during Saffron Walden's trial of the century, when Walden was 'infested with gangs of thieves and poachers', and John Player coined the phrase, 'this well-ordered town'. Magistrates attempted a clean sweep through the criminal fraternity, seemingly rounding up every thief they could find and staging a big show trial of the 'gang'. This 'gang' image was part of the popular conception of crime, and other small Essex towns such as Foulness, Fordham and Witham also went in for large-scale prosecutions as a show of strength against 'gangs'. In the hands of crime-busting mayor, C.B. Wilkins, it was a policing effort of extraordinary single-mindedness and for a while was the entertainment of the day, as large crowds of onlookers fought to get into the court.[28]

It all began with the accidental discovery that the yields from similar loads of barley were showing considerable discrepancies. As events moved on swiftly in the late winter, the gaol was full to bursting, dozens were interviewed, over 20 came to trial, some were jailed and ten men transported. What emerged was a diverse collection of offences of considerable complexity, of years of opportunistic thieving. Most of the booty was malt, that most central of Walden products, but also barley, wheat, hops, turkeys, ducks, hampers, guns, ferrets, nets: in fact anything they could lay their hands on and either eat for supper or sell for beer. To make matters worse, some of it had been taking place right under the noses of the foremost businessmen, particularly the malting owners, and often involving their own trusted employees. There was no mercy. Sentences of 7 or 14 years' transportation were imposed on James Fish, William Green, James Hall, Joseph Housden, George Ling, Francis Marshall, William Phillips, James and George Richardson and John Stacey, the largest number ever.[29]

The success of the prosecution turned on the willingness of some of the men to betray their fellows, as a result of which immunity from prosecution was given to William Richardson, who exhibited admirable contrition, and to 'Rusty' Housden, a 32-year-old 'fellow of notoriously bad character'. He fitted the common image of the habitual criminal, shifty and opportunistic, without compunction, for whom regular work, highways labour, poaching and theft were interchangeable forms of income: 'I work at anything I can get to do — it's not very particular to me. I have not had a day's work since harvest; I am obligated to the parish', he told the court with a swagger. Housden was a man as disliked among his own as by the authorities, a cocky, 'Bill Sikes' kind of a character who had bullied others to steal: William Stalley deposed that Housden threatened him with a billhook; George Richardson said Housden laid him down and threatened to stick him if he said anything; William Richardson himself claimed Housden had led him on to steal. But the magistrates were nevertheless prepared to play ball with such immoral types in the cause of a well-ordered town. While lesser thieves found themselves on the dreaded hulks bound for Australia, and their families on the parish, Housden walked away with impunity, his sister commenting 'the biggest rogue has escaped'. His position in town being untenable, Housden was set on a ship for New York, starting a new life in North America at public expense.[30]

Thus for Rusty Housden, crime did pay, whereas for the Walden ratepayers, it cost dearly. Some of the richest men in town, including some malting owners who had lost goods, were well rewarded out of the public purse for their willingness to prosecute. There were also travel expenses, searching houses, apprehending prisoners, watching at the gaol, fees for several constables night and day over two or three weeks, prisoners' food and other expenses. To add up the costs of this extraordinary exercise is to realise the full import of the term 'the well-ordered town'. That ratepayers were prepared to countenance this level of expenditure on crime is itself indicative of confidence in the ability of the town to police itself, in the importance of order and protecting property.[31]

Threat to the Sessions

The extremely expensive purge of 1833 did not put an end to crime in Saffron Walden, even though it cleared up many old offences not proceeded with, since only one provable charge would be needed to effect a sentence. Relative to the rising population, total convictions were not excessively high. However, in the villages around Walden in 1832, according to lurid press stories, crime was out of control, particularly in remote parts such as Clavering, Arkesden and Elmdon: 'Notwithstanding the numerous apprehensions which have lately taken place of gangs of thieves… very little impression appears to have been made on those left behind, as depredations of all kinds continue to be committed with impunity upon the property of farmers within their reach'. One such farmer found, the morning after his wheat was stolen, an abusive letter pushed under his kitchen door, with this four-line verse: 'We poore are ground into the dust/ And now to rob and steal we must/ Your dogs we'll kill — your corn we'll seize/ So now old Flint, act as you please'.[32]

But the dividing line between the well-ordered town and the local countryside was not perhaps as demarcated as magistrates liked to pretend. There was a reluctance to admit that people could live in town and commute out to plunder and steal, or use outside receivers. When John Barker absented himself from parish stone-breaking work to rob young Rebecca Plum at Littlebury, he must have known she was *en route* to Walden to pay her father's rent, and thought he had more chance of getting away with it by intercepting her out of town. Market towns were also focal points for the surrounding rural society, and the August fair was a Mecca for pickpockets, thieves and highwaymen, from as far away as London. Daniel Porter, taking a nap at the fair, allegedly had the shoes stolen off his feet. Others 'contrived by getting up show fights to plunder many of the unwary'. A Little Walden farmer William Kent, visiting the fair, suffered the theft of his pocket book containing £30–£40, a huge sum. Furiously riding home, he fell off his horse, hit his head and died.[33]

At least in town miscreants could be instantly hauled before a Justice, rather than sent at great expense to Chelmsford. But then came the unthinkable: a threat to take away the right to hold Quarter Sessions in Saffron Walden, and consternation knew no bounds. This was a by-product of the Municipal Corporations Act (see chapter 3), but seems to have come as something of a shock, even to the

Dissenters who were otherwise delighted with the new legislation. According to the Tory press the news was a 'cruelly mortifying' blow, and the 'wing-clipping tidings came upon them like a thunderclap'. Not so the lesser mortals of the town who, Braybrooke informed the Home Office, were celebrating: 'the news of the Session being done away with has been hailed by the lower orders with joy, and they now openly avow that they shall in future escape unpunished'. Immediately the worthies swung into action to protect an institution which embodied so much of their civic pride and self-importance, facilitated targeted local justice and enabled the exercise of considerable power over the 'lower orders'. No one was more appalled than the Mayor, John Player, who had looked forward to the time when Dissenters like himself could become Justices. He had only just taken his long-awaited place on the bench and fought vigorously for its retention, adamant that it was a huge 'advantage to have a magistracy local and accustomed to the inhabitants whose object may fairly be said to prevent crime rather than to punish offenders… Distant punishments are imperfect in their affects: when removed so far from the centre of crime, they have but little influence over vicious companions.' County magistrates, he said, would not be aware of mitigating circumstances, and over-severe punishment would be a waste of borough funds.[34]

Player master-minded the campaign to keep the Sessions, arguing for Walden's importance, as the centre of a 24-parish Union, and petitioning through the new Town Council about the 'irreparable injury' if they could not administer justice on their doorsteps, for the trouble and expense of going to Chelmsford would deter a lot of people from undertaking prosecution. The appeal failed, to the burgesses' 'deep disappointment and regret', and there was no response to their request for a deputation. Player wrote again, this time adding the impressive argument that Walden was contributing more revenue than Cambridge, a sum of £30,000 a year, largely from the rich malting businesses, which needed the protection of local policing. He repeated that 'the nearness of conviction and the certainty of punishment are highly useful… in a town they import vigour to the operations of the law and tend to prevent many offences and to curb those excesses which too frequently expand themselves into enormous and heartening crimes. The punishment of an offence 27 miles off apparently lessen its enormity in the eye of any where the offence is committed'.[35]

By way of example, he said, the magistrates had dealt with a widespread incidence of thieving of root crops, by making a strong example of the only persons caught and frightening the others away. That year, 1836, was a year of serious shortage, with the poor stealing from the fields and 'no means short of a systematic watch prevented depredation'. A young brother and sister, Joseph, 32, and Flora Augar, 20, were transported for stealing a shillings' worth of potatoes from Lagdens in Castle Street, Player saying he regretted 'that no respectable person could be found to speak to the previous good character of these delinquents'. At least eight others were 'deeply implicated' and some had fled the town to escape prosecution. The poverty of those given this exemplary punishment may be judged from the fact that the town paid £2 for Flora Augar to have some new clothes.[36]

After this brilliant mixture of economic, practical and moral arguments, an audience with the Home Office was eventually granted and thither at considerable public expense went an all-party deputation led by Player. What won the day apparently was an allegedly unsolicited intervention by Lord Braybrooke, via an 'influential and exceedingly weighty communication to Lord Russell'. Pointing out that he owned half the acreage, Braybrooke made much the same points as Player, adding that, 'perhaps the certainty of immediate punishment and the little trouble which attended conviction deters offenders and actually prevented crime'.[37]

He also made some rather exaggerated claims about the achievements of the magistrates, commenting that, with 'one exception', the existence of a local court had kept trials down to no more than six a year. This was misleading on several fronts. In 1832, there had been a huge rise in game convictions, which seldom went through Quarter Sessions but were dealt with summarily the morning after nocturnal forays: it was freely admitted in a parliamentary return later on that these persistent poachers were not in the least deterred by there being a local court, as Braybrooke well knew, spending thousands of pounds protecting his coverts from their depredations. Secondly, the improved record-keeping at the Town Sessions showed there were dozens of petty offences every year. Thirdly, in 1833, the 'one exception', the malt trial gathered together numerous hitherto undetected offences dating back years. The following year, 1834 there were not six cases, but ten and the year in which the Sessions battle was being fought, 1836, was itself one of the busiest at the court, as Player later admitted. Braybrooke's 'exceedingly weighty communication' may have been effective, but his letter was somewhat economical with the truth.[38]

However, the Sessions were saved and Player was a hero, although he later commented that 'Lord B certainly took not little credit to himself for what he did in order to obtain that point'. There was much celebration at the news, loud cheering for the mayor, church bells ringing a merry peal and an excellent musical band parading down the High Street. The first Sessions under the new system took place, with Vicesimus Knox, the new Recorder, now earning a salary of £60 a year, later joining fellow worthies in their traditional junketings, an evening of 'the utmost harmony' at the *Rose & Crown*. At his first Sessions as Recorder, Knox complimented the town on having so little crime, a somewhat odd statement, since Player later referred to the 'unusual number of criminal cases in my mayoralty'. What with the expense of a new Walden gaol also being made a condition of keeping the Sessions, there was a high price to pay for local justice. But the laws were framed by and for men of property, and property must be protected at all costs from those bad characters who did not respect it.[39]

Bad Times or Bad Characters?

The emphasis on 'bad characters' rather than what is now called 'social crime' was part and parcel of the public relations exercise which, reinforced by sensationalist newspaper stories, helped build up an image of a habitual and alien criminal class, quite separate from the ordinary poor, avoiding the link with poverty and distress. If the 'respectable' poor could be encouraged to distance themselves from and inform upon the 'idle', this would drive a wedge between the two and isolate the latter. Yet historians have found that the existence of a 'criminal class' as such was largely popular fallacy. Crime related to family background, the state of farming, personal pique, distress, illiteracy, unemployment and other variables, facilitated by opportunism. Thefts were higher in winter and in times of distress. Most law-breakers were poor. Most items stolen were of little value. Previous convictions could make people unemployable and therefore prone to further crime.[40]

Some people seemed to follow a downward spiral to transportation. It would be no good George Savill, a 29-year-old illiterate labourer, pleading hunger as the reason why he tricked a grocer into handing over five loaves of bread, two pounds of cheese and some butter. It was a planned scam, he had stolen in the past, he was a 'bad character' and this time he must go. So was 19-year-old William Fuller, who took an iron chain from a farm, but had been in trouble before and compounded it by trying to break out of prison. He was 'sulky and obstinate' and no asset to an orderly town. Nor was 39-year-old Elizabeth Reed, illiterate and subject to fainting fits. She had never been in prison, but was judged yet another 'bad character with very indifferent connections and former course of life' and taking a large piece of calico from Robson & Day drapers was a serious offence, so it was off to the hulks. All these cases were in 1830, a year of increased distress.[41]

So were these crimes of poverty *per se*, or were their perpetrators irredeemably bad types? This was clearly the crux of the decision facing magistrates, who had access to networks of information to help them decide. The pathetic nature of the food, clothing and other trivial items commonly taken scarcely suggests large-scale, organised crime waves. But as alarm over pauperism grew, employers, magistrates and property-owners no longer tolerated even mild purloining. How to explain why people, often very young, were expensively prosecuted for all sorts of sordid little episodes, like 16-year-old Henrietta Salmon who, leaving her servant's job without wages, foolishly pocketed some silver spoons, only to throw them away over a hedge on her way home? What was the magisterial mentality which dumped young girls of 14 or 15 among ruffians in the county gaol, ordering as much 'hard labour as befits her age and sex'. Why did John Emson prosecute two lads, James Savill and Stephen Barker who, eating bread and cheese in his kitchen, took 1s.3½d left lying around by his servant: 'I hope you will forgive me this time, I will never do so any more' said one, suggesting he was contrite: but they were both jailed, and one was whipped as well. Two other boys, William Esland and William Douce, caught scrumping apples from Chater's garden were at least offered the option of joining the military to escape gaol. Not so the 13-year-old whipped and jailed for taking a whip stock, or the 10-year-old in gaol for ten months, some with hard labour. Presumably magistrates deemed harsh punishments justified in trying to deter youngsters from a life of crime, so they would not end up like James Lucas who, although only 17, had four previous convictions by the time he was transported for stealing threepence-worth of linen napkins. There seemed to be an increase in such prosecutions from 1836, which suggests a link with the New Poor Law. Across the country, peaks of recorded crime also often coincided with troughs of agricultural depression.[42]

It does underline the depth of poverty at the bottom end of society, than even a penny horseshoe was worth risking prison for. There was, of course, a reasonable chance of getting away with it, but not all miscreants were bright enough to do so. William and James Augar, transported ten years for theft, were identified because they absent-mindedly left their dog behind in the Walden shop they burgled. The other stories above also suggest little skill in the art of thievery. Most of those indicted were at the bottom of the heap: surviving presentments for the 1820s and 30s show that, as elsewhere, the vast majority were labourers. The tender years and at least 50% illiteracy among many of the offenders, even after a quarter-century of public education in the town, also became clearer from 1841, when the Sessions clerk began recording age and literacy of the accused (see chapter 11). Whatever the depravity of these delinquents, it seems a sad business, but there was nowhere else to send them: until the mid-nineteenth century, children were treated the same as adults in criminal matters, and separate reform schools for juvenile offenders did not appear until 1854.[43]

Poaching

Nowhere was the question of 'bad times or bad characters' more acute than in the world of the poacher. Many of the Walden men imprisoned in the county gaol were young poachers, but the increasing number of offences against the game laws differed from the ordinary run of petty crime in several ways, as regards those affected financially, the range of attitudes to the offence and the potential scale of the business. Firstly there was the property aspect: whereas anyone — rich, middling, poor — might lose out to ordinary thieves, there was only one person in the borough who lost game to poachers, and that of course was Lord Braybrooke, for he owned nearly all the ancient woodlands and newer plantations around Walden. Some like Pounce Wood were temptingly close to town. The number of coverts had increased with the eighteenth century landscaping of the Audley End estate, which created small clumps and belts of woodland, ideal for pheasants, so in this sense landowners brought this problem on themselves, as they did by passing laws which made poaching so profitable.[44]

The first Lord Braybrooke allegedly neither knew nor cared about poaching. But shooting parties were part of the third lord's social whirl. Once out shooting with a party of gentlemen on his extensive demesne, Braybrooke 'getting through a hedge, passed one of his feet through a snare, which had evidently been set for the purpose of catching hares, and it held his Lordship so tight that he became a complete fixture until he was released by the attendant keepers'. Game preservation was an expensive business. In addition to the normal salaries for gamekeepers and warreners, required anyway to curb predators, there were extra payments in winter 'for men assisting in night watching for poachers'. This might amount to £50 or more over a quarter, in addition to powder and shot for guns, and items such as 'serving summons on poachers', 'going to Chelmsford to appear against poachers', and 'paid to Gibson for beer for men going at night £3.11.3'. Thus, any vestiges of paternalistic semi-tolerance to a once-customary practice had gone.[45]

One would expect lesser ratepayers to be unhappy at paying maintenance for poachers in the county gaol, a sum which was reasonable when game prosecutions were few, but much higher as they grew: from 1833–4, the Saffron Walden Corporation received a bill for over £110 to keep 22 prisoners, nearly all poachers, for various periods in the county gaol. Sometimes overseers asked Braybrooke to contribute. Nevertheless the game laws were tolerated as a part of the natural order of things. The town knew the value to stability of having resident nobility, and Braybrooke's tenant farmers would have to accept game eating their crops.[46]

As a way of mollifying any opposition, successive Lords Braybrooke conferred sporting rights in the form of a somewhat mysterious Walden custom known as the 'privilege shoot', whereby townsmen with game certificates could shoot over 200–300 acres on his property near town, including Herberts, Turnip Hall and Brick Kiln Leys Farms and part of the Roos Farm (see chapter 9). At one time it was quite common for landowners to make these kinds of concessions or 'indulgences', in order to retain the support of farmers and tradesmen, and such rights were greatly prized and difficult to revoke. In Walden part of this concession involved old charity lands, and it was a matter of some irony that, while the unenfranchised poor were prosecuted if they took a rabbit for the pot, better-off burgesses could shoot game on fields which had once belonged to charities set up for the poor! But of course, it helped legitimise the lord's own rights in relation to the wildlife in his woods. They offered an edge to the poacher: on one occasion, the beadle offered a reward for information about the theft of 17 brace of partridges and four brace of hares from the 'privilege' lands.[47]

Secondly, attitudes to poaching differed from the normal run of property theft. The tempting commodities were edible and sellable, there was the thrill in the sport and pride in the skill, far more attractive to the young under-employed than the alternative of humiliating parish work on the highways. Whereas even the most ignorant pilferer must have had some inkling that they were breaking the law, many of the poor did not regard taking game as illegal, but as something they were entitled to. Snaring rabbits or taking pheasants seemed no more crime than taking blackberries, nuts or birds' eggs. This was Nature's bounty, available to all. The law might say that the person who owned the land now also owned its wildlife, but the poor could not, would not, accept it. However, the romantic view of the poacher as a rugged loner taking the odd rabbit for the pot is only one part of the picture and perhaps belonged more to an earlier time than to the post-war period.[48]

This suggests a third contrast to town crime was (with the exception of the 1833 round-up) the sheer scale and intensity of poaching. By converting woodlands into game preserves, landowners opened the way for a different breed of more organised poachers to work in gangs on a regular basis to supply a ready market. Town policing could scarcely be called a 'war', but this was the military word increasingly apt in poacher-gamekeeper altercations. Two of those transported after the 1833 malt-stealing trial, John Stacey and Joseph Housden had previously been jailed for assaulting a gamekeeper and taking his gun. Occasional bitter encounters involved gangs of poachers 'drawn up in battle array' against forces gathered by gamekeepers. An exceptionally ferocious encounter in the Elmdon woods of John Wilkes became a two-hour affray which ended with fractured bones, smashed skulls and broken teeth, after which 17 men from various villages were transported. Nothing quite so vicious occurred in Braybrooke's plantations, but on one occasion, his keepers, Joseph Tinworth, Simon and John Powell were targeted by three Littlebury labourers, William, James and John Richardson. They got off lightly, and it may have be that Braybrooke intervened for leniency.[49]

An order to Braybrooke's keepers not to carry firearms was no help. One gamekeeper was shot at by Isaac 'Old Spring' Barker near Pounce Wood, and the same year there was yet another bloody battle near the Audley End mansion, when three gamekeepers had a 'fearful conflict' with half a dozen poachers, two of whom had guns. And so it went on. Surprisingly — since gamekeepers were being murdered at a rate of two per year nation-wide — it was not until much later that a Walden gamekeeper was killed in one of these altercations. No hint of this rural war appeared in Lord Braybrooke's many speeches at the annual agricultural shows, his one annual opportunity to talk to the poor *en masse*. He was more likely to wax lyrical: in the mid-forties, with incendiarism spreading round Essex, Braybrooke spoke only of the loss of game preserves to railways, warning that people would 'see no smoke from the chimneys of the old family mansion at Christmas' and strangers would come, so that those who 'have driven the landowner from the hall of his forefathers will regret they have been parties to such a result'. Was it therefore in homage to some such rural-idyll lost world that he had spent thousands of pounds waging war against poachers? His words reveal a gap in understanding the lives of the poor, which no amount of philanthropy could fill.[50]

The more one reads of these skirmishes, the greater seems the contrast between the well-ordered town and its lawless hinterland. But was this due to an increase in poaching or to a decrease in tolerance? The game laws had existed for some time and there was plenty of anti-poacher legislation in the eighteenth century too. However, the treadmill was becoming a commoner deterrent, and penalties for night poaching increased to a maximum two years' hard labour, with the option of transportation for persistent or armed poachers. Magistrates could still exercise discretion and in Walden most were summonsed for trespassing or being found in possession of snares or other game offences, rather than night poaching. Snares were easy to make: 'One of his Lordship gamekeepers on walking round some fields much infested with poachers, found a few days since, sixty-five snares set about at about the distance of a rod from each other'.[51]

But it was not just changes in the law: there was genuinely a huge expansion of poaching, helped along by the ease with which game could be disposed of via butchers, beer-shops or carriers. The county gaol was bursting at the seams with poachers, even though only about half of those indicted were actually proved guilty. By 1831, one sixth of all convictions in England were for game offences. The actual number of undetected offences must have been phenomenal, since it has been estimated on a national scale that recorded poaching cases reflected only one-tenth, and maybe only one-twentieth, of the actual convictions. Thus Walden was reflecting a general pattern. Recorded game convictions here, normally under ten a year and often at nil up to the early 1820s, went up dramatically from that time onwards. In the middle of the particularly harsh winter, January 1829, there were said to be 25 poachers in custody in Walden. During the first year of the New Poor Law, April 1835–April 1836, out of 29 Walden prisoners in Chelmsford gaol, 20 were poachers, mostly serving two or three months.[52]

Contemporary critics felt the game laws must be reformed. The resulting Game Reform Act of October 1831 banned the sale of game and said it was no longer the monopoly of the gentry. But, although it remained in force till 1880, poaching offences actually increased. It was not uncommon for the magistrates to pass judgement on poachers several times a week: from October–December 1832, the Town Sessions opened on at least ten occasions for a variety of game offences, including trespass, night poaching, and, snaring: 'imprisonment seems to make no impression on the numerous persons who are daily committed for this crime', commented the Essex press after one Walden case. The vestry's attempts to ban dog-ownership for those on relief may have been linked with their use for poaching.[53]

This fact, that the game laws were failing to deter, was admitted by the Clerk of the Peace, C.T. Masters, who said that poachers also stole malt, corn, turnips, fruit and fowls. So poachers were seen as thieves by any other name. Many were young men, and at least almost half the convicted poachers were guilty of repeated offences: of the 45 named from 1831–5, at least four had three convictions and 16 had two convictions within this period. Masters believed there was a group of Walden men for whom poaching was their principal occupation:

'The offenders against the Game Laws are continually brought to justice but the repeated commitments of one and the same person for the crime of poaching does not seem to lessen the evil. The temptation to poaching being great in this neighbourhood there are 20 or 30 dissolute characters who seldom do any work and no doubt live chiefly upon the gains from their nightly excursions.'[54]

The rise in poaching, whether young men's bravado, organised gang warfare, a business opportunity or an echo of traditional hunter-gatherer rights, was part of the wider context of the well-ordered town. There were many reasons why poaching increased, but it was not likely to decrease while poverty remained such a problem. In the sense that poaching carried echoes of defiance against the established order, some historians have also seen it as a form of labourers' protest, but sporadic riots, incendiarist fires and anonymous threatening letters were different from most types of everyday crime, and require looking at in more detail.

Chapter 7

'Tumultuously Assembled Against the Peace'
Labourers' Unrest

'With divers other persons to the number of three or more riotously and tumultu-
ously assembled against the peace for the purpose of procuring an increase of wages'[1]

On Monday 13 December 1830 John Player was due to meet Lord Braybrooke
on Gallow Hill to discuss highways improvements. Instead he received a message: 'I am desired by Lord Braybrooke to acquaint you that he will not be able
to attend the meeting on Gallow Hill tomorrow morning as he is obliged to be at
Newport prison to dispose of the rebels committed yesterday'. The note was
from Martin Nockolds, one of scores of special constables hastily sworn in to
deal with the famous 'Captain Swing' rioters, in the surrounding countryside.
Named after a mythical figure, the 'Swing' troubles had been spreading throughout southern England since the previous August. They mostly consisted not of
'riots' but of combinations of labourers and others marching together to farmers
to demand higher wages and, in some cases, to smash threshing machines which
were reducing the availability of winter work.[2]

In spite of the fact that Walden escaped trouble, 'Swing' proved to be a seminal
event in terms of class relations, in poor law policy, in philanthropy, allotments,
education and many other aspects of life in the well-ordered town. Although north-
west Essex did not see rebellion on the same scale as some other parts of southern
England, the reactions to and aftermath of the riots deserve far more attention than
they have hitherto received in the annals of the Walden poor.

Food Riots

In dealing with the local manifestation of 'Swing', the third Lord Braybrooke
had precedents from both his predecessors who, as leading magistrates, had
also had to deal with outbreaks of labourers' unrest. In the run-up to Walden's
famous 1795 food riot, the elderly first Lord used his influence to defuse the
worsening crisis by trying to rescue the amateurish Corporation, by subsidising
grain and by stamping down on avaricious men who were trying to capitalise
on high prices. But once the mood of the poor worsened, he brought in the

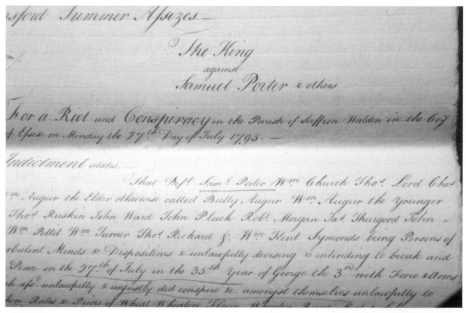

Fig.7.1 *The indictment at the Essex Assizes of Samuel Porter and others for riot and conspiracy in Saffron Walden in July 1795. Porter was the only one who spent any length of time in prison. In later life, after five years behind bars, he returned to Walden and became a respectable maltster.*

troops, responding to an urgent appeal from the Corporation: 'A very alarming riot has taken place here in consequence of the high price of provisions'. The total of 1,254 food tickets given out to the poor underlines the seriousness of the situation. The wider significance of the food riots was as a very public demonstration of the capacity of local people to rise *en masse* in defence of their rights and, although there was considerable sympathy for their plight and the episode was quite gentlemanly compared to later protests, the point was made that Walden folk had a breaking-point. Town worthies might recall, whenever there was a sniff of discontent, the events of '95 when the people had, for one memorable day, taken over their town.[3]

Although this was an unusual occurrence in Walden, overall such events were not at all uncommon: throughout the country, between 1790 and 1810 there were over 1000 riots. They were part of the local political scene, a method of bargaining for a better deal, rather than a direct challenge to the *status quo*. Essex experienced such disturbances in 1740, 1757, 1765 and 1772, the latter including Saffron Walden. In 1795, other Essex towns going through this trauma included Colchester, Braintree and Halstead, although the Walden riots were the most serious. The Walden rebellion shared the characteristics common to most such riots: real grievances, disciplined tactics, relevant targets and the avoidance of unnecessary violence. But there was a high price to pay for the scapegoat of the day, cooper/carpenter Sam Porter, who was indicted for riot and conspiracy, and languished in prison for five years, before being released and helped back into employment by A.F. Gibson.[4] [Fig.7.1]

Lucky Cooper — Well Order Town

Boca Riot
p 125 6 o 7

Only four years later, in the time of the second Lord Braybrooke, the high price of provisions provoked a further crisis, and this time the parish officers acted decisively, appointing a special committee, providing cheap stocks of wood, turf and potatoes, increasing the allowances for children and providing extra unemployment work on the roads. The vestry clerk, Robert Browne later reported that he had given out payments to as many people in one week as in the previous six weeks. As poor harvests and high prices continued, the bakers in town were called together to offset any further threat of riots, by making a special 'Assize of the Making of Bread' aimed at 'obviating the distress which the industrious Poor are likely to suffer from the effects of the late unfavourable season in raising the price of wheat and other grain'. Wet weather had dramatically reduced the yields from the barley, wheat and potato crops, and this doubled the cost of living.[5]

Threatening Letters

Trouble was this time averted in town, but in 1800 an uglier mood emerged out in the surrounding countryside, where labourers threatened incendiarist attacks on millers and shopkeepers, and even on parsons who would not intervene to help them. The Corporation clerk, Thomas Halls had passed on to him two anonymous letters threatening arson and murder, testimony to an anger and despair which echoes down the years and which gives the lie to the version of events generated by the ruling classes. In words of the poor which were seldom heard, an anonymous Clavering labourer in a badly-spelt letter threatened to kill the overseer and burn down the mills and churches unless flour prices were reduced: 'we had least di as live for we ar All most starvd I myself hast got a Wilfe and 6 Children and thay low me 4 and 6 a weak', he complained. The second letter-writer said they had patiently borne hunger, but could take no more and in a land of plenty they must be given more to live on. Cursing farmers, factors and shopkeepers as being worse than the lords, he threatened to destroy their families and, in a more specific anti-establishment protest threatened: 'We mean to behave well to eveary minester that will red this in the Church if not he is a ded man by night or by day we by all means disstroay the King and Parlement'. There were said to be similar letters in circulation elsewhere.[6]

In an accompanying letter, Halls said there was no information about the senders but the Corporation was ready to take any measures necessary, although Saffron Walden itself was not affected: 'we have nothing of the kind here, and all appear to be quiet'. The second Lord Braybrooke, although privately anxious to obtain assurance that troops from Chelmsford would come if necessary, also advised discretion so that the letters would be kept secret: 'I enclose two unpleasant letters… the Justices did right in sending copies of them to the Duke of Portland, but I rather hope no public admission will be thought right, for fear of informing more mischievous men of the contents of idle letters which they might otherwise have never seen.'[7]

This proved to be wise, as the threats did not materialise, but there was always an awareness that they might. Walden seems to have remained quiet during the next danger period, immediately after the French wars when the inevitable post-war slump led to widespread unrest, not helped by an appalling harvest in the summer of 1816. There were protests in parts of East Anglia, the worst being the 'bread or blood' riots at Ely, for which several were executed and others transported; and in Finchingfield, Halstead and elsewhere in Essex. As crime increased in the 1820s, there were sporadic outbreaks, for instance in 1827 at Henham and Finchingfield. Then in 1830 came the 'Captain Swing' riots which, unlike the eighteenth century troubles concerned with the price of basic foodstuffs, centred on wages and unemployment. Although north-west Essex was less affected than some other counties, the so-called 'riots' did cause a considerable stir and, although the riots took place in the countryside, they still caused noticeable alarm within the town.[8]

The 'Captain Swing' Riots

The third Lord Braybrooke had his ear to the ground and cannot have been unaware of the tensions building up, as poor harvests were followed by bitter winters, just the kind of conditions which had led to trouble in the past. The machinery of philanthropy moved into action in the town, with extra handouts from the Benevolent Society and a widening of the allotment scheme only recently established (see chapters 8–9). The overseers ordered 3,000 bushels of coals to sell cheaply to the poor, and the surveyors organised extra work for the unemployed. There had been hard winters before, but this time it was different. It was a time of political tension, of revolution abroad and agitation for Reform at home. There was an expectation of change. During the cold dark days of November and December 1830, a new radicalism arose among the rural labouring poor who normally never dared to openly express their anger and dismay. For a brief period, they were somehow galvanised into an unprecedented display of solidarity and largely non-violent protest. It was then quite extraordinary for large groups of men, including many 'respectable' types, to descend quite openly in daylight on farmers to demand higher wages. One particular target of the disaffected labourers was the hated threshing machine, blamed for reducing the amount of winter work available, and in some places there was a 'maniacal enthusiasm' for destroying these.[9]

Those in charge of law and order in Walden could not fail to notice that the country appeared to be dissolving into revolution. In the pages of *The Times* and in the county press, there appeared an alarming collection of reports on fires, riots, wage demands and machine-breaking all over the southern counties. In the beershops and taverns, at box club meetings, on road gangs and through kin and neighbour contacts, the same news was circulating: that a huge rising of labouring men, demanding higher wages, was taking place in rural England. Beginning in Kent, it spread in waves, fed at first by a lack of resolution among the authorities. When the Government changed in late November 1830, attitudes hardened. Rioting broke out in Norfolk and just over the Cambridgeshire border near Walden, night watches were instituted and soldiers called in on occasion. The riots reached Suffolk and into Essex, where Steeple Bumpstead was in turmoil for over a week in early December 1830. As the days went by, there were reports of riots at Fowlmere, arson at Bishops Stortford, machinery destroyed at Dunmow. The troubles were moving ever closer to Lord Braybrooke's district.[10]

Preparing for Trouble

Braybrooke was deeply concerned, but the evidence must be sought by reading between the lines. There are small signs that he was taking sensible precautions at his home farm in Audley End. The farm accounts for December 1830 are suspiciously full of extra jobs for regular labourers, suggesting he was bringing forward a number of winter tasks and giving jobbing to more men than usual, keeping them occupied with unloading and grinding barley, tying hay, making hurdles, brewing, catching rats and moles, cutting underwood and planting trees so that they were much too busy to be discontented. Later he was to boast that in 1830 'when there were an amazing number of poor men out of work, he employed many of them in making a new plantation, and never went into that now without recollecting it with pleasure'. Braybrooke was also clearly protecting his own farm, for in December he paid men to watch the premises and bought them two great coats to keep warm and, most significantly, spent £2.16s on a new gun from Furlong's gun shop in town. Thus, men were being paid extra to guard the farm and at least one of them was armed.[11]

Braybrooke was also actively drawing up plans to deal with riots in the surrounding area, for he sent off to the Home Office for a copy of regulations recently alluded to in a circular letter from Lord Melbourne and already adopted in Sussex. He did not, however, admit to the Home Office that any problem was likely, writing somewhat prematurely on 1 December: 'I am happy to say this district is perfectly tranquil at present, and the poor less ill off than in former seasons', a clear reference to the allotments. But the discreet methods used by his father in 1800 for a couple of isolated writers of threatening letters, were not appropriate to this large-scale movement. Even as he wrote there was widespread unrest developing over the nearby Cambridgeshire border, and it was spreading down the main road into north-west Essex. The most crisis-torn week of his life was about to commence.[12]

The North-west Essex Riots

On Tuesday 7 December, Braybrooke's 'perfectly tranquil' district erupted. There had been a wave of protests over the county boundaries near Walden the day before, and now he received an urgent summons from Elmdon, where neighbour and fellow JP, John Wilkes of Lofts Hall was in difficulties, confronted by about 100 labourers demanding wage rises. According to a press report (which was afterwards refuted), they had first of all gone to the parish church 'where the respectable inhabitants were assembled for the purpose of considering the state of the parish. The mob immediately locked the parishioners in the church, left a portion of the party to watch the doors, whilst the remainder went to the residence of Mr Wilkes, and demanded that twelve shillings a week should be paid to the labourers.' Immediately Braybrooke rode to Wilkes' home, where they swore in 56 special constables, hastily gathered from various villages, from Elmdon, Clavering, Wendens, Littlebury, Wimbish, Arkesden and Newport. They included some Walden men, mostly Braybrooke's own employees. The speed with which this was done suggests that the 'specials' had been hand-picked beforehand, for the 'prevention and suppression of any tumult, riot or felony… during the present distressed state of the country'. Together they 'very speedily quelled the disturbance', lodging seven ringleaders in Newport Gaol. There was trouble at Chesterford the same day.[13]

Next day, a Wednesday, at the *Rose & Crown* in Walden's Market Place, Braybrooke swore in a further 19 constables from Langley, Hadstock and Wimbish, suggesting that he was nipping in the bud any potential trouble from these villages. There was a lull on Thursday but on Friday 10 December, two other parishes, Arkesden and Henham suffered protests and once again Braybrooke swore in a further 33 special constables, five of them prominent Walden worthies. The mood was getting uglier: at Henham, two men who refused to take part in the wages riot were assaulted and threatened. As often happened, only a handful of alleged ringleaders were picked out for punishment, although not charged until three days later. A degree of coercion was also displayed at Arkesden where the rioters 'struck for an advance of wages and proceeded to several barns in the parish, as well as to the fields where any men were at work, and compelled them to desist, at the same time unharnessing the horses'. A story got about, but was later denied, that the strikers besieged the vestry and defied Lord Braybrooke's order to disperse. A later report about the Arkesden incident suggested that the men had not been 'driven to acts of insubordination by want' since the 13 ringleaders had in their pockets six silver watches and a total sum of £4.9s between them on the day of their arrest, even though it was the day before pay-day. Lord Braybrooke rode forth and his constables once again put the ringleaders behind bars at Newport Gaol, which must have been bursting at the seams by now.[14]

But worse was to come next day, Saturday 11 December when, a mile away from Arkesden, the much larger village of Clavering saw a mass turnout of around 300 men all assembled together to demand higher wages. This was an unprecedented expression of anger and despair, for such high numbers would include almost every labourer for miles around. On this occasion Braybrooke allegedly had to dash over from the Sessions at Walden, where he was meeting other magistrates. At Clavering 23 of his 'specials' were 'very active', apprehending 13 of the 'principal disturbers'.[15]

That was the end of a hectic week for the third Lord, but the mood of the poor continued unhappy for a further week. Sundays were riot-less days generally, but Braybrooke was determined to defeat all idea of revolt in the other villages. The unrest now seemed to be moving further south, and on Monday 13

December, Braybrooke took on board a further 65 special constables, 30 of them from the very poor parish of Widdington, which suggests that there was much discontent there. The others were taken from Debden, Newport, Clavering, Henham and a further four from Walden, including the vicar's three sons. Next day was the busiest 'swearing-in' day of all, for another 132 men from Birchanger, Ugley, Elsenham, Berden and Stansted took their oath: the total of 73 sworn in one day from Stansted suggests that this was a particularly tense trouble-spot. Finally, at the end of a fortnight of high drama, another score of specials were sworn in, and there the threat subsided. By this time it had affected at least two dozen villages, and required policing by at least 320 special constables. Most of the rioters in this part of Essex were non-violent, at least towards farmers, albeit harsher on their own kind who refused to strike: at Finchingfield a labourer was dragged across two fields by rioters.[16]

Braybrooke's strategy, presumably following government guidelines, paid off. A *cordon sanitaire* was thrown around the entire district, over a wide rural area encircling Walden, from Littlebury in the north down to Elsenham in the south, from Wimbish in the east to Elmdon in the west. Almost every sizeable parish around the town contributed its share of special constables to suppress riot before it could break out, so that only four major incidents were reported and all in the first week. Similar troubles occurred elsewhere, such as Steeple Bumpstead and Finchingfield. In Chelmsford, 500 troops were called out, a command centre set up and 450 special constables, half of them mounted, were appointed. The entire exercise was unique and quite extraordinary.[17]

Policing the riots was an expensive business. Hiring horses and carts cost over £25, and there were generous fees for the 'specials' (seldom among the poorest anyway) who earned five shillings per day, more than half the normal weekly wage of a labourer. A number of others elsewhere in Essex later claimed large rewards from the government. Even in Essex, which was one of the less disturbed counties, the total bill for rewards ran into many hundreds of pounds. This underlines the use of informers to keep Braybrooke and other JPs in touch with events, so that they could quickly mobilise armies of special constables in advance and nip any potential trouble in the bud. The occurrence of only four riotous villages does not, therefore, prove that all the others were entirely quiescent.[18]

Punishing the Rioters

Throughout 34 counties, a total of 1,976 rioters were tried, of whom 19 were executed, 481 transported, 644 imprisoned, a few fined or whipped, and 800 acquitted or bound over. By the 21 December, it was reported that all the riotous areas in Essex had quietened down, but there were so many court cases pending that the Essex press ran out of space to print the details. Of the 123 indicted in the county, 31 were acquitted, 23 rapidly transported (including two from Stansted for maiming a lamb), and the remaining 69 imprisoned with hard labour. It was a harsh retribution, but in the Saffron Walden area Lord Braybrooke seems to have acted to soften the blow.[19]

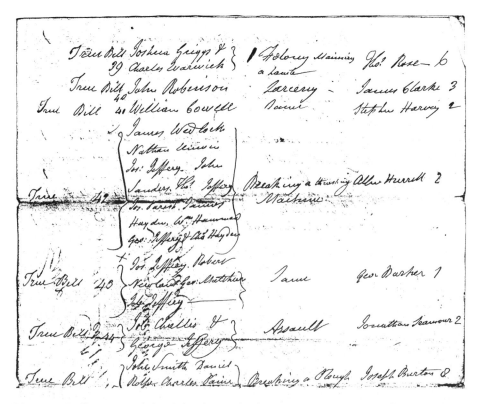

Fig.7.2 *Indictments of the Arkesden and Clavering rioters (True Bills 42 and 43), originally charged with breaking a threshing machine in December 1829, but their actual convictions at the Essex Assizes were for rioting for higher wages. True Bill 44, which deals with an assault charge, also relates to two of the local rioters.*

As with policing, so with punishment: Braybrooke believed in selectivity to maximise deterrence and minimise further protest: 'on these occasions success depends in great measure upon as few persons as possible being committed'. Braybrooke picked out known troublemakers, minimised arrests and in suitable cases intervened on behalf of some local men. Over a quarter of the 92 Essex convictions came from this area including ten from Arkesden, four from Clavering and six from Henham. All were imprisoned, normally with hard labour, for periods of two to six months. Like most of the Essex 'Swing' prisoners, they were predominantly labourers. Although some were initially charged with breaking a threshing machine, this was changed to the less serious one of trying to procure increased wages through tumultuous assemblies. [Fig.7.2] It may be that Braybrooke influenced this. He was able to prevent some Elmdon rioters being jailed (although two were jailed for assault), and obtain remissions of sentence for three of the Arkesden rioters. Five of the 14 Clavering and Arkesden men had previous convictions, and would have been picked out as known faces. George Matthews, for instance, a Clavering rioter, had once spent two years in prison for stealing barley. It was the others who particularly worried the authorities, for the high turnout in villages like Clavering indicated participation in riots by many ordinary 'respectable' labourers.[20]

Causes of the Riots

There was much earnest questioning for years afterwards, as Parliament, through its poor law survey sought to discover why some parishes were more riotous than others. Historians have noted that most of the troubled villages were large, open ones with more tradesmen, many under-employed labourers and a tradition of Dissent. The survey also asked why the riots spread as they had. Of the 20 (out of 50) Essex parishes who bothered to answer this question, causes suggested mostly centred on low wages, unemployment, harsh game laws and general distress. Among places which did not reply was the unhappy village of Clavering, where almost every labourer had turned out in protest, and where 313 people were on relief. The person who sent in the return, John Newport, had been a special constable during the Clavering riots, so he should have known the answer. But he was also a farmer and overseer, to whom the size of the protest must have been a huge shock. At least one part of Essex found that the riotous villages were now the quietest, since 'the most turbulent spirits' had been banished.[21]

Obviously deep distress was the background to unrest, but it does not explain why some villages rioted while others, equally poor, did not. One influence, it has been surmised, was geography, specifically the nearness of the village to main highways along which news of riots elsewhere was more easily communicated. Rather than thinking in county terms, it is much more instructive to look at north-west Essex, east Hertfordshire, south Cambridgeshire and west Suffolk as a linked area, ignoring boundaries, for this better illustrates the day-by-day spread of the riots, and it certainly seems that the trouble around Walden spread southwards down the main road from Cambridge. All four riotous villages — Clavering, Arkesden, Elmdon, Henham — were within a few miles of the main Cambridge–London coaching road, as were many of those where 'specials' were recruited. Through travelling artisans, coachmen and carriers, the news could be passed by word-of-mouth and the newspapers transported, to be read aloud in alehouses, shoemakers' shops, blacksmiths' forges and other meeting places such as market day gatherings: Walden market was on a Saturday and the local riots took place the following week.[22]

All this is speculative, but it raises the idea that there was in existence in some villages, but not so noticeably in others, a core of politically-minded individuals who, hearing the news from Kent and elsewhere, were eager to join in and stir others to follow. The comment made afterwards by Martin Nockolds, one of Walden's special constables, suggests that some individuals egged on others: the riots he said, were due to 'want of employment and inadequate relief in some instances, and increasing depravity in others… a strong tendency towards exciting vindictiveness and desperation'. The curate of Chrishall said as much, blaming the riots in nearby Elmdon on 'inflammatory paragraphs in some of the public papers', although historians have found there was only 50% literacy among those recorded. But simply hearing about the riots elsewhere could encourage others, equally desperate, to follow suit, so long as there was a feeling of resentment and a leader among them. Yet in Walden, although men had rioted in 1795 and although there was 'insubordination' in 1835, all was quiet in 1830.[23]

Aftermath

This is because the 'Swing' riots were essentially a rural phenomenon, breaking out in villages, not towns. For all the dire poverty, there were still more job opportunities, more road work, more charity handouts, more shops to pilfer from, more woods to poach in around Walden. In any case, as emerged much later, in the 1833 trial quoted earlier (see chapter six), the malt-stealing and other scams dated back some years: thus the undeserving poor were supplementing their income very nicely with ill-gotten gains! It would have been unusual if the town poor *had* joined the protests. Yet in Walden the aftermath of 'Swing' was triumphalist, homing in on allotments, the town's great answer to all the labourers' troubles, as the vital ingredient which kept their men content: 'While many other parts of the county were the scenes of the most fearful excesses, committed by the agricultural labourers, this district presented a happy contrast not a single offence of the nature to which I allude was committed'.[24]

Launching the Clothing Bank, the appearance of which was directly linked to the trouble only four months before, John Player praised 'the good order which remarked this place during the last winter', proving that the poor appreciated the philanthropic efforts on their behalf; and criticised the rioters for lack of gratitude: 'in the past winter when riots and commotions, when calamitous and appalling fires disgraced or disturbed other districts, the poor of our own parish were quiet and orderly, and conducted themselves in a praiseworthy manner'. Even more dubious was the claim, by Poor Law assistant commissioner, Ashurst Majendie, that Walden labourers actually helped police the riots: 'when fires and riots were prevalent in many of the adjoining parishes, this altogether escaped the infection. Not only did the labourers refrain from joining the mobs, but they went out under the orders of the magistrates to assist in putting down the riots.'[25]

This statement was, to say the least, very economical with the truth. Likewise the fanciful suggestion that allotment-holders were all special constables in waiting. In fact, there were few labourers at all among the score or so of special constables enrolled in Walden, and those who were, worked for Lord Braybrooke anyway, as did another who was a bricklayer. The others were gamekeepers, farmers and landowners, prominent townsmen and sons of the vicar, whose living was in Braybrooke's hands. It was really not surprising if such men were chosen as special constables in preference to ordinary labourers, but why make such a grossly misleading claim? It all seems to be part of the public relations exercise which followed the riots, which themselves hardened attitudes towards a drastic reform of the old poor laws (see chapters 4–5).[26]

Majendie also described an odd incident in the town itself during the time of 'Swing', when huge numbers of labourers allegedly volunteered to watch a house threatened by arsonists: 'It happened at this period that (by an ill-timed joke, as afterwards appeared) the notice "This house to be burnt" was written with chalk on several houses, and among others, on that of a principal promoter of the allotments'. Did this really happen? Could the 'principal promoter of the allotments' be John Player himself? There was another curious incident when Player, by then surveyor of highways, received an anonymous note, a few weeks after the riots: 'Sir, Unless you immediately attend to your duty by removing the vast accumulation of filth from the streets now (beyond precedent) almost impassable you may expect very soon to hear further from Swing'. Had the labourers' action already become a joke? Jokes can be euphemisms for ill will, and other houses were chalked. The threats were perhaps taken more seriously than anyone admitted, for in January 1831, only a few weeks after 'Swing', there was a tightening-up of fire-fighting arrangements in the town. The fire brigade dated back some years, but now drew up new regulations and purchased a new engine, with the help of various insurance companies with local agents. The uninsured could also use the fire engine if they paid two guineas to the overseers (five guineas if outside the parish). If there was a fire, however, the engine could not leave without order of a committee member.[27]

Officially played down and roundly condemned as they were, the riots produced only short-term improvements. Local wages went up that winter, according to Thomas Rickman, the architect engaged to build the new church spire: in a note explaining his bill for the job, he told the spire committee that labour costs had risen by 5% between December 1830 and April 1831. The number of men employed by Lord Braybrooke may have increased in the early 1830s, but this could have related to building work on the estate. In some other areas farmworkers' wages went up for a time, but they did not increase at Audley End (see chapter 1). The outcome of the protest was a great disappointment to the poor, compounded by their gaining nothing from political Reform two years later, and suffering the body blow of the New Poor Law five years on. More widely, 'Swing' made the authorities realise that the poor law was no longer hiding the cracks, or rather deep chasms, in the system. Even areas which had escaped riot were deeply worried by it. One response came in the shape of the horrifying Union workhouses a few years later. Another was a widening of philanthropic endeavour, the discussion of which forms the second half of this book. As well as the effects on the allotment scheme and clothing bank, the 'Swing' period also influenced the setting up of the British School in Walden, although this was some years later (see chapters 8, 9, 11).[28]

Since the outbreak of 'Swing' in north-west Essex appears milder than those elsewhere, it has not previously been perceived as particularly important here, even though almost a quarter of the Essex convictions concerned men from north-west Essex. This was largely thanks perhaps to Lord Braybrooke, John Player and others who understood so well the need for public relations exercises for the maintenance of a well-ordered town, and hence the absence of direct references in most town records has left the riots largely absent from Walden annals. Yet it *was* hugely significant that, in the hierarchical system of the time, men were prepared to risk everything — job, home, respectability — to march openly and seek betterment.

The riots left their mark. The panic induced on the allotment committee and John Player was palpable (see next chapter). Nor is it too fanciful to suggest that, after playing so intimate a part in putting down the riots, Braybrooke's mindset would forever afterwards be affected by the memory of 'Swing'. The rebellion was undoubtedly a watershed. Relationships could never be the same again. Some historians link the rise of Primitive Methodism with the need for the poor to make sense of what happened to them in the 1830s (see chapter 12). Others believe that protest, far from being abolished, simply went underground, in the form of arson. Only a tiny, desperate minority actually lit the flames of incendiarist fires, but they were often tacitly supported by the crowds who gathered to watch and refused to betray the perpetrators. Incendiarism, the disaffected labourer's ultimate weapon, was only a sporadic phenomenon but became very much more common in Essex as time went on.[29]

Rural Incendiarism

If Walden labourers were quiescent in 1830, they certainly made their feelings known five years later, during the workhouse fire, an occasion on which the lower classes were reported as behaving quite scandalously and cheering the flames, a demonstration which rather dented their earlier reputation for orderly restraint (see chapter 5). More commonly, however, incendiarism was a crime of the countryside, where there was less chance of detection. Arson was viewed as a very serious crime, as evidenced by the hanging of 26-year-old Joseph Bugg, after a notorious incident in Manuden, during the troubled summer of 1816. During another year of distress, 1829, only a few miles from Walden, a devastating fire at Linton carried away stacks, barns, implements, cottages and animals, the destruction covering a total area of 1½ acres. Thousands of people turned up to watch the execution of three young men found guilty of this and another incendiary fire.[30]

In spite of this severe punishment, from 1830 onwards, arson became more widespread. Where once shopkeepers and millers were blamed for the troubles of the poor (as at Clavering in 1800), now farmers were targeted. In most cases no one was caught, for a wall of silence met investigators, in spite of the carrot of large rewards. An Elsenham farmer, Michael Phillips, hit by a wave of incendiarism in 1832, unavailingly offered a huge £50 reward for the capture of the person who set fire to six stacks on his farm, insisting that he would pardon all the incendiarists 'except the one who actually put fire to the stack'. That same winter, Lord Braybrooke informed the Home Office of an even worse outrage, the poisoning at a Radwinter farm of cattle, poultry, oxen and fowl with arsenic: someone clearly loathed the farmer, Frederick Giblin, but Braybrooke blamed it on a 'gang' who had 'recently committed every sort of depredation with impunity'. He was sorry to send such a report, but had to admit that 'petty offenders have very much increased throughout this division, though the lower orders are very quiet and apparently not discontented'. Increased philanthropic efforts in Walden from this period onwards may well have related to events in the countryside, for the well-ordered town was not an island, and its welfare could not be separated from the lawlessness of its hinterland.[31]

Things quietened down a little in the late 1830s, but returned at epidemic levels, hitting Essex during the deeply distressed years of 1843–4. Nationally, arson cases increased by almost a third between 1831–7 and 1838–44. In Essex, from only two or three recorded fires in both 1842 & 1843, the number leapt to 21 in 1844 and 19 in 1845. These included many villages around Saffron Walden, with at least 30 recorded incidents of incendiarism in north-west Essex between 1844 and 1851.[32]

The year 1844 was particularly bad, with at least five fires locally, and Manuden and Clavering were hit more than once, but over the years many villages saw such blazes. Arkesden, Chesterford, Debden, Hempstead, Littlebury Green, Newport, Radwinter, Sampfords, Wicken, Wimbish: all suffered. Comments in the Essex press, who were inhibited, became a regular feature and followed a pattern: of the fire, 'little doubt exists but that this was the work of a vile incendiary'; and of the farmer concerned, 'one of the most humane and benevolent men in the neighbourhood'. Thousands of pounds of haystacks, crops, livestock, barns and other farm buildings went up in smoke, and insurance claims were rife. Farmers were terrified, particularly if they knew that these dreadful acts did not displease the peasants: the crowds who cheered the Walden workhouse fire, and ate roast meat from burnt beasts at Manuden, were not that unusual. As a further twist, disaffected labourers sometimes left Lucifer matches, by then conveniently invented, on farmers' doorsteps as a warning. Not all fires were linked to distress, but a study in neighbouring Suffolk, a similar agricultural area to north-west Essex, showed there was a direct relation between periods of distress and unemployment and outbreaks of arson.[33]

And what of Saffron Walden in these troubled times? Even as arson in Essex quadrupled through a decade, the lower classes enjoyed their customary day out at the Saffron Walden Agricultural Show, which Lord Braybrooke found a convenient platform for annual displays of paternalism and pride. In 1842, he reminded the gathered crowds of how he had set up a woodland creation scheme during times of distress. Speaking at the 1843 show, he claimed that such societies had transformed relationships, teaching farmers to help their neighbours more. In 1844, for reasons naturally unconnected to the burning stacks, now reaching his own neighbourhood, Braybrooke exhorted farmers, who bore no blame for agricultural distress, to put in more capital so that the poor man could find work. The press might give the wrong impression if he spoke of 'certain subjects', such as 'those dangerous or doubtful questions which if handled unskilfully or but imperfectly expressed or understood were not calculated to do much good to the cause they all had at heart'. More boldly, in his 1850 speech, Braybrooke joked about 'the cunning man of Walden', saying that there was 'a great man so called and that during the time the fires were so prevalent in Cambridgeshire a lady sent to consult him as to their cause. Now he was on the treadmill.'[34]

In July 1846, suspected arson came to Walden town centre. A row of shops in Market Street (now King Street) suffered two mysterious fires within a fortnight. The first began in the stables of *The Hoops* Inn, but pains were taken, as in the reports on the workhouse fire a decade earlier, to stress how townsfolk responded magnificently when the fierce blaze, raging for an hour and a half, threatened to destroy all the buildings nearby: 'great assistance was rendered by the thousands assembled, more particularly the females, who appeared to vie with each other in extinguishing the flames, and to whom too much praise cannot be given'. Nevertheless James Wedd the saddler lost his house, and there was damage to Henry Hart's premises and to the Day, Robson & Co grocery / drapery shop. No motive was suggested, but Allen Hopwood, who owned *The Hoops*, was also a small farmer at Sewards End and elsewhere. Then only two weeks later there came a second fire only 20 yards away from the first, in the loft of Cowell's butcher's shop, necessitating the rescue of cattle. This time the possibility of arson had to be admitted and it was 'much feared that this is the work of an incendiary... it being considered remarkable that it should commence in the loft, and not in the lower part of the building'. These fires fuelled the campaign to establish a professional police force in the town (see chapter 6).[35]

To list all the fires, even those which were reported in the press (for many were not, for fear of inciting copycat crimes), is to receive an impression that during these years Walden sat in a potential ring of fire, surrounded by a countryside periodically likely to flare up with anger and despair. During January and February 1851, the countryside around Walden was lit by flames on at least seven occasions, one after the other, including two in Walden parish: 'We regret to observe that the crime of incendiarism seems greatly on the increase in this neighbourhood', was the press comment. After a fire at Manor Farm, Great Chesterford, extinguished with the help of Braybrooke's own engine, and others soon after at Ickleton and Wimbish, the most spectacular of all was the huge blaze at Tiptofts, Cole End, just outside Walden. This attracted hundreds of townsfolk to watch Thomas Westrope Gayton's farm ablaze. The flames lit the sky as three large barns full of grain and several farm buildings disappeared, to the value of over £3,000, undoubtedly caused by an incendiary. In spite of a large reward, a few days later another farm in Walden parish, Sadlers near Little Walden also lost a barn full of oats. Two weeks later yet another huge blaze destroyed buildings at Pinckneys Farm, Radwinter and once again the press was puzzled as to why anyone should target someone so popular: 'The matter has caused considerable excitement and alarm among the neighbouring farmers, as it is difficult to assign a motive for the act, Mr. Emson being a large employer and bearing an unexceptionably good name amongst the labouring population'.[36]

In spite of this dreadful catalogue, some continued to pretend it was not happening and took the line of one prominent MP that 'the peasantry were not in any degree implicated in the crime so prevalent... it was the work of a few persons perambulating the county'. But the more enlightened saw things differently: arson was caused, said Suffolk landowner Sir Henry Bunbury, by low wages, frequent dismissal through weather, lack of resources to fall back on and a deep dislike of the New Poor Law, which was 'too cold, revolting to the feelings of the labouring class'. If the poor were better treated, he suggested, 'you will have no more fires, nor will a Secretary of State's mind be taxed to imagine incendiaries perambulating through Suffolk'. In fact incendiarism continued sporadically in north-west Essex throughout the rest of the nineteenth century.[37]

Conclusion

Few Saffron Walden elites, even if they recognised the truth of Bunbury's analysis, officially acknowledged the existence, let alone the causes of all this unhappiness. At times John Player seemed to be near to grasping the truth, writing about allotments just before the 'Swing' episode: 'Those who seem out of the reach of poverty — who are placed as it were above the contemplation of the under provision of the fabric, know not the importance which the labourer attaches to a quarter of an acre of land'. The 'under provision of the fabric', as he called it, by such dramatic and dreadful outrages like incendiarism, proved that they were not all, and not always, simply helpless victims of a deeply unequal society in which they had no voice. The more desperate among them evolved some devastating methods of fighting back, and these crimes of protest carry a different message from crimes of gain, for here there was no obvious material advantage, and everything to lose. Deplorable though they were, these fires represent a public statement by the alienated sections of the poor, highlighting the growing tensions in society.[38]

If it is difficult to understand why people should burn down the farms which represented their only opportunity of a livelihood, perhaps the devastating piece of reportage which emanated from the very poor village of Clavering, six miles from Walden, almost two decades after the 'Swing' riots, is relevant:

'Here is a farmer from Clavering, an area notorious for its incendiary fires, speaking to the Morning Chronicle's rural correspondent: "A man with a family of five children will be nearly able with 6s. a week to buy bread enough, if he buys the coarsest flour; his rent he generally gets out of his harvest money; his clothes he gets by some means or other — people sometimes give them to him — and then, when he is unemployed… we keep him in the workhouse. So you see, sir, he is amply provided for, even with wages at 6s. a week".'[39]

As the writer commented: 'Calculations are made with the greatest possible nicety, not so much to ascertain how much he can live upon, as how much he can live without'. The memory of the 'hungry Forties' lingered long in the stories old men told to the next generation, who continued out in the countryside to grapple with the same underlying poverty their fathers and grandfathers had known, a situation which eventually led to the 'revolt of the field', the farmworkers' union action of the 1870s. With such dire poverty continuing, it sounds very much as though threatening letters, wages riots and arson achieved nothing in the end, but this is to assume that the elite version of events is the only one. However, as another nineteenth century writer put it:

Fig.7.3 *This engraving of Audley End, made in 1831 soon after the 'Captain Swing' riots, captures the idyllic illusion of rural England, so contrasted to the reality of most poor peoples' lives.*

'Clearly the articulate upper classes monopolise the historical record and we end up with a vision of well-meaning reformers and zealous improvers generously serving the needs of the labouring poor. The record however does show that the poor did act in the promotion of their rights, and riot and tumult must have played some role in forcing action for the benefit of the victims of development.'[40]

The second half of this book will offer many examples of these philanthropic reformers at work in their moral crusade, providing allotments and benevolent societies, charities and clothing clubs, prizes and provident societies. The need to promote an illusion that things were better than they were is reflected, too, in the rural-idyll paintings and engravings of the time. [Fig.7.3] But the source material is indeed largely monopolised by the articulate providers of the bounty. Were they zealous and well-meaning, or were they forced into action by the 'riot and tumult' of the poor, or at least the worry of what the poor were capable of? The discussion of crime in these two chapters, while of necessity telescoping a huge subject, serves to emphasise how the lives of the poor were at this time rather far removed from John Player's 'well-ordered town'. Pauperism and crime were the two great challenges, and certainly the poor law and criminal law were formal controls on which order depended. But there was also this informal method of social control, the widespread and widening use of philanthropy not only to aid distress and demonstrate concern, but also to offset rebellion and inculcate deference and gratitude. Its best-known expression was the Saffron Walden allotment scheme.[41]

PART TWO: RESPONSES

Chapter 8

'A Tendency to Prevent Depredations'

The Allotments Scheme

'The allotment system has already produced such excellent effects to justify the most sanguine expectations of further benefits.... it has a tendency to prevent depredations'.[1]

The Saffron Walden allotments were famous in their time, their holders being 'among the most industrious, happy and comfortable of their class,' and Walden praised as the town which 'took the lead in this county in encouraging the allotment system, from which such extensive and beneficial effects have already flowed'. What is less well-known is that allotment schemes in the early nineteenth century were directly linked with the threat of unrest among the poor, and that Saffron Walden was one step ahead of the game: here allotments were dreamed up *before* the 1830 'Swing' riots, whereas most other schemes appeared after 'Swing' and even more so in response to arson later on. Certain notables of Walden, particularly the third Lord Braybrooke and 'Gentleman' John Player, were then able to claim that Walden had no riots because its labourers were contentedly digging their plots. This idea gained credence simply by being repeated on many occasions, even though in neighbouring Suffolk there were some parishes which had both allotments and riots.[2]

This is not to say that allotments were not extremely important amenities, offering as they did a unique opportunity for the poor to produce some of their own food. Saffron Walden deserved credit for being one of the first towns in the country to adopt them, at a time when allotments were still controversial, in fact a burning issue of the day. But to accept the official version of events at face value is to lose all the nuances which reveal so much about the mindset of the men who were at this time actively building Walden into the 'well-ordered town' it became only later in the century. Approaching the scheme as a vehicle of paternalistic philanthropy and social control, rather than in its original poor law context, is to see it in a very different light. The allotments in their early days then emerge, not simply as an altruistic effort for the poor, but as part of a carefully-crafted attempt to create among potentially restive labourers an illusion of independence and an attitude of grateful deference, thus defusing all thoughts of rebellion against an unfair social system.

Early ideas

The idea of allowing labourers an allotment garden, defined as a piece of land cultivated by the occupier for the production of crops for himself and his family, was nothing new. They existed in the Middle Ages and in Elizabethan times, while 'Diggers' later set up colonies, from which they were evicted in 1649. An influential journal, *The Gentleman's Magazine*, started publishing articles about allotments in 1765. As poor relief rose, the subject of allotments came up in Parliament: from 1782 it was possible to put aside ten acres of waste near poorhouses for use as allotments, but further attempts at legislation in the 1790s failed, although the 1801 General Inclosure Act showed some progress. The agricultural reporter, Arthur Young noted great demand for allotments among Essex labourers and in 1801 published a pamphlet on the subject. It was Young who penned the resonant lines about the labourers' lot: 'For whom are they to be sober? For whom are they to save? … For the parish? If I am diligent, shall I have leave to build a cottage? If I am sober, shall I have land for a cow? If I am frugal, shall I have half an acre of potatoes. You offer no motives; you have nothing but a parish officer and a workhouse. Bring me another pot.'[3]

Locally, surveyor William Robinson of Walden Grove, a critic of enclosure, in 1814 attacked 'the baneful practice of cutting up little farms' and made the radical suggestion that the problems of the peasantry would be relieved if they had smallholdings again. Over the border in Suffolk, a far-sighted landowner Sir Henry Bunbury was a famous promoter of allotments, particularly after the 'blood or bread' riots of 1816. The notion of giving the poor a small stake in the land on which they toiled remained revolutionary for a long time. Some people felt that income supplements like allotments would encourage the poor to procreate too much. Given the small size of most plots, this was far-fetched to say the least. A group called the Labourers' Friend Society, prompted by post-war distress, was founded to campaign vigorously for more allotments. There was increasing parliamentary interest, and a breakthrough occurred in 1819 when the Select Vestries Act allowed up to 20 acres of parish land to be rented out as allotments, increased to 50 acres in 1831. Unfortunately this provision was little used at first, and considerable opposition ensured that legislation remained permissive, not compulsory. Up until then, the few allotment schemes which had appeared tended to be in the manorial type of village. In some places clergy helped with allotments, and one early experiment took place in the early/mid 1820s in Chesterford when the rector (who later became the Bishop of London) arranged for labourers to have half-acre allotments.[4]

The context of the allotment scheme was the poverty question, yet in Eastern

[handwritten margin note:] Rev. Blomfield Vicar prev. Curate *[handwritten:] Vicar*

England, where distress was commonplace, progress was slow and there was more activity in other regions. Throughout the country, an average of 42% of parishes had some kind of scheme, whereas in Essex less than a third by 1833. Not so Walden where, as often happened, the paternalistic lord of the manor took a strong interest, in conjunction with pro-active parish overseers. A later claim by the Horticultural Society that Walden was 'the first town to adopt the parliamentary provision of allotting land to the poor' cannot really be verified, but Walden was well ahead and, once provided, the allotments rapidly acquired a mythology of their own, and were described in terms of philanthropy.

Lord Braybrooke and Allotments

The third Lord Braybrooke read about allotments in the influential journal, the *Quarterly Review*, and from some of the hundreds of pamphlets in circulation on the subject, being impressed by three publications, and especially *A Peasant's Voice to Landowners* by John Denson of Waterbeach, Cambridgeshire, although he disliked the author's aggressive tone. Since Denson attacked the 'scourge' of large landowners whose avarice and cruelty produced wretchedness and immorality, the booklet seems a surprising recommendation. However, after visiting Waterbeach in the spring of 1829, Braybrooke realised the importance of such schemes being managed by landowners rather than tenant farmers: 'Whoever neglects these precautions will not give the experiment a fair trial, and assuredly endanger its success'. He found Waterbeach holders had half-acre plots but would have preferred a whole acre, and Denson was emphatic about this aspect: 'To effectually benefit the Labourer, so that he may have a useful resource when out of employ, be enabled to pay his way, and have the comforts of life within reach, he ought in no case, to be the occupier of less than an acre'.[5] Braybrooke agreed that, under favourable circumstances, a hard-working labourer and his family could manage an acre, and it would offer work for young sons. Yet in spite of similar evidence from a scheme at Bassingbourn, he was against such large plots here because, he rationalised, men should manage small plots first, for fear that failure would give the whole scheme a bad name. It was also true that smaller slices made the limited cake go further, larger numbers could be listed as beneficiaries, for publicity purposes, and labourers would be less disinclined to work so hard for other masters. Because of the small plot sizes, Denson was extremely critical of the scheme which emerged in Saffron Walden: these would give no independence from poor relief, yield an income of only £3 a year, not even enough to pay rent on a cottage: 'he will remain the same heartless, degraded being as before'. It is therefore clear that, while quoting Denson as an authority, Braybrooke took no account of the central plank of his philosophy.[6]

The first allotments in this area were not in Walden, but in Littlebury, another part of Braybrooke's demesne. Having researched the subject, he thought there would be 'no harm in trying the experiment', although his subsequent arrangements suggest it was rather more calculated than that. The 'experiment' was set up in a large field on the hill behind Littlebury Church, where 34 plots were laid out, varying in size from 31 to 47 rods, at a rent of threepence per rod. The results, he reported, were excellent, with abundant crops in the first season, all rents paid and no complaints or improper conduct. An innovation of particular significance was the issue of prizes for the best plots to William Rider, John Parish senior and James Freeman. The holders, probably Braybrooke's own employees and/or tenants, co-operated fully, so success was guaranteed, and a survey by the Vicar of Littlebury, showed that, after deducting rent and other expenses, the 1s.3d a rod profit tallied with similar findings elsewhere. Braybrooke pronounced himself amazed at such profits, quoted in the *Review*, 'little thinking that they would so very shortly be realised in my own neighbourhood'. Moreover, the allotments were so popular that he was trying to provide more near to cottages in distant hamlets, for instance among 13 of his Wenden employees. This popularity proved, he felt, the success of the system.[7]

Spade Husbandry Committee

If the Littlebury scheme was an experiment, it had scarcely begun before a similar one was being discussed in Walden, reflecting a degree of haste for some reason. A committee was formed, its most energetic member, and very much Lord Braybrooke's right-hand man in the town, John Player, the 'able superintendent' required, who did all the clerical work to which we owe details of the scheme: 'I held the onerous office of overseer that winter', he later wrote, 'and thought something should be done to help the labourer without taking more from the farmers'. Player saw that such a scheme held a perfect symmetry: 'It is clear that the able-bodied are only to be assisted with the means of earning a subsistence, not with money without a return of labour'. Thus allotments would 'create a medium population between the debased poor and the farmers and to this class we should look for trustworthy domestics as a class of characters who not having been so greatly pressed by want, have superior feelings of integrity and uprightness'. John Player, for all his pompous speeches, held quite radical views on allotments, rather different from the official *laissez-faire* attitude to the subject: 'landowners employ as few as possible, neither philanthropy not public expediency would make them do otherwise, so it needed the law'. His most radical suggestion, that the government should force landholders to offer 25 acres out of every 1000 in a parish to be let to the poor as allotments, was obviously fanciful. Already Player had realised that the indifference of farmers was the greatest obstacle to success. In fact the Walden scheme succeeded only because a tiny minority of town landowners supported it.[8]

The first minuted discussion about allotments took place in December 1829 at a time of great distress, when Lord Braybrooke chaired a meeting of professionals and tradesmen, some of whom owned land, but very few farmers. Out of this was borne the Spade Husbandry Committee, a somewhat confusing title since spade husbandry was a different scheme from allotments (see chapter 4). At this historic meeting wealthy maltsters and bankers Jabez and Wyatt George

Gibson, who owned a large number of fields around the town, set the ball rolling with the offer of 4½ acres near the chalkpit off Little Walden Road, which became known as the Lime Kiln Field. The plots were not free, and the landowners, praised for their generosity, were perhaps receiving a higher return than for an agricultural tenancy. But the poor did not seem to mind, as the idea took off straight away. When next they met the committee found a list of 40 applicants, which soon increased to 75, suggesting that they actually needed 15 acres for they felt that 'every applicant if their condition entitled them to it should be allowed a piece of land as early as may be'. Those 'entitled' would now, after all, be not only family men but also 'single men of good characters'.[9]

Lime Kiln Allotments

Still with only the Gibson land on offer, the committee nevertheless set to work in the early spring of 1830 to draw up the list of rules. By now there were 85 applicants wanting the first precious plots on the only field the committee had so far found, Lime Kiln, some asking for as many as 120 rods, so there clearly was a demand for the larger plots suggested by Denson. But the committee decided on a maximum size of 40 rods, with some only 20–30 and only one man, James Taylor who had eight children to feed, was given more. Preference was given to those living nearest with the largest families: at the end of the evening the committee were satisfied that they were providing for all the Castle and Church street families with five or more children. This initial idea, aimed at targeting the greatest potential drain on the rates, was not sustained for long: compared to further sites acquired later, Lime Kiln holders had an average of almost 4½ dependent children per family, whereas the average went down to 2½–3 or even 1½ or less later on. Thus the requirements were rapidly downgraded. There was no discrimination on grounds of character, apparently, and it is noticeable that among the first batch of 24 names, there were at least half-a-dozen who were later in trouble with the law and lost, or were threatened to forfeit their plots.[10]

On a spring morning in early March 1830, the new allotment holders met on the field off Little Walden Road, to draw lots for the plots. By adding on the wives and children, the committee was then able to claim that the allotments were already helping 154 people. The committee were delighted to see that all the plot-holders 'cheerfully took possession of the allotments offered to them upon the terms proscribed', and in the first printed report Braybrooke praised the 'degree of spirit and energy highly pleasing to the Committee, and encouraging the hope that this first effort to ameliorate their condition was duly appreciated by those for whom the benefit was intended'. Appreciation was thus, from the start, part of the package, even though the landowners were getting a good deal: the chalky soil of Lime Kiln Field was £2 per acre, but the allotment holders were charged more than this.[11]

Meanwhile there was still not enough land. A general appeal having failed, the weeks went by and a personal letter was sent to three local landowners. This asked them to offer land for rent to 'furnish the opportunity to many industrious Hands of employing themselves and their families in work of the most suitable description', but it produced no further offers, even though the carrot of lessening 'the growing burthen of parochial rates' was dangled. The three recipients of the appeal letters were all wealthy men who could have helped: grocer/draper John Emson never replied; rich maltster Thomas Archer Catlin said he needed his ten acres himself; corn factor John Archer, whose family owned a great deal of land, responded only by doing free ploughing, and that probably because one of the sites adjoined his own garden, and he was worried about the boundary line. There were others who could have offered land or helped in some way, but did not.[12]

Park Wall Allotments

Curiously at this stage, Braybrooke himself was still holding back from offering land, a delay of several months which certainly built up expectations. When he finally moved, the poor were queuing up, for it was an 'extremely eligible' prime site of seven acres beside the Audley Park wall (now Saxon Way). He wanted £3 an acre, more than the plot rent elsewhere and this at a time when average land rents in southern England were said to be rather less. Although this made it something of a commercial proposition for the lord, found from the pockets of the poor, and although it represented an infinitesimal part of his holdings, the arrangement was nevertheless clothed in the garments of philanthropy, and Braybrooke praised mightily for this 'considerable sacrifice'.[13]

Only 38 of the 48 applicants, mostly living that side of town, could be accommodated with 30–40 rod plots, although there was always the ambitious applicant, in this case Samuel Legerton, who wanted three or four times as much. The men were exhorted to 'cultivate these allotments in the best manner, recollecting that the better you do by the Land, the better the Land will do by you'. Their labours, so near the town, were 'very visible to neighbours and gave them a good example of industry'. A tide of goodwill enveloped the scheme: John Archer, he who would not offer land, did plough; the Vicar waived tithe; Lady Braybrooke had a well dug, her husband paid for fences and footpaths, Player planted a hedge and Gibson erected gates; Rivers of Sawbridgeworth handed over 300 apple trees; and the Horticultural Society offered prizes. These went first to George Butcher, Adcock Carter, William Barker, William Savill, William Richardson senior, James Barker, William Moull and Ratcliff Wright. The society members enjoyed 'watching the operation of the plan, and pointing out such improvements in the culture of the land, as from time to time occurred to them. They were also better enabled to judge of the comparative merits of the occupants, who were not a little gratified by the interest evinced in their proceedings.' All were motivated by ensuring 'the least possible expense to the parishioners in general', since they hoped to prove that allotments would reduce rate bills. Paying an unannounced visit the committee 'found many of the holders or their families at work... were gratified with the progress made... gave a few hints on the most judicious modes of cultivation'. Sadly, not all the poor were impressed: the hedge, gates and notice-board were vandalised.[14]

Meanwhile Jabez and Wyatt George Gibson wanted to provide allotments for their own employees, but were persuaded that the proposed site, Railey field on the Thaxted Road, would be more useful for people living nearby: they too received £3 an acre for another 11 plots. Now, with 78 plots on three sites, 450 people were benefiting, 'no inconsiderable portion of the labouring classes in the town'. As Player said, it was better for the community if ten acres could benefit 50 families rather than just one family. With Braybrooke away for the summer, there were no more committee meetings for three months, and one wonders if the members noticed the unrest, already simmering elsewhere in the country, which was to lead to the 'Captain Swing' riots six months later (see chapter 7). But through that first heady summer of 1830, apparent harmony prevailed in Walden, everyone was too busy to lounge around street corners, they had to start in the early hours to find time and wives and children could help too. Moreover, the town was awash with cheap fresh vegetables: 'With respect to the apparently improved habits of the poorer classes, and the decrease of idlers in the streets of Walden during the last year, the Committee confidently appeal to the testimony of many of the inhabitants; and they learn from the same source, that the town has been, throughout the summer, supplied with vegetables from the allotments, in greater variety, and a reduction of one half in price, as compared with former years'.[15]

Allotments and Labourers' Unrest

When the Committee began meetings again in the autumn, all rents were paid and every individual seemed perfectly satisfied with the proceedings of the committee. But then things began to alter, slowly at first but gathering momentum as distress was increasing again. The law allowed only 20 acres for parish allotments, although Braybrooke now added on some private ones at Holmer Cross, east of Little Walden Road. However 28 of the plot-holders wanted bigger plots, one asking for an acre to support his family, and a further 30 new applicants appeared. This meant that at least another ten acres must be found. This sudden demand for more plots spurred the committee to ask the Saffron Walden Corporation for use of charity land. Meanwhile Player issued a sympathetic statement, the timing of which seems significant, pointing out how the town was trying to help the poor man. The next meeting, on 9 November, was not recorded, even though Lord Braybrooke was probably there so it was clearly not just a sub-committee. This was very odd, for secretary Player was normally a meticulous clerk. At this point in the official minutes, it is very clear that the whole tenor of the Spade Husbandry proceedings temporarily alters, from one of benign and busy benevolence to one of sheer panic. It was the time of 'Captain Swing' and, although no specific reference appears in the minutes, to read them in conjunction with other allotment documents, and knowing that the riots were going on, is to realise that people were deeply worried.[16]

It is now realised that there was a close correlation between the appearance of allotment schemes and the pattern of rural unrest: a study in neighbouring Suffolk found that 1829 was one such period. It was therefore no accident that Braybrooke's initiative appeared when it did, aiming to make independently-minded men too busy and too grateful to go on the march. The plan worked. It was not until mid-November 1830 that the 'Swing' troubles came this way, setting alarm bells ringing. John Player, in an unpublished letter to *The Times*, urging the adoption of allotments, said he was reluctant to bother the new government 'in these critical times', a clear reference to 'Swing'.[17]

After meeting only three times in September/October, with a small attendance of six or seven, the Spade Husbandry Committee, who now had a lot to talk about, met at least a dozen times from late November through December, with far higher attendances: 17 on Monday 29 November just before the riots hit north-west Essex, 26 on Thursday 9 December while they were going on. On the first day of December, just as Lord Braybrooke informed the Home Office that the district was tranquil, Player was urgently summoning a large gathering of farmers, landowners and others at 8.30 a.m. in the town workhouse: the invitation underlined the word 'particularly requested to attend'. All of a sudden, offers were eagerly forthcoming. Mr. Nicholls, the tenant of five acres of Erswells Charity land in Thaxted Road, was given compensation to relinquish his tenancy immediately, so that the field could be set for allotments. A committee was appointed to investigate further land near Castle Street where about 25 men were waiting for plots. The Gibsons offered Warners field and the Catlins, they who previously had none available, suddenly found two spare acres in Copthall field by Ashdon Road. There were also seven landowners, some of whom had taken no interest before, anxious now to offer spade husbandry and other farm work. The whole scheme was moving into higher gear and clearly all this was connected with the unrest, by now spreading rapidly through Cambridgeshire, Suffolk and Essex. The meeting was adjourned to the following night (which was unusual) and it was 'particularly desired that such intended meeting be communicated to the principal landholders in the parish, in order that they may have the opportunity of knowing what measures are taking under present circumstances to employ and benefit the poor'.[18]

This meeting was not recorded, but the following week (on the same day as the Elmdon riot and just before the Arkesden and Clavering outbreaks) another urgent summons resulted in a large gathering on Thursday 9 December. Finally, some of the bigger farmers of the area were sitting up and taking notice: here were John Allen of Sewers End, John Salmon of Shire Hill, Henry Smith of Audley End, John Clark of Roos, John Rickard of Castle Street farm and the Spicers who were involved in various farms. The talk must all have been of 'Swing', but the official minutes record only that there was still a shortfall of land, in spite of the addition of Nicholls, Warners and Copthall fields. Once again, the Gibsons intervened, offering to hire the Turners Charity land at the foot of Windmill Hill, and re-let at a lower rent as allotments. Unusually, the Turners Charity committee called a special meeting at the old workhouse, in the middle of the 'Swing' period, to sort this out and, again exceptionally, minuted the decision in their account book.[19]

It was time to call the plot-holders together to tell them the good news, 'having an anxious desire to afford all the holders as well as new applicants every reasonable accommodation'. This was again an unprecedented large gathering, and a clear tribute to local events, albeit that the minutes give nothing away. It was also very cleverly timed, for men at elite-organised meetings could not be simultaneously plotting rebellion against those elites. Indeed, as they stood to hear about all this increased beneficence, their fellows in Arkesden had that very day been on the march. But in Walden all was quiet. These events occurred between 7 and 17 December 1830, precisely the period of the riots. And so it was that by the time the disgruntled labourers of nearby Clavering, Elmdon and other north-west Essex parishes started demanding to earn more than seven shillings a week, the labourers of Saffron Walden, whose earnings were slightly higher anyway, had apparently been sweetened by the energetic concern of the town elites who had — fortuitously or by design — brought in allotments in advance of crisis, and —probably by design — extended them at the right moment to nip potential protest in the bud.[20]

Allotments and Social Control

With the crisis over and the rioters punished, it was time to sort out the details of the new plots, and to boast of Walden's achievement . Each allotment-holder was now seen as 'a special constable ready to protect public order in moments of difficulty, because he has now an interest in maintaining it', and Walden labourers praised for their restraint: 'during the last winter when disturbances agitated the country at large, our own poor were perfectly quiet – notwithstanding their wages were very low'. The link between allotments and unrest was made manifest as Player later wrote: 'When disturbances exist, it is not the time to frame a remedy — it must be done before, unaffected by terror and with the declared view of benefiting those for whom it is intended'. This was exactly what the Walden worthies had so cleverly achieved.[21]

A self-congratulatory public relations exercise began, which went on for several years, Lord Braybrooke personally paying for the publication of a report on the first year of operation: 'Those who considered the experiment as visionary and impracticable, may be convinced of its useful operation… had exceeded their most sanguine expectations'. Some plot-holders, he claimed, reported that the yield of 20 rods of vegetables was more than double their rent, quite apart from the 20 rods of potatoes. Ignoring the extra costs of seed, manure and tools, none of which was given, Braybrooke estimated a profit of £10–£12 per acre, most of which would be circulated in the parish. If this was so, then a man with an acre could have doubled his normal income, but of course no one had an acre. The Committee preferred to stress how *little* land was required to benefit so many people: only 15 acres to start with, doubling by 1833, but never in this period more than half-a-percent of the parish acreage.[22]

Later, Player also pitched in with his own 'comparative statement', although only 11 of the 36 invited turned up to hear him rally the 'superior' classes to provide allotments, in order to 'materially lessen that galling and degrading weight of poverty which inevitably casts the unassisted poor upon parochial relief'. But any real empathy with the poor, stressed during the time of the riots, had already reverted to a utilitarian rationale. Allotments prevented the poor from 'eating the Bread of a dishonourable dependence', but there was no need for the superior classes to worry that labourers might get ideas above their station: 'we would utterly abrogate the preposterous idea that the labourers can by this system become independent — because Society is formed of consecutive and dependent links'. Here was the final denial of the dreams of Denson and other advocates of the labourer's acre.[23]

The constant stream of articles and letters continued throughout 1831 and into 1832, with reports on the Walden scheme being sent by Braybrooke to influential figures like the Prebendary of St Paul's and even the Whig Prime Minister Earl Grey. Writing to the Vicar of Finchingfield, Player repeated his arguments that farmers could not be expected to pay higher wages, but it was immoral to just give the poor money when what they needed was the chance of some land: 'Our parish contains 7000 acres and is it *too much* to devote 40 or 50 in allotments for the poor, who could not possibly obtain land near a town like ours without benevolence assist them?' In another letter, to the Essex press, Player again promoted allotments as a kind of cure-all: 'Surely no system can be better adapted to encourage an attachment in the labourer to the soil of his birth. A land of freedom should have no paupers but those of absolute necessity... but the hand of the willing and industrious labourer should be enabled to find for himself, some fruits to sweeten the routine of the toil which he is doomed to experience.' Only a few months later, Player's own survey of employment in the town underlined his own naivety in maintaining the fiction that there was farm work available if only the 'idle' would look for it (see chapter 1). Nor was unemployment work on the roads permanently reduced. Those who ran the allotments must have known this, and were perfectly aware of where the real problems lay, but relied on philanthropy and self-help accompanied by a moral crusade to supply the remedy.[24]

Financial Effects of Allotments

Some of the financial claims made for allotments were also a little suspect. By 1831, there were eight allotment sites, potentially benefiting 700 people (including wives and children) and Braybrooke and Player were anxious to prove that allotments could lower rate bills. Braybrooke was positive that allotments had reduced claims for poor relief, although he admitted that 'many causes must have conspired to produce this desirable result'. The Poor Law assistant commissioner, Ashurst Majendie, probably briefed by Player, also claimed that rates had gone down and 'the most competent judges ascribe much of this improvement to the allotments'. There were many other published reports on the Walden scheme in influential journals of the day, often harping on this rates/allotments theme. Comparing the various articles and letters suggests some weaving of

Castle
Hedingham

figures and extracts to suit arguments. As a result of all this publicity, in 1832 Player found himself in an embarrassing situation when the journal of the Labourers' Friend Society, which existed to promote allotments for the poor, misquoted figures. This led to much correspondence, and Player felt bound to deny the figures and quote the right ones.[25]

Various reductions in roadwork expenditure and poor rates were claimed for different periods, from 1829–33. Given the variables of weather, wheat prices, harvests, illness and other factors which influenced under-employment and reliance on outdoor relief, quoting such short time spans was of dubious validity, and there was little evidence that allotments alone permanently reduced applications for poor relief. A comparison of early 1830s lists of allotment holders, highways workers and regular employees suggests, in very broad terms, that possibly about two-fifths of plot-holders enjoyed fairly regular employment, two-fifths were frequently unemployed, and one-fifth in and out of work. Even these vague estimates suggest that allotments were not significantly reducing the need for poor relief, for at least two-thirds of the allotment-holders' names continued to appear in lists of those 'on the road' (so far as can be ascertained, given duplication of names). A more sinister possibility is that the overseers denied poor relief to those who had allotments. In one of his many statements, Player said that the allotments committee was working 'in conjunction with the parochial officers' to lessen the rate burden. As an offshoot of the vestry, the allotments committee clearly worked closely with that body, since reducing rates was a prime motivation. One year, the vestry threatened to deduct 20 shillings of unpaid allotment rent from James Saggers' poor relief unless he paid up. On another occasion, it was the vestry which confiscated John Dubery's plot and took him to court for the rent owed.[26]

Some contemporaries were unconvinced by claims that allotments reduced poor rates: after Braybrooke's first report appeared in the *Quarterly Review*, a writer commented: 'It is evident that this profit is only a transfer from the farmer to the labourer; but that if it diminishes the poor rates to the amount of the profit, then Peter pays Paul'. After elaborating an economic argument, he suggested emigration, not allotments alone, was the answer as there was simply not enough work available for labourers: 'it is a positive absurdity to suppose that the residence of a man, wife and family on an acre of potatoe ground places him in the garden of Eden'.[27]

It must have been tough on a man who already did physical labour through a 12-hour day (when in work) to set to on his allotment, either early in the morning before his day-job, or in the evening, but many did so and unwittingly played into the hands of a system which legitimised keeping their earnings below a living wage. The low wages could be further glossed over by stressing that the labourers were contributing to the local economy: there was 'a constant creation of capital, which otherwise would not have existed'. Some rather suspect claims were, in any case, made about the monetary value of such self-grown crops. Player said that an allotment 'affords the labourer an honest opportunity of making from 2s. to 3s. additional provision weekly for his family'. This would add up to an extra £5–£8 per year (less than Braybrooke claimed), but the breakdown of costs at Littlebury suggested the annual profit was scarcely a shilling a week, since seed, tools and manure all ate into income. The exaction of rents seems particularly inappropriate. The Walden overseers' accounts show that during the winter of 1831–2, for instance, rent receipts amounted to £130, money which surely the toiling gardeners could have been allowed to keep, in view of the fact that allotments were supposed to relieve poverty. It is therefore difficult to see that labouring families were much better off in terms of income.[28]

Benefits to the Poor

The benefits, of course, were not only financial. Many poor people simply appreciated having a little bit of land. Cultivating their own patch, producing food for themselves and the community life of the allotment: this was something they could relate to, and many took pride in their plots. Allotments were undoubtedly popular, otherwise they could not have used them to serve the ends of the 'well-ordered town'. They offered exercise and companionship, an escape from small overcrowded cottages, and some small measure of independence. Allotments are still valuable supplements today, but at that time they were of greater importance to men who had no other assets. The little plots gave back some residue of the old way of life of the peasant, and this was, as Player said, a noble labour. A correspondent of Lady Braybrooke's commented that allotments changed people, made them happier: 'no cowering over the embers in winter, no hanging over gates and lounging in summer — the garden occupies all their leisure hours'. Observers were pleased to note how much the labourers enjoyed their plots: 'The effect on the habits and comforts of the labourer has been most beneficial. The attachment of the labourers to their small occupations is increasing. Many spend their hours of leisure and sometimes a whole day, there. They have now something they may call their own.' This was confirmed by Thomas Ives, a carter, who 'bore strong testimony to the benefit he had derived', and a maltster who said 'he had never realised how good it would be to have a small piece of land'. There was also appreciation from an old man, normally stuck with very low wages on the roads, who commented that he and his aged wife had comforts through two winters which they could never obtain before.[29]

However, the views of most allotment-holders do not appear in the records. It would be interesting to know the feelings of those who failed, for there was a high drop-out rate among those who originally expressed interest, with about a third changing their mind in the first year. Player always realised that allotments were not suited to what he called 'the debased poor'. This would include many of the most troublesome labourers at the bottom of the pecking order, like single, under-employed, young men, who would find digging less exciting than poaching as a method of supplementing income. The sick poor were not fit enough to cultivate them, and the truly destitute could not afford them. Allotment-holders were slightly more literate than the 'debased poor': two-thirds of the early tenants were sufficiently literate to sign their name, compared to only half among those committed to Sessions. Some types were most definitely not welcome, such as 'an idle shoemaker to whom we were desirous of giving a fair trial but who cannot any longer possess the land, seeing it tends to mar the whole of our proceedings'. This suggests that the system shook out the unsuitable, for worthies felt unable to embrace this radical idea without attaching to it a moral agenda. In this they were not unusual, for similar motivations prompted many such schemes. Giving evidence to a parliamentary enquiry, for instance, G.W. Gent, a landowner who let out 30 allotments in Steeple Bumpstead and elsewhere, maintained that the plots made the holders better behaved. The truth was that the men who took allotments led hard lives and allotments, whatever their utility, could not turn them into saints.[30]

Allotments and Morality

That allotments were not cure-alls for social ills becomes apparent when collating the various problems recorded in the minutes. Initially the allotments were to be restricted to respectable men, for it was essential 'to draw a more definite line between the idle and profligate and the really industrious'. This attempt to build social control into the allotments system by restricting tenancies to those of unimpeachable character, became impossible in practice. Such transgressions must have clouded 'Gentleman' John's image of the 'rural-idyll' associations of allotments, for it is obvious from his writings that one side of him was idealistic in the extreme, seeing these humble plots as far more than mere vegetable patches. 'Do-gooders' like Player never seem to have addressed the twin faults in their logic: firstly, that those at the bottom of the heap and therefore most in need of character improvement were least likely to take part; and secondly, that even among 'respectable' men, the much-vaunted spirit of self-help was not sustainable on so small a piece of land.

Even among the one or two allowed larger plots, poverty beckoned. James Taylor, presumably the same one given such on Lime Kiln because he had eight children to feed, nevertheless stole a loaf when he was in Chelmsford and went to prison for a week. The allotments committee, however, realising it was preferable to feed Taylor's large family with his allotment vegetables rather than their rates via poor relief chits, allowed him to keep the plot 'in consequence of distressing family circumstances which led to his crime'. Even though Taylor's fall from grace had occurred far away from Walden, it still counted as a transgression against the sixth rule of the allotments. Likewise William Saggers lost plot and crops after commitment to Cambridge Castle for a misdemeanour, although he later got it back. It was not easy to enforce the allotment regulations. Although these were handed out to new plot-holders, often with a lecture — 'the tenants are liable to lose their occupations by misconduct, those whom good motives might not influence, are bound by a tangible recognisance to their good behaviour' — allowances had to be made.[31]

Most of these rules caused problems. [Fig.8.1] Keeping the land in good heart (rule two) was obviously sensible, but where were townsfolk to find manure? Most lived in tiny cottages or crowded tenements with no gardens and no space

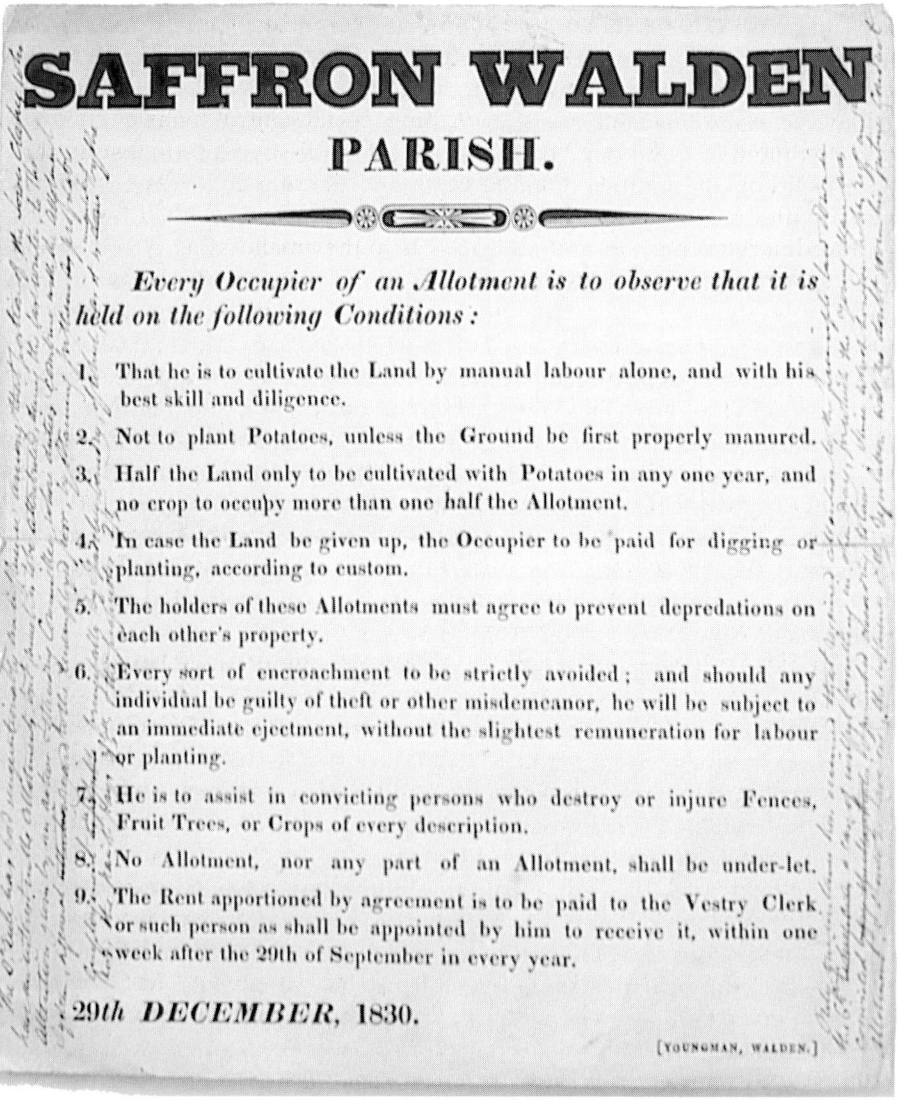

SAFFRON WALDEN
PARISH.

Every Occupier of an Allotment is to observe that it is held on the following Conditions:

1. That he is to cultivate the Land by manual labour alone, and with his best skill and diligence.

2. Not to plant Potatoes, unless the Ground be first properly manured.

3. Half the Land only to be cultivated with Potatoes in any one year, and no crop to occupy more than one half the Allotment.

4. In case the Land be given up, the Occupier to be paid for digging or planting, according to custom.

5. The holders of these Allotments must agree to prevent depredations on each other's property.

6. Every sort of encroachment to be strictly avoided; and should any individual be guilty of theft or other misdemeanor, he will be subject to an immediate ejectment, without the slightest remuneration for labour or planting.

7. He is to assist in convicting persons who destroy or injure Fences, Fruit Trees, or Crops of every description.

8. No Allotment, nor any part of an Allotment, shall be under-let.

9. The Rent apportioned by agreement is to be paid to the Vestry Clerk or such person as shall be appointed by him to receive it, within one week after the 29th of September in every year.

29th **DECEMBER***, 1830.*

[YOUNGMAN, WALDEN.]

Fig.8.1 *Saffron Walden allotments rules.*   *SW, Museum.*

for a pig-sty, but needed manure to grow potatoes, the most bulky, nutritious crop for the poor. John Player, who wandered round the allotments on a regular basis, kept a notebook full of admonitions on rule three. Rents were another trial for men of irregular income. When Samuel Taylor left town without paying up, his wife was warned 'not to sett off potatoes as it would defraud the parish of rent'. Lost marker posts made rule six about encroachment difficult to prove, and rule six sounds distinctly unfair, using allotments here as a lever to good behaviour elsewhere. But this sort of thing, social control by any other name, was commonplace. All in all the rosy glow of the first year soon lost its shine.[32]

When Lord Braybrooke pointed out that five crime-less Sessions had coincided with the early years of the allotment scheme, he was asked 'whether this extraordinary exemption is at all traceable to the ameliorating effects of letting land to the poor?' But shortly afterwards, John Cornell and William Moul lost their plots after being found leaving work with bundles of wood, and the same year labourer James Miller was given notice to quit after being convicted of 'a violent assault on Pomfret while Assistant Surveyor', and his father's request to take over the plot refused. Pride in the crime-free years took another knock at the 1833 malt-stealing trial (see chapter 6). It transpired that all the time that Player and Braybrooke were lauding the contented, crime-less, vegetable-growing town, some of the lower classes were reaping their own harvest of illicit malt, oats, hops and other commodities. It was a great disappointment, the more so since two of those implicated, William Richardson junior and Thomas Lord, were actually allotment holders themselves. The latter absconded, and the value of his crops was given to the vestry clerk.[33]

Nor did allotments stop people taking game, though it might have been hoped that cultivating in all their spare hours would make men too tired to go out on nocturnal poaching expeditions. At least two holders, George Warren and Philip Augar, were ejected after being found guilty of game offences, James Douce after stealing potatoes and James Erswell jnr after receiving stolen property. One of Braybrooke's tenants, Adcock Carter who 'misapplied his property' not only lost his home but was also given notice to quit his allotment. Altogether there were thus at least 14 ejections for 'criminal' activities in the first decade of the allotment scheme. So far as one can tell, most of these men were labourers, often living in Castle Street or Church Street, and therefore probably from the communities at which moral improvement through allotments had been aimed. Some of those who lost plots later regained them, after expressing contrition, but there were many other warnings or ejections for excessive weeds, sub-letting, keeping a beerhouse and, most commonly, rent arrears or growing too many potatoes. John Player's allotment notebooks in the later 1830s are littered with complaints: 'bad state', 'badly farmed', 'too much corn'. No sign of this tarnished ideal appeared in Player's celebrated *Sketches* of Walden, where he would see allotments in misty-eyed myth as 'a vast garden'.[34]

By the time this was published John Player was a sick man. In 1841 he resigned his post as secretary. With his death at the age of 60 in 1846, there went the chief publicist and promoter of the allotments, not to mention a meticulous taker of minutes. After his resignation, there followed a period of far more perfunctory and less tidy records but he must have been losing his grip for some time as those now running things, bootmaker Charles Baron and maltster Joshua Clarke were appalled when they inspected the allotments in 1841 to find how weedy and uncultivated they were, with too much corn, paths in a slovenly state and no marker posts, so that there were constant complaints about encroachment on each other's land, and still lots of unpaid rents. The conclusion has to be that the attempt to use allotments in their early years as a means of inculcating good behaviour was not an unqualified success and their overall contribution to the desired 'well-ordered town' was perhaps more in image than reality. The decline in allotment standards took many years to improve, but by the late 1840s the Committee were receiving better reports. However, increasing demand could only be met by dividing up existing allotments, which suggests that it remained impossible to persuade farmers and other landowners to rent out land for those on the allotment waiting list, the problem which had bedevilled the scheme right from the start.[35]

Allotments and Farmers

The antagonism of farmers towards Saffron Walden's allotment scheme has seldom been noted, as it was hidden from the official minutes; but the scheme emerged largely because it did *not* have to rely on farmers. As was the norm in this part of the world, it happened only because a very few wealthy independent men not only owned land near enough to where people lived to be of use, but were also persuaded that allotments were the key to social order. Contrary to what was claimed, this was not really at any great sacrifice in most cases, and the good rent and fulsome praise received in return made it a good investment. But at least they did take part. If the scheme had had to rely on farmers alone, it would never have taken off at this time, for in East Anglia they were by no means of the same mindset as large landowners like Braybrooke. A recent study in Suffolk and Norfolk, a cereal-growing area similar to north-west Essex, found that allotments represented a power struggle, not only between farmers and labourers, but between tenant farmers and landowners, a clash of market-led capitalism versus morals-motivated paternalism. Those farmers who finally turned up to the emergency gathering during 'Swing', for instance, did not respond to the crisis with offers of allotments. As one commentator put it: 'the farmers appear to grudge rather than rejoice at it'. The same situation was found almost everywhere, and this was a major reason why the allotment movement failed to spread more widely in this period.[36]

Farmers, particularly the larger ones, might dislike allotments for a mixture of reasons, feeling that the provision diluted their own control of the fluid labour force they liked to have available when required; labourers might be too tired or busy to work hard; they might pilfer seed corn or manure for their own use. But mostly, it seems sadly to be the case that most (though not all) tenant farmers were 'jealous of such deductions from their holdings... and they object to the increased independence of the labourers'. Many saw no advantage to

156

themselves in giving the poor a stake in the land. They had their own worries, often were only tenants themselves, and letting land to labourers could only make things worse.[37]

Both Braybrooke and Player confirmed locally this general state of affairs. Braybrooke later expressed surprise that such schemes in north-west Essex were largely confined only to his farms in Walden, Wendens and Littlebury, and castigated those farmers who 'continue so indifferent to their own interests, so averse to innovations, and so tremblingly alive to the deduction of a few acres from their holdings'. If he felt so strongly, why not offer more land himself? It is not clear whether he followed his own advice to put an allotment clause into new farm leases. Player also complained that 'the farmers do not look upon it with a friendly eye — they now, I believe, commend it for its practical bearings, but are prone to say "there are too many farmers by half" meaning the Little Holder is not an acquisition'. Both men were frustrated that farmers could not embrace this key to preventing unrest: Braybrooke said that raising men up through allotments would create 'a better feeling in agricultural districts'; Player was totally convinced 'that to restore the peasantry to a better order of feeling, and to benefit them effactually no system can be adopted as good as allotments'. Farmers remained unconvinced, at least until labourers starting burning their stacks.[38]

The campaign to spread allotments went on through much of the nineteenth century, for there were many individuals and societies who dedicated themselves to the movement, but progress was very slow. Although a few other allotment schemes appeared in the area, a later claim by the Horticultural Society that, following the Saffron Walden scheme, allotments had 'been wisely and happily extended over many parts of the Kingdom' over-simplifies the true situation. An age of *laissez-faire* condemned allotments to remain among the whims of philanthropy and, notwithstanding admiring comments in official reports, the attitude was that if allotments were such a good thing they would spread of their own accord. But they did not, because they were not compulsory, and farmers ruled Essex on their own terms. The lack of response may have actually worsened relationships between landowners, farmers and labourers.[39]

In any case allotments could not make up for the fundamental and very deep inequalities in society. There came a time, in the mid-forties as the fires of the incendiarists burned, when even Lord Braybrooke recognised their limitations and frankly admitted that the allotments which he had pioneered were not a panacea. Forgetting Denson's earlier 'warning voice' that only an acre would do, he told an audience of agriculturists:

'His neighbours encouraged him to try it when nothing has been ascertained of its practical working, and it had succeeded in that neighbourhood; but he should deceive them if he said it would be a remedy for all evils. It would be a good thing if the system could be extended, but he did not think it would do a great deal for the labourers. There were times when a man had leisure and had a large family when he might cultivate an allotment advantageously; but the most exaggerated view of a half acre allotment would not furnish the labourer with that which was necessary.'[40]

157

Conclusion

In fairness, given the opposition, Braybrooke's achievement in setting in train the provision of something like 58 acres of allotments over his three parishes (33 in Walden, 22 in Littlebury, 3 in Wendens), was a considerable one. Although himself thoroughly wedded to capitalistic farming enterprise he cultivated, as did some other members of the landed gentry, a streak of old-style dutiful paternalism which seized on allotments as a way of encouraging respect in his own locality, and defusing unrest. But there was little substantial improvement in the labourer's lot. The lord was too much imbued in the mores of his class to truly understand the poor, and spoiled his gesture by asking for rent and expecting praise for what was in effect a commercial arrangement. Even the prizes given for well-kept allotments were small fry for one of the richest men in the country. Posterity has, however, given Lord Braybrooke much of the credit for the allotment scheme, in fulfilment perhaps of the lavish acclaim poured on him at the time by the *Quarterly Review*: 'The nobleman may depend on it that the patriotic and humane experiments… will be remembered to his honour long after half the statesmen of his day are as much forgotten as if they had never breathed'. Indeed it was Braybrooke's contribution, rather than Player's, Gibson's or anyone else's, which was immortalised in the parliamentary report on allotments in 1843: 'There are a good many about Walden. Lord Braybrooke, I believe is a great encourager of them,' said a witness at the enquiry.[41]

In reality, the genuine utility of allotments to the poor was hijacked by elites for their own ends, in the process bending the truth about benevolent landowners, holders' profits, rate reductions, effect on crime and moral behaviour: almost a campaign of sustained disinformation. The reason why Saffron Walden's allotments received so much attention was largely because the subject was under national debate in the wake of the 'Captain Swing' riots, in the quelling of which one of the scheme's chief advocates, Lord Braybrooke, had played so intimate a part. The town elites, who had tried the idea mostly as an experiment among several others, to cut the rates, were able to capitalise on this interest to publicise their achievement. In the process they convinced themselves, and apparently many others, that Saffron Walden had no riots because it had allotments. On the plus side, it has to be said that allotments were a very radical idea at this time, for the very thought of giving the tiniest shred of independence to the common labourer was anathema to some. In some ways, the propaganda and social control aspects — the only way to make the idea acceptable — did increase provision so the poor did ultimately benefit by having more allotments. Allotments *were* a very radical idea and most parishes lacked the commitment to provide them.

In time the social control element of allotments became secondary. After the death of their early advocates, and with 'Captain Swing' no more than a folk memory, the novelty wore off. With the usual problems of rent arrears, poor cultivation, encroachment and broken rules, the little plots became ordinary amenities rather than a prestigious pioneering initiative in the gift of the rich, and they could no longer be used as an attempt to bribe the poor into good behaviour. The Spade Husbandry Committee even stopped meeting in 1858, or at least there were no recorded meetings for ten years, although someone must have been collecting rents.[42]

Today, although Limekiln and Parkwall plots have gone, and there remains a temptation to bury allotment land under bricks and mortar, there are still allotments at Windmill Hill and elsewhere in the town. New generations of independent-minded individuals, albeit unused to manual labour in the fields and digging without hunger gnawing them inside, still enjoy their allotments which remain an important and much under-rated facility. A great camaraderie exists among allotment people even today, which makes one wonder whether these humble vegetable patches, rather than removing all ideas of sedition from men's minds as was claimed in 1830, may actually have cemented working-class solidarity and made them less, not more, inclined to doff their caps!

On one occasion Player proclaimed 'A grand feature in the allotment system, in my opinion, is that it supersedes the necessity of forcing high and unnatural wages from the farmer'. This was a dubious claim but it could be said that the entire allotment scheme came about because of the impossibility of doing just that. Likewise other forms of philanthropic endeavour — charities, societies, educational and religious outreach — were made all the more necessary, in order to cover the cracks in the system and maintain the 'well-ordered town'. This is the theme to be explored in the remaining chapters.[43]

Chapter 9

'A Quality of Evil Peculiar to Themselves'

The Walden Charities

'As now administered, such charities are often wasted, and often mischievous. In many instances being distributed on the same principle as the rates of the worst managed parishes, they are only less pernicious than the abuse in the application of the poor rates, because they are visibly limited in amount. In some cases they have a quality of evil peculiar to themselves.[1]

Poor Law officials, in their published comments about the administration of charities, stated that in many places they were often mismanaged. In Saffron Walden, however, the Charity Commissioner who visited the town only two years later concluded that, by and large, the local charities *were* carefully administered, albeit that there were some dissenting voices to this view. This chapter is a description of the old charities, the arguments which they generated and the ways in which the approach to philanthropy was altering in a time of deepening poverty.[2]

Saffron Walden, like many towns, had a seemingly impressive tradition of charitable effort. By the nineteenth century, there were a large number of charities in the town, administering income from bequests of varying value, often tied up with land or annuities.[Table 9.1] They owned a small proportion of the parish land, the income from which was directed specifically at the poor, often at the sick and aged, or those with large families. They offered a variety of benefits: in any one year there were in theory a small handful of apprenticeships, six or seven gifts of money or clothing and a number of weekly doles of bread; when vacancies arose, there were up to 30 Almshouse and 30 Charity School places. It sounds a lot, but spread between several hundred families, it cannot have made much of a dent in the general level of poverty, although even small gifts like regular loaves were eagerly taken up. Some towns reckoned the poor could receive in cash or in kind an average of a shilling a week from charities, but in Walden this can only have applied to a small minority.[3]

Charity trusteeship was a popular office. It made men feel good about themselves doling out gifts, not from their own pockets via the poor rates (as did overseers or guardians), but from sums donated by benefactors long since safely dead. An analysis of the voluntary work done by the leading lights in town

Charity	Aims	Benefits (in 1830s)
Adams' & others	Grammar School of Walden.	£40 p.a. (closed until 1844).
Almshouses	Almshouses for 30 poor people.	£825.17s.6d. p.a.
Barlee's	Help apprentices.	Once every six years.
Bromfield's	Clothe & put forward apprentices.	£21 p.a. (about 2 or 3 boys p.a.).
Penning's & others	Charity School.	£72 p.a. (30 poor children).
Erswell's	The Poor ('twenty shillings money').	£66 p.a.(60-100 recipients).
Falkland's	39 poor women ('eleven shillings money').	£21.19s p.a.(39 recipients).
Howard's	Clothing poor of Walden & Littlebury.	£42.7s p.a.(34 old people).
Hubbard's	Bread for poor.	6s.8d. p.a. (almost worthless by 1830).
Leader's	Bread for poor.	£21 p.a. (about 12 people).
Martin's	Deserving poor at Audley End & Walden.	£3.6s.8d. p.a. (about 10-18 old people).
Pennystone's	Bread weekly to the poor after church	About 25 people.
Rand's	Poor in Castle Street.	£5 p.a. (worth very little by 1830s).
Sparrow's	Honest industrious poor inhabitants.	£10.8s. p.a. (6 or 7 people)
Suffolk & Turner's	The poor.	£66 p.a. (3 apprentices in 1834)
Symond's	Repair roads at Sewards End.	
Edmund Turner's	Audley End & Walden poor.	£41 p.a. (40 poor recipients)
Thomas Turner's	Bread for poor, etc.	£45 p.a. (mostly bread after church)

Table 9.1: *some Saffron Walden charities, 1818*

shows that almost every one of them had some charity connection, and to be a trustee was one of the most prestigious in public life. Nor was it hard work. Apart from treasurers and secretaries, the remaining trustees on most charities might find the rewards exceeded the burdens, for some met only once or twice a year to compile an annual list, while the regular weekly doles of bread were left to the vicar and churchwardens to sort out.

Apprenticeships

A few of the gifts were greatly prized, in particular the handful of apprenticeships paid for by Broomfields and Turners Charities, and by the parish. These were much sought after, and it is unlikely there were ever enough to go round. Something of the changing economy of the town can be gleaned by analysing the actual apprenticeship documents. The vast majority of these were in town, but lads were still sometimes sent out to local villages or even occasionally to London. In the first half of the nineteenth century, opportunities most commonly occurred in shoemaking, tailoring, blacksmithing and the various building trades: from 1815–50, surviving documents relate to 15 shoemakers/cordwainers, 18 tailors, 15 building and 23 other trades. About half of the apprenticeships were with Walden masters, and the other half divided between local villages, Essex, London, Cambridgeshire and elsewhere. Some years there were three or four more applicants than places available, and disappointment would ensue if employers declined to accept candidates, or there was no master available or the lads were deemed too young or too old, for children as young as 11 were put forward. Occasionally boys from outside Walden were nominated, an example being Charles Barker from Bassingbourn who applied to Turners Charity in 1837, although no master was found and, earlier Benjamin Barker from Wimbish who was apprenticed in Debden, via the Turners Charity.[4]

The trustees seem to have been diligent in sorting out over-subscribed places, paying premiums of around £10–£15, and maintained an interest afterwards in the behaviour of both apprentices and masters. They must obviously have chosen boys whom they thought would behave and benefit, taking action if not. When local carpenter Charles Pledge applied for his 16-year-old son John to be apprenticed to a shoemaker in the town, the trustees were clearly worried that the master, Charles Jeffery also sold liquor and tried to protect John's morals by making it an express condition in the indentures that 'the boy shall on no occasion be employed in the public house now kept by Charles Jeffery'.[5]

On occasion all the apprentices living in town were summonsed to attend a trustees' meeting to give an account of their progress. One such summons, to a meeting on Easter Tuesday at the Town Hall, went out to apprentices of cooper Thomas Patient, bookseller Henry Hart, baker James Barker, carpenter Robert Hunneybell, shoemakers Josiah List, Thomas Brand and Charles Jeffery, gardener William Chater, tailors John Francis and James Housden, basket-maker George Prior, miller James Clayden and wheelwright Nathaniel Guyver, so clearly all these were operating charity apprenticeships at this time. One year, they discovered that shoemaker apprentice, 20-year-old Alfred Augar, had not turned up for work for the past eight months and ordered his master to fetch him back. On another occasion, when carpenter's son Elias Bird left his job, instead of punishing the boy, his indentures were transferred 'in consideration of the master's conduct', which suggests that his master Robert Hunneybell had treated him badly. The same master was in trouble some years later for refusing to pay wages or find work for his 15-year-old apprentice: this time the trustees told the boy to summon Hunneybell before the magistrates. Masters were similarly admonished if they did not summons defaulting apprentices.[6]

In addition to the charities, there were also some apprenticeships arranged by the parish, and there seems to have been liaison with charity trustees. The general impression is of a system quite carefully organised, which must have owed something to the statutory protection which existed for parish apprentices. The rules and conditions would be a price worth paying for most parents and children. But how were these lucky few chosen? With up to half the population aged under 20, apprenticeships could be an option for only a tiny minority, so such an opportunity must have depended heavily on knowing the right trustee and behaving in the right way. But a labourer's son seemed to have as much chance as a tradesman's son, while orphans and children of widows were looked on favourably. Very occasionally, an apprenticeship was offered to rescue a youth from a life of crime, albeit at a distance: '£15 allowed for Henry Barker, son of Samuel Barker aged 15, if a situation can be found for him out of town, on his return from the Reformatory'.[7]

The Livery & the Almshouses

At the other end of the age range, and also much valued, was 'Lord Howard's Livery', legacy of the first Lord Braybrooke, still given out by his successors on Christmas Eve to 34 aged and infirm poor of good character, from Walden and Littlebury. Each man got a coat, waistcoat, breeches, shirt, hose, shoes and hat; and each woman a gown, coat, shift, straw hat, hose and shoes. The Charity Commission found the charity carefully administered by the third Lord Braybrooke who was still 'particular in requiring the two vicars to see that the recipients appear in their new clothes in their respective parish churches' on Christmas day, Easter day and Whitsunday morning and evening services. No doubt the fortunate few little minded parading in their excellent outfits, wearing them with pride. One such was, 84-year-old Master Parmenter: 'His person was well-known, having for many years been bent nearly double, and been accustomed to wear Lord Howard's clothing'. It was surely worth cultivating a good character to keep warm in winter.[8]

Likewise with the Abbey Lane Almshouses, a much-desired place to end one's days. [Fig.9.1] Of all the charities for the elderly, this was undoubtedly the most desirable, for it brought other advantages such as fuel and treats. Originally the Almshouse had been a 15th century foundation by the Guild of our Lady of Pity, intended for the 'succour and sustenance of XIII poor men, such as

Fig.9.1 *The Almshouses in Abbey Lane, opened in March 1832, offering good accommodation with various 'perks' for 30 elderly residents.*

be lame, crooked, blind and bed-ridden and most at need'. In theory social control was built into its earliest regulations, with early rules forbidding drunkenness and other bad behaviour. The ordinances required attendance three times a day at religious services, while residents were admonished if they haunted alehouses or kept evil company and, if they 'stubbornly use themselves towards the Dame or rail uncomely on any persons' or purloined Almshouse property, they were liable to be evicted. This was unlikely to be strictly enforced even in earlier times. An old person removed from the Almshouses would only end up on the poor rates. In the nineteenth century, with increasing numbers in distress, the Almshouse was even less the sort of place where the average pauper was likely to find a final home. It existed largely for the more genteel aged poor.[9]

By then the old Almshouses, erected in 1782, had become dilapidated. As with many other improvements, it was during the troubled 1830s that the long-standing plan to replace them came to fruition. The new building, costing £5,000, provided homes for 30 old people, plus hall (with a large fire eight months of the year) and chapel. The earlier provisions stipulated lodging, board, firing, drink, potage, visitation, burial and common alms. They remained well provided for, receiving a weekly cash allowance of 5s.6d, a further quarterly payment of 2s.6d, and 1s.6d in Lent instead of fish. They also received seven quarts of beer weekly, and special treats at Christmas, with free medical advice and the services of a resident matron. The trustees could afford all this because the charity was remarkably well endowed with an annual income of £950, from 280 acres of Wimbish land, a further 130 acres in Walden, 4 messuages and 22 cottage tenements. Land exchanges at enclosure had benefited the charity too. Some of the building money was borrowed, some rentals increased and there was also a sale of timber from the 280 acres in Wimbish owned by the almshouse.[10]

There must always have been many old folk who looked on longingly at the privileges of the lucky few who had these comforts. In 1841, when there were several hundred over-60s in Walden, there were still only the 30 places available, hence this fine provision made little impact on the problem of poverty among the elderly, and many old folk continued to live in dismal conditions. These may well have included those now living in the very run-down *old* almshouses in Almshouse Lane. According to Lord Braybrooke, the former almshouses, instead of being pulled down, were rented out for ninepence per week to poor widows, thereby 'affording an asylum to a class of person too frequently left without any habitation'. It seems odd, however, that they were paying rent for shabby dwellings without all the perks enjoyed free by the luckier aged poor nearby in the new Almshouses.[11]

These included jollifications on opening day. When the new accommodation was ready, there was a concert and the Almshouse inmates 'were removed to their new dwellings; and after being well supplied with wood and coals, were plentifully regaled with a good old English dinner, and were allowed to bring such of their relatives as had been accustomed to live with, or attend upon them, to partake of their much-enjoyed entertainment'. Nowhere in Essex offered an institution with such extensive benefits, it was claimed. It was not mentioned that these benefits derived from the generosity of earlier generations. In the normal fashion of the day, the inmates' party was followed by one given by the mayor and aldermen for local gentry, 'a sumptuous dinner' in the Almshouse hall, in honour of Ald. Thomas Smith who had been a zealous Master of the Almshouses since 1816. By all accounts the Almshouses were well run: the Charity Commissioner apparently declared of the charity that 'he never saw one conducted better'.[12]

Nevertheless the institution attracted controversy. Although over half the inmates were Dissenters, hence no religious discrimination was practised, nevertheless the trustee membership, complained John Player, exhibited no such balance. Instead the trustees practised 'the systematic exclusion of persons where opinions were not strictly accordant with those of the Corporation'. The original rules, he also pointed out, stated that one of the 'Brothers' who ran the Almshouses was supposed to be elected from among the inhabitants, which would of course include Dissenters. This drew forth an angry riposte in the Tory press. The question not addressed by Player or anyone else was discrimination on other grounds. The inmates were variously described as 'aged ratepayers who owing to misfortune or infirmity have been reduced to poverty' or 'decayed tradesmen or yeomen'. The 1851 census confirms that ex-labourers and their widows were rarely to be found there: farmers' widows of which there were nine, were the most common, while the others included a mixture of backgrounds: shoemaking, dressmaking, milling, butchery, plumbing, innkeeping, grocery and building trades.[13]

Discrimination

To obtain an Almshouse home, Charity School place, set of livery, apprenticeship for your son or any larger handout, was a question of knowing the right people. A clue as to how the system worked, slipped out during one political rumpus, when Tories accused Radical candidates of seeking votes by making 'repeated promises to the poorer burgesses of snug houses for life in the Almshouse'. By inference, this suggests that this was precisely how the Tory trustees had organised the task, for when demand outstripped supply, there must have been some means of deciding who was to receive charity. However, recipients were not, according to the Charity Commissioners, discriminated against on grounds that they had already been given parish relief. A random check suggests that many people did indeed receive both. Priority always went to the needy aged, disabled and sick, but it seems logical that, with limited resources, trustees would use local knowledge as to who the most deserving were amongst any others, although this cannot have been an exact science.[14]

There was nothing new in this. For many centuries attempts had been made to couple some kind of social control into charitable bequests of food, fuel or clothing: indeed the donors often enshrined this in the wording of their bequests. By the nineteenth century most of these prohibitions looked decidedly quaint and cannot have been adhered to. The Pennystone Charity, for example, reflected a mid-seventeenth century concern by excluding 'all persons in the least suspected to be witches or wizards'. Less dated was the reservation of the eighteenth century Sparrow's charity doles for honest, industrious, poor Walden inhabitants who were 'aged, overburthened with young children, or should accidentally meet with any other misfortune in the world, happening to them not by their own neglect'. This distinction between bad luck and bad behaviour was a vital one. Likewise Erswells' Charity beneficiaries must not be 'common swearers, drunkards or adulterers, nor live scandalously in their conversation'. More specifically, the Erswells' trustees, at least in token, went on asking at least until the 1850s specific questions about school and church/chapel attendance, cleanliness of house and children, as well as the normal questions about settlement entitlement. [Fig.9.2] Looking at a sample from 1852, the answers given by the poor indicated that all belonged to the parish, most of them having gained settlement by being born in Walden, some by hiring land or by marriage, service, apprenticeship or other occupational reason.[15]

Thus the system persisted as of old, that those who could at least simulate 'respectability' had the best chance of receiving limited handouts. For instance, some of the weekly bread doles were available only after the church service. The success of these efforts should not, perhaps, be taken too literally, for the poor were canny too and had learnt to manipulate for as long as the charities had existed. The worthy trustees knew this happened, and to some extent the whole process could be viewed as a game of bluff. But those deemed completely undeserving, and particularly young, able-bodied males, were largely left to fend for themselves. It is also worth noting that labourers were not the only ones receiving help: many of those receiving charity handouts were in trade, so presumably not much better off.

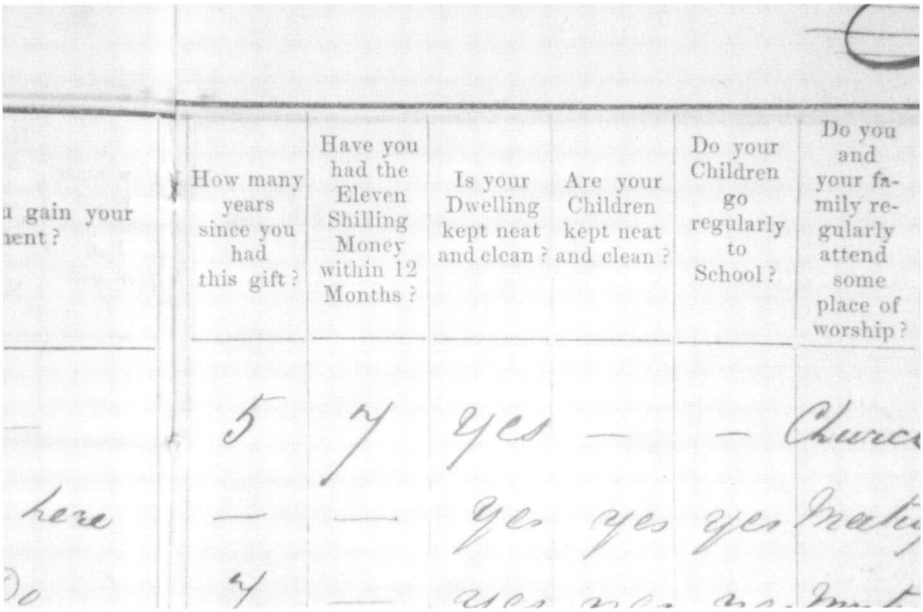

a gain your rent?	How many years since you had this gift?	Have you had the Eleven Shilling Money within 12 Months?	Is your Dwelling kept neat and clean?	Are your Children kept neat and clean?	Do your Children go regularly to School?	Do you and your family regularly attend some place of worship?
	5	7	yes	—	—	Church
here	—	—	yes	yes	yes	mati
Do	4	—	yes	no	no	Inn t

Fig.9.2 *A page from Erswells Charity records, illustrating the controls built into charity handouts, to encompass domestic cleanliness, parenting, school and church attendance.*

To some extent, the old Walden charities contain grey areas, such as lost benefactions and missing records, which are unlikely ever to be fully explained. One such was the curious custom of the 'privilege shoot', whereby successive Braybrookes allowed certain townsmen to shoot over some of their property, as a privilege in exchange for sporting rights to include old charity lands (see chapter 6). These had once been isolated fields belonging to the charities, Almshouses or Grammar School trustees but adjoining the Audley End estate and spoiling the shooting. Hence the gentleman's agreement, made by the first Lord Braybrooke, regarding shooting rights. Later on a rent was paid to the charities. In other cases pieces of land, including some charity lands, were exchanged for others, so that he could enclose the originals within his new park wall; he had, however, obtained an Act of Parliament for these transactions. The Charity Commissioner did not appear to condemn the custom, but a remark that most of the rent-charges in the Almshouse accounts 'had their origin in a practice which in principle is most objectionable', may be a veiled reference. But during one of the debates over the charities, Tories accused Radicals of promising the richer burgesses 'unlimited sport over the Charity Lands' if they were elected, inferring that this was Tory tradition too. Such indeed were the perks of office. One wonders what the poor thought of it, as they themselves were prosecuted for taking wild animals. Still it was in no man's interest to abolish the 'privilege' and it continued well into the twentieth century, with names of participants posted in the borough each year.[16]

The Charity Commission

The old charities, regulated by Tudor and Stuart statutes, were in need of an overhaul by the nineteenth century. Investigating commissioners were working from 1818, there was a wide-ranging commission in 1836, while the Charity Commission we still have today was appointed in 1853. The 1830s were a time of increasing central interference into local affairs and, following on from the investigations of the Poor Law and Municipal Commissioners, there came this third visitation, from the Charity Commissioners, in 1836. There had been complaints from other areas, which had been festering for some time, alleging maladministration of charities, undemocratic decision-making and preferential treatment. The Commissioners came to towns all over the land, ostensibly to check that the hotchpotch of thousands of charities were being run properly. In reality the enquiry was linked to the New Poor Law, whose commissioners had expressed concern that paupers were drawn to towns because of the existence of indiscriminate charity handouts which were 'often wasted, and often mischievous'. Walden was one of the places investigated, for the Liberals, now a force on the new Town Council, were stirring things up about the way the charities were run. Although the Charity Commissioner James Wishaw largely gave Walden an all-clear, his report highlighted some of the inner workings of the old town charities, but the correspondence he received, now preserved at the Public Record Office, reveals that the published report omitted many of the disputes. Putting these sources together, it is clear that there was discontent about the way some of the old charities were administered.[17]

The Commissioner expressed his 'entire satisfaction' about the management of the eighteenth century Falkland's charity, finding there was no discrimination regarding religion or parish relief, towards those old folk receiving the clothing or food tickets. Yet complaint had been made by one of the Radicals, William Thurgood, that the treasurer, Rev. Nicholas Bull was not a proper person to be a trustee because he had not submitted accounts for two years. Although the books were found to be in order, the vicar's name did not appear on the new body of trustees, leading the churchwarden Thomas Frye to beg Mr Wishaw to speak up for 'our highly valued and esteemed vicar' and put in writing that he was not guilty of 'this foul calumny in the eyes of the public'. Mr Wishaw, however, declined to interfere in the selection of trustees.[18]

This was not mentioned in the published Charity Commission report, nor was a dispute about the sixteenth century Lettice Martin Charity, which gave small sums to 'the most aged and deserving poor women residing at Audley End' and to 'all the most necessitous poor belonging to Walden, a preference being given to the aged and sick'. The treasurer, Mr Wilkes of Lofts Hall, Elmdon, described by his solicitor as a 'man of very retired habits,' was accused of failing to invest the charity's funds, thereby losing potential interest. Wilkes, who had 'very unwillingly' been treasurer for 25 years, only because no one else would do it, replied that the trustees were not businessmen and no one realised the money was supposed to be invested. He cleared up the matter by donating the sum, while complaining it was 'making him pay rather dearly for the trusteeship', having already paid £80 to the charity funds out of his own money when Searles' Bank went bankrupt in 1825.[19]

While these two disputes were left out of the published report, the Commissioner's intervention to reinstate the Grammar School was included (see chapter 11). He also tightened up the rules and co-ordinated the arrangements, so that people could not receive more than one money handout in the same period. A check on 127 people who received two charities in 1841, for instance, confirms that this was obeyed to the letter: no one got both. The privileges of the Audley End village residents were also curtailed a little by excluding them from one of the town charities: these cottagers, who already enjoyed the security of Lord Braybrooke's estate housing, schooling and other forms of patronage, were the most privileged in charity terms too, for every family received the '25 shillings money', the old people got a few shillings from the Lettice Martin charity, and the mothers loans from the Lying-in Charity: this was started by the Hon. Miss Neville in 1807 for the relief of poor women lying-in at their homes in Audley End, enabling them to borrow sheets and baby clothes made by schoolchildren. It could be that the town poor resented the extras which Audley End people received.[20]

Trustee Elections

The Charity Commissioner's investigation, like those of his poor law and municipal predecessors, added fuel to the flames of political controversy in the town. After the enquiry the Whig/Liberal Dissenters complained that people went on charitable trusts to push their own 'peculiar political and religious views', while the Tories mocked what they called the 'Jacobinical antics and unmanly attacks upon men so much their superiors in every point of view'. Many in office, they pointed out, 'had been trustees for 10, 20 or 30 years without having the slightest charge of misappropriation or exclusiveness ever before brought against them'. But much to their chagrin, the Liberals narrowly squeezed through a petition to the Lord Chancellor for a new body of 'more honourable men' as charity trustees. In the course of an acrimonious debate, the Tories in fury accused the opposition of 'malignant falsehood' and 'villainous tricks'. At the last minute, extra Tories were hauled in to defeat the motion, but the 'moderate Whig' Mayor John Player used his casting vote in favour of the petition. The Tories' supporters then organised a counter-petition putting forward their own list of 'highly respectable inhabitants' for the trustee positions, leading the Liberals to counter with a third petition containing yet another set of candidates.[21]

At the end of this astonishingly ferocious row, the issue had to go for consideration to the Master of the Almshouse. Although he too was a Tory, the new trusts did emerge with a more evenly balanced membership of nine Conservatives and six Liberals, albeit that five of them were labelled by the Tory press as 'Radicals of various degrees of destructiveness'. The other 'Reformers' failed to be elected and those who were did not obtain any of the influential officer positions which all went to staunch Conservatives. Two weeks later it was reported that the Radicals were 'still nursing their wounds from the charities debacle', but at least the charities had been reformed.[22]

The Saffron Walden charities, many of which had existed for centuries, held rather dull meetings and dealt largely with very modest handouts, thus became caught up with much else in the bitter sectarian divisions of the 1830s. The arguments seemed to have little to do with concern for the poor, whose welfare (although the New Poor Law was causing much distress) was not the issue. Status mattered more, and reforming the charity trustees was part of radicalism, for the issue of Dissenter rights was constantly brought to the fore. The Dissenters, however, had already made their mark on philanthropy. They knew that the collection of limited charitable bequests was of little real use as a palliative to the poor. A free weekly loaf was better than nothing; an occasional '20 shillings money' handout would be eagerly accepted for buying shoes and other necessities; and the more remote chance of obtaining an apprenticeship for your lad, a subsidised place at the Charity School, a retirement home in the Almshouse or a set of good quality new clothes was much to be desired. But it was not enough to act as a real sedative when the number of poor continued to grow. By the 1820s, increasing distress, linked as it was with threats of immorality, irreligion, illiteracy, crime and protest, dictated some fresh, more co-ordinated response, coupled with a moral crusade, to fulfil the vision of 'the well-ordered town'. There remained a worry about people taking advantage of the system, and one excellent way of gauging need was by personally visiting the poor in their own homes.

Visiting the Poor

To be poor in Saffron Walden in this period was to be the subject of much sociological enquiry. Every now and then any harassed resident of the mean streets might open their door to be confronted by a well-dressed gentleman or lady asking them to sign their marks on rate forms or petitions, attend a celebratory dinner, subscribe to a clothing club, have their homes lime-washed against cholera, their children vaccinated against smallpox, maybe offering extra fuel or blankets for the hard weather. They might be asked whether they went to church, owned a bible, sent their children to school. Religious tracts were handed out every week, and uplifting volumes could be borrowed.

John Player seems to have been particularly fond of knocking on doors, but this was also one pursuit where the worthy women of the parish could do their bit. Indeed the women of England had been specifically exhorted to visit the poor in their own homes, in order to prevent distress turning into unrest. What with filling in forms and answering questions, paying over their weekly pennies, receiving blankets and tracts, a greater contact grew up between the classes which, reproduced in countless towns all over the land, played its part in spreading knowledge about the lives of the poor. This more personalised relationship also made less likely any rebellion against the system which produced so much poverty in the first place. In addition, visitors could utilise the opportunity for moral uplift, 'connecting more closely the different classes of society, thereby producing a mutual interest and good feeling and a door is thus opened for moral and religious improvement of those in the humbler walks of life'. This was not fanciful, for these visits could be far more effective than evangelism at a remove, as the town missionary recorded: 'on visiting her today she told me that it was being *visited* at her own *house* that made her first begin to think about her soul's salvation'.[23]

Visiting was also a form of market research of its time and, as a result of such gathering of a body of evidence, there might emerge a new form of philanthropic outreach. For instance, in 1836 during the annual listing of those excused rates, householders were asked to sign their name or mark, providing a good indication of the progress of literacy among the poor. It may be no coincidence that a new school opened two years later (see chapter 11). Another outcome might be the formation of a new society to tackle perceived need. Such societies tended to follow the same broad pattern, with the setting up of a committee with officers, AGM and voting, a high status figurehead, the choice of secretary and treasurer from among the upper tier of elites, and a committee of hard-working members who gave their time and talents voluntarily. A list of worthy subscribers was an absolute essential, and it was no doubt something of a status symbol to be *seen* to be giving money away. Thus philanthropy was of benefit to the donor as well as the recipient. In this period, however, a sharper edge became more apparent, an insistence on participation by the recipient too. The Saffron Walden Benevolent Society was a prime example of such an approach.

The Benevolent Society

With Lady Braybrooke at the helm, the 'Saffron Walden Benevolent Society for visiting and relieving the aged, afflicted and distressed poor, of every denomination' was formed in 1828, a time of deepening poverty. The society did not appear out of nowhere, and indeed the Braybrooke ladies were noted for their kindness. The Hon. Miss Neville had been running since as long ago as 1807 a 'Lying-in charity'. Later on there were also some subscription charities run by the Braybrookes using donations from the rich. The Benevolent Society may well have been an extension of these ideas, necessitated by increasing distress.

The Benevolent Society had at most £90–£100 to spend each year on the poor, sometimes less, which made them careful with their resources. A list of those to be visited would be compiled, but mostly for the winter months, and visitors recommended whether they should stay on the list. Overwhelmed with need, within a few years the Society adopted a condition that, apart from the sick, relief would be given only to those who had lived in the town for a year. At first there was also a geographical limitation, excluding those living beyond Mount Pleasant (near London Road), Copthall Buildings (in Ashdon Road) and Lime Kiln (off Little Walden Road), even though some of the most destitute lived in the more remote parts of the parish. On the eve of the New Poor Law, although it strained the finances, they decided to distribute sheets to the poor in Little

Walden and Sewards End if they contributed a quarter of the cost. Likewise in 1848, outlying cottagers were able to buy 135 blankets at a price of 1s.6d each. Those who were helped were not given money — which after all could be spent down the beerhouse — but in the form of tickets for food such as meat, oatmeal, rice and flour; useful items like coals, wood, clothing or other necessities; and, for those 'afflicted with lingering illness', a stock of linen and blankets was collected. The distributions could be generous: 'The Benevolent Society distributed 100 pair of sheets and a quantity of blankets to the deserving poor of this place'.[24]

Whereas charity trustees were invariably male, the Benevolent Society was essentially staffed by well-to-do ladies and it was, like other forms of philanthropy, a chance to cross the sectarian divide. A body of 25 lady visitors, ten of whom were daughters of worthies and the others wives, all worked together: the names are familiar ones — Gibson, Robson, Humphreys, Dunn, Archer, Fiske, Emson — a mixture of Dissenter ladies and Anglican ladies, going forth in pairs once a week to knock on the doors of the poor. Their participation was vital, for the Benevolent Society was not concerned only with benevolence. Its parallel aim was to improve the physical and moral conditions in which the poor lived. The handouts were, in some sense, secondary to the reports of the visits which took place every week and which resulted in 'a considerable increase of cleanliness amongst the poor and in many instances a disposition gratefully to appreciate the benefits afforded'. A decade after their founding, they could report that, helped by the weekly inspection of dwellings, 'the general character of the poor is improving'. Whether recipients were permanently converted to greater domesticity is open to question. Deference could be only skin-deep, and acquiescence to the gift relationship does not constitute proof that people necessarily welcomed the value-laden raison d'être of the voluntary societies, but rather that they understood only too well the strategies required for survival.[25]

Reading between the lines of the annual reports, it seems that the poor were, in any case, not always overtly humble and grateful and could be 'prone to ingratitude', taking favours for granted, but after all, they had so little in the first place, reasoned the worthy ladies. And so they kept up the good work, feeling that only by entering 'abodes of vice and wretchedness' and inspecting wants, could they do the work properly. Accordingly they 'would discourage none from visiting… [although] it is far from being always of a cheering character… [but] might help them cultivate the right feelings'. It was probably, for many of these genteel ladies, the first time they had seen what real poverty was. Detailed descriptions did not appear in the minutes, but the squalor can be imagined through other testimony such as that of the town missionary (see chapter 12). Apart from any ulterior moralistic motives, it was very much to the credit of worthy ladies that they were willing to call upon this 'very suffering class of their fellow creatures'.[26]

For many the prime motivation was religious, an essential aspect of Christian activism. It was also social and part of their position in society, to be seen to be doing good. It is not easy to separate out the precise mixture of humanitarian, egotistic and economic feelings which motivated each person, be it for hobby, prestige, civic pride, social betterment, assuaging guilt, denominational activism, neighbourliness and so on. It seems to have been a channel for radicalism in the broader sense, and also helped to legitimise the middle-class way of life. There was little concept that such help could fundamentally alter the system which produced such deep poverty. It was a benevolence which relied on an unshakeable belief in the natural hierarchy of rich and poor as ordained by God, 'who, in the wise ordering of His providence, has been pleased to make so great a variety in the circumstances of the human family'. One should not entirely judge this from the perspective of today, for even such basic aid could be a lifeline, and without this religious impulse, even less would have been done. As the town missionary recorded on one occasion, when visiting a very poor family where the father had been ill and unemployed all winter: 'The woman told me today, if it had not been for one of the visiting ladies, they should almost starved, I think it is true'. On the other hand, the missionary also received frequent complaints about families seldom visited, because they lived in rural outposts.[27]

Nor is it satisfactory to gloss over the hypocrisy of their position, for it should have appalled the good ladies, seeing the reality of the situation, that only the slender resources of a voluntary body of spare-time do-gooders like themselves could stand between survival and destitution for some. The Benevolent Society always found far more needs than it could meet, and every year appealed for more subscribers. In 1829, particularly (a year of acute distress), the ladies reported 'demand found to be greater than means for supplying it'; and in 1834 (the year of the New Poor Law), they noted how 'severe illness meant they could not afford sustenance and some had suffered because of no help at this time'. In view of these constant appeals for more donations, it seems likely that the majority of people were not over-generous to any one cause (although one must take into account the large number of public subscriptions going on). Worries about mendicity are still with us today, when poverty is less visible, but at that time humanitarian and utilitarian concerns were even more in conflict: that the successful classes must of course help the destitute, but not do anything to encourage pauperism to the detriment of society at large, an ideological dilemma. Thus the ladies sought to make a 'distinction between sober and industrious and those of known disreputable character'. To prevent abuses, no one could be relieved without being visited first. Only the more deserving would receive help since, although people lived in difficult circumstances, they could not condone 'the painful discovery of deception or other disagreeable traits of character'.[28]

The question arises as to what use was made of the ladies' 'painful discovery'? The answer seems to be, as in the running of the allotments, a close co-operation with parish officers. Information about the parish allowances already given was first of all sought from the deputy overseer, R.D. Thurgood, because the society aims stressed that the 'assistance afforded by the society is not intended to supersede the relief provided by law, but to be the means of procuring additional comfort for the distressed'. There seems little doubt that this flow of information was two-way so that, as well as obtaining names of those on poor relief, the ladies also passed onto the overseers their observations about character and circumstances. The new society might thus have served a more sinister purpose: to be, under the guise of a kindly outlet of 'do-goodery' for genteel womenfolk, part of an overall scheme of control. Information gained from all this visiting and from Poor Law proceedings and the administration of justice must surely have been passed around quite freely, for frequently the same men, or their wives, sat on many different organisations. A magistrate with a wrong-doer before him would have access to a network of informants. In this sense, the good ladies were spies!

As an antidote to this somewhat cynical view, it has to be said that most of those helped were just ordinary, poor old and sick folk, and the society minutes record only three rejections: 'The cases of the Widow Barrett, John Augur and Woodley are dismissed, owing to bad character'. That those on the receiving end were playing into the hands of the philanthropic, by helping to legitimise an unfair society, cannot have been a concern to the hungry and cold. Most of the time the monthly reports were pleased to note 'an evident feeling of thankfulness has been raised for the acceptable addition to their comparatively small comforts'. For those who behaved well and were in genuine need, the Society could be a vital and valuable extra and, although always short of funds, over a period of 17 years they helped people on 2,587 occasions, many of them old and infirm or widows, with emergency action in cold weather. One year, 200 calico sheets were purchased to lend to smallpox victims. The numbers helped averaged about 140 a year over the period 1830–50, with peaks in years like 1834 when the old poor law was being phased out, 1837 when there was an influenza epidemic, and 1841 when fever was prevalent. As the restriction on able-bodied outdoor relief bit deeper in 1838, a town-wide survey was organised to discover the wants of the poor.[29]

It is apparent from the records of the Benevolent Society that this embodied a different approach from the old, fixed charity handouts. Not only were there visitors, female involvement, subscribers and some flexibility, but also crucially a feature much respected in nineteenth century society, an element of self-help and thrift: that the food, fuel, clothing or linen were not entirely free. Three-quarters of the cost was paid for by rich subscribers, but the recipients must pay the other quarter before they could receive relief. Thus the poor were contributing towards their own benefits. The poor must be encouraged to 'adopt habits of frugality', as it was specifically not to be a mendicity society, which could be abused by those who were not really in need. This anticipated the hardening of views apparent in the Poor Law report, that it was 'evil' simply to hand over cash or goods indiscriminately to the poor. This approach became a cornerstone of other initiatives in this period, targeted specifically at the deserving poor. Yet, paradoxically, these handouts continued to carry a large expectation of gratitude and deference. The next chapter will take a closer look at the way in which worthies used philanthropy as a lever to influence the poor towards an attitude of self-help, hard work and thrift, in other words as social control.[30]

Chapter 10

'Peerless Gems of Charity and Goodness'

Self-help Philanthropy

'… no small pride to the humble recipient when coming from one moving in so exalted a sphere, and who added a double lustre to his high station by the peerless gems of charity and goodness with which it is his study to adorn it.'[1]

The exalted, high-status, charitable person referred to here, shaking the hand of one of his humble townsfolk at the agricultural show, was of course the third Lord Braybrooke, a description which sums up much of the tone with which philanthropy was organised. But philanthropy in Saffron Walden in this period, as elsewhere, became a much more dynamic and adaptable resource, able to respond to changing circumstances, unlike the old charities whose outgoings were largely fixed by bequest. This chapter is an exploration of these changing attitudes, which had begun to emerge in the late eighteenth century, but which were most noticeable from the 1820s, and the role of such 'loaded' philanthropy in maintaining a well-ordered town. The dates of foundation of many new initiatives suggest a strong link with existing or potential crises, a rationale which 'Gentleman' John Player understood perfectly, insisting that it was no good seeking solutions when panic reigned: remedies must be put in place, in anticipation of problems, and then announced with full publicity, so that recipients appreciated what was being done on their behalf, and would not rebel later on. Player became a master of this activist approach.[2]

Thus it was no coincidence that it was in 1828–9, a period of deepening distress and unrest, that a benevolent society, a religious tracts society and then the allotments were set up; nor that within months of the 'Captain Swing' riots, a clothing bank began operating in the town; nor that a labourers' prize system appeared 'that very week' that the perfidy of various employees was uncovered at the 1833 malt-stealing trial (see chapters 8, 9 and 12). There was clearly also a direct connection between the proposal to abolish all outdoor able-bodied poor relief and the founding of two provident societies, both in 1838, for the Guardians had been specifically told to 'prepare all those who are likely to be affected by it for the change which must necessarily take place' (see chapter 5). It was also quite normal to exploit the public relations value of the various urban initiatives as potential adjuncts to the comforts of the poor even if, as in the case of the cattle market, the Museum and the Institution, such things were remote to their concerns. By the 1830s, these projects joined a wide array of societies in Walden requiring huge inputs of energy, time and resources, and for some formed a respectable outlet for radical activism.[3] [Table 10.1]

The impression is therefore one of a local system which could, when occasion demanded, react swiftly and pragmatically to any increase in distress with its attendant threat to the *status quo* and social order, trying when possible to be pro-active rather than reactive. Whether this exemplifies the deliberate use of philanthropy as social control, or just shows how kind people were, has been greatly debated among historians, but this chapter offers some local evidence which, at the very least, suggests mixed motives. The power to add small extras to the meagre resources of the lower classes was bound, given the attitudes of the time, to carry an accompanying moral agenda. This was increasingly an agenda based on the ideals of thrift, self-help, hard work and respectability, which would help build a finer layer among the poor, who would reject the immorality of the idle. The hierarchical society remained an assumption, but this more robust expectation seemed to be growing alongside the old emphasis on gratitude and deference, although these qualities continued to be appreciated by benefactors who naturally wanted some return for constantly dipping into their pockets. The stress on making the poor more independent suited the harsh new order, and offered some middle ground between the opposing impulses of a Malthusian hardness about pauperism and a Christian desire to help those in distress.[4]

The Clothing Bank

The Saffron Walden Clothing Bank was founded in the spring of 1831 in the immediate aftermath of the 'Captain Swing' riots, to meet an obvious need, but also to demonstrate how much the town was doing for its poor. Clothing institutions were one of a number of measures such as savings banks and lending libraries generally in favour in the early 1830s as a means of spreading 'habits of piety and self-command'. John Player was secretary of the Clothing Bank, which was indeed just that: it was not a society supplying clothes as the Bible Society supplied Bibles free of charge; it was a bank in which they saved 'for the purpose of supplying poor persons with comfortable woollen and other wearing apparel, blankets, sheets, etc. during the winter'.[5]

Volunteers, who included ladies, collected the pennies of the poor, 'readily and cheerfully brought to the Bank at all Seasons'. Rich subscribers nominated each poor person, who then had to save twopence a week, which was topped up with a further penny from the subscriber. At Christmas 11 shilling clothing tickets were issued and there was a big shopping spree (upping the profits of the town drapers), the members afterwards parading their new clothes for approval before their benefactors 'in order that they may see the money is not improperly expended, and that the articles purchased are suitable to their wants'. Distribution day was always a 'day of cheerful gladness throughout the town'

Date	Name	Aims included
1812	Bible Society Auxiliary	Distribute Bibles among poor.
1815–17	National School	Anglican education for poor children.
1818	Savings Bank	Induce habits of economy among poor.
1818	Missionary Society Auxiliary	Religious outreach.
Formed in 1819	Horticultural Society	Encourage good habits among labouring classes.
1826/40	Prosecution Associations	Prosecute offenders & offer rewards.
1828	Benevolent Society	Visit & relieve aged, afflicted & distressed poor.
1829	Religious Tracts Society	Distribute tracts to poor homes.
1829	Spade Husbandry Committee *?*	Provide allotments for the poor. *?*
1831	Clothing Bank	Encourage poor to adopt habits of frugality.
1831	British Schools Auxiliary	Non-denominational education for poor children.
1832	Literary & Scientific Institution	Disseminate useful knowledge.
1832	Mental Improvement Society	Ditto.
1832–5	Museum	Ditto.
1832	Natural History Society	Ditto.
Formed by 1833	Agricultural Society	Encourage industry, thrift, long service among poor.
1835	Reformers' Registration Club	Recruit members to Liberal Party.
1838	New Provident Society	Help the poor to save.
1838	Provident & Friendly Institution	Ditto.
1838	Union Book Society	Disseminate knowledge?
1840	Church Union Society	Anglican outreach.
?	Society for the Suppression of Vice	Improve morality among poor.
1840s?	Temperance Society	Campaign for temperance (hall built 1849).
1842	Town Mission	Visit poor, read Scriptures, send children to school.
1848	Nonconformist Society	Campaign for civil and religious liberty.

Table 10.1: some Saffron Walden voluntary initiatives, 1812–48

with tickets carried from house to house and goodly bundles deposited in cottages. A surviving ticket of 1832 shows how Sarah Mackey was nominated by Wyatt George Gibson, the shop to supply 'useful clothing, linen or flannel to the full value for eleven shillings… the articles provided are invariably to be taken, as soon as purchased, to the subscribers by whom the parties were nominated for their inspection and approval'. Others who took part in the early period included James Douce with seven children, William Augar with six, the widow of John Searle, and an elderly couple, Thomas Erswell and his wife, aged 89 and 80.[6]

Any failure to pay meant a twopenny fine for subscribers, or a loss of sponsorship for the poor, 'as one very material feature is to induce the poor and children in particular to provide for the future'. A few were rejected, but the Clothing Bank proved enormously popular with those who could afford it. Only eight months after starting, a sum of £130 was spent on 'useful cloth, linen and flannel for the working classes', all thanks to the donors, who had 'the gratification of knowing that their poorer neighbours very highly value this interesting institution'. Without the Clothing Bank, 'it is probable not a sixth part would have been so applied'. Success bred success, and more people joined. Two years later there were 431 members whose 41,800 pennies plus bonus amounted to a large expenditure on clothing, which 'very materially benefited a great many families'. In its first 13 years the organisation spent a total of almost £4,000 on its worthy objects.[7]

One should not detract from the achievement of the Clothing Bank, whose popularity spoke for itself, and indeed it remained in existence well into the twentieth century. But in its early days, instead of simply lauding this excellent institution in its own right, it was yet again hijacked as a vehicle of elite propaganda: 'The benefits derived by the lower classes of society, from the attention of those in more elevated situations, or affluent circumstances, are by no means of rare occurrence in this town'. Notwithstanding the two-thirds contribution of the poor themselves, the elite organisers received the greatest praise. John Player was largely credited with its efficiency, due to the 'ability which he brought to bear upon its formation, the zeal and perseverance with which he carried out all its details and to the spirit of cheerfulness and right feeling which he infused into all its operations'. On other occasions tribute was paid to the ladies of the town, whose 'indefatigable exertions had been the chief means of extending its benefits to so great a number of their poorer townsfolks'. And of course the Braybrookes were endlessly praised, for they were large contributors, always preferring to give well-publicised voluntary donations, received with gratitude, rather than be forced to pay compulsory, thankless poor rates.[8]

Other aspects niggle: did the poor mind parading before their benefactors in their new clothes? what of those who could not afford to subscribe? were people in the hamlets (often the poorest) excluded from the scheme? Large though the uptake, many were left out, for they lacked enough to live on, let alone save. Nor was there any place for the failures of society: just as fallen allotment-holders might lose not only their plot but their crops as well, so Clothing Bank depositors convicted of thefts or misdemeanours could, in theory, be expelled and forfeit all the money they had already deposited, although it is not clear whether this ever occurred. But if the most destitute and least respectable *were* left out, how could such schemes raise the general moral standard of the poor? Such fundamental questions were never addressed. The concern was that the poor should show gratitude, while simultaneously contributing to their own benefits, which large numbers of them embraced with enthusiasm, for the clothes were one-third free.

Savings Banks

In this same spirit of self-help the savings bank movement had been founded, although Essex as one of the poorer counties was not among the best areas for savers. Savings banks were part of a general growth of ideas such as life assurance, annuity schemes, building society and co-operative movements which all began to appear at the end of the eighteenth century. Contemporaries viewed the savings movement as part of the great march of progress: that vaccination would banish disease, fever hospitals eliminate infections, Bible societies eradicate ignorance and savings banks banish poverty. By 1829 there were at least 487 of these savings banks throughout the country, and almost half of the accounts were small amounts. The 15 savings banks in Essex showed a similar pattern, and also held the funds of 173 friendly societies and 56 charitable societies.[9]

The Saffron Walden Savings Bank began in 1817 (continuing until 1893), set up under 'the impulse of benevolence, locally to serve the less opulent part of the community, by inducing habits of economy', also holding funds for 41 charitable institutions over a wide area. At Saffron Walden Savings Bank, any deposit over a shilling was accepted, the money was perfectly safe, and interest was payable only to small savers. By 1829, the Walden Savings Bank was looking after a total of 965 accounts, but together they totalled only £33,000, because more than half of savers had less than £20 each and only a dozen had over £200. This, it was felt, proved that it was achieving its object of helping those with small savings, and had not been abused by the rich. The doors of its High Street office opened on Fridays for two hours, its secretary in 1848 being a local chemist, Jeptha Miller. A contemporary writer recommended the higher classes to become involved in the savings bank movement, in order to redeem the less reputable aspects of friendly societies.[10]

Friendly Societies

Among those making use of the Savings Bank repository were friendly societies from the town and rural area. By 1829, the 21 society deposits amounted to almost £2,272. In some form, the germ of this idea might be traced back to medieval times, when the Gild of Corpus Christi in Walden aimed 'to pay 8d. a week to the brethren in accidental poverty, sickness or other mishap and to pay for the churching of poor women, and the burial of poor strangers'. In the mid-eighteenth century there was a 35-strong 'brotherly and friendly society', the Rose Benefit Club, meeting at the *Rose & Crown,* but this seems to have been a more middle-class organisation. But the superior classes did not invent this idea for the lower classes: it was self-generated, for friendly societies were part of a long tradition of mutual aid among the poor. A more working-class affair perhaps was that on show in the Bishop Blaize woolcombers ceremony, likewise the Friendly Society of Shoemakers recorded in Walden in 1785. Friendly societies must have existed then in Walden, for some of those receiving thrift prizes in the 1830s had been saving since the 1790s: John Elborn's record went back to 1793 and James Brown to 1799. An entry in the parish meeting book of 1795 also confirms the existence of such clubs among the poor: 'mayor has been pleased to say that he will make application to the Clubb (*sic*) in order to have John Wisby taken in again'.[11]

Nationally, membership grew dramatically from 50,000 in 1793 to 704,000 in 1805, and Parliament went on constantly enquiring and legislating on this important subject, the key to reducing poor rates, it was thought. From 1829 friendly societies had to be registered and over an 80-year period to 1870 there were 19 Acts, 5 enquiries and a Royal Commission. There were many variations, including independent town societies, county societies with local branches and large national orders with affiliated local groups. These were the three types most prominent in Walden in this period, but there were also a great many informal, and largely unrecorded, clubs based in drinking establishments. Popularly known as 'box clubs' (because the contributions were put into a box), they were the source of much angst among elites, and a strong element of their motivation to provide alternatives. They were condemned at the turn of the century by the agricultural writer, Arthur Young and in Ipswich the famous social commentator, John Glyde wrote a detailed criticism in mid-century of these clubs: 'The working classes are too easily led by the flattering proposals of publicans, who for sinister purposes are desirous of having clubs meet at their houses'. Lord Braybrooke was particularly scathing about these efforts and often warned against their evils: 'too many of these clubs may be properly called publicans' clubs for the publicans reap the only benefit from them'. Both as JP and as Guardian he had often spoken to people who had lost all their benefits when such clubs broke up after people had paid into them for years.[12]

This was not the only reason for opposition. Club nights were popular social occasions and for those who attended, buying a little warmth and companionship today might be of rather more appeal than saving for tomorrow. There was a belief that such clubs impoverished men already poor, that money (which might have come out of ratepayers' pockets as poor relief) went to the bar, not the box. But many members of the working class also found the more disreputable pub clubs of no practical use, and for some time had tried to organise their own friendly societies, with regular meetings, strict regulations and carefully-kept accounts.

Self-help

By the early nineteenth century, Essex had 353 friendly societies, and by 1815 total membership had reached over 20,000. The numbers went on growing throughout the nineteenth century, with at least 21 in the Walden district by 1829, more than doubled by 1845, many of them in the local villages. This suggests that almost every village had one or more of these groups, which is very significant indeed, for it demonstrates a widespread willingness for collective organisation which not only promoted working class culture, but also offered some self-generated cushion of independence from parish relief. Most of these clubs, like those recorded at Arkesden, Radwinter and Ashdon, also met in village pubs. Some clubs, like the one in 1833 at the *White Horse* in Great Chesterford, lasted a century. Some villages, like Clavering, had more than one, in fact three, run by and for working men, tradesmen and junior tradesmen. Many of these societies catered largely for artisans with more regular income.[13]

In Saffron Walden, however, there was at least one attempt to form a club for poorer men, the New Union Society, formed in 1822 at the *White Horse*, a Gibson pub run by William Hodson. This specifically excluded tradesmen and anyone earning more than 12 shillings a week. The price of membership, however, seems rather high for labourers, every member paying five shillings for entrance, then two shillings per month, which included beer, reducing the temptation to spend extra. The payouts for this sacrifice had to be attractive and after one year's membership, sick or lame members could have eight shillings a week, provided their incapacity was not caused by quarrelling, drunkenness or whoring. For breaking a limb, there was a £2 extra. There was £5 for a funeral, and members could also claim £2.10s towards a wife's funeral. But payments to the box had to continue during sickness, thus reducing the benefit payments to six shillings. After nine months, the payment was cut by half.[14]

Meeting on the first Monday each month, with the addition of a midsummer dinner, the rules suggest a moral and pragmatic approach. The limitation to 51 members under 35 targeted a manageable nucleus of the younger, fitter types. Members guilty of theft or felony were excluded and, if anything, the regulations were, at least in theory, more rigorous than anything imposed on them by the superior classes. There were fines for failing to pay up or refusing to attend a member's funeral (unless the member had died of smallpox), and forfeits for divulging secrets and pretending. Fourpenny forfeits were imposed for swearing, fighting or smoking in the club room; one shilling for 'any member upbraiding a brother member on account of his age or calling'; and 2s.6d for getting drunk, gaming or 'behaving in any manner disorderly'. This was a society determined to be respectable![15]

A decade later the 'Friendly Society of Tradesmen' was formed at William Spicer's house (another Gibson pub), *The George Inn* in Hill Street, its title clearly embracing artisans rather than labourers. [Fig.10.1]The stewards were James Housden and Thomas Wilson, with William Turner as clerk, receiving a payment of five shillings on each feast day. This club, with the motto 'Blessed are the Peacemakers', had two special dinners each year, with forfeits for anyone

Fig.10.1 *Articles of agreement of the Friendly Society of Tradesmen which met at the George Inn from 1831.*

chewing tobacco or who was 'drunk, swares, curses, gives the lie, quarrels, challenges to fight, or games or demands silence or casts reflections, contradicts the majority in any one thing'. Most of these forfeits were only twopence, but there was a huge 2s.6d fine for anyone divulging secrets. Members in prison could rejoin when they came out, but were excluded if they joined any other box society, suggesting an element of rivalry between these clubs. Numbers were limited to 51 members under 30 who, when sick, received seven shillings a week for the first year, thereafter only four shillings, plus help with funerals. Anyone becoming lame away from home could obtain help, but curiously, only up to 43 miles distant.[16]

Other aspects suggest that Lord Braybrooke's fears about drinking may have been justified, for there was a ruling that each member, in addition to his four shillings quarterly in the box and five shillings entrance fee, must spend sixpence at meetings. There were even precise directions as to how the liquor was to be disposed of, with one member acting as butler dealing with four horns of liquor and making sure everyone was regularly topped up. Furthermore there was a provision that if any member died within the parish, then 25 shillings out of the box had to be spent at the club house, presumably on the wake refreshments, rather to the benefit of Mr Spicer. There were two feast days, on the Tuesdays after Lady Day and Michaelmas Day, traditional high points in the agricultural calendar, when Mr Spicer's profits could be expected to rise further.[17]

Other societies known to have existed included one at the *Cross Keys*, and another in 1837 at the *Duke of York*, its membership limited to just 40 under-45s, but it kept going until 1886: in exchange for an entrance fee of three shillings and a monthly payment, it offered sick pay, funeral expenses, and a payout at Christmas. Sadly, most records of most such clubs, a vital part of working class life, have disappeared. It cannot have been easy to keep them going, particularly in times of distress. Surely the destitute, who most needed help, could scarcely save much at all? Even a well-funded society was stretched by a bad harvest which put everyone in distress at once. There also seems to have been little long-term provision for widows, fatherless children or people too old to work, who would have to fall back on poor relief and charity handouts. The small societies always thus had great financial limitations, although since club benefits helped keep down poor rates, overseers might in deserving cases temporarily keep up 'club' payments until a man was fit again. An example was John Barker who worked as a maltster but hit hard times from 1829. The overseers gave outdoor relief for various needs, but also on at least six occasions between 1829–33 gave sums between three and ten shillings 'towards club'.[18]

Later on, a different kind of society appeared in Walden, one which, like the box clubs, was run democratically by the members themselves but, unlike them, enjoyed the backing of an umbrella organisation to which it was affiliated. These tended to flourish later in the century, as the smaller independent ones disappeared. There were several such affiliated societies in Walden: the Shepherds, the Foresters and the Oddfellows. The latter, meeting at *The Hoops*, seems to have been the earliest and some of its records survive in the town today, since it remains part of the Cambridge lodge. The earliest register of the Manchester Unity of Oddfellows, Saffron Walden branch, does not begin till mid-century, but the biography of its earliest recorded member is typical of many. Carpenter Charles Pettit of Castle Street was admitted on 30 April 1845, at the age of 20. In fact most members when they first joined were young men, wisely insuring themselves against the vagaries of fate from the beginning of their working lives. Married to Eliza in 1853, Charles paid 27s.9d per year contributions. If taken sick, he would then receive 14 shillings benefit for the first year, then 7 shillings for the rest of his life. (Both contributions and benefits could vary with other members.) His wife died in 1906 and Charles in 1909, after 64 years membership of the Oddfellows, during which time he had received over £100 in sick pay, concluding with a funeral benefit of £10.7s.[19]

Among 13 others who joined in the 1850s, all were in their twenties and all remained members until death in the early twentieth century. Significantly, all were small artisans. These early Walden Oddfellows included blacksmith Elias Pettit of Radwinter Road; bootmaker Josiah List of Gold Street; groom Laurence Dorne, carpenters Henry Wisken and George Harvey, cooper J.T. Hughes, upholsterer Charles Earnshaw and hairdresser L.W. Burningham, who was treasurer of the lodge for 51 years. Out of 58 men who joined from 1851–71, 21 were in the building trade, but less than half lived in Walden, suggesting that even when their work took them elsewhere, they went on paying contributions. There is much scope for further exploration of this little-known aspect of working-class life.[20]

In summary, the friendly society movement was clearly a multi-faceted one in Walden as elsewhere, its functions varying over time. Women do not seem to have taken much part in this period, but it was very much to the credit of poor men that they tried so hard to provide for their families, and surviving records suggest the existence of a grassroots movement towards self-help among working men, not only in town but also villages. It is revealing, perhaps, to look at the sentimental and dignified wording enshrined in their lists of aims and rules: 'that brotherly love would prevail... assisting each other in the hour when we most stand in need, that of sickness and dire distress... by mutual compact we may be enabled to support each other, and smooth the rugged road... by moral certainty insure a something in sickness, and convey us with decency to the grave...'. The emphasis here is all on helping each other, in teamwork and friendship, to get through hard times and avoid the shame of a pauper funeral. The early ones were financially insecure, but they must have collectively made a huge contribution to preventing poverty from turning to destitution in many cases. Clearly friendly societies simultaneously performed many functions: social gathering, mutual aid, moral support, working class fraternity. Together with prohibitions on absenteeism, lying, quarrelling, fraud, theft, swearing, fighting, smoking, chewing tobacco, bad manners, drunkenness, gaming and disorderly behaviour, they suggest either a fierce determination to be respectable citizens, or a strong desire to appear that way.[21]

So were these genuine expressions of working class respectability? Or were the strict rules framed with half a mind to convince pious worthies, who perhaps disapproved of the poor having fun, that all was above-board at their meetings? Could it be, given the culture of imbibing and the independently-minded nature of those who joined such societies, that something more subversive went on? After all, the Tolpuddle Martyrs were found guilty of forming a friendly society, indicating their association with sedition. This was certainly the impression in 1792 when the Saffron Walden Association for Suppressing Sedition threatened to confiscate the licences of any publicans who suffered 'seditious or treasonable clubs in their houses'. Interpretation is problematic, but surviving records in Walden do provide one of the rare bodies of evidence to counteract the illusion that the well-ordered town, if it became such, was entirely of elite construction. That thrift, self-help and philanthropy itself were *not* the exclusive invention of the well-off, is proved by the widespread incidence of these self-help societies. Many of the better-off did not appreciate the extent to which the poor already helped each other, for workhouses would have overflowed had kinship, neighbourliness and mutuality not flourished in working-class communities. Nor did they always understand the importance of social outlets as a psychological safety valve.[22]

The Town Hall Club

The friendly society movement, while seen as laudable, had financial limitations and could not, some felt, be left to its own devices, particularly with the New Poor Law threatening to withdraw able-bodied outdoor relief altogether. In 1838, the Walden Guardians were told to advise the poor to be prepared for the change (see chapter 4). Village clubs had disappointed people, said speakers at the agricultural show that year, and with bread prices likely to rise, the better-off must assist labourers to save. There was also the moral aspect: although the more respectable friendly societies seemed to echo middle-class concerns about thrift, self-help, independence and upright behaviour, yet their riotous feast days, link with public houses and opportunities for seditious talk generated suspicion. As always, John Player was at the forefront of a further exercise in philanthropic social control, the provision of a provident society to teach the poor to manage their money better and encourage the habit of saving. He went so far as to publish a pamphlet on the subject, written in the form of a dialogue in the vernacular, designed to be read by the more literate working classes. It was not too difficult for old-style paternalism to reassert itself, and thus it was that Walden acquired elite-generated and elite-run provident societies, the best documented of which is the 'Saffron Walden Provident & Friendly Institute', popularly known by its meeting place as the 'Town Hall Club', since one very important tenet of its existence was to dissociate the benefit society from its association with alcohol. This was formed in 1838, the same year when the Gibsons gave up running pubs and a period of increasing emphasis on temperance.[23]

The stewards of the friendly societies were requested to be present at the initial meeting at 12 o'clock on 31 January 1838, and the other names listed are all the familiar ones: Gibson, Player, Catlin, Emson, Fiske, Humphreys, Robson, Day, Burrows and a dozen other leading lights of the town. But something unusual was going on, for the discussion appears to have been set for exactly the same time that a similar meeting was taking place a few yards away in the *Rose & Crown*, only this other meeting was chaired by Lord Braybrooke. Braybrooke had been campaigning on behalf of the Chelmsford Provident Society for some time, and was now setting up a local branch in the town. The Town Hall meeting sent a deputation across the road to ascertain whether the two bodies might co-operate, but returned saying that no discussion could be admitted. The townsmen echoed a feeling that 'the town should have its own society independent of any other'. They decided to go ahead and print a handbill to call a meeting to start their own society. In some ways this is a curious episode, for what had happened to Player's friendship with Braybrooke? Having worked so closely on the allotment scheme, they were now for some reason in a situation of rivalry. This reflects the continuing strong belief in town autonomy, and there was clearly a lot of personal prestige attached to being at the forefront of these initiatives.[24]

However, both societies, set up 'to accelerate the condition of the poor man', flourished. The stewards of the friendly societies were invited to the inaugural meeting on 12 February 1838, when the Town Hall Club was proposed by Player 'for the relief and maintenance of members, their wives and children, in sickness and advanced age'. Workers as young as 15 could join, initially up to the age of 55, but in 1850 this was extended to the age of 65. There was supposed to be a minimum weekly payment of ninepence, which would entitle members to a sick payment of five shillings a week or, if they paid in more, up to a pound. If incurable, there was a half-pension for life. For the over-65s there was a pension of between 2s.6d and 7s.6d a week.[25]

185

Fig.10.2 *Certificate of membership for the Saffron Walden Provident & Friendly Institution.*

With a banker (W.G. Gibson) as treasurer and an attorney (C.T. Master) as secretary, the finances and administration were in sound hands, its respectability fully established with the appointment of medical consultants, a committee of town and village worthies, and a collection of distinguished trustees, mostly with 'Hon.', 'Sir' or 'Esq.' appendages, although not of course including Braybrooke. Well-wishers also gave subscriptions and donations to launch the institution. Some of the working-class members joined the committee, an unusual occurrence in the annals of Walden philanthropy at this period, suggesting that a new spirit was abroad. They included an ironmonger Isaac Buck, journeyman currier George Barrett, gardener John Siggs, three other town and four village men. Upon joining, applicants had a medical examination certifying they had no disorders, family background of insanity, consumption 'or any other disorder which is likely to incapacitate him for his work'. This obviously excluded those who were likely to be irregular contributors. The Town Hall Club did well, by 1846 having backing from 60 honorary members, and contributions from 273 ordinary members from the town and a wide rural area. Some of the sums paid in seem pathetically tiny: in 1839 Richard Reynolds and Frederick Forkin were putting in only about sixpence or sevenpence a month. Outgoings varied but years of particular distress, like the mid-40s, are reflected by dramatic increases in sick pay.[26] [Fig.10.2]

A remarkably complete register from 1839 lists members with their occupation, parish, sickness insurance amounts, payments, pensions and the dates of joining and leaving, the latter only at their death. The register demonstrates that much of the strength of the Town Hall Club actually emanated from outside the town. In 1845–6, for instance, almost two-thirds of the 263 members came from surrounding villages, although still the largest numbers were in Walden. No individual village had a large membership, the biggest branches being at Ashdon, Radwinter, the Bumpsteads, Hinxton and Clavering, with a scattering in Hadstock, Arkesden, Castle Camps, Sampford, Linton, Littlebury and Bartlow. But Clavering membership increased tenfold in the 1850s. The experience in Clavering may have been typical of many, showing how an enthusiastic agent, in this case the British School master, William Savill, could promote the idea: 'Several clubs were established at the beerhouses demoralising to the members and of little avail in sickness. In 1853, I undertook the management of a branch of the Saffron Walden Benefit Society and we soon numbered 150 members, the beer house clubs were closed'. Savill himself joined as a young man in 1848, qualified for a five shilling pension on retirement and a £5 funeral payment on his death in 1898 (see chapter 11).[27]

Although the destitute could not take part, there was a strong lower class element among membership. Of the 114 men and women who joined up to 1850, half were labourers, while most of the others were small-income trades, including some farmers and schoolteachers. In town, the social composition differed. Among 25 Walden members registered joining pre-1850, over a third were labourers, the remainder being servants, gardeners, grooms, maltsters, and one each of waiter, currier, shopkeeper, clerk, printer, butcher and a solitary woman dressmaker. Once joined, the majority went on paying their dues until old age or death. Among labourers who joined as young men and remained their whole lives were William Cornell jnr who joined age 18 in 1845 and was still on the books as an old man in 1888; James Erswell, a Castle Street agricultural labourer who joined at the age of 19 and remained a member till his death 38 years later; and 17-year-old Alfred Eldred whose 65-year membership ended only with his death in 1910. Among others whose membership could be traced over a long period were Obadiah Barker, a gardener of Castle Street who joined aged 22 in 1844, moved to Great Chesterford and brought up his family there, but continued his payments to the Town Hall Club until 1882, then moved to Cambridge and died in 1902, receiving a £3 funeral grant. There were many other examples.

The Town Hall Club was clearly an important institution, carefully designed and continuing in existence for at least a century. Its graduated contributions meant that workers could pay in according to their means (and hence receive more sick pay), there were no age barriers, and even rudimentary old age pensions. But it seems surprising that so few Walden people joined, for in town there were only 69 members out of 1030 households, which suggests that the elite-generated Town Hall Club, although more secure than the pub clubs, was not as popular as they were, lacking the conviviality and democracy of their own self-generated organisations. The Town Hall base was clearly aimed at separating saving from alcoholic temptation. In addition, there were of course many of the poorer poor who could not afford subscriptions. Among those who did save, there were still problems, seldom recorded. But the Saffron Walden town missionary, who called regularly on the homes of the poor, found that provident societies were no panacea, as the wife of a sick man told him: 'his wife complained of only having five shillings per week from his benefit society, it was owing she said to a certain number of men being ill that they had so little. I asked if no one gave them anything besides that, she said no one'. If this was true, this suggests the rather disturbing possibility that those who had private benefit might actually be refused public relief: the Poor Law Commission had hoped that fear of the workhouse would force people to save for themselves. Another problem was that when the society member died, his widow and children lost the advantage of a lifetime of saving, as the town missionary reported of a family where the father died three weeks earlier: 'he had in his lifetime, received a pension of seven shillings per week, so now they are left to the world'.[28]

The Provident Society

The other factor which reduced membership of the Town Hall Club was the existence of a strong rival. In 1838, on the same night, Saffron Walden acquired not just one, but two new provident organisations, part of a flurry of activity which occurred during that year. In some parts of Essex, this and other forms of philanthropic outreach linked with fears of the upsurge in Chartism and, although there is no overt evidence in Walden, some such thought may well have been in Braybrooke's mindset as he set up a local branch of the Essex Provident Society. The parent society had been set up over 20 years earlier specifically to discourage people from joining beerhouse clubs. In 1838 it had a total of 1,962 members in Essex and a stock of £10,403.[29]

It was common for landowners to subscribe themselves to such county societies in order to increase the financial base as a further attraction for labourers to join. With his county interests, Lord Braybrooke was an enthusiastic supporter and regarded such societies as 'the best things that were ever instituted'. There already existed an Audley End Benefit Institute, to which he contributed. Although he did not go so far as to make provident society membership a condition of getting work on his farms, he would attempt to persuade a new man by paying his entry money 'even though he had worked with him only a week and advised other farmers to do so'. The paying of this entry money gave the Provident Society an advantage, and this may be why by the mid-forties, the society had a membership considerably higher than that of the Town Hall Club or any one friendly society. Starting with 40 members in 1838, the numbers trebled within two years. By 1843, Braybrooke reported 277 members, with a capital of £20,000. In the years that arson peaked in the Essex countryside, the widespread distress dramatically increased membership to 401, but also made unprecedented calls on the society funds, which were able to bear the strain: 'last year which was the most sickly one which has been known here for a considerable period, its members were relieved to the amount of £254 without reckoning the payments for births and burials'.[30]

Braybrooke invariably plugged the Essex Provident Society during his annual speeches at the Saffron Walden Agricultural Show, where thrift prizes were an early innovation. At first he was able to highlight people who had been saving for decades, men like William Saggers, aged 59 in 1842, who had been saving for 28 years. But there were few of these long-term savers, and the prize then had to go to labourers or servants who had managed a year or less: William Stock, however, who was only 18, had been saving for four years. Braybrooke was particularly keen to encourage young men to establish good thrifty habits, and winners included a number in their teens. But he also exhorted family men to take advantage of the society: 'the best thing a man could do for himself and family', he told the audience at the 1843 agricultural show, 'was to contribute to a benefit club. The best society of the kind in Essex he believed to be the Chelmsford Provident Society'.[31]

The Agricultural Show

For Lord Braybrooke the Agricultural Society's annual show was the ideal vehicle for propaganda of his hobby-horses before thousands of his neighbours. The Essex Agricultural Society had been founded in 1793 by landowners to encourage progressive farming, but also to promote hard work and deference among labourers by offering prizes for temperance, long service and refraining from claiming poor relief. There were therefore early precedents for Lord Braybrooke's Walden initiative, although it was claimed to be 'the parent of all similar ones in Essex'. Apart from its serious agrarian purpose, it was designed to improve relationships between classes and this was said to have succeeded: 'many landlords had become more fond of farming, so more attached to the soil, getting to know their neighbours and helping them more'. Although Jabez Gibson contributed largely before his death, Braybrooke took a lot of the credit, particularly as he built the Agricultural Hall (now part of the Museum) for its meetings. Indeed Braybrooke said it was the most gratifying achievement of his life. He liked to look ahead a century and muse that 'in the next generation we have candidates coming forward with a pedigree of good conduct, going through three generations and saying 'my father gained a prize at the Saffron Walden meeting in the middle of the late century, and my grandfather at the beginning'. [32]

There were three aspects of the society which impinged on the lives of the poor. The one which touched the most people was the show day itself, an exciting event 'like a holiday in Walden', attracting in its first years crowds of about 6,000, from a wide area, and greatly enjoyed by all. When else was it acceptable for the poor to gather in large numbers? As well as 'all the beauty, wealth and intelligence' of the neighbourhood, there was a glittering guest list including, on one occasion, the Lord Mayor of London, on another the American Ambassador, while it was particularly popular with worthy ladies who on one occasion were likened to 'benignant stars, shining upon and cheering their humbler neighbours around them'. The subsequent newspaper report occupied an entire seven-column broadsheet page in the Tory press. For no one was it more exciting than for Lady Braybrooke, who kept a scrapbook of these press reports, but failed to cut out an article in a London paper which, in 1836, claimed the Agricultural Society had dissolved through disagreements. A breakaway group of north-west Essex farmers was formed as a result.[33]

Prizes for the Few

The second feature, the central part of the day, was the handing over of prizes to the most skilful and most deserving labourers. This idea had begun in 1828 with the Horticultural Society, mostly a middle-class affair, but also for 'the comfort of the poor', including cottagers' prizes for well-grown apples, pears, potatoes, cucumbers, onions, cabbages, celery, turnips, flowers and so forth. Established in 1819, they organised regular horticultural exhibitions in the grounds of Audley End House and these developed into annual shows. Later they also offered prizes to allotment holders, and this idea merged seamlessly into the wider agrarian and moralistic aims of the Agricultural Society. It was not felt sufficient merely to reward the ability to plough a straight furrow or to raise the most lambs, but an edge must be added to the proceedings. The organisers did not pretend otherwise: 'the object of this Society is to revive those habits of industry, and to discourage that feeling which relies on indiscriminate parochial support, and which has nearly extinguished those industrious habits'.[34]

This was very much along the same lines being enshrined that very year in the New Poor Law, an association confirmed by the Vicar of Elmdon, Rev. Robert Fiske who said that the societies 'will have no unimportant bearing in connexion with the new poor law, and that it will be shown that the ancient spirit of self respect and independence of our peasantry is not extinct'. Thus, thrifty saving habits, long service with one master and, most laudably, refraining from claiming poor relief were put on a par with the old farming skills. It was of course considerably cheaper to offer the carrot of a prize for good workmanship among the few, than to raise agricultural wages across the board, but the ruse worked, and very soon the prizes were said to be raising up the labourers. Over the first ten years, out of 242 prizes awarded at Walden, just under half of the total prize-money went to poor men, as opposed to the purely agricultural skills. Right from the start, those who never or seldom claimed poor relief, in spite of great poverty, were the heroes of the prize-giving and a speaker was cheered when he said 'the bringing up of a large family without parochial relief… is not only highly creditable to the man, but is beneficial to us, and to the next generation, because it tends to produce good members of society'.[35]

For the top man in the low-relief stakes, there was a prize of far higher status and monetary value than the rewards for farming skills: it was a fine clock, valued at five or six pounds (equivalent to several months' wages), an example of which is still preserved in Saffron Walden Museum. [Fig.10.3] Recipients of this valuable object included James Marshall who received prizes on five occasions over a seven-year period, having worked for the same Roos farming family since he was a child, and brought up eight children without relief. His father William Marshall was also rewarded for bringing up a dozen children without poor relief, and came to the meeting in the coat he had worn for 44 years, saying 'although on one occasion he lost his harvest and had sickness in his family, he would not ask for parish relief; he said that he had friends because he was industrious and careful'. Indeed the Clarks from Roos Farm obtained prizes for these faithful family retainers on at least nine occasions in ten years. The message of all this was clear: 'It is not

Fig.10.3 *One of the clocks given to the person who had claimed least parish relief, awarded each year at the Saffron Walden Agricultural Show.*

only by what we give to our poorer neighbours that we do the greatest good; but by bringing forward the examples of industry and virtue which we see exemplified in so many cases before you (cheers)'.[36]

A closer scrutiny of the prize-winners suggests that the virtuous examples represented a very tiny and unrepresentative proportion of the poor. Prizes in the non-agricultural sections came only by personal recommendation and, looking at the Walden recipients over a ten-year period, there were only a dozen or so families making such nominations, principally Lord Braybrooke and his tenants, the Clarks at Roos Farm and the Smiths at Audley End, and occasionally the Spicers and the Gibsons. Obviously the largest employers were likely to have the most candidates, but even so it seems excessive that Braybrooke recommended almost a third of the Walden prizewinners. Braybrooke made particularly good use of the show to publicly reward his own staff, among whom were some who had spent their whole working lives at Audley End, such as 57-year-old William Spicer who had worked there for 41 years. Others included Thomas Stacey who got five shillings for his 27 years, Joseph Webb who twice received prizes, first for 26 years and for 35 years' service as shepherd; and John Symonds who was Braybrooke's manservant for 19 years. Others who probably emanated from Braybrooke's patronage included, in the low-relief category, 55-year-old Charles Kidd who had a disabled wife but had brought up six children. There were Kidds working as woodwards for Lord Braybrooke. There was Henry Lindsell who had fathered 19 children and widow Lucy Reed who had placed the most daughters in respectable service. Thus the show was something of a platform for Audley End estate personnel.[37]

Although it was an agricultural society, the vast majority of farmers were not mentioned in this period as recommending labourers, the exceptions being Braybrooke's tenants at Audley End and Westley farms, who put forward Robert Miller for 52 years, Edward Francis for 31 years, Joseph Watson, aged 69 for 44 years and Edward Webb for 33 years' service. But then most farmers employed by the day, so long service was a nonsense. Nor did many town businesses take part in the non-agricultural categories. Bootmaker Charles Baron nominated his two long-serving employees, Thomas Clark, and 67-year-old Charles Lacey for their virtual half-century of service each, but the biggest firms, the Wards and Hockleys, builders who between them one year employed 130 workers, never seem to have recommended anyone in this period. Thus the prize system, at least in its non-agricultural offshoots, was often just a reward for those who already had considerable job security. While it was very laudable for Samuel Harris to save with a benefit society for 32 years, and never seek a farthing from the parish, it was made easier because, by the time he received the coveted clock first prize, he had been an old retainer with the Gibsons for 41 years. Likewise Wyatt George Gibson's manservant William Burgess and maidservant Frances Mason, who were publicly rewarded for their 32 and 23 years' service.[38]

Even among the lucky few, the prize-giving in time became a hollow exercise, for there were only a certain number who could qualify: hence the lack of any prizes in some categories some years, and the appearance of the same men who had received prizes for the same achievements before. Out of the non-agricultural sector prizes given out to Walden men between 1833 and 1844, almost a third received awards more than once; most of these repeats were in the 'least benefit' section where more than half of the prizes in this period went to people who had them before. The inference is that these long-term positions were few, and it was very difficult for others, even when regularly employed most of the time, to totally manage without relief through their whole lifetime, for poverty was a life cycle occurrence. To some extent this was recognised and minor lapses allowed for: 61-year-old James Hodson, Braybrooke's man who got a second prize in 1838, had received some poor relief 30 years earlier and on one occasion since, to help him bring up the nine of his 16 children who survived. Did these life histories always tell the whole truth? In 1836, the clock prize for least relief went to William Barker, a long-term employee of Braybrooke, said to have been married for 50 years. If this is William 'Rags' Barker (who died falling from a haystack two years later), there was something odd going on, for he had received poor relief on several occasions, had once been indicted for theft (though found not guilty) and had been married 45 years, not 50. One wonders how many other stories were a little ornamented.[39]

Elderly retainers like Barker would apparently enjoy being paraded to applause, in his case showing off 'with great apparent pride and satisfaction' the coat in which he had been wed 50 years earlier. This was at the show dinner, for which tickets cost the equivalent of almost a labourer's weekly wage. The prizewinners were all special men and deserved their moment of fame, but the whole spectacle leaves an uncomfortable feeling that their rustic pride and goodness were being exploited for other purposes. Contrary to the grand claims made, in no way could this prize-system in this form offer anything for casual labourers who at this time did not qualify even as candidates, let alone winners. While the prizes raised up a few, the vast majority were left out, for elites always passed over the fact that long service, regular saving and avoiding poor relief were possible only for those in regular work.

Moral Uplift

The third aspect of the show and the subsequent dinner was a vital reinforcement of the moral import of the prizes, the making of somewhat patronising and exaggerated speeches, invariably greeted by cheers. Putting together these speeches, year by year, offers insights into what was going on not only at the agricultural show but also in all the other forms of philanthropic outreach in the town. It was, for instance, important not just to do good but to be *seen* doing good: 'from scenes like these', glowed one gentleman, 'it might be expected that the lower orders would become more respectable, and rise in the scale of society'. They might then become like old-fashioned 'splendid specimens of the peasantry', or young couples 'after many years of frugality and industry, basking in the sunshine of their cottage, and greeting their children as they return from scenes like this, loaded with prizes'. There were frequent references to the money which members were giving away as prizes, trying to raise labourers in the social scale but 'we do expect that they will deserve the kindness shown to them'. The attempt to use the prize system as social control was made manifest, for education in moral habits was essential for 'then the Walden Society will not have laboured in vain, and whatever expense we may have incurred will be repaid by the advantages of increased good order and mutual good will amongst all classes of society'.[40]

After the euphoria of the early years, Lord Braybrooke's speeches acquired a new edge during the 'hungry forties' when, to demonstrate solicitude, the president would publicly exhort the farmers present to offer more jobs, such as digging ditches, during the hard winters to come. Speeches along these lines were noticeably more common in the years of distress when the countryside of Essex was lit up by incendiary fires. On one occasion he referred directly to the link between unemployment and crime: 'The poor man when once out of work became discontented, his family were in misery, and he was soon tempted to do that by which he would lose the good character he had for many years maintained'.[41]

In summary, given the background of extreme poverty in the surrounding countryside, the prizegiving must be seen for what it was: an elaborate charade, a staged drama in which Braybrooke took the lead, worthies the supporting roles, with walk-on parts for family retainers, and an audience of the local populace enjoying a rare day out. Historians have noted the significance of agricultural shows as vehicles for 'rural-idyll propaganda of the well-ordered and hierarchical society'; as philanthropic extravaganzas to offset the threat of Chartism which aimed to stoke the fires of democracy in working-mens' hearts; and they would seem to fit the bill perfectly for the process of so-called 'hegemonic incorporation' which sought to bring the poorer classes on board the ways of the worthies. The whole exercise, with its one-sided prize system, pseudo-paternalistic atmosphere and obsequious back-patting could be seen at this time as an investment towards the well-ordered town. The shows continued for many years, and in later times lost much of this moralising baggage.[42]

'Bearing their Misfortunes Quietly'

At one of these shows during the 'hungry forties', Braybrooke congratulated the people on the great decrease of crime, 'showing that the poor had the good sense to bear their misfortunes quietly'. This last phrase has a resonance which perhaps Lord Braybrooke did not intend, but rather sums up the meaning of the entire panoply of glittering prizes for the few and crumbs or less for the undeserving, which typified the lottery of being poor in those difficult times. Of course the hindsight of history can mislead. Looked at from another angle, it could be said that the more recalcitrant poor were to some extent able, through a reluctance to 'bear their misfortunes quietly', to influence the course of events, albeit indirectly and inadvertently; that, far from elites providing remedies to problems, it was actually the poor calling the tune, dictating some response. Perhaps philanthropy was not a simple one-way process of social control, but a much more subtle interplay. If one were able to penetrate the day-to-day handling of charity, it would no doubt reveal much manipulation by at least some of the poor, and plenty of middle-class people who did not take part in what the likes of Player and Braybrooke saw as something of a crusade, to splice philanthropy with a moral agenda. Even a seasoned campaigner like Player reflected at times an ambivalence about charity which is still with us today, anxious to help people but worried about fraud and ingratitude.

But he and his ilk were surely wrong to draw such rigid divisions between dependence and independence, for in a mixed economy of welfare, to claim relief, to accept charity, to pay club monies and to run an allotment might all be necessary at different stages in the cycle of life. Taken altogether philanthropy was an essential part of this network of strategies, and relationships would have been far worse without it. The poor would then surely have rebelled long before the fairly peaceable 'revolt of the field' in 1872. But the existence of that movement of protest, albeit in the next generation, demonstrated the limitations of philanthropy when deep distress set in for a prolonged period.

Moreover, the fact that the poor accepted the tangible gifts on offer does not constitute proof that they deferred to elite values in these matters. It is evident that poor people would not turn down handouts when in need; that they would agree, in order to clothe their children, to subscribe eightpence to a worthy fourpence to make a shilling; that many genuinely enjoyed gardening their allotments; that they saw the sense in saving for old age, sickness and funerals; that they would be proud to receive a prize for sticking to the same secure job for decades. But this demonstrates only an understanding of all the strategies needed to survive in an unfair society. Inculcated values of gratitude, self-help and respectability could not be handed out like blankets, bread or even a much-desired plot of land. In fact the 'moral crusade' could only be ultimately effective when coupled with the self-respect which came with regular employment, a living wage, better housing, public health and basic education.[43]

At this time, however, it looked as though the extensive and ingenious system of targeted, controlled philanthropy to simultaneously relieve distress, prevent unrest and bring the deserving poor into the fold was the way forward, and much energy was expended on its construction. Not least of all these efforts were the parallel themes of a great deal of nineteenth century philanthropy: the education of the poor and religious outreach, the themes of our final two chapters.

Chapter 11

'A Suitable Degree of Education'
Schooling for the Poor

'I have reason to believe that no backwardness exists here on the subject of education; but on the contrary both the members of the establishment and those who
dissent from it, under whatever denomination are equally impressed with the
duty and the expediency of giving the poor a suitable degree of education. I say
a suitable degree, for anything beyond that would be mischievous.'[1]

Thus spake Vicesimus Knox Esquire, well-known Essex barrister, Deputy Recorder of Saffron Walden, at the conclusion of the largest criminal trial ever held
in the town, that of the malt-stealing 'gang' in 1833 (see chapter 6). The link
between crime and illiteracy generally would draw confirmatory nods from
attendant luminaries but there was also this contradictory, yet deep-seated belief, that too much educating of the poor would be 'mischievous' for, destined
as they were to take their allotted place in the hierarchical society, what was the
point of their learning too much? If poor people became too clever, they might
get ideas above their station and begin to question the *status quo*; if they learned
to read too well, they might look into seditious pamphlets, as was feared in the
1790s when Tom Paine's revolutionary *Rights of Man* was banned from the town
bookshops (see chapter 7). Nevertheless they needed educating out of the mo-
rass, a moral training away from a life of crime. This was the paradox which lay
at the heart of educational endeavour. Such ignorant, myopic elitist pronouncements, with their arrogant denial of wider educational opportunity, were only
very slowly becoming outdated, but one small victory had just occurred in 1833:
in that very year, as Knox made his blinkered statement, the Government finally
conceded the need for some limited central intervention, and for the first time
offered small grants towards the building of new schools.[2]

His claim that Saffron Walden was not backward in education does not necessarily indicate that it had gone very far forward, and it comes as no surprise
to learn that, just as in the nineteenth century, early educational endeavour in
Walden was equally subject to the expediency of politics and the whims of philanthropy. Fifteenth century schooling initiatives were restricted by the Abbot
of Walden, and even the dedication of Dame Jane Bradbury in founding the
Grammar School a century later did not much advance the education of the
poor. The Charity School, founded in 1715, was a step in the right direction, but
not until the late eighteenth/early nineteenth centuries did this vital subject

become a focus of attention. This chapter is an examination of why and how this expansion of elementary schooling for the poor took place, the difficulties encountered, and the place of education in contributing to the well-ordered town of elite desire.[3]

Schooling for the Poor

The scale of need in elementary education in Saffron Walden can be estimated from an 1825 survey which found 427 poor children aged 6–12, the age group mostly targeted. By the 1830s, there was an expanding collection of 'educational' establishments in Saffron Walden. The 1832 trade directory lists about a dozen day, boarding and other establishments, but there were several others not mentioned such as the Audley End school, the Gold Street school of industry, Abbey Lane infants and various dames' schools. Schools were of varying quality. Some were clearly not intended for the unwashed, judging by their titles as academies or seminaries. Of such degree must have been the Church Street establishment run by Miss Isabella Spicer, whose pupils had their own reserved seats in the south aisle of the nearby parish church. A much more workaday institution was the 'school of industry', known since the seventeenth century and more common in north-west Essex than other parts of the county. 'Industry' normally implied girls learning needlework, working long hours and selling the garments to finance the school. A small school of industry for girls operated in Gold Street, Saffron Walden, later converted into the girls' British School. No details are available, but it may have been similar to the one at Hadstock, its produce of quilts, caps, neckerchiefs, bonnets and tippets eagerly bought. Such exploitation of young lives was commonplace, but the dressmaking skills acquired would be of use in future life.[4]

Much more common were dames' schools, humble establishments with limited educational aims, often run by poor widows or men to eke out their income. In Saffron Walden, at least one was run by an illiterate woman, Betsy Bird in Castle Street. There were in 1807, at least 153 of these dames' schools in Essex. Parents paid a few pence a week for child-minding, needlework, maybe a little reading. In town there were at least five such places in 1824, but elites did not approve of these establishments, judging by a survey the following year which described 71 children rather disparagingly as 'supposed to be educated or in private school'. Over a decade later, about 150 children were still attending dames' schools, and in the 1840s, 'the state of the children in some of the small schools in Town' remained a worry. In spite of criticism, dames' schools were a remarkably persistent feature of the education scene, presumably because these simple establishments were nearer to the culture of the poor, offering what poor parents wanted — cheap childminding and some basics — without the attendant moral high-ground of elite-driven educational endeavour.[5]

The Charity School

Free schooling was available for a small minority, but it was very limited in scope and came with a moral agenda. The earliest public provision for the children of the poor, the Saffron Walden Charity School, exemplified the attempt to blend schooling with social control. In the early eighteenth century, as the old Tudor educational foundations declined, there had arisen a fashion to bequeath charity schools for the poor, amounting in time over the whole country to about a thousand in number, most of which later fell into decline. Early in the nineteenth century, small charity schools were recorded locally at Heydon, Stansted and Walden, but there were only about 37 in the whole of Essex. Charity schools had originally been linked with the work of the Society for the Propagation of Christian Knowledge (SPCK), which association of education with religion, although it initially enabled public schools to get going, was ultimately to prove a bar to educational progress until the late nineteenth century.[6]

The religious emphasis was paramount in the Saffron Walden Charity School, founded during the heyday of such foundations in 1715 by charitable individuals and boosted with £500 left in the will of Thomas Penning and other bequests. A church-going requirement was seen as one of the civilising influences, and once a year the children were given new clothes, worth up to 20 shillings, to wear on Sundays as they 'decently go together immediately before the beginning of divine service to the parish church of Saffron Walden and being then and there seated shall reverently attend such service'. A Charity School children's gallery, originally at the west end of the church, was later repositioned in the north aisle. The Charity School committee, 'the most substantial honest and reputable inhabitants', met in the church court room to allot places to 'children of the poor inhabitants of such town unable otherwise to give their children learning to be cloathed taught and instructed to read write sew and knitt'. Places were for children aged 7–14, for the respectable offspring of 'poor persons of honest lives and conversations', and those who misbehaved lost their membership.

The numbers, judging from a list of 1838, appeared fairly evenly divided between labourers' and tradesmens' children. How they chose the lucky few, out of so many who could have benefited from a place, is not otherwise spelt out, but no doubt the trustees, taken from the ranks of the usual Anglican worthies,

Fig.11.1 *The Charity School uniform of blue breeches, coat and cap made the pupils quite distinctive even after they were absorbed into the National School.*

198

formed their own ideas about the most deserving. From 16 places in the early eighteenth century, numbers rose and, before its pupils were absorbed into the new National School, there were 13 boys and 13 girls, still chosen annually by the minister and principal parishioners. The pupils, who stayed for only three years, would be quite distinctive walking to church in their uniform, which for boys consisted of blue breeches, coats and caps paid for, as were the bibles and writing materials, from the charitable income. [Fig.11.1] However, the charity schools were limited in their aspirations, for their principal aim was purely 'to condition the children for their work in life'. A few were helped towards literacy, but it was never going to achieve much for the mass of poor children.[7]

Sunday Schools

The more common method of educating the poor was through Sunday schools, an often under-rated aspect of early education, and the true beginning of improved mass schooling. Although the first recognisable Sunday schools began only in 1780, they spread within a few years to Hadstock and possibly other villages near Walden. In the early years of the century, there were already hundreds of children attending Sunday schools at the Independent and Baptist chapels and the Parish Church. The 1851 Religious Census demonstrated the popularity of these free institutions, with over 600 Sunday scholars, half of them at the Parish Church, an impressive number, albeit offered only basic literacy.[8]

They were popular because they cost nothing, did not interfere with children's weekday earning power — essential to the economic survival of many poor families — and offered occasional treats: one Christmas 'the Church Sunday school children, 90 in number, received each a plum cake and half a pint of beer'; in summer there might be feasts, concerts and sports, as when 380 Anglican day and Sunday school children were entertained in the Agricultural Hall and on Castle Field: 'its good effects are already apparent', commented the press, 'a great number of poor children who scarcely ever attended a place of worship, or receive any kind of instruction, have now the benefit of both: and the anxiety of the parents to send them to, and the readiness of the children to attend at, church must be a source of gratification to those active and zealous individuals who devote their time to this benevolent object'.[9]

Studies in neighbouring counties show that by mid-century the Anglicans, with a presence in every parish, attracted most Sunday scholars, almost two-thirds of the total in both Cambridgeshire and Suffolk. With two-thirds of children attending generally, the Sunday school movement reflects energies devoted to a cause which was seen as *the* key to the future of a church or chapel. Recent research suggests that this denominational control was more important than general social control. The wider significance of Sunday schools was that they helped to make the better-off classes aware of the very low level of even basic literacy among the poor, and out of this grew some early experiments in day schooling which eventually diminished the importance of the Sunday arrangements.[10]

Day Schools

All these early piecemeal provisions were just tinkering at the edges. The real turning point was the foundation in 1808 of the Royal Lancasterian Society (later changed to the British & Foreign School Society, hence the term 'British School'), which drew its support from Quakers, Congregationalists and Baptists but also Evangelical Anglicans. Its inspiration was Joseph Lancaster, a Quaker from a humble background, who did not advocate a particular doctrine, but based teaching on the Bible and general Christian principles. Lancaster was a remarkable man who adapted ideas suggested earlier by Andrew Bell, evolving his own monitorial system, a utilitarian, factory-like method of organising schooling. In the British Schools, hundreds of children could be taught with just one master, thereby saving money, through issuing information to older children trained as monitors. The monitors learnt small nuggets of information then issued them to huddles of younger scholars, who then had to repeat, memorise and trot them out next day. Thus the lessons proceeded and, since learning was rewarded, it was cheap and efficient mass schooling. It sounds crude now but, with a competent teacher, it was a huge improvement on the standards of the day and became the key element in spreading discipline and basic literacy to hitherto untamed youngsters, and in the wider spread of elementary education for the poor, not only in Britain but in over 50 other countries.[11]

Lancaster's success was disturbing to the Church of England, who were aroused from their lethargy by a redoubtable lady, Mrs Sarah Trimmer, who pointed out that Anglicans were in danger of losing control of education. Frightened that through this non-denominational brand of schooling, Nonconformists would use schools to recruit the poor to their chapels, they responded. The result was the National Society for Promoting the Education of the Poor in the Principles of the Established Church (hence the term 'National School'), whose title expressed their aims, with strong emphasis on doctrine, liturgy, Catechism and the Book of Common Prayer. The Bible was used to teach reading, with a subordinate place given to writing and arithmetic, plus needlework for girls.

Although founded slightly later, in 1811, the 'National' schools movement spread more widely than the 'British' one, because they were well placed to receive the support of the Anglican elite who ran towns at that time and, in the countryside, a ready-made network of newly-energised parish clergy. While the non-residence and indifference of the latter had once been a hindrance, they now realised that education was the answer to 'correcting that disposition to idleness, and in many cases, intemperance, which of late years, appears to have gained ground amongst the labouring poor: of reviving that spirit of industry by which alone parish rates can be relieved'. They also tried, among their very poor and underprivileged scholars, to spread cleanliness next to godliness. The Essex county branch was set up only one year after the National Society, its ambitious plan to establish National schools in every town and village. Within a few years, there were 7,000 children, and this trebled within a decade. Unfortunately, like the old charity schools, the National Schools unashamedly pursued fairly minimal educational aims 'not to educate overmuch' but to train children as 'diligent, useful and religious members of society in the class to which they belong'. And so once again religion, so essential as catalyst and inspiration for outreach, also proved to be a straitjacket resisting change for generations.[12]

Saffron Walden National Schools

Both National and British schools developed in Walden, but their foundation dates were over 20 years apart. The first reference to paying a master was in 1815 and by October 1817 there was a new school built by subscription in Little Church Street (now Museum Street). In 1818, however, the boys were recorded as being taught in the repaired Grammar School room in Castle Street, so presumably the new building was only for girls. The National School made use of what turned out to be an illegal diversion of endowment given for the redundant Grammar School. The running of the old Grammar School had been entrusted to Saffron Walden Corporation but, like many another Elizabethan foundation, it was under-funded, declined and was closed altogether in 1802, the Corporation maintaining that they could not find a suitable master. They made occasional unsuccessful attempts to remedy this, but the demise of the Grammar School proved a neat solution to the problem of funding the National School, supplying a repaired building and master's salary, an arrangement which the Walden Corporation, accustomed to manipulating at will local resources to suit local needs, got away with for 20 years.[13]

Over the years disquiet built over this, both among Dissenters and churchmen. The vicar's son, who had unsuccessfully applied for the mastership, protested about the 'misapplication of the funds of the Grammar School in this town'; John Player felt it absurd that the children of the poor were better provided for than those of 'the middling ranges'; and other Dissenters that, since it was run for Anglicans, their children 'were altogether virtually excluded from any benefit to be derived from it in its altered form'. Although Lord Braybrooke defended the Corporation, saying they had kept scrupulous accounts, the regulatory mood of the 1830s spelt the end of such *ad hoc* arrangements. When the Charity Commission investigated the Walden charities in 1836, they severely censured it as 'a flagrant breach of trust' and the job of reviving the old Grammar School was put into the hands of new trustees. Nevertheless, it was a further eight years before it actually re-opened, greatly helped by a generous bequest of £1000. Its first pupils were very largely from middle-class families.[14]

The National School also benefited from the funds of the old Charity School, as happened in many other places, taking over their endowed scholars. This arrangement continued for over half a century. As well as this, the National School received the scholars' weekly pence, which had to be paid even in absence, and the proceeds of an annual service where the children intoned dour hymns with words like: 'Clouds o'er our infant years are spread/Our minds are dark, our hearts are dead'. After the sermon, given by some distinguished cleric, the collection could raise £50 or more. Nevertheless, expenditure still often exceeded income. A happier occasion, for the children at least — 'happy little innocents' as they were called — was an invitation by the second Lord Braybrooke, watched by many ladies and gentlemen from Walden: 'Amongst the numerous festivities at this season perhaps there has been nothing more gratifying to a benevolent mind than one given by Lord Braybrooke in his great hall at Audley End on New Year's Day to the National Schools in his neighbourhood, where his Lordship entertained near 300 poor children with roast beef, plum pudding, etc.'.[15]

As well as helping the town schools, the Braybrookes also provided a school to serve Audley End, Littlebury and Wendens where many of their employees and tenants lived. This began as a Sunday school with over 80 children, enlarging by 1818 to a day school. It is not clear whether this or the town one was the 'new working school for girls on Dr Bell's plan', the personal concern of the Braybrooke daughters, who received much praise for their kindness. It was not uncommon for high-class ladies to patronise schools in this way. With others helping, this was virtually a school of industry, with payments of fourpence for every shift sewn, sixpence per shirt and a shilling for a pair of stockings.[16]

Meanwhile, within a year or so of opening, the boys' and girls' National Schools in town were claiming a total of 320 pupils, although this declined by the 1820s. Staffing was one of numerous problems: masters at the boys' school became ill, left because of low salary, or were dismissed for neglect or incompetence. Apart from the innovation of 'Smart's Boys' Singing Club' every Tuesday evening, education was basic but, with only one master controlling so many children, the immaturity of the monitors caused problems at first: Ed Stokes lost a month's pay after 'receiving a toy from a boy as a bribe', John Hodson and Henry Gatward were detected 'in talk most indelicate and obscene and that in Church' and William Mole stole malt from Messrs Gibsons. Discipline could be harsh, however: William Smith was confined without food in a coal hole, James Wright flogged for stealing a watch, Charles Byatt expelled for very base and insubordinate conduct. But things settled down and the National Schools quickly became part of the town fabric, attracting a fairly even mix of artisans' and labourers' children. In 1840 the committee re-affirmed their commitment to the monitorial method, but it was becoming increasingly frowned upon by government inspectors who said the monitors were too young and 'positively detrimental to the moral character' of schools in Essex, where they found only about 20% of the children could read with ease, and said the answer was more and better teachers.[17]

The National School always struggled financially, their troubles exacerbated when they lost the use of Grammar School money. Relationships with the vicar, Rev. Nicholas Bull were not always good: there was an incident when he accused the National School committee of insubordination after they refused to accept new hymn-books offered. When the old vicar died, a ruling that the committee was in future to be chosen solely by the vicar was resisted by the new incumbent, Rev. Ralph Clutton who felt that this would upset the school's supporters: 'it is owing entirely to the interest felt by the subscribers that the school exists at all', he wrote. Their support was all the more essential to afford a new building, for they had lost the old Grammar School premises in 1844 and, with girls occupying Little Church Street, the boys had to carry on somehow in a temporary home. At a time of deep distress, this was no time for the National School to go under, for there was an upsurge of educational outreach at this time, not unconnected with the spread of arson through Essex (see chapter seven). Clergymen were convinced 'that the frightful indifference in many cases of incendiarism evinced by villagers… is in no small degree to be attributed to the vices which are inseparable from ignorance, and stimulated by want'.[18]

But the vicar was probably less worried about this than about denominational competition, for Dissenter-run schools had been growing in popularity since the early 1830s, and many clergy cited this in their requests for grants for new schools. By the mid-forties the new Boys' British School in East Street had three times as many pupils as the Boys' National School (see below). Clutton was also concerned about the need for a National Infants' School, using the Little Church Street building, to offset the influence of the Dissenters' infants' school which, in his view, took children away but did not give them correct religious teaching. It is not altogether clear which of the two infant schools, with 85 children, was the one criticised by an inspector in 1850: 'the mistress is a little deaf; the noise in the school is intolerable and the order very defective. They are nice children. The brick floor is miserably cold, and I am certain must be very injurious to the health of the children'.[19]

Wisely, Clutton retained Braybrooke's goodwill, and when in 1845 a purpose-built National School went up in Castle Street, the third lord loaned the extra money not available through grants from the National School Society and 50 or so subscribers, and himself subscribed an annual sum. New government grants made available from 1844 also helped. The new vicar's efforts paid off for, soon after opening, the National School numbers began to climb again, perhaps at the expense of their rivals. But it had been the pressure from the Dissenters which forced the pace of change, long before a British School actually appeared. They had led the way with both Sunday and infant schools and campaigned to have the Grammar School revived, thereby depriving the National School of both funding and premises. They also seem to have been the driving force behind a Bible Society survey of Saffron Walden in 1825, which revealed deficiencies in schooling for the poor.[20]

Surveys of Education

This survey, aimed at increasing the number of children attending school and the number of Bibles in poor homes, was ostensibly ecumenical, but the Dissenters led the way. As usual, it was the indefatigable John Player who had revitalised the Bible Society Auxiliary and, at a time when evangelical outreach was coming to the fore, instigated this survey through its members. Therefore, in November 1825 the worthy gentlemen of Saffron Walden, Anglican and Dissenter, went forth in pairs together into the mean streets of Saffron Walden and knocked boldly on 328 doors, about a third of all the families in town asking about the ages of 1,120 children, whether they did or might attend Sunday or day school, the willingness to pay school pence and the possession of Bibles. The poor were used to these visitations, which we would find so intrusive, and their contribution to this piece of market research provided a useful snapshot of education in the town and hamlets, where school participation varied dramatically, as it did street to street.[21]

The team of 16 visitors included several with a particular interest in education, including the Baptist minister, Rev. Josiah Wilkinson who ran a Dissenters' day school, and encouraged Sunday schools; Thomas Archer Catlin who was a strong supporter of the National School; and Quaker Wyatt George Gibson, later to become principal benefactor of the British School: his brothers Jabez and Francis and other leading lights of the town also helped. This was a considerable task. Those who drew the short straw with Castle Street, for instance, visited 76 families with 333 children between them. Even before the results were published, it was said 'many children have entered the schools since the investigation', suggesting it had proved a useful exercise. Player collated the results, and resisted pressure from Catlin to leak the results before the meeting at which they were to be discussed. Catlin, later praised for his 'unwearied diligence in the promotion of the best interests of the National schools', may well have been anxious about a survey which might show his school in a poor light, but Player assured him that, in spite of the opposing views on the committee, he would act impartially, not push his own politics.[22]

Lacking a key, the results of the survey are hard to interpret, but suggest that most families said that they attended church or chapel, and about four-fifths of the over-sixes were claimed to be in day or Sunday school, whether Church, Dissenter or private. The questionnaire also placed great emphasis on the possession and readability of Bibles. They found, not surprisingly, that Dissenter families were more likely to own Bibles. In the area which included the Independent chapel, every family had a Bible, whereas in the Castle Street area, although adjacent to the parish church, a quarter of the poor families did not possess this essential volume. This last aspect was the easiest to remedy, and the Bible Auxiliary, of which Wilkinson was secretary, moved quickly in response. The survey took place in November 1825, was reported in December and by early January Player was asked by the Bible Auxiliary to superintend the distribution of 64 Bibles and Testaments according to the list.[23]

The big divide underlined by this and by various county surveys was a geographical one: whereas no part of town claimed more than 4% of children 'without education', out in the hamlets (where families seem to have been larger) between 18–20% were in this lamentable state. In 1839, 17 years after this survey, it was still reported that Sewards End had 'neither Sunday nor Daily School of any kind', something of an indictment of Walden philanthropy. These rural outposts of Walden parish, were probably more typical of other poverty-stricken villages of north-west Essex, which could be decades behind town progress. A survey of 1818 had showed that some villages were luckier: Chesterford and Heydon had the benefit of bequests for education, while Debden and Newport possessed paternalistic resident gentry: Lady Vincent at Debden paid for the education of 90 children; the Smith family from Shortgrove Hall supported many

Newport children requiring schooling. Meanwhile, some villages had no school at all, Wimbish catered only for girls, and the Chrishalls were served only by Sunday schools and dames' schools. Thus there was a hugely disparate provision across the county, although heroic efforts were going on to remedy it. Schools needed sufficient population, funding, energetic clergy, interested landowners, good teachers, premises, none of them easy to generate in this area of scattered labouring communities, where the chance to learn to read depended very much on where you lived. It could be that the first time a poor country child had much education at all was if he spent some time in the workhouse.[24]

The Workhouse School

For the comparatively small numbers in the old High Street town workhouse, under the old poor law, education had been minimal, or at any rate is seldom mentioned in records. In 1806, it was decided by parish officers meeting in the workhouse that Thomas Andrews should 'learn the children of this House as before', which suggests that some sort of instruction was in place at least by the early nineteenth century. A decade on, when five children of one poor family were taken into the workhouse, the question of schooling was raised, and it was about this time that the older workhouse children were sent to the new National School, although the following year the sum of two shillings was paid to instruct children in the workhouse. In 1833 there was a record of a schoolmistress being given a trial, but most of the time children were looked on as being fit to contribute to the work of the institution.[25]

The New Poor Law had an effect on schooling. In Clavering, where the vicar had been running his school in the village workhouse, he lost the accommodation without compensation. When the Ashdon overseers sought to continue helping five children with '2 guineas which have hitherto been paid out of the poor rates towards educating poor children', the Saffron Walden Guardians refused (although the vestry went on helping poor children until 1847 when Lord Maynard gave Ashdon a school). Such children, gathered from the 24 constituent parishes, might in future find themselves living in the big impersonal Union workhouse in town. In 1837, at a time when there were 28 children in the Union House, the Guardians were told to provide schooling but it was difficult to find teachers, as the salary was low, the hours long and the work unrewarding. Their duties were wider than in ordinary schools: not only to teach reading, writing and arithmetic to the boys, and reading, spelling, needlework and knitting to the girls, but also to live in and superintend their conduct, and help the master and mistress in their duties. Here they had a role in the welfare of the children as well as their education. But it was a role which was of lowly status and not clearly defined, as became clear at Walden when teachers tried to improve the children's conditions and came into conflict with the other workhouse officers, who perhaps saw the children purely as young paupers.[26]

The first workhouse schoolmaster, William Hasler was reprimanded for 'improper interference' in the duties of the medical officer, allowed a further trial but eventually given notice because he was said to be inefficient. The second one stayed only a few months, to be followed in 1840 by Robert Hodder who, with his wife as schoolmistress, had previous experience in a Devon workhouse. By now the joint salary had risen to £65, presumably in an attempt to obtain a better quality couple. Very soon the Hodders applied to introduce the Bell monitorial system into the workhouse school, a sign that they were trying, in spite of the discouraging environment, to give the children the standard educational offerings of the time. But within a few weeks Hodder was suffering from the violent temper of matron, Ann Burkmyre, and he complained that she was under-feeding the pauper children. The complaints built up to a scenario reminiscent of Charles Dickens' *Oliver Twist*. Mrs Burkmyre, described as 'a noisy violent woman over whom the unfortunate husband has little or no control', had been keeping some of the children's rations for her 30 fowls. The Guardians ignored Hodder's complaint, so he secretly kept aside samples of meals for them to weigh, which they duly did and found he was right: the puddings were five ounces underweight, the bread an ounce short, the cheese half an ounce short and the meat only half the quantity it should have been. The potatoes were just served by guesswork and Hodder had seen matron throw bread and pounds of potatoes out to her fowls.

For how long had this dreadful woman, who had been there since the workhouse opened six years before, been under-feeding the already distressed workhouse children? This was not revealed. She was merely reprimanded for not weighing the rations properly, and for punishing a child with undue severity. The incident was disguised in the official records, which simply minute 'no evidence of fraud in the stores', the matron being told off for keeping too many chickens and a rule that food was to be weighed in front of paupers in future. Sadly for the workhouse children, Robert Hodder, the hero of the hour, received no credit and suffered the fate of most 'whistle-blowers', being forced to leave his job with a somewhat muted testimonial, as the salary was greatly reduced. In fact there was a complete change of personnel, with the master, mistress and nurse also leaving, so there was a fresh start and a public scandal was avoided.[27]

Workhouse children were not necessarily all orphans. In the Walden area it was not uncommon for a few children to be plucked out of a pauper family and put in the workhouse, in preference to giving relief to the whole family. Here they were treated like little adults. A recent study in Hertfordshire also found that most workhouse children were with a single mother. Others might be illegitimate, orphaned, deserted or with parents widowed, infirm, jailed or transported. Towards mid-century, among the 74 children in Walden Union, two-thirds were there because there was no one else to look after them: 'it is evident that for these children the school alone can supply the place of paternal or maternal care', commented the school inspector. Reports on the workhouse schools varied from bad to fair: 'teachers took great pains to improve the children, as did chaplain. The boys as usual are much better writers and arithmeticians than the girls, but the latter are certainly making progress', was the comment in 1847. Yet the following year, after Mr and Mrs Mark had left with a good testimonial to take a proper teaching post in Littlebury, the inspector remarked on the deficiencies they left behind for their successors, the Caslakes. He recommended — and the Guardians agreed — various changes to form two separate mixed schools, divided by an open door, and improvements in literacy and materials.[28]

The curriculum began to expand into husbandry, geography and history but it was difficult to improve standards with a shifting population of pupils, numbers fluctuating in 1850, for instance, between 36 in summer and 90 in winter. Henry Caslake worked from 6 a.m. till 8 p.m. but earned only £35 a year with accommodation, and after all his efforts, there was a poor report: 'this school has never risen above mediocrity and has varied considerably in proficiency at my different visits. There appears to be a want of systematic attention.' Throughout the rest of the school's existence, the jobs of workhouse schoolmaster and schoolmistress remained of low status: between 1864–79, there was a succession of eight couples in the posts, most staying only between one and four years. Fortunately, in 1880 the workhouse school closed and the children transferred to the Boys' National and Sewards End schools.[29]

As well as schooling, there was some training for the young. In the early days, some workhouse lads asked to be apprenticed to the Navy, but generally the authorities at first objected to apprenticeships, in case it encouraged poor parents to rely on this type of help. But it became clear that the vicious circle of pauperism could not be broken unless young people acquired skills. Around mid-century, the school inspector commented that, while girls were well trained, there was not enough for the boys to do 'in consequence of which they continually return to the workhouse. Five of them were at my first visit actually in the able bodied men's ward, having thus relapsed into pauperism'. The Guardians agreed that the oldest boys could be 'selected to attend to the horses and gigs of the Guardians on Board days', while others would learn agricultural skills on a piece of hired land nearby. Later on the girls were taught to milk cows and learn dairy skills. According to a later report, 21 boys and 23 girls were able to find jobs after such training. Thus some effort was made to help pauper children to make their way in the world.[30]

A Workhouse Boy

And it was not impossible. Little is known of ex-workhouse children, but William Savill seems to be one who made it. Mocked for having been born in a workhouse, he is said to have retorted: 'You would never have had the sense to get out of it!' The son of an agricultural labourer, he grew up to be a remarkable self-made man. [Fig.11.2] A 13-year-old lad of this name was recorded among 98 inmates at the Union in 1841. At some stage he also participated in the improved education available at Saffron Walden British School in East Street, and next appeared in the records, aged 18, having moved six miles away to revive the failing British school in Clavering, a village where church and chapel were set against each other and education was the battleground. Very soon the normally critical government inspectors were describing the idealistic teacher as 'a very respectable and deserving young man… who is keeping a boys' school with

Fig.11.2 *William Savill, Clavering British School master, who spent part of his life in Walden workhouse, but also attended the Boys' British School.*

rising success'. Attempts to re-open the girls' school failed, but the boys' school in 'this remote and rather disheartening neighbourhood' went on expanding, with young Savill keeping his 55 boys 'in excellent order and under a course of steady progress, which exhibits itself in the general demeanour of the children as well as in their classes'. In the vacations he attended the Borough Road training school in London, passed the examinations, and ran the Clavering school for 15 years, surviving numerous difficulties.[31]

Perhaps through his own background, Savill always felt empathy with 'the poor and ignorant population of this remote village' and devoted himself to their welfare: he ran night schools, brought in a doctor, encouraged them to save in benefit societies, found work for the unemployed by personally visiting Yorkshire industries and helped dozens of others to emigrate to Australia and America. By the time the school was forced through the 'payment-by-results' grant system to close in 1862, William had managed to combine farming with teaching, and became a full-time farmer, employing many young people. In the 1880s, concerned at the illiteracy and ignorance of religion among his young farmworkers, he gave land and money for a new British School, which he continued to support for the rest of his life. Finally, William Savill retired to Saffron Walden, died greatly respected and was buried in the town cemetery, a short distance from his beginnings. Today Savill Close, on the site of Clavering's old school, is named after this former workhouse boy.[32]

Pressure for Change

William Savill's great fortune was to be the right age to attend the Saffron Walden British School, which was not established until 1838, 30 years after the parent society had begun. In a market town so strong on Dissent and therefore fertile ground for educational outreach, it is relevant to speculate as to why it took so long. On the face of it, the town was already well provided with various establishments, including the Rev. Josiah Wilkinson's academy for Dissenters' children in Baileys Lane, which was overtly religious and moralistic in its objects. The relatively novel innovation of infants' education was also catered for, and the Abbey Lane Infants' School even had a specialist trained teacher, Elizabeth Rumsey. But disapproval of private schools with no specific Christian connection, remained, a concern made manifest when some 'friends to education' from the town and vicinity wrote to Parliament denouncing the idea of factory schools. Similarly, the stepping-up in 1839 of school grant and inspection systems, also initially aroused deep suspicion through its centralized and secular associations. This was true of Anglicans too who heard a visiting bishop giving 'a very good sermon in which he plainly set forth the evils of the new system of education by the government plans or in other words the evil arising from having no settled and true faith to follow no creed, and the great probability of its making the children infidels altogether'.[33]

Political pressures were also a strong influence on the expansion of education at this time. Chartism was reviving in the late 1830s and, although not identifiable in Saffron Walden, its potential influence on the poor was elsewhere counter-acted by increased activism in churches, chapels, charities and schools. The Liberal press promoted popular education as the remedy for Chartism: 'Tranquillity may have formerly been insured by the absence of enlightenment; but that season is past'. Worries about law and order in these years were also reflected in the Police Act of 1839, for many, like Vicesimus Knox, perceived the link between irreligion/illiteracy and crime: 'The best mode of preventing the necessity and cost of police establishments, penitentiaries and transportation is the preventive system of a general plan of national education', it was thought.[34]

With population in Walden expanding, and various surveys confirming slow progress among growing numbers of poor children, there was ample evidence that the National Schools were not meeting all the needs. The year 1838 was significant. The list drawn up for the Coronation dinner underlined how many children there were in town. Able-bodied outdoor relief was due to end and a new school, like the new provident societies, might help redress the balance for the poor (see chapters 5 & 10). Wyatt George Gibson, who took over as chairman of the Guardians that year, was in the thick of all this, and also belonged to a faith and a family which had long supported educational outreach, appreciating that education helped provide the respectable workforce required for their business interests.

The Gibson family interest in Dissenter education could be traced back at least 20 years, via their support for the British & Foreign School Society (hereafter BFSS), who never ceased calling for more schools to be opened, a campaign which intensified from 1829 onwards. As early as 1818 both Wyatt George and his father, Atkinson Francis Gibson were regularly donating sums as life governors of the BFSS, and the latter did so annually up to the year of his death. From the 1830s other prominent Walden dissenters, including Joseph Green, Richard Day and Thomas Spurgin, were regularly donating small sums too, while John Player gathered donations and sent in reports. From 1831 a Saffron Walden Auxiliary Society persuaded other Dissenters like Robert Paul and Hannibal Dunn to make donations to the BFSS and organised public meetings in the town.[35]

This coincided with increased allotments activity, agricultural show prizes and the clothing bank, all linked with the 'Swing' riots the previous winter (see chapters 8 & 10). The 'Swing' connection was spelt out by the BFSS itself with strongly-worded resolutions, appalled that out of 700 prisoners on trial during the riot years in the agricultural counties, only 150 could write or even read with ease and nearly all were ignorant of religion. They called on 'all who are friendly to the religious education of the poor, to exert their influence in their respective neighbourhoods in the support of existing schools and in the establishment of new ones'. For funding, the BFSS pledged to help those who wanted to establish a school for 50 boys and 50 girls on the Society principles. There were never more than 50 British Schools in the whole of Essex, and it is easy therefore to underrate their importance, but after these exhortations, some new British schools appeared in the troublesome north-west areas, including Dunmow, Stansted and Thaxted. In May 1838, the year that a British School opened in Clavering, the Society again earnestly recommended schools to be established in the districts where the agricultural peasantry lived. This repeated BFSS campaigning and the coinciding of various religious, political and personal influences surely was the wider context for the establishment of Saffron Walden British School, although, being locally funded, it managed to run for nine years without affiliating to the parent society.[36]

Saffron Walden British Schools

However strong the evidence, to found a completely new public school for the poor still required a massive leap of faith, for schooling was notoriously difficult to fund, but eventually it came about. The new boys' school was sited in East Street (and the later girls' school in Gold Street), an area which the 1825 Bible Society survey had suggested contained large numbers of Dissenter families, probably because the chapels of the Baptists and Independents were all on this side of town. Since nearness to school was a factor, it was built 'with the simple aim of benefiting the locality in which it is placed' to serve a different neighbourhood from the National Schools. To begin with, the Boys' British had a great advantage over the National School, starting out in a handsome new building, given rent-free by the Gibsons. [Fig.11.3] This included a large schoolroom, a smaller classroom, and two-bedroom teachers' accommodation. There was also use of the charity land up to Cates Corner, where selected boys were later given allotments. After an initial meeting in July 1838, by November over 40 applications had been received and the school opened its doors, averaging around 100 boys for the first three years. The new school catered for boys aged 7 to 14 (although the majority left by the time they were 12), who paid fees of twopence per week. School visitors were appointed, and it was run by a committee meeting monthly at first, later quarterly, with George Stacey Gibson serving as treasurer for 45 years, and secretary Joshua Clarke also in the post most of his life until 1890.[37]

Appropriately, Wyatt George Gibson was the president, and among his contributions was heating and lighting for an evening singing class, run by the master, William Jenkines, who had been sent by the committee for musical training.

Fig.11.3 *Boys' British School, East Street, built by Wyatt George Gibson in 1838.*

This gave rise to a much-quoted incident in which an Anglican member of the committee complained about the extra expense and queried why boys needed to learn music. Wyatt George, visiting the school, admonished the critic who had once been his banking partner: 'Nat Catlin, thou had better study thy own business' and walked out again.[38] Generally, however, Dissenter/Anglican rivalry was kept out of sight. The British School committee sought to appease the National School committee, changing their meeting night so as not to clash, inviting the vicar onto the managing committee (although he appears not to have taken part), opening the school to all religions and adjoining parishes, and framing an opening resolution of masterful diplomacy:

> 'Whilst this meeting is deeply sensible of the value of the laudable exertions of those Gentlemen who have hitherto devoted their time to the cause of education in conducting the various schools now in operation in this town it is nevertheless of opinion that additional provision for the instruction of the poorer classes is highly desirable and that is expedient to establish a school on the British system'.[39]

A year after opening, the British committee invited the National committee to take part in a joint survey to find out how many children in town were not going to school. They were prompted perhaps by a diocesan survey of education sent round to all parishes in 1839, the results of which re-emphasised the huge disparity between educational provision in different areas. This recorded

211

in Essex 148 day schools, 140 dame schools, 35 Sunday schools, 4 charity schools, 24 middle schools and 3 schools of industry. In Saffron Walden, the vicar scarcely bothered to answer some questions, vouchsafing no information about Sunday school, buildings, finance and non-attendance. But he did reveal that a total of 480 Walden children were attending some kind of school. The National Schools, which could accommodate up to 300, were clearly under capacity with a total of 169 day and Sunday. In addition a further 100 attended 'schools of higher classes'. The vicar himself superintended a recently-established adult school attended by 120 on average.[40]

Most worryingly, there were still 150 children attending dames' schools, and this could have prompted the Dissenters to organise another Walden survey, because 'a considerable want of education exists in the town among the poorer classes'. The National School committee, with apparent reluctance, agreed it was necessary to co-operate in 'visiting the houses of the Poor and pointing out to them the advantage of sending their children to one of the two schools'. Pairs of National/British visitors were assigned to seven different areas, as in 1825. For some reason it was a further nine months before the survey papers were delivered. After this, neither National nor British School records mention the survey again. Did this attempt at ecumenical co-operation founder? This is unclear, but it was, at any rate, followed by a dramatic rise in numbers at the British School, where 'admiration has been warmly expressed as to the improvement of the children both in learning and behaviour'. Speaking at an annual meeting, John Player optimistically waxed lyrical: 'Opposed in its design to no other institution the British School has preserved the even tenor of its way... so long as the great ends of education among the classes for whom it was intended, are fully answered, the highest wishes and hopes of its founders are realised and secured'.[41]

These 'highest wishes and hopes' continued to be realised in the first few years as numbers quadrupled, leading within five years of its foundation to a glowing report from the school inspector that the school was 'in a very prosperous condition'. Already by 1843, 281 boys had benefited, numbers were growing rapidly and there was even a high attendance rate (140 out of 160). Jenkines the master, now in his late thirties, received accolades also from the parents who gave him a silver cup 'as a testimony of their respect and affection, and as a reward for his care and attention to their children'. The occasion was a celebratory sit-down tea for 400, including committee, subscribers, parents and children in one of the Gibson maltings. The British School zenith of 190 scholars coincided with a low point in the fortunes of the National School, which was in deep financial trouble in the early 40s (see above).[42]

But then came a challenge. The old vicar died and the new one grasped the nettle of the National School problems. The Anglicans built their new school in Castle Street, and now it was the turn of the British School to feel the draught of competition. After reaching a peak of almost 200 boys in 1844, almost its capacity, numbers dropped rapidly by 40% in just three years. Attendance rates were still good, but urgent remedies were required, particularly as expensive floor repairs were needed. The action decided upon, to apply for government grants, deeply upset the much-respected, if rather old-fashioned master, already unhappy because his application for increased salary had been refused. But school finances left little room for manoeuvre, with almost two-thirds going on the master's salary, leaving little for heating and repairs. The income in 1846 was only £87, of which £35 came from subscribers, £35 from school pence and £17 from local collections. Although known as a British School, they had not yet affiliated to the British & Foreign School Society. By deciding to do so, they would qualify for grants, and secure the future of an institution into which so much effort had been poured, and the need for which, in the face of illiteracy, distress and unrest, was greater than ever.[43]

Moreover, Jenkines' star had fallen. The monitorial system was out of favour, and there was now an adverse report from the school inspector, who said Jenkines was 'very faithful to his duties, but not of the most modern training'. As a result the Boys' British was 'considerably deficient in ethos, and the mass of the school is neither in high discipline nor making any remarkable vigorous progress, although a few top boys are very fairly instructed, and in collective answering, appear to know everything'. There was a sense of crisis in the school. Normally the committee met only quarterly, but they now had a number of meetings to discuss a proposal by Francis Gibson, seconded by George Youngman, that 'the efficiency of the school would be increased by placing it in connection with the British & Foreign School Society, with a view of receiving Government aid'. It was a move opposed by only two members, the Independent minister, Rev. Frederick Pollard and local surgeon, Thomas Spurgin who said that such action would materially injure the school, and objected strongly to 'government interference in the education of the people of this country, as not only wrong in principle but injurious in practice' (a remarkably similar argument to that used a few years earlier by Anglican critics). This desire to retain local autonomy could be found in other areas of public life, such as policing (see chapter 6). Gibson was sure the school subscribers would agree to affiliate, and was willing to risk resignations: 'The 2 or 3 of our friends who are so decided in their opinion that no government aid should be received threaten to leave us, this I regret but I hope others may be found who entertain more favourable views'.[44]

Economics won the argument against conservatism, as it was becoming impossible for schools to survive without outside help, which was dependent on a more professional approach to teaching. Jenkines felt bound to resign, feeling unable to teach without monitors or cope with the standards required. In a poignant farewell letter, he thanked the committee and asked for help in finding a job 'as I shall be quite destitute when I leave my present one'. Eventually he found some work at the bank. This sad departure had an even more tragic outcome, for the following year his wife, Elizabeth, aged only 43, committed suicide by hanging herself from a door at her home. At the inquest it was said that her mind 'had been seriously affected for a considerable time past, chiefly owing to her husband having left the British School, of which he was the respected master many years'. No mention of this appears in the minutes.[45]

Affiliated to the BFSS, the Boys' British never looked back. Under a new head, Edwin Chennell, out went the old monitorial methods, and in came pupil teachers, the brainchild of a former poor law assistant commissioner, Dr Kay Shuttleworth, based on his observations of pauper children in Essex and elsewhere. To qualify for grants, the British School signed indentures for its first three pupil teachers in 1848, and all proved excellent, especially Samuel Willett, then aged 15. Praised for his diligence and energy, 'universally beloved by the children of the school, and respected by their parents', Willett later returned to follow his old mentor, Chennell as master of Walden British School, remaining over 20 years. By the 1850s, numbers were high and the curriculum included geography, history and drawing, the main problems being — as with all schooling for the poor — absenteeism and keeping the children long enough. But then this British School, unlike many others, was aimed at the working-classes, and succeeded very well, as school inspector Matthew Arnold noted some years later. A sample analysis of those boys whose parents can be identified in the 1841 census confirms that at least a half were sons of labourers, and the others of small tradesmen such as shoemaker, carpenter, bricklayer, maltster and smith.[46]

Rather less detail is known about the Girls' British School, but Dissenters viewed girls' education as important too. A recent study of private girls' schools (excluding dames' schools) in Essex, Hertfordshire and Bedfordshire, found that private Dissenter girls' schools exacted high standards from their pupils and were popular with parents. The Girls' British School seems to have grown out of what was an industry school for females at the bottom of Gold Street. Miss Margaret Jeffs became the first mistress of the Girls' British in 1847. Three or four years later, with 76 girls registered, inspectors found everything fair, improved or improving, the mistress 'respectable', the instruction 'modern'. By 1851–2, with numbers doubled to 150, a new school in Roos Lane with staff accommodation was being built, a new mistress being sought and a committee of 'the kindest and most considerate ladies' being constituted. In the late 1850s, there were four pupil teachers to help organise a roll of 238 girls, well over capacity, some as young as three, although only about a third attended regularly. To their credit the school offered most of the subjects taught at the boys' school, with the addition of course of needlework and domestic economy. Nor did the school seem to suffer the same financial problems as the boys' school. It is worth noting that the BFSS contribution to educational facilities in the town also included the Saffron Walden Training College in South Road, founded in 1884 for non-sectarian training of infant teachers on kindergarten lines, continuing for well over a century.[47]

Progress in Education 1800–50

At the end of this half-century of educational endeavour, what had been achieved? Quantitatively, the picture looked impressive. Little by little, elementary education of the poor grew from patchy provision into a focus of local and national activity by the 1840s. The 1851 census showed that nationally there were already 2.1 million children at day school, and the numbers rising rapidly, with two-thirds in grant-aided (mostly church) schools. Walden had over a score of educational establishments, although many were academies and seminaries catering for better-off families. Parliamentary returns in 1845 counted 537 day and 289 Sunday scholars, while the 1851 census described 733 children as scholars, over 13% of the population, with 32 school teachers. Of the 212 who applied for the Erswell's charity handouts in 1852, almost all recipients claimed that their children attended school regularly, 118 being church families, and 87 chapel-orientated. This is likely to have been exaggerated: a recent study of Walden schools found that right up to the early twentieth century, absenteeism was rife.[48]

Out in the countryside, 'a very large proportion of villages in Essex have no daily schools in operation, and although much good is effected in Sunday schools, they cannot supply the deficiency'. Provision was much improved since the early nineteenth century, but many rural areas were still decades behind town education facilities and standards. From the 1840s, Government inspectors visited schools, bringing terror to teachers' hearts. In Essex they found the clergy struggling, unhelped by farmers who were often Dissenters. But the improvements they demanded were not affordable and, whatever the efforts put into schools, educators were always up against the deep, endemic poverty of this region. That schools did materialise, in spite of this, further underlines how driven clergy and worthies felt about the links between education and religion, morality and law and order. Nonconformist activism and the reaction to it was also the catalyst for much activity.[49]

In terms of quality, rather than quantity, however, there was still a long way to go. The benchmark was the ability to write one's name, and on this basis nationally about two-thirds were literate by mid-century, but this slid to half in poorer districts. Indeed it was claimed in 1845 that Essex was the sixth most illiterate county in England, two-thirds of its 63,000 children having no education at all: Essex 'famous for its agriculture and Nonconformity, is not less remarkable for the ignorance of the bulk of its population'. In the 1840s the Government's Committee of Council on Education, produced an 'educational/moral map of England', the title of which rather expresses the official view of what schools were for. Based on the simplistic measure of the number of grooms signing marks in marriage registers in 1844 as compared to a few years earlier, Essex again appeared in the region with the worst illiteracy in the country, 46% of men signing with marks, its 'ignorance', like its degree of pauperism, well above the national average. There was also more 'improvident marriage', less saving and more crime committals than the average.[50]

This measurement of marks in marriage registers, although a crude indicator, can be applied to the local scene. In the 1840s, when male illiteracy nationally was a third and female a half, something like twice as many brides and grooms in Clavering Parish Church signed with a mark: some men were still illiterate in the 1890s. At Saffron Walden Parish Church, marriage register marks for some reason suggest a dramatic drop in literacy levels in the early forties, particularly among women, afterwards improving. Over the period 1837–51, these figures suggest that between 40–50% of men and women in Walden were still signing with a mark.[51]

The vast majority of those unable to sign were from labouring families. Although such illiteracy seems sad enough, marriage entries were of course a cross-section of *all* classes. Narrowed down to the poorest people, those excused from paying rates, the picture looks much worse, for as many as 84% of the 533 non-ratepayers in Walden (in 1836) signed their rate excusals with a mark. In certain parts of the parish, such as the remote outposts of Little Walden, this figure rose to 97% of non-ratepayers. Other evidence suggests that around half of those excused rates were small tradesmen. Many perhaps had been children before the National School was opened, so had little chance to learn.[52]

Narrowed down still further, to the lowest of the low who ended up in court, figures are not available until the early 1840s, when the Walden Sessions clerk began adding to some of his records information about age and literacy of the accused. This may be a more reliable source than either marriage registers or rate lists, but unfortunately the information was given for only 38 accused in this decade. This limited sample suggests that the median age of the literate defendants was several years higher than that of the semi-literate or illiterate. If this pattern was typical, it suggests that lack of education among the young did have a link with crime, as worthies knew, so that the system was still failing those who needed it most, for many of those committing petty thefts were young people.[53]

The indifference of parents was often blamed. People might pretend to send the children in order to qualify for handouts like the Erswell's charity, but the fact was that children had earning power, which could be a vital addition to low family income. As the incumbent of poverty-stricken Widdington put it: 'where no rewards are given, the poor… are unwilling that their children should be kept in school and prevented thereby earning a trifle by keeping shop etc'. In Castle Street, for instance, all the older children were expected to work, so none were described as scholars in the 1851 census. Even the minimal school pence were a drain, but Sunday schools normally were free and did not interfere with work, and these were very popular, which suggests the poor were not entirely averse to education. Blaming the poor for their poverty was essentially a diversion, to hide deeper problems, for economic realities could not be ignored.[54]

The third Lord Braybrooke once commented that as a magistrate he saw many who said they had been to school but could not read or write: he would 'be happy if the observations he had made would have the effect of inducing many of them to frequent the beer house less and to bring up their children better'.[55] Some poor parents in his audience, relying on children's income, might have silently thought that there were other reasons which could not be understood by one who had lived in the lap of privilege all his life. Those who visited the poor found a different reality:

'This is a very distressed family… her husband had had no work for more than two months… (had nine children) I asked her whether they went to school, she said no, they had no money to pay for their schooling… This is also a very poor family and pleads great poverty, they have only three children they do not go to school, because they cannot afford to pay for their schooling.'

These were just some of the first-hand testimonies uncovered by the town missionary, decades after public schooling for the poor had begun in Walden. Their parents, born before the education expansion took off, could not teach what they did not know themselves. Theirs was a generation which endured all the hardships but without the compensations of learning. More than once, the town missionary also met adults deeply saddened by their inability to read, like the old man who very much wanted to learn:

> 'His grand daughter could teach him to read but could not explain it to him when he had read it... he was able now to read a few easy words, but he did not understand it... I found the poor old man to be very anxious but totally ignorant, so I told him I would come up to his house some times in an evening, and explain some passages of Scripture to him, the old man seemed so over joyed, tears started in his eyes as we parted.'[56]

In the first half of the century, a great deal of time and energy, which could have been well used in educating the poor properly, seems to have been wasted in pursuing religious indoctrination and sectarian rivalry at the expense of wider literacy. A great deal more could perhaps have been achieved quicker without ideologies intervening. But this is to assume that other social, economic and cultural circumstances would have permitted such faster expansion: it may be that a conservative society needed time to fully accept the absolute need to fund education more fully. Meanwhile, without this religious impetus, how could education have expanded, particularly in poor rural areas? The evangelical drive did put in place the beginnings of an infrastructure of buildings, personnel and funding mechanisms which laid the foundations for the future.

From the perspective of a more secular age, this evangelism is easy to underestimate, but helps explain why worthies devoted much of their lives and part of their wealth to education and other forms of philanthropy. There were many men and women whose Christian beliefs necessitated an absolute obligation to do good works, albeit that much of it now appears highly selective, purely cosmetic or deeply hypocritical. Indeed this was so important a motivation that it deserves a final chapter to itself, for an understanding of the role of religion, and its effects on the poor, helps us to understand more fully the well-ordered town of Saffron Walden.

Chapter 12

'No Man Careth for our Souls'
Religion and the Poor

'Saffron Walden, highly as it is favoured with the means of grace, yet contains within it, Streets for which no other means seem adapted to the condition of their population than those the committee have selected in sending to them a Missionary... were the feelings of the Cottagers expressed in the language of Scripture, it would be "no man careth for our souls".'[1]

By the 1840s, the New Poor Law was biting hard and all the efforts of the visiting ladies and philanthropic gentlemen were more vital than ever in providing some small relief for the destitute. In 1842, there appeared yet another organisation to deal with the poor, the Saffron Walden Town Mission. But whereas other visitations dealt largely with material needs, this one was intended to concentrate entirely on saving the souls of the poor. No reason was given for its appearance, but the seeds of its being could be found in the tradition of religious activism in the town, and in a need to combat the growing forces of unrest. Chartism was abroad once more, incendiarism increasing in the countryside and immorality rife. Large numbers of the poor were not great churchgoers, and indeed were prone to blame the churches for not helping them more. Long before, not far from Walden, some half-literate labourer had once threatened to 'set fier to that god dam Metten and all the pepel that is thear in for... the Church doth fale...'. (see chapter 7).[2]

The church was still failing the poor, and it was essential to evangelise more energetically. If they would not come to the church, then the church must go to them. So urgent was this quest that it could not be left to volunteers or ministers, and therefore a full-time paid missionary was employed, whose job it was to call personally on the poor people in the parish, not to give away blankets or clothing tickets, fuel or food, but purely to give spiritual sustenance. His first report (above), containing his initial impressions, marked the beginning of a remarkable 20-year campaign to reach those for whose souls, concluded the missionary, no one else cared.

Yet, as the missionary remarked, Walden was indeed amply 'favoured with the means of grace', that is, there was no shortage of places of worship to choose from, with Anglicans, Independents, Baptists, Quakers and Methodists all active in the town. Roman Catholics were not mentioned in the survey: indeed there was strong anti-Catholic feeling at this time. The Nonconformist chapels, representing both Old and New Dissent, were not isolated enclaves but, in most cases, were widely linked in all sorts of ways, both official and informal, to networks of others of their denominations right across the district and beyond. This was an essential part of their strength, while others were the involvement of lay members, the attraction they held for the important middle class section of the population, the installation of discipline and the call to evangelism. These same advantages also gave rise, however, to some serious problems which, in the face of increased sectarian rivalry, the threat of labourers' unrest and the daunting challenge of implementing the New Poor Law, brought the churches and chapels under great strain in their object of spreading Christianity among the poor. Churches were by no means always united either with each other or within their own denominations. The particular focus here, a neglected study, is the relationship of the poor to religion, particularly in Primitive Methodism, and to the Saffron Walden Town Mission, the archives of which have only recently come to light, and which reflect the evangelical and ecumenical efforts made to reach the poor. It becomes clear that religion, one way or another, was *the* essential background to the maintenance of the well-ordered town.[3]

The Religious Census

First it is useful to look at the unique survey of religious adherence, the Religious Census of Sunday 30 March 1851. The results shocked the Victorian Establishment since, nation-wide, it revealed that although seven million people attended services that day, over five million did not, mostly the poor; worse still, about half of attenders went to non-Anglican services. This invaluable snapshot of public worship over the entire country is full of caveats for the historian: local events, weather, illness, double-counting, unco-operative clergy, incomplete and rounded-up returns all counsel caution regarding the figures given below. But its findings that the poor were largely ignoring religion and half of churchgoers were Dissenters are generally accepted.[4]

The survey of the nine churches in Walden parish counted 2,545 attenders in the morning, 2,879 in the afternoon and 888 in the evening. The table [table 12.1] broadly indicates the relative support for the different denominations, Anglican, Independent, Friends, two Methodist and four Baptist meetings (one in Sewards End). At least a quarter of the morning attenders, and rather less in the afternoon, were Sunday scholars. Around half the townsfolk, it seems, went to church, chapel or Sunday school that day.

The Church of England still had the allegiance of a sixth of the parish population, but the Dissenters between them had more, although some came from out of town. This was of course a survey of congregations, not core membership, which was much less. Not all church attenders were self-motivated. The Almshouse residents and Charity scholars had little choice, while the carrot of charity enticed others, and certainly this was the case in Stansted, for instance, where churchgoing was tied in with clothing handouts. Many very poor people lived too far away to walk to church, but there were other reasons for non-attendance. A decade later, a poor woman told the Walden town missionary

Denomination	Morning	Afternoon	Evening
Anglicans	942	1042	491
Baptists (4)	908	965	177
Friends	50	43	—
Independents	545	609	—
Methodists (2)	100	220	220
Total	2,545	2,879	888

Table 12.1 Religious Census, Saffron Walden: Church/chapel attendance, 30 March 1851 (Baptists include meeting room at Sewards End).

that 'she went occasionally... but her husband never went, because he had not clothes to go in'. Seating arrangements were also discouraging, the poor often relegated to pews without views. Seats at the western end of the parish church north aisle were once said to be 'consistently vacant', because they had traditionally been allocated to the servant class. Later on, under a different vicar, seats were allocated in the middle and south aisles.[5]

There was plenty of spare space in most churches, which had been built on optimism. On that spring day, there were over a thousand empty seats throughout the various buildings, and very few were filled to capacity. This worried people, albeit that various excuses such as illness were given. There may have been some generalisations: for instance, the evening service noted at Baileys Lane Upper Meeting on Sunday actually took place during the week. Such raw figures also disguise the vibrancy of church life: the General Baptists, who got only 76 at their afternoon service, could attract up to 200 to winter evening lectures.

The Quakers

The emptiest building was that of the oldest Dissenting group, the Quakers or Society of Friends in the High Street. Recorded in Walden from at least 1656, their early persecution was long past. Quaker meetings were held in silence, members speaking only when moved by God. In Essex, as elsewhere, the Quakers were numerically in decline, particularly among the poor. But Quakerism was a close society, with strong kin and business ties over a wide area, and its significance was not to be judged in numbers attending. Their strong, silent, pacifist ways responded better to a system of small, quiet meetings, which was traditional to certain families: Bush, Day, Green, Impey, Robson, Wyatt and of course Gibson were some of the few. Largely funded by the Gibsons' and others' subscriptions, the Quakers were a force to be reckoned with in Walden life.[6]

Quaker rules counselled members to avoid all tale bearing, be just in business, bring up their children 'in godly conversation, plainness of speech, behaviour and apparel', provide for the poor and have nothing to do with bearing arms, alehouses, sports or gaming. Some local members continued to refuse to pay church rates or tithes, which obstinacy invariably cost them far more than the original payment, yet they went on refusing time after time. Such action set the wealthier Quakers apart from others of the middling sort. Wyatt George Gibson, a traditional Quaker who still habitually used 'thee' and 'thou' in conversation, suffered the seizure in 1834 of £70 worth of malt because he refused to pay £56 of 'church rate so called'. The following year, his malt valued at £118 was seized to cover church rates and five years of Great Tythes. Similarly in 1836, Day & Robson grocers had soap seized from their stocks, while Joshua Green forfeited umbrellas, coal scuttles, warming pans and other goods from his shop. It was an embarrassing situation for those fining them, to whom the Gibsons as Conservatives were allied politically, as well as being the bankers for the town.[7]

Like a number of Quaker families all over the land, the Gibsons were involved in the drink trade, which did not appear to contradict the Friends' exhortations against 'all unnecessary frequenting of Alehouses or Taverns, excess in drinking and intemperance of every kind'. Yet the Gibsons ran maltings, owned a large chain of pubs and brewed highly popular ales. A resolution passed in 1830 by the Friends' locally suggests that spirits, not beer, was the main cause of 'great immorality and misery'. However the growing temperance movement may have been what prompted Jabez Gibson, in his final years, to provide a borehole water supply for Walden as a safe alternative to beer, and his surviving brothers to unburden themselves of their pub empire (see chapter 1). One way and another, Saffron Walden's history was intimately linked to that of the Quakers, albeit that numerically they appeared so insignificant in the 1851 religious census, mustering only 50 attenders in the morning and 43 in the afternoon, though there was space for 400. The Quakers looked after their poor, but the figures suggest that the number of poor attending these silent, contemplative meetings was not high.[8]

The Independents

By contrast, the religious census confirmed the strength of the Independents' (Congregational) chapel in Abbey Lane. Their roots went back to 1665, when Dissenters were still being persecuted. Early influences in various villages came from across the Cambridgeshire border. As conditions improved, the Walden congregation began meeting in a barn in 1689, then moved to a new building a few years later. [Fig.12.1] Their fortunes varied in the eighteenth century, and the break-up between the Baptist and Congregational sections of the church in 1774 was a major upheaval (see below). In spite of this, the congregation recovered so well that by 1811 they were strong enough to build the present-day chapel, later enlarging it to accommodate more people. The Independents based

Fig.12.1 *The old Independents' chapel built in Frog's Orchard, Abbey Lane, in use from the 1690s until 1811, when replaced by the present building.*

their teachings on the Bible, and particularly objected to the state running the church. In Walden, as in many independently-minded market towns, this had great appeal. Here in 1851, 545 heads were counted at morning service or Sunday school, and 609 in church or Sunday school in the afternoon. Even this high figure was said to be below the average attendance of 700. Such strength enabled them to exercise, through their membership system (as did other Dissenting denominations) a reasonable discipline on those on the roll.[9]

On the other hand, since Dissent tended to attract rebellious types, it was not uncommon for argument and, on occasion, deep schism to occur, and such rows tend to stand out in the surviving records, giving the erroneous impression that these serious-minded seekers after truth spent much of their time arguing with each other over doctrinal matters. One example was Robert Driver Thurgood, later to be a leading worthy and political Radical, and in 1819 already a young man of headstrong views, who thoroughly upset the tranquillity of the Abbey Lane congregation by his 'pernicious sentiments' and 'unsanctified tempers'. In his case, to the grateful relief of the chapel, he resigned voluntarily because of new insights. It was a performance he was to repeat again in his old age. In 1825, the congregation was also shocked by the downfall of Searles' Bank, for this family were prominent members, and some felt thoroughly let down. Commercial success was seen as evidence of God's grace towards the godly, and therefore bankruptcy was far more shameful than today.[10]

One pastor, Rev. William Clayton, was particularly zealous, as evidenced by the numerous disciplinary rebukes among his 165 members. During his time, people were admonished or even dismissed for 'deplorable misconduct', 'open and scandalous immorality', 'drinking to criminal excess', cruelty to wife, the

222

sin of intoxication, profane language, contentious disposition, absconding from creditors, or even if their conduct appeared suspicious. Clayton himself may have departed under something of a cloud, having quarrelled with his hearers. Clashes between pastors and members could occur, for the chapel was run by the people, and not by some distant bishop or other official. In addition, there was opposition from outside critics, a particularly striking example of which was the satirical broadsheet circulated in 1826.[11] [Fig.12.2]

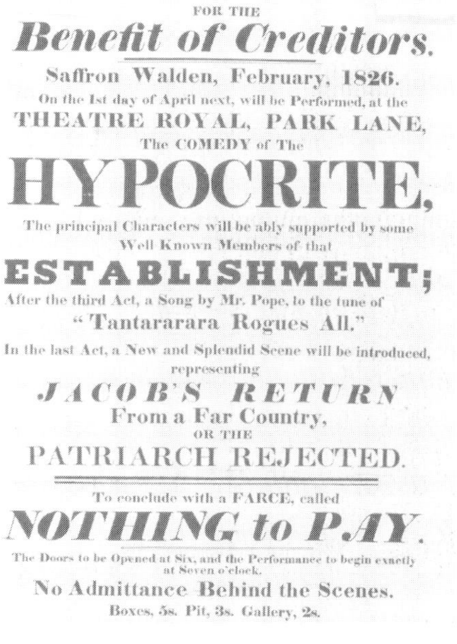

There were also of course plenty of good reports and new members recruited and it was a measure of the strength of such gatherings that wrangles and even schism did not permanently damage the chapel. In Essex generally, the Independents were losing their Evangelical edge by the early nineteenth century as compared to some of the other denominations. But Abbey Lane was on the ascendant, extending its mission along with Baptists outwards into 'the once degraded and immoral hamlet of Little Walden', where in 1852

FOR THE
Benefit of Creditors.
Saffron Walden, February, 1826.
On the 1st day of April next, will be Performed, at the
THEATRE ROYAL, PARK LANE,
The COMEDY of The
HYPOCRITE,
The principal Characters will be ably supported by some Well Known Members of that
ESTABLISHMENT;
After the third Act, a Song by Mr. Pope, to the tune of
"Tantararara Rogues All."
In the last Act, a New and Splendid Scene will be introduced, representing
JACOB'S RETURN
From a Far Country,
OR THE
PATRIARCH REJECTED.

To conclude with a FARCE, called
NOTHING to PAY.
The Doors to be Opened at Six, and the Performance to begin exactly at Seven o'clock.
No Admittance Behind the Scenes.
Boxes, 5s. Pit, 3s. Gallery, 2s.

Fig.12.2 *A satirical broadsheet circulated in 1826 in reference to the new Abbey Lane chapel's architecture which, with its gallery, resembled a theatre, while its services were seen as shows and its adherents mocked as hypocrites. Obviously there are some 'in' jokes here which are lost on us!*

Frances Player, by then John Player's widow, paid for a chapel. The large numbers attending Abbey Lane services must have included poorer people, enjoying the fellowship and spiritual solace. The chapel was particularly popular with women, of whom there could be twice as many as men members, although most of the administration was in the hands of males.[12]

But, although poorer folk attended services, they appeared to take little part in its organisation. This was a chapel dominated by the middling sort who were increasingly important in small-town life, and membership covered a range of trades and professions. Leading lights in the 1820s included maltsters John Clark and Samuel Porter, ironmonger Robert Paul and of course, after his move to Walden in 1823, 'Gentleman' John Player. Player regarded his role as treasurer of the Abbey Lane Trust as the most honourable of all his many public offices, and was also a deacon. These were the type of strong-minded people whose energies laid the foundations for much of merit in the town, and who were often at the forefront of initiatives to help the poor, but also caught up in sectarian and internal rivalries: in the later 1850s, there were further schisms, resignations and departures. It seems that the path of Dissent was seldom without its chasms. But out of the earnest searching for spiritual truth at Abbey Lane, there arose three more chapels in the town.[13]

The Baptists

These other chapels were all Baptists, and by 1851 their congregations, including a mission room in Sewards End, amounted to almost the same as the Anglicans. But although united by their belief in baptism through immersion, the three town groups were all completely separate from each other. The oldest, the Hill Street group, were General Baptists and therefore Arminian, believing that everyone could be redeemed through faith, while the London Road group was Strict and Particular and hence Calvinist, signifying a belief that only the select few were chosen for redemption. The Baileys Lane group varied over time from mixed membership to Particular.[14]

The 'Old Connexion', the General Baptists had been founded in 1711, apparently by a group of people disaffected by the preaching at Abbey Lane. Their chapel in Hill Street was replaced in 1791, and preachers funded through a small but vital endowment which kept them going when numbers dwindled in the nineteenth century. Surnames like Bird, Coe, Erswell, Finton, Grainger, Housden, Hodson, Hurry, Jeffery, Moul, Nichols, Seamer and Willis can be found in the records. Numbers were very low in the late eighteenth century, and by 1851, their morning/afternoon services attracted only 47 and 76 people respectively.[15]

By then the General Baptist congregation had recovered from the Cundill affair which threw the small community into disarray in 1824–5. Linen draper James Humphreys, who later became one of the new wave of Liberal councillors, as a trustee had his political skills sharpened by having to deal with this unpleasant business. The pastor of 30 years' standing, Stephen Philpot died in 1821, and his place was taken temporarily by the Rev. John Cundill who claimed he was owed money and refused to leave. On one occasion, he took possession of the pulpit, with his wife, infant in arms, standing on the stairs. This led to scenes 'in which the Constable was the chief actor and of which violence was the distinguishing characteristic', but prosecutions were avoided and after many months Cundill, now destitute, accepted a £50 pay-off. Another chasm was crossed, and the Hill Street chapel lived on until 1957, the last General Baptist church in Essex.[16]

The other two Baptist churches also both owed their origins to Abbey Lane. In 1818 a young member there, John Dane Player (a relative of 'Gentleman' John Player) left for doctrinal reasons and started prayer meetings, which resulted in the Strict Baptist Church. A chapel was built in London Road which, at the time of the 1851 survey, was filled with 190 attending both services. This continued until the early 1840s. In fact the Players over the years had associations with all three Baptist groups, as well as Abbey Lane. The third group, also Calvinist, was by far the largest. They regarded themselves as the original congregation at Abbey Lane chapel, but in the 1770s there were disputes about baptism which later led to the expulsion, out of the blue, of their minister. Leaving behind only a small group at Abbey Lane, they formed the Upper Meeting, later building a chapel on the corner of Baileys Lane and continued attracting members from a wide area. As a boy visiting Walden, John Player attended the Upper Meeting.[17]

Their head-count on census day 1851 exceeded the Independents, with 591 adults and children in the morning and 699 in the afternoon, plus evening lectures, for which an attendance of 600 was claimed. The popularity of the Upper Meeting owed much perhaps to the Rev. Josiah Wilkinson, who was pastor for almost 40 years from 1809. He had come to Walden as a young man aged 23, and within a few years trebled the roll of 80 members. With his arrival, the Upper Meeting became Particular Baptists, reverting to mixed membership after his death. Whereas the chapel had been born in schism, Wilkinson had a gift for building bridges with other dissenting groups and helping ecumenical mission, particularly the Bible Auxiliary. During this time, they also helped Baptist chapels in Ashdon, Thaxted and Langley, while Dissenters later worked together to mission Wimbish, Debden, Hadstock, Radwinter, Sewards End and Little Walden. The Baileys Lane (now Audley Road) building remains a thriving Baptist church today.[18]

The Wesleyans

The newest denominations in town were the two groups of Methodists. The Wesleyans arrived in the early 1820s, and the Primitive Methodists in the late 1830s, both of whom eventually settled in the Castle Street area. Earlier attempts to plant Methodism in this area had not grown to fruition, although the famous Calvinist preacher George Whitefield drew huge crowds when he spoke on Walden Common on 21 June 1739: 'Preached at Saffron Walden... to about 2,000 people... wherever I go, people fly to the doctrine of Jesus Christ', he recorded in his journal, visiting also Wimbish and Thaxted. John Wesley once described nearby Bishops Stortford as something of a spiritual desert and the nearest he got to Walden was to visit Wimbish. Wesley never wanted to found a separate church, but to reform the Church of England from within: nevertheless Methodism, retaining similar doctrines but with a distinctive style, broke away after his death in 1791. This 'New Dissent' reached Saffron Walden 30 years later.[19]

The story of how the Wesleyans came to town is a well-known one, thanks to the rather ardent memoir published about their first lady preachers, Miss Charlotte Sophia Steigen Berger and Mrs Henrietta Elizabeth Webster. [Fig.12.3] Voyaging out from a genteel existence in London, these wealthy ladies became known for establishing Wesleyan preaching rooms in various places, and in 1821 were invited to tame the depraved poor of Walden, of whom they had been told: 'there are many heathen here who regard neither God nor man and attend no place of worship'. Undaunted, the 'truly heroic' Methodist ladies came to Walden, preaching in the open air, in a barn, then a chapel, only much later in 1865 erecting largely at Miss Berger's cost the present-day chapel in Castle Street. The only other Wesleyan chapel seems to have been at Little Chesterford.[20]

When the good ladies finally moved to Walden, they decided to live beside the 'moral wilderness' of the overcrowded courts and yards of the residuum.

Fig.12.3 *Miss Charlotte Steigen Berger, one of the two founders and spiritual leaders of the Wesleyan Methodists, and donor of the present-day Methodist chapel in Castle Street.*

This deliberate choice of situation, albeit in a fine house securely gated, led to considerable harassment, stone-throwing and vandalism, while in the chapel itself 'rough boys behaved ludicrously, drunken men talked loudly and profanely and certain lewd fellows of the baser sort acted with scandalous indecency'. There was a famous trial at the town's Quarter Sessions where the Recorder, then Lord Braybrooke jailed the young ringleaders, his lordship promising an end to persecution and giving 'a manly exporation of the law on passing the sentence, which it is hoped will have much weight with the populace, great disturbance having been occasioned by the thoughtless and profane for some time past at the several places of worship in this town' (see chapter 6). This episode and others suggest that some sections of the poor were actively hostile to religion.[21]

However, by 1851 the preaching ladies, acting as lay evangelists for there was no resident minister, were attracting 150 to evening services and 100 in the afternoon, with plenty of spare seats. As with Josiah Wilkinson among the Baptists, so Miss Berger was very much the early inspiration for the Walden Wesleyans. But they were not destined to remain the only Methodists in Saffron Walden for very long.

The Primitive Methodists

Starting in the Midlands in 1810, the Primitive Methodist Connexion had separated from the mainstream Methodists, now grown rather staid, and been steadily spreading around the country ever since. The difference from other traditions was not so much in doctrine as in style: the 'Prims' practised outdoor preaching, had several unique aspects and took a very experiential view of Christianity with extempore sacramental customs. As a result, their services were exciting and dramatic. It has been said that the Wesleyans were a religion *for* the poor, but the Primitives became a religion *of* the poor. This was true in the distressed areas which lay on Walden's doorstep, for this was a rural mission organised from the town.[22]

Like the Congregationalists, the Primitive Methodist influence spread south from Cambridgeshire. They first missioned Walden via the fenland parish of

Upwell, a hotbed of Dissent, which in 1838 appointed two missionaries, Messrs B. Redhead and J. Jackson, to go forth and plant new chapels in areas of their own choice. In late April they set out to do so, allegedly taking only one day to walk a quoted 40 miles to Walden, where they woke up next morning to find 'a country town of some importance; and on making inquiries they ascertained that there was no Methodism there nor in the neighbouring villages'. Obviously, for the 'Prims', the Wesleyans did not count. In agrarian metaphor much used in PM parlance, they decided that Walden offered 'a fine field for usefulness' and in 1839 began to cultivate a harvest of souls. Although open-air preaching was claimed to be unusual in Walden, they stirred up interest by preaching in the open air in Castle Street, the Market Place, the Common, Little Walden and outdoors in many villages like Chesterford, Newport, Hadstock and Arkesden. Disapproval of large gatherings of the poor in any one place, particularly when such excitement was engendered, may well have set tongues buzzing in more respectable middle-class religious circles.[23]

Primitive Methodist energy was extraordinary. One Sunday in May Mr Jackson preached at Debden in the morning, Wimbish in the afternoon, Radwinter at teatime and Ashdon in the evening. The efforts paid off. Societies were founded in many villages, open air meetings progressed to barns or cottages, and in time Sunday schools were opening and a few chapels being built over a wide circuit, all missioned from Walden. Labouring and artisan families, especially women, flocked to the stimulating services. At Chrishall, virtually the entire congregation was composed of agricultural labourers. At Dick Turpin's birthplace, Hempstead, where local pastimes included bear-baiting, the preachers converted 'some who almost equalled him in daring wickedness'. At Clavering, 'a few pious females' persuaded a sympathetic landowner to give a tiny plot of land for a chapel, to which hundreds came. [Fig.12.4] Lack of winter meeting places was a restriction, but there were up to two dozen preaching places in the first decade, gathered in the Walden circuit. Unpaid and half-literate lay preachers, often labourers themselves, would commonly tramp up to 15 miles on their day off to preach at distant chapels. Underpaid ministers, remaining *in situ* only three or four years, needed great stamina to do their pastoral visiting over this 28-mile long circuit: one minister apologised for not fulfilling his visiting duties because 'in consequence of several very bad corns his feet are very tender'.[24]

The astonishing Methodist outreach reached out not only across north-west Essex, but well into west Suffolk, south Cambridgeshire and east Hertfordshire. All this work was organised initially from Upwell, who complained about the expense, and later by the General Missionary Committee, until the circuit became strong enough to stand alone in

Fig.12.4 *The Primitive Methodist banner across the doorway of the Clavering Methodist chapel, built on the same Hill Green site as the original 1844 chapel, and missioned from Saffron Walden.*

1850. Ten years later the Walden-based ministers were part of a large organisation of 45 local preachers, 24 class leaders, 9 Sunday schools, 7 chapels and at least 27 other preaching places. And yet the Walden membership itself was quite modest, recorded at 30 in 1841 and remaining around 40 from 1850 onwards, although the 1851 religious census showed 'hearers' amounting to up to three times as many, filling the chapel to capacity.[25]

The Walden 'Prims' had no rich philanthropists to fund a chapel, no high-status patrons, but instead rented an 'unceiled, unfloored' barn once used by the Wesleyans, opening for worship on 30 June 1839. Five years later, though still penniless, they decided to refurbish it, and appealed to the mayor, magistrates and other influential gentlemen who were pleased to assist, being 'convinced that much good was resulting from our labors, especially among the poor' and thus the improvements were paid for. In 1847 another 'kind friend' gave £10 towards a new Primitive chapel in Walden, presumably in Castle Street where they were recorded in 1851. The village chapels were mostly run by labourers, but Walden drew members from a slightly wider social spectrum, with small artisans like bootmaker George Shepherd of Commons End, though unfortunately known for being rather 'violent and quarrelsome'; sweetmeat manufacturer Daniel Porcher of Millfield, once rebuked for intemperance; and gardener Joseph Bird of Mount Pleasant. Methodism has been seen as a religion of control which undermined traditional working class culture based on the beerhouse, and many were the 'fallen', with at least ten Walden members rebuked for drunkenness in the early years.

But in spite of occasional problems, the Walden Primitive Methodists were a busy and popular society, with their tireless preachers missioning, processioning, holding camp meetings on the Common, protracted revivals and 'love feasts' (a sort of communion). It was a whole new panoply of activity, particularly enjoyed by women, and quite a few young people, some of whom rose to become class leaders, Sunday school teachers and local preachers. The 'Prims' were unique in offering opportunities for the poor to be leaders, even chapel trustees, in spite of widespread illiteracy. The glowing obituaries of very ordinary, poor country folk, often women, appearing in the denominational journal, though stylised, are extraordinary: when else would peasants rise above archival anonymity?[26]

The circuit seems to have really taken off from 1843–6 with the work of two particularly charismatic ministers, Edward Rust and Robert Eaglen, a young family man with a gift for conversions. [Fig.12.5] Later on, preaching at Colchester, Eaglen was credited (probably wrongly) with converting Charles Spurgeon. He and Rust left the circuit 'thriving spiritually and temporally'. It was a time of immense deprivation, the 'hungry forties', and many found solace in God. Circuit membership doubled from 1847–50, and doubled again within four years: 'the country seems under deep religious impressions', proclaimed one minister, 'the fields are white already to harvest!'. Their achievement in garnering several thousand labouring souls, traditionally the least religious, was literally halved by the devastating impact of the 1850s 'spirit of emigration': 'Many of Our Local Preachers, Class Leaders and most influential members have emigrated, many others are on the eve of emigrating. This is the engrossing topic of conversation in many of our societies, some of which have been quite shaken, and almost everyone seems to be unsettled.'[27]

Prejudice was another problem faced in more backward outposts of the circuit. The dramas of revivalism — loud singing, hellfire-preaching, emotional cries and violent conversions — which attracted some, equally aroused mockery in others. As the Wesleyans had suffered earlier, ignorant youths played mayhem during their services: several were jailed after interrupting services in Clavering. But Anglican landowners and employers could also oppose. Those who lost their jobs through religion were advised to band together to form associations to campaign for parochial relief, then 'the persecuting clergy would be rebuked for their folly, and warned not to afflict the parishes by their unrighteous interference with the consciences of the poor'. More superior

Fig.12.5 *Rev. Robert Eaglen, Saffron Walden Primitive Methodist minister in the early 1840s. It was Eaglen who, with his fellow minister Rev. Ernest Rust, oversaw the wave of revivalism in the surrounding villages at this time.*

churches perhaps found the exponential growth of this working-class denomination rather disturbing, its conversions impermanent, its teachings shallow and its services too affecting for the impressionable poor. There could scarcely be a greater contrast than the quiet, serious Quaker meetings and the noisy, demonstrative 'Prims' services.[28]

By far the worst problem they faced, however, was the sheer endemic poverty of the Walden area, so typical of the cereal-growing lands of eastern England. The Primitives were habitually poverty-stricken. In their first decade of existence, the members of Walden chapel were able to contribute an average of only 1½d per week each to the collection. Some of the ministers, who worked extremely hard, received in the early years a salary of only £18 per year, sometimes in arrears. This was no more than the worst-paid labourer. Although preferring pastoral visiting, they were constantly diverted into fund-raising to pay off endless debts on buildings, which eventually extended to about two dozen chapels over the entire circuit. Year after year the quarterly gathering complained of agricultural distress, often very poignantly: 'Some of our members have had to seek a refuge in the Union House of Industry and many have left because they could not pay their class monies while children were wanting bread which the parents had not to give them. We are sorry anyone should leave the Society on account of poverty, but so it is, we know not of any corrective.'[29]

These were men who laboured face-to-face with the poor and found, as one quite articulate old man put it: 'Solomon rather stepped over the mark when he said the sleep of a labouring man is sweet whether he eat little or much, he said he had often gone to bed hungry, and he could not sleep so well as when he had had a good supper'. Persecution, prejudice and poverty took their toll but, whenever there was a lapse, the Primitives simply made a renewed evangelical drive, organising 'protracted meetings' which went on all week, working groups of people up to a high pitch of feeling, announcing with confidence 'we are expecting a general and mighty revival'.[30]

One aspect hard to assess, however, is the relationship between this 'religion of the heart' and labourers' protest: did the little chapels subdue latent unrest or ferment it? Nineteenth century Methodism was strongly associated with socialism, for a number of working-class organisations, such as friendly societies and early trade unions, modelled their meetings on Methodist lines, suggesting this was where their leaders had been nurtured. The 'Prims' preachers differed from their Dissenter counterparts, springing from the same roots as their hearers, outside the social whirl of the middle class chapel milieu. Although there is little overt evidence in this area that rebellious labourers and religious labourers were related (indeed a large proportion were their womenfolk anyway), Primitive Methodism was allied to education, self-help, a sense of self-worth and social justice which channelled energies and was to have repercussions in future generations.[31]

In summary, Primitive Methodism was full of problems and contradictions, but it reached the poor, and hence its records form one of the few accessible aspects of working class culture in Walden in this period. There is no reason to doubt that for many poor folk the little chapels transformed arid lives into something special, that their faces glowed as they left the chapel, as described so well in one of the best social histories ever written, *Joseph Ashby of Tysoe*. While evangelical overdrive had characterised the early years, later times saw the 'Prims' becoming part of the town fabric and attracting their own loyal local following — the Farnhams, the Elsoms, the Reeds — although other denominations never quite lost their suspicion, well into the twentieth century, of the upstart newcomers and their noisy, emotional ways. Finally, of course, in the 1930s the town Primitives united with the Wesleyans and since then most of the village chapels, which these humble folk had dug into their not-very-deep pockets to provide and maintain, have been consigned to oblivion by our materially-rich but spiritually-impoverished age. The little-known story of the Saffron Walden Circuit Primitive Methodists has needed telling at greater length, for it qualifies a general impression that the poor were not interested in religion.[32]

The Anglicans

And finally, what of the Church of England in this town packed with Dissenters? The large emphasis on Dissent in Walden tends to suggest that the Anglicans were in retreat, but the strength of support among the Establishment was never seriously under threat. Everywhere the Church of England, stimulated by the Dissenting challenge, the much-disliked toleration act for Roman Catholics and the threat to social order of the rebellious poor, had emerged from eighteenth century torpor to rethink its approach. A half-century of effort was reflected in the 1851 census figures which showed that St Mary's Parish Church attracted 942 to morning service, of whom a third were Sunday scholars, rising to 1042 in the afternoon, with 491 at evening service. All this was well below capacity, but this was of course one of the largest churches in Essex. It was also well-funded, with income from endowment, tithes, donations and other sources.[33]

The central figure through the first half of the nineteenth century was the Rev. Nicholas Bull, who came to Walden as a young man in 1804, at a time of great challenge and change. He was revered by the ladies of the church, who once presented him with a fine new gown, a gesture to reflect 'regard for the ordinances of that church, the characteristics of whose ritual are, truth and holiness' and testimony against 'the intolerance of popery on the one hand, and the malignity of sectarianism on the other'. On his death in 1844, there was an outpouring of grief among all denominations, 'each one appearing as if he had lost a father, or a dear and affectionate friend'. During Bull's 40-year incumbency, the church became much more active: Sunday and National schools were founded, adult education began, and renovations undertaken, all visible statements of a renewed Evangelical thrust, pushed along by the Dissenting challenge. Major works included the building of an organ, new pewing, chandeliers for the roof, and of course the new steeple, a necessary repair, but also one full of symbolism, a major, eye-catching reassertion of the pre-eminence of the Established Church (see chapter 1). Church events also expanded. On one occasion, the church held a popular *Messiah* festival, but rowdy youths constantly caused disruption. Leading churchman, Henry Smith went outside and 'supposing he had found an offender gave Mr. White's son of Castle Street a beating'. After such demonstration of muscular Christianity, Mr Smith presumably returned to worship.[34]

The vicar could also be a prickly character at times, and had his share of controversy, with the National School committee over hymn-books, with the overseers regarding the parish pall and not least alongwith his churchwardens in an acrimonious dispute with the new Town Council over their use of the old corporation room above the south porch (see chapters 4 & 11). Bull was also involved in a religious argument of extraordinary intensity which unfolded among the Board of Guardians.[35]

Religion in the Workhouse

Nothing more signifies the importance of religion in nineteenth century society than the fact that the issue which most upset the Guardians in their early and very difficult years was not regulations, diets, personnel, migration, vaccination or any of the other myriad and irksome duties, but the type of religious service on offer to the inmates, for most of whom this was probably the least of their worries. But it was no side issue for some of the Guardians. In the early months of the new system, they used to allow lay members to come into the House on Sunday evenings, to explain the Scriptures to the illiterate poor who could thus 'hear the consoling truths of the Bible instead of spending that sacred day in idleness or loose and unprofitable conversation'. The Guardians were positive that this had helped defuse the spirit of insubordination at the time of the workhouse fire. They were therefore, like many other Boards, incensed when the Poor Law Commission interfered with these arrangements, announcing a plan to appoint expensive Anglican chaplains instead. This particularly upset the Dissenters on the Board, especially Wyatt George Gibson and John Player. The Commission, being more concerned to placate the Church of England, under-estimated the importance of Dissent in towns.[36] Gibson and Player felt that dissenting preachers should be allowed equal access to the Union, and that paupers should be allowed out to chapel. Not all the Guardians agreed, but over half voted in favour and a resonant statement was prepared:

'Liberty of conscience being the inalienable right of Englishmen it would be inconsistent with the spirit of the British constitution to deprive a man who has not been guilty of a breach of the moral or national law of the privilege of assembling with his fellow Christians in acts of Worship whether in church or chapel. .. regulation would be at variance with the feelings of a great proportion of the ratepayers both among churchmen and Dissenters... it does not seem equitable to provide religious instruction to one class... it would be placing churchmen and Dissenters upon an unequal footing.'[37]

The statement was sent to the Poor Law Commission but, curiously, accompanied by a long letter from the Guardians' clerk, Robert Driver Thurgood, also a Dissenter but no mere lackey of the Board, which hinted that the Gibson/Player influence had swung the vote, but some disagreed. Other workhouses, he pointed out, had found it led to drunkenness among those let out, and allowed troublesome preachers into the building. The assistant commissioner agreed that such a system would be abused and 'the Lords day to be regarded as a day of licence rather than of devotion, and the religious privileges which it would confer to be disregarded'. Instead he recommended a chaplain be appointed at a salary of 50 guineas.[38]

Gibson and Player reduced the internal opposition, but still the Commissioners prevaricated. Stories went round the town that Mr Gibson and Mr Player were just scoring political points, rumours which they strongly denied, insisting they were 'actuated solely by principle and not by any factious opposition'. Thurgood said there were few Dissenters in the workhouse anyway, and Gibson made clear that Quaker poor were especially provided for in their own society and 'would never be found within the walls of a workhouse'. The affair reached crisis point, with both Player and Gibson threatening that unless this was agreed, 'they could no longer conscientiously attend the meetings of the Board of Guardians'. The resignation of such prominent figures would have undermined the operation of the new statute, and other members 'implored' the assistant commissioner to agree, while the chairman, Lord Braybrooke, suggested a compromise, otherwise the Board would lose some valuable members, and their departure would be 'followed by every description of opposition and annoyance within their reach, on the part of the main body of dissenters'. This strongly suggests that the New Poor Law was not universally popular.[39]

Finally a compromise was allowed: well-behaved inmates could attend their own church, and there would also be a chaplain for those too infirm to go out. But there remained a ban on lay preachers, distrusted for proselytising, and once more Gibson petitioned, for banning laymen would otherwise 'excite a prejudice among the reflecting part of the public upon whose good feeling and co-operation the Guardians have confidently relied for assistance'. The minutes disguise the seriousness of this dispute, but the original correspondence gives a different picture. By now the entire Board was prepared to resign because they too perceived the vital link, which the Commission ignored, between religious freedom and Dissenter support for the New Poor Law. There was yet another disagreement over the chaplain's salary, Bull the vicar scorning the paltry £50 on offer. With the Anglicans now angry too, there were no Sunday services in the workhouse and Braybrooke pleaded 'if the workhouses are left without chaplains, there will be a greater and a more awkward clamour against the new law than has yet existed'. Somehow it was all resolved, and permission to take the workhouse pulpit also extended to the Independents and Baptists. Braybrooke, caught between all this wrangling, soon afterwards faded from sight, opening the way for his uncompromising vice-chairman, Wyatt George Gibson to take over and the workhouse religion issue quietened down.[40]

Sectarian Divisions

This heated correspondence exemplifies the power of religion to divide a community, a common state of affairs in the history of Dissent in Walden. The urgent need to mission the poor could produce co-operation, as exemplified by the ecumenical education survey of 1825 (see chapter 11). Crises like the Irish potato famine would see the churches making common cause, joining together for a packed united service at the church which, alongwith other efforts, raised £150 for the victims: 'all party feelings, whether political or religious seemed subdued and forgotten before they reached the sanctuary'. But times were changing and the ecumenical movement in Walden was about to hit a sticky patch. With Whigs (overwhelmingly Dissenter) in the ascendant, both centrally and locally, the Established Church felt threatened. In Saffron Walden, the cooler atmosphere was reflected in the support given to the Bible Society which by 1837 lost much of its impetus: 'very few of its former eloquent advocates being present, and it was observed by many that the harmony which a few years ago subsisted between the clergy and laity of the Church of England and dissenting ministers and their congregations in regard to this institution appeared to be rapidly passing away'.[41]

Lord Braybrooke blamed it on the 1834 Municipal Corporations Act, 'the

Dissenters being almost as numerous as the Church men and opposing each other upon all occasions, whereas before there was no bone of contention'. Newly emboldened to speak out about long-standing grievances, Dissenters brought to the fore in Walden and many other towns their complaints about the privileges of the Church of England, particularly the long-standing issues of tithes, which demanded a tenth of agricultural produce on titheable lands; and church rates, which obliged parishioners to pay for repairs to the church fabric (although clergy were responsible for the chancel). John Player might appeal for them all to co-operate as brethren 'instead of perpetuating civil feuds and local matters of strife', but he was also stirring up feelings in favour of civil registration. At present churchmens' births, marriages and death were automatically recorded, whereas 'the dissenter however wealthy and respectable must go cap in hand to request an ignorant parish clerk to record every alteration in his domestic circle, and to request him to overlook, if beyond the stipulated period, any unintentional infringement of the legislative law'.[42]

The causes of Dissenter resentment of Anglican privileges, and the latter's hostility to such pressures, were legion and, following the Dissenter inroads on the Town Council, sectarian arguments intensified, with thinly-veiled references to the new men as 'fanatics', and accusations of insider dealing in trade. More dramatically, a call to disestablish the Church of England surfaced in Walden in 1834, the year when a failed attempt was being made in Parliament to redress the church rates issue. A faction in town, labelled 'men of straw' by the Tory press, were gathering signatures for a Parliamentary petition to disestablish the Church altogether. Church men in various local parishes retaliated by organising their own anti-disestablishment petitions, and the Walden one against these 'bitter church-hating agitators' was claimed to have been signed by all the 'respectable' people and also by many of the humbler classes.[43]

The campaign for disestablishment (which never succeeded) was, however, less vociferous than the church rates agitation. By the late 1830s, a passive protest by a few strong-minded Quakers, had become an active crusade among many others in Walden, beginning with yet another Dissenter petition, continuing with an allegedly 'gross and fallacious statement' about church improvements such as the steeple and organ, and ending with yet more petitions and counter-petitions. This was not unusual at the time: nationally, some half-a-million Dissenters signed a petition organised by the Church Rate Abolition Society. About 40 Walden Dissenters subscribed to the Braintree Anti-Church Rate Society, where silk manufacturer Samuel Courtauld fought a turbulent campaign, which culminated in a test case in the House of Lords. Further attempts were made in Walden by a 'squad of church-hating agitators' in 1839–40. In 1848 a Nonconformist society was established at the Abbey Lane chapel, part of its aim being to study references to civil and religious liberty and prepare petitions to Parliament. Papers were read at a preliminary meeting in the Girls' British School, and flysheets distributed round the town. Participants included members of the Thurgood and Spurgin families. The issue rumbled on for many years, but church rates were not finally abolished until 1868. Meanwhile several other Government measures placated Dissenters, notably civil registration, allowing chapel marriage ceremonies and the 1836 Tithe Commutation Act, which put an end to centuries of litigation on this subject.[44]

Evangelical Outreach

What, it might well be asked, had all these wrangles to do with the poor? Eventually the various churches realised that such disunity undermined the urgent need to evangelize the poor who, notwithstanding Methodist and Baptist missioning, stayed away from church and chapel in large numbers. Worthies of all denominations felt sure that the poor could not find their way to God without their personal, paternalistic intervention. And so was born in 1842 a remarkable experiment in Evangelical outreach, the Saffron Walden Town Mission. The new Dissent of Methodists, Wesleyan and Primitive, seem to have been the only ones to take no part in this otherwise ecumenical initiative.

The roots of the Town Mission might be sought 30 years before in the formation in 1812 of the Saffron Walden Bible Society Auxiliary, designed to disseminate the Scriptures in the town, the villages of north-west Essex and abroad. This began as a high-status organisation, with a one-guinea subscription (ten guineas for life members), Braybrooke as president, the local MP, mayor and aldermen as vice-presidents and a battery of the great and good in committee. But it was also a committee which got off its seats and went out and about, knocking on doors. Early surveys suggested that about three-fifths of those visited could not read. At first the money to buy and distribute Bibles came pouring in, over £400 in the first year and they were able to spread their efforts round many local villages. The bankruptcy of the Searles, strong supporters of the Bible Society, caused a setback, and they were blamed by at least one person for 'uselessly spending a part of the Capital in collecting together a number of individuals to speechify, and compliment each other on their respective abilities'. But, as with so many aspects of Walden life, it was the move to the town of 'Gentleman' John Player in the mid-20s which revitalized the society. Around this time, also, the Saffron Walden Auxiliary of the Missionary Society, which had been founded in 1818, also acquired a new lease of life. There was clearly a renewal of mission at this time, with greater efforts made to get Bibles into poor households. The various churches worked in harmony in the Bible Auxiliary, apart from the sectarian problems of the 1830s.[45]

A religious tracts society, which had faded away, was also revived by Abbey Lane chapel — significantly in 1829, the same year as allotments began — to embrace all denominations. There were also at various times a Society for the Suppression of Vice, and a Temperance Society whose agent was William Kelly. The latter met much opposition when first started, but later expanded. In their first year, the Tracts Auxiliary lent 200 volumes and distributed 5,000 tracts, some at Audley End fair, such titles as 'Divine cordial' and 'Soul's conflict' being 'cheerfully received, diligently read and highly prized in the dwellings of the poor'. One particularly zealous member took on himself to visit 100 families per week, engaging them in religious conversation and reading the Scriptures aloud to small groups. As a result, some started going to church and morality improved: 'The profligate and vile have become moral and decent in their habits and prophane husbands have become affectionate to their wives and tender to their offspring'. There were never enough subscribers, but the few enthusiasts, who included women, by 1835 had given out a total of 10,000 tracts, doubled two years later. Its reports are full of phrases like 'days of abounding iniquity' and 'moral contagion' and they were constantly expecting 'a new era' to begin. But there were long gaps between meetings and financial support and enthusiasm fell away.[46]

Significantly perhaps, its demise followed soon after the resignation due to illness of John Player in 1843, for he had been a leading light. In its early success, however, can surely be found the germ of the idea which emerged as the ecumenical Saffron Walden Town Mission. The essential difference was that the earlier efforts had all been part-time and voluntary, whereas the town missionary was full-time and salaried.

The Town Mission

The Quakers, particularly Wyatt George Gibson, were a moving force behind the Town Mission, their influence revealed in the careful accounts and minutes, as well as the compulsion to reach the heathen poor. By the time that the other churches met together, in the Town Hall in February 1842 to discuss the subject, Gibson had already begun the hunt for a suitable person, via the British & Foreign Mission Society to 'to visit, read Scriptures, engage in religious conversation, urge people to observe Sabbath, distribute tracts and try to get scriptural education for children of the poor'. Philanthropic handouts minus moral uplift would not do, as noted at the agricultural show: 'unless the prizes of the society were accompanied with sound scriptural education they would be unavailing'. The energetic Baptist pastor, Rev. Josiah Wilkinson was also an enthusiastic supporter and Anglicans were generally outnumbered by Dissenters, but all agreed on the object, the missionary to receive £65 a year to work full time among the poor.[47]

Such organisations were becoming more common in towns at that time, having been pioneered in Glasgow in 1826, using evangelical doctrines as written for the London City Mission, but with a simplified statistics collection. The town missionary carried other advantages beyond those stated, for he also supplied social intelligence, to help with decisions about poor relief, charity and law enforcement. By employing a person independent of the churches, they hoped poor people would open up more. As with Benevolent Society and Clothing Bank visitors, the missionary could produce reports on immoral habits, the prevalence of sickness, school attendance, literacy, family size and domestic arrangements of the poorest, many of whom lived in the ramshackle tenements on back land, or in the more rural outposts of the town. Hence at least one of the missionaries, unlike more genteel middle-class visitors, deliberately sought out remote communities such as Redgates and Painters, populous slums such as Cains

236

Buildings in Castle Street and Copthall Buildings in Ashdon Road, and even itinerant residents in the various lodging houses, and in the streets and at fairs.[48]

The longest serving of the four missionaries, remaining from 1842–50, was the first, Peter Johnson from Clerkenwell, a man who proved to be of 'irreproachable character'. His first impressions, quoted at the head of this chapter, confirmed the desperate need to mission the poor. Within a month of his appointment, he had already produced a list of 654 dwellings to visit, which was two-thirds of all those in the parish. If they all turned out to be poor, this included almost every household in Debden Road, East Street, Lime Kiln, Foundry Lane, Copthall Buildings and Horn Lane; two-thirds in Sewards End; one-third in London Road; half in Bridge Street, Castle Street, Church Street, Gold Street and Little Walden; and one-quarter in the High Street, Butter and Pig Markets.[49]

Some reports were better than others. Audley End had its busy school, and the almshouse inmates enjoying a religious service on Sunday afternoons, courtesy of Lord Braybrooke's chaplain. Likewise, Little Walden, which Dissenters had missioned many years before, was 'highly favoured, and the people of that place seem fully to appreciate their privileges'. By contrast, Sewards End had 'no religious service, stated or occasional', a gap which was later filled by the Baptists, and by the Anglicans in 1847 with a chapel-of-ease, the site given by a local landowner and the building paid for by subscription. Johnson's initial impression was that many of the worst households, whom he identified particularly in Sewards End, Castle Street, London Road and Debden Road, were totally outside the influence of the church. Freed from most administrative or preaching duties, he could concentrate on the pastoral. Working 40–45 hours a week, he made well over a thousand visits in the first six months; after eight years, the tally amounted to 40,000 visits, reading the Scriptures more than 25,000 times and giving away thousands of religious tracts. Such concentrated, personalised evangelism must have made a difference, not only to those visited, but to the committee members, who every month heard the missionary read out the details of life in the mean streets, so contrasted to the bustling, well-ordered town flourishing a stone's throw away.[50]

The missionary was told specifically to 'seek out those who neglect public worship and are living in sin and pay special attention to such. This class being the one to which a Missionary is principally needed'. Many lonely, old and sick people enjoyed his visits, and once he had to be reminded that 'the main object of the Mission is to visit and reclaim the ungodly and vicious, rather than the religious part of the community'. But the committee were well pleased at the end of his eight years' service. Likewise his successors, Stephen Harber and William Perry did well and money seemed no problem, the mission being funded by subscribers, notably the Gibsons, and augmented further by legacies. Unfortunately most journals have not survived, other than one scrap of paper which records some of those visited in July 1858: a 'man in prison', Widow King who lived 'near the new pond', Maria Bradford of London Road, John Hodson of Castle Street, Mary Fincham of Sarah's Place and Elizabeth Houseden of Foundry Lane.[51]

In time, however, the drive which brought the Saffron Walden Town Mission into being seems to have lost its edge. After a rather unsuitable Primitive Methodist

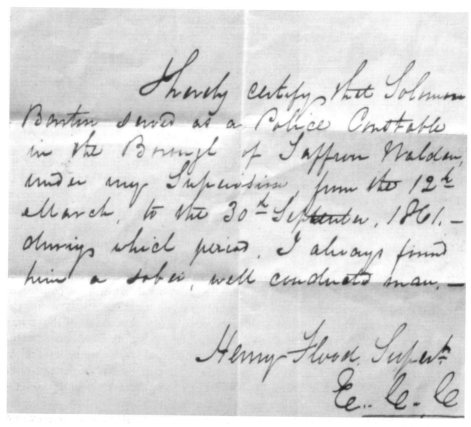

Fig.12.6 *The reference given to Solomon Barton, ex-policeman, the last full-time missionary employed by the Saffron Walden Town Mission.*

candidate was put aside, the job was given to ex-policeman Solomon Barton, who came with personal recommendations from the local superintendent, Henry Flood. [Fig.12.6] Barton, who lived in London Road, worked hard, visiting on average about ten households every day. In the course of a year he completed more than 3,000 visits, sometimes staying two hours for 'all the poor people seem to like me to visit them'. He read the Scriptures over 1,300 times to those who could not read, and gave out over 2,000 tracts to those who could.[52]

Barton, like the other missionaries, kept a journal, but his is the only one to have survived, a remarkable document, the more authentic because the missionaries were instructed to keep strictly accurate records. None of those visited were identified, apart from one undated note which shows he visited the *Swan* and the *Castle* lodging houses, and lists Mrs Judd of Church Street, Mrs Stanton of the *Swan*, Castle St, Mrs Smith of Foundry Lane, Mrs Cooper and Mrs Moore of Sewers (Sewards) End Road and Mrs Ferman of Little Walden. From its closely-written pages can be traced many attitudes of the day, not only to doctrines and morals, but to the economic and social conditions of the poor: on religious and moral questions, the missionary was unswerving in his strict stance throughout a year of recorded visits; the other matters provoked in his kindly heart a greater dilemma. His time in Walden coincided with years of particular distress, and this may have worsened conditions he reported.[53]

Barton's primary task was to tell the good news. Although the vast majority of his visits were to women in their own homes, curiously, the doctrinal questions recorded all came from men, sometimes quite complex issues such as Biblical texts, the deity of Christ, the Trinity, deism, pre-destination and Universalism. Reactions to his calls at first varied from mild interest to indifference, but gradually he won them over: 'During the last three months the inhabitance of the Town and parish, has received me generally speaking very cordially. Odd ones has born testimony that they have been benefited by my visits.' He clearly had a gentle charm, winning round the hostile: 'he rose quickly from his seat, his countenance changed, and he looked like a man that is out of his mind', he wrote once, but by the end of this visit, there was a smile and a handshake. The missionary's brief was to avoid religious argument and all discussion was firmly redirected towards the simple but momentous Arminian message of hope he carried into the homes of the poor: that however bad someone was, it was never too late to be forgiven and find salvation. In a context of destitution and prostitution, petty criminality, chronic illness and low life expectancy, this assurance carried a greater resonance and sometimes there was good news to tell, as with 'a woman who has rather an indifferent character till of late. This last twelve months she has reformed her character... I believe her to be a true penitent, she attributed these convictions to the death of her two children. Her husband who is not a very steady man ridicules her about those feelings.'[54]

The missionary must show none of the spiritual vacillation now penetrating the wider world, via Charles Darwin's *On the Origin of Species*, no troubling knowledge of how man descended from the apes, but an absolute certainty of Biblical truth. He must ensure there was a Bible in the house, to read from it, and perhaps help the semi-literate to learn the words with him. Not only the overtly sinful, but also — and with great urgency — the blameless dying were addressed with cruel candour: 'I said to her you had better think about another world, as I do not think you are long for this; it is useless for me to flatter you, you have a soul to save'.[55]

Barton's other great challenge was to distinguish between the genuinely needy and the mendicant. At first, he often displayed a hard attitude towards shallow protestations of poverty, on one occasion refusing to help an 'old practitioner', on another commenting 'there are very many about that acts the hypocrite for what they can get for their temporal wants'. With others he might conclude: 'there is a great deal of deception about but there cannot be any in these people'. The number of occasions on which he refers to this confirms that these social reports were part of his function. As time went on, however, he discovered the appalling depth and spread of poverty in town and countryside and, faced with a cold, sick, half-starved figure scarcely covered, lying on rags on the floor, could not help feeling increasing empathy with the poor. Then his respectful recommendations for material aid to be given became more frequent and more urgent: 'if there is a little charity to be bestowed those cases which I name this month, I believe is in greatest need, as my attention has been drawn, once or twice to the poverty that is in the town or parish'.[56]

Barton's brief to make a clear distinction between the spiritual and the material wants of the poor was often untenable, and the descriptions became more graphic. Those with no furniture, food or fuel, ex-prisoners, recently-confined women and those just out of hospital without home support, battered and deserted wives, the illegitimate and illiterate, the delinquent, the depressed and the drunk, the dying and the insane, prostitution and incest, disease, disability and debt, unemployment and malnourishment: all this and more, Solomon Barton saw and wrote down and read about every month to an audience of well-dressed gentlemen and men of the cloth, the leaders of the community, who learned from him what the Walden poor were experiencing. What action they took is not recorded, but it is difficult to imagine that Wyatt George Gibson or his generous son George Stacey, obeying their faith, did not quietly do something.

The missionary himself was not supposed to remedy physical poverty, but he wanted to do more to save their souls. His predecessors had also wanted to extend their work beyond the purely visitational, but Johnson's request to read Sunday evening sermons to the then church-less folk of Sewards End was not encouraged by the committee. Harber was allowed to organise a Bible class at a room in Castle Street for the inmates of the lodging houses, and other young men wanting to learn the Scriptures, and Perry tried to develop an evening adult school. But there was always a worry that this type of outreach was moving away from the original purpose of the Town Mission, and intruding on the territory of the churches.[57]

Solomon Barton took the mission to places others seldom ventured, calling on rough types in pubs and lodging houses, and visiting various homes straggling in the fields, miles from anywhere. No one else ever came there, and the lonely women asked him to run a cottage meeting, so that their menfolk would turn up. There was a short-lived experiment at Chapel End near Little Walden, and a more sustainable one at Sewards End, where a sympathetic landowner allowed the use of a barn. This was visited also by people from Painters and Cole End who crowded in on summer evenings: 'a great number of boys collects to gather there, and hears the scriptures read, and hear prayer and also a number of men who I dare say never goes to any other place of worship', he reported. Barton himself found the meetings rewarding, for his people became more willing to discuss religious feelings with him: 'there was a person told me on Sunday evening last, they thought I poured out my very soul for the people, this is very encouraging', he wrote on the last page of his surviving journal. At the end of his first year, Solomon Barton felt he was really getting somewhere, and was full of plans to pay out of his own money to light up the barn for winter meetings.[58]

But then it all came to a mysterious end. Barton's final journal entry, having filled up the book, records one of his Sunday evening meetings, and no more journals survive. The committee could see, perhaps, that the Town Mission was developing in a different direction, one which might be suitable in a city needing a mission hall but could not be justified to the town subscribers, who already supported a plethora of church buildings, and were paying out specifically for someone to visit the poor in their own homes. A few months later, they minuted dissatisfaction with the present arrangements and suspended them, giving Barton notice. When he bade farewell three months later, there was a sour note: 'The Journal was not read being considered unsuitable and not connected with the subject of the Mission'.[59]

A vague plan to replace the missionary with a Bible woman did not materialise, although they later decided to spend £40 on a missionary to evangelise the navvies on the railway being built at nearby Audley End. Later on George Stacey Gibson erected an Iron Meeting Room at Debden Road near the railway bridge, in use until 1870, with services and Sunday afternoon reading/writing classes. The Gibsons continued to support mission well into the twentieth century. But of the Town Mission itself, we hear no more. Perhaps it had just come to the end of its natural span, as had two of its chief supporters, Francis and Wyatt George Gibson who both died, each leaving legacies which were invested in railway shares. Clearly Barton left under a cloud. Had he grown too close to the poor, losing the objectivity expected of a professional social worker? Were the churches worried about the appearance of informal meetings which appealed more to the poor than church services? Perhaps the committee decided that the Primitive Methodists were more suited to reach the poor. Solomon Barton seems to have been a kind man. The lonely old folk, in particular, must have missed him.[60]

Conclusion

At the start of the twenty-first century, it is difficult to imagine how religion was once so all-pervasive. Out of the relative apathy of the eighteenth century had arisen a renewed Evangelical drive, closely linked to deepening poverty and unrest. Tremendous efforts were put into evangelising the Walden poor, through Sunday and day schools, missions and visitations, Bible distributions, church refurbishments and, in the case of the Primitive Methodists, recruiting the poor to teach themselves. Though temporarily weakened by sectarian divisions, the Walden denominations learned to work together again in the Town Mission, Christian activism on a full-time, face-to-face basis. It is fashionable to mock their seriousness, yet on this foundation much was achieved and, without it, the poor would have been even worse off and even more disaffected.

And yet... there remains the evidence of Solomon Barton's unique journal, extracts of which appear as a postscript, offering rare and authentic glimpses into the actual living conditions of the Walden poor at the end of the period under discussion in this book. Here, spread over 260 pages and about 50,000 words, it becomes clear that a half-century and more of worthy endeavour, statutory and philanthropic, had achieved very little for those at the bottom of the heap. The reasons were many but the fact was that the system made it extremely difficult for the majority of the poor to rise out of their difficulties. Some blamed the poor themselves, deepening the distinction between the respectable and the residuum, and increasing philanthropy to validate the system and prevent unrest. The strategy *seemed* to work. Saffron Walden by the 1860s, soon to acquire a purpose-built hospital, branch railway, new waterworks, modernised Town Hall and other improvements, appeared busy, prosperous and peaceful. But there were still many who did not share in the bounty, and Solomon's journal tells us the reality behind the facade. Theirs are sad and depressing stories but, whether or not those visited were 'old practitioners', they were also citizens of Saffron Walden and, on the backs of such, the town we enjoy today was built.

This book therefore ends with a question: if the social conditions of the poorest were still at this deplorable level, 70 years after Tom Paine's revolutionary remedies had been banned from the Walden bookshop, was the orderly town in reality merely an elite illusion, designed to obscure the fault-lines in a deeply unequal society? It is true that the history of Saffron Walden in the first half of the nineteenth century was a subtle, complex interplay of many forces, and it cannot be that social control alone explains them all. At the very least, however, Solomon's journal is a thought-provoking commentary on the true lives of the poor, and raises a question-mark as to whether there really existed in this period such a place as John Player's 'well-ordered town'.

Fig.12.7 *Castle Street.*

Postscript

Solomon's Journal

Journal of Saffron Walden Town Missionary, 1861–2 (extracts)

November 1861

a very distressed family… her husband had had no work for more than two months… he used to drink very much at one time but not so much lately… nine children… I tried to introduce religion to her, but their poverty seemed too great to think about religion, I really felt very much for the poor children, it seemed such a fearful way to bring them up in, really it is a mystery how they live according to the woman's account…

a family I personally know to be very dark and wretched… one of the most ignorant families in Walden… she still seemed to think it very strange that any one should have such a regard for such people as them, I asked if no one ever visited them, she said a Missionary used to come round once or twice a year…

this woman is mother to one of the lowest of the unfortunates, I asked her how she came to allow her daughter to lead such a life, she said she could not help it, she said she never received anything from her …

the most distressed family I have ever visited, I asked her how they came to be so distressed, she said they was obliged to get into debt to bury two of their children, some time ago, and her husband was out of employment and when they were called upon to pay they could not, and the creditor took their goods, I asked her if they were so distressed in their bed rooms, she said they had nothing in them, not even a bed, only some straw in a piece sacking on the floor…I believe what the woman said was right, I asked the neighbours a few questions about them, and they said they had their goods taken from them, and they said her husband was a steady man, he did not spend his money in drink like some, I really felt for the poor people, if I had had it in my power, I would have relieved them…

… a very young woman… lives in a very distressed state in a small room on the second floor and has nothing in it but one old chair a stool and an old bedstead I did not see any bed there was some thing laid in the middle of it an old shawl laid over it…

I visited various families on Ashdon Road… they said they wished there was a cottage meeting at one of the Houses, then perhaps the men would go in the evening, indeed I think my self it is very necessary there should be some thing of the kind…

a poor woman who lives in North End… she went to Church, but she could not get the relief she seemed to want … neither she nor her husband could read…

once lived in Pleasant Valley... they removed into this house to be nearer to Chapel... I said I thought it a great pity the daughter should lead such a bad life, the mother said she could not help it... both her girls had turned out bad... I then turned my attention to the girl... I told her how every one looked upon them as disgraceful... she said she would be glad if she could get out of it, she said if she could get a place of service, she would like it better, her mother said she would have to alter or go to the Union...

this woman has a family of eight children and is very poor, she did not plead poverty so much as some but I think she is a woman of great trouble, I told her I could sympathise with her and that was all I could do in that respect...

visited the one Bell and Castle Lodging House at the Castle I found Six Travellers, and some Children... one of the men presently talking to me about teetotalism... they all listened with very good attention, and especially one young man... they thanked me for my visit.

afflicted and she has been for some years with rheumatism... she seemed very surprised when I went in the House, I asked her if the Missionary never visited her, she said he did once or twice some years ago but not of late, I said did no one visit her, she said the Curate once upon a time, but very seldom...

this young man is deaf and dumb, lodging in a house where I called today... he wrote on a slate and said he wished he could hear me... he showed me a Bible that was presented to him at the deaf and dumb asylum... I hope he was a good young man, but that I must leave with God...

this old lady... began lamenting the loss of a son, that had left England, with out assigning any particular reason, and it appeared that this son was in good circumstances in life, he rose till he became Mastorman in London, so became higher in life than her other children...

this man in a very desponding state of mind... he had no fire and was walking about the House, with his hat and great coat on, I asked him if he had any one belonging to him living near, he said he had one son in London and one in Debden... I told the neighbours I thought it was quite unsafe for him to be alone...

visited eleven families in the neighbourhood of Painters, and read the Scriptures with some of them, they all seemed very pleased to be visited and to hear the scriptures read, they said it seemed such a heathenism place just round that neighbourhood...

January 1862

On calling at this House I expected to find the inmates in a very dark state of mind, having previously heard that the man was an infidel... the woman began to bewail her troubles. She did not tell me decidedly that her husband ill treated her, but I understood her to say as much, she also said her family was a great trouble to her, and that some people who had called at the house in times past, had spoken very cross to her, and said there were no pity for her... she appeared a clean industrious woman... neighbours said... she had been in that low state of mind she was sent to the asylum once...

I found the woman ill in bed and the house in a very desolate state, though she had a daughter at home quite a young woman, but had brought her up in such a way that she knew nothing, not even the way to clean a house, and the neighbours do not like to go in, they are such strange people, I have been unable to get admittance into the house before today, I went up stairs to the woman, and found her by all appearance in a dying state...

said she wished I would give her husband a good talking to when I saw him... her husband was not altogether unkind to her, but neglected his home... he was fond of Drink, and company...

their dwelling not being visible, standing at the back of other houses, I found an old man ill, lying on a bed in an old back place, more like an out house than a bed room... he pleaded poverty, indeed their dwelling looked the picture of it, as the room was dark where he lay... I read the Scriptures to him by the light of a candle...

a very careless family and never attend any place of worship... I fear there are several in that neighbourhood of the same kind...

a family I have given some extra visits, on account of the old man, whom I promised I would teach to read, but I found he could not read to understand what he read but had to spell every word..

he is dray man at the Brewhouse, I told him I am afraid it was a place of great temptation, he said it was, and he should prefer some thing else...

February 1862

Just had a child die a few days before, rather ill, yellow jaundice... the folly and anger of leading such a life as I have known them to have led... the impression seemed but very slight upon her, she rather lamented the loss of her child and her own affliction...

the mother, a son and daughter, and a man who passed as the daughter's husband, and I fear it is only to pass as such or more, wretched still, for I have seen her walking the streets with her sister, who is an unfortunate, and was in bed only a few hours before, having given an untimely birth to an illegitimate child... the old man the father of the child, had died only three weeks before... they only laughed at what I said, I think it is the most hardened family I ever met with...

a young woman who was only confined three days before... about her work. She could not afford to pay any one for attending upon her...

Sewars End... this man came into a house where I was, he had a great deal too much drink... Told him about hell — this conversation did not appear to suit him, as he rose from his seat and left the room...

this poor man is very ill... he frequently has a relapse of it... and I am sorry to say in an unconverted state, and I fear rather hardened in sin... I said I feared it would take him off... the surgeon told him the same thing... I am sorry to say his wife seems in the same hardened state, I believe they never go to any place of worship.

family lived at back of The Swan yard — I spoke to them about some unfortunates I have known them to harbour... they had all left now and they did not intend to have any more, but still she said she thought there must be places for such to live... I said there were a great many of that kind, as was not drove to it... I fear they are bad characters, though they were very kind to me.

visited this poor woman several times… seems very much cast down… as she sat sewing I saw the tears drop down her eyes… I asked her what made her so low spirited…the woman is penitent, but wants encouragement in the place of this strong language.

this old man very ill in bed, he is Dropsical… he never had religion explained to him so clearly as I had explained to him that day, and I am thankful to say he is not the only one, that as told me the same thing even people that did not have anyone come to visit them, now tells me to come as they like my company…

a poor woman, who is living with her son at Little Walden. Began pleading her poverty. I asked her if she had no parish allowance, she said she had, but had to pay sixpence per week for her lodgings and some other odd pence for other things, so she had only about one shilling and sixpences per week to live upon. I said I must allow that was not much to live upon, but no one was without their troubles, some more and some less, the whole family seems very poor.

this poor man very lame, having had a misfortune and been kicked by a horse… he never had scarcely any sickness in all his life before, though he was getting a very old man… they live close to the farm where he has worked for many years, though they may not be any better off for that.

a very poor family who live in North End… the woman pleaded great poverty… they had six children and her husband had only nine shillings per week… they are in difficulties at this time, for the poor woman is expecting to be confined very shortly and cannot obtain any assistance by way of charity as they are between two parishes. They formerly lived at Littlebury… they do not allow anything from the Parish… she belonged to Walden and her husband belonged to Littlebury… it was not in my power to relieve her…

this poor woman seems very ill… pleaded great poverty on account of her husband being out of work so long…indeed I find that a general complaint this month, men being out of employment and people plead great poverty…

this old lady ill in bed… very contented… had only Parish allowance and sixpence per week to pay out of it for rent… She said she wished I could come every day…

two people at this house one of them was a very old practitioner, she began begging of me, I told her I could not give to all, so I would not give to any, then they could not disagree…

too weak to converse much, he said he felt himself going very fast… he said he felt he was a sinner… doubt whether he had nourishment enough, one of the neighbours told me they thought neither him nor the family had sufficient, he wished me to pray with him, I did so…

April 1862

this family…seemed to have a comfortable home for poor people, the family looked clean, but the woman complained of great poverty… she said her husband was a labouring man, but lost a weeks work occasionally… there were seven in the family…

young people, they have only one child, but the woman complained of great poverty and said her husband had been out of work three months, I believe it is quite true as I have seen the man standing about the streets a very long time, I am sorry to say they are a very careless family, and ignorant of religion, I do not think they go to any place of worship, from one month to another…

he had very bad health... now quite unable to follow his employment... not be able to return to his native town... cost him to bring his family here... he was supported from a club he was in, that brought him in ten shillings per week, and in the course of a few weeks that would be taken off to five, and he has now a doctor to pay out of it, his poor wife seems in great distress... if I had it in my power I felt I could have given the poor man the money out of my own pocket, I hope Providence will provide the means for the sake of the poor family...

this woman has been ill for nearly twelve months, she complained of being very much neglected... no one cared for her or gave her anything, I told her I cared as much for her as any one else, but I had nothing to do with giving charities, mine was a higher mission... she attributed the neglect as she so called it, to a false report, that had been raised about her...

a young woman without any children, she has been very ill of late and unfortunately her husband has been out of employment for some time, and I much doubt whether she has sufficient nourishment as she still remains very weak...

an old man... he is frequently asking me to relieve him, I believe he is in want some times, I have given him sixpence myself... I fear strong drink was at one time a great besetment to him... says he has not forgot the words I said to him, I hope that was a caution to him, not to give way to Drink so much...

this woman complained of great poverty, and said her husband had been out of employment all winter, she said all the children had been ill, she said the visiting ladies did not come in that neighbourhood, therefore they never get relieved. This woman is not one who generally pleads poverty though always looks distressed in the house...

a very wretched distressed family... a daughter 19 years of age... formerly living in Stennets Yard... I fear there is not very good works there on a Sunday as I have seen once or twice a quantity of low looking men, come out of the house... the mother always complains of the conduct of her husband, and says he spends all her money and leaves the family destitute... she told me before she went to prison, she had not cloths to go in, I think the woman is to be pitied...

her complaint is I believe a decline, a complaint that requires nourishment, but it is out of the way of all visiting ladies, and her mother told me they had a family of 8 children, and her husband is only a farm labourer and gets but very low wages...

May 1862

those are three poor families, they are continually pleading great poverty, they have formerly been to my house to ask for relief, I told them I had nothing to give them... there does not seem to be that anxiety and industry about them, which I would like to see, there always seems something slovenly about them, and careless...

a very poor distressed family, indeed they are nearly all alike in those Buildings, but however poor and ignorant they are, they are very civil... some of them had never been into a place of worship in their lives, though they were then men grown... stand in the yard of an evening, and speak openly, when the men were home, for there were many in the yard had no regard for God...

this woman is in the most pitiable state, it really is fearful to see her, she is quite unable to speak, though she is very patient in her affliction, I think she really is to be pitied, however bad her character may have been, I look upon such as all the more to be pitied, not having one glimpse of hope, my heart yearns over such, taken as it were death is staring them in the face, and starving to death as it were by inches, because she cannot partake of any sustenance... I hope God will have mercy on her soul, for it is awful to think of suffering so much hear (*sic*), and hearafter.

a young man who is suffering from deceased (*sic*) heart... I believe incurable... I told him those times when he felt worse ought to be a great warning to him, and especially as he appeared in a dying state... he evaded all my attempts by speaking of different things respecting this world...

on visiting the Lodging Houses this month, I only found one at the Castle, a woman to whom I was going to read the scriptures, but she walked out of the room, I hope she will be led to see her state by nature before she is called away to give an account of the deeds done in her body. I have frequently spoken to the Landlady of this House about her soul...

June 1862

very poor family, and I think is deserving a little charity... husband has been very unfortunate as it regards his work... has been working in a malting nearby all winter at very low wages in the place of a boy because he couldn't get anything else to do, he is now working at Wenden for a short time at the railway, the woman looks careworn, she is very civil but destitute of religion...

this case is a very hard one... I believe the woman to be a very industrious person, though a bad temper. Had a child before she was married to this man... She has gone into such depths of iniquity, but still she seems to like to hear good things, and she cannot tell me more about true religion than one half of the professing people...

many out of employment a long time, I do think they are in want of bread, I know the children have been out to beg, the man formerly worked at the brewery, I believe he left in disgrace from what I have heard, but it is hard for the children to want food...

their means are but very scanty... altogether I think the poor people are almost at their wits end...I believe they are deserving a little assistance, by way of charity.

she is very lame now. She tells me she never had any relief whatever, and her husband is only a farm labourer. I believe there are visiting ladies and other visitors in that neighbourhood, but she says they do not visit her because she supposes she has offended them... she is very blunt in her way of speaking but I think straight forward, though I may be deceived in her, I think she is very poor and needs some little assistance... the woman who lodges there looks very distressed, I believe the woman is in want, she told me she had only a crust of bread to eat, and she appears to have scarcely any cloths, she makes gloves for a livelyhood...

this man is suffering from an internal complaint I believe he has tried almost every thing and had good advice. But it has done him no good... he paid two shillings and sixpence for the medicine each time... his wife poor woman has little hopes of his recovery... it is very discouraging for the poor young people, he is unable to work...

a very poor ignorant woman till of late… her son had broken out again, she attributed it to a persons company, whom he had been in… one of the neighbours was speaking to me about the disturbance, I told them I believed the woman to be a good woman… they said she had got some bad ones about her, I said she couldn't help what they did…

July 1862

a young man who is subject to fits, I believe he is well known to most people, he receives parish allowances. But I do not think he is able to get sufficient nourishment… so very sinking at his stomach, a continual gnawing as it were… I believe him to be in very great need, indeed his suffering is very great…

the woman told me her husband was gone away and left her… he was at one of his relations, who is living at Walthamstow…he was in such a distressed state of mind, they did not know what to do with him… I do not know how the woman obtains a livelihood unless it is by her needs. She has two children, she keeps them very clean, she appears a very industrious woman… her husband has been sent to the asylum… he has since died.

this poor old woman is getting very feeble, and really is unfit to be left alone, she fell down in the house one day and had to lay for a very long time before she obtained assistance… she has a daughter who is very kind to her, she pays her house rent for her and one shilling per week for a woman to go in occasionally to attend upon her… I really feel she is not fit to be left alone, therefore if she had a trifle allowed her with that of her daughters, she would be able to have some one with her…

this family I believe is in great distress, they are depending upon one of the sons for livelihood, and he has been out of employment for a very long time, but there are many things in the way which prevent them from being relieved, … they are living in a house which is considered to be their own, but I believe they had a great deal to pay on it… they are keeping children belonging to one of the daughters… it lays very hard upon parents, when children are so unruly… they are a very ignorant family about religion…

this poor woman is in a most pitiable condition, she is so much afflicted… her husband is also a very great sufferer, it really is the most pitiable case I ever known, they do not complain, but such as these are often in the most need…

the poor woman has been very ill during this last month of the fever… I believe they lie on a bed of straw, the first time I went up into the bedroom, she had scarcely any cloths on the bed, and the pillow of her bed had an old shirt of her husbands laid over it by way of a slip… her husband behaved very bad to her and spent his money in drink and she has a family of eight children..

on visiting these Buildings today, I met with those two men, they are of that wretch ignorant family, one of them I do not think never entered a place of worship in all his life time… I forced my conversation upon them but they made very little answer…

I visited the one Bell, and White swan, but found none present. On visiting the castle, there I found eight or nine, I talked to them some time about the importance of the souls salvation. But there was only one that answered me…I gave them three or four small tracts, they began to read them very readily, I then left, warning them to seek to flee from the wrath to come.

a very distressed family… seldom appears to have any change of raiment, the clothes she wears they really are very bad, today she scarcely had any shoes on her feet, I did not make any remarks about it, but only asked her how she got on in this world, and she spoke as if she was thankful, because she was able to get bread. I know she has two or three great girls, which ought to be out at service…

August 1862

she wept very bitterly to me, and said she did not know how she should obtain a livelyhood as she was quite unable to work at present, I asked her how much money she received per week, she said two shillings, and she had one shilling and 6d to pay for her house rent, so she cannot have saved much out of it…

she took very great notice of what I said… I was afraid the people were all so very careless about the soul, they would not come in… my receptions are very cordial in those buildings and all the lower parts of the town and parish, much more so than among those who profess to know some thing of religion…

this is an unfortunate… she seems now to resolve to break off her evil habits… she seemed to find excuses, I daresay she feels ashamed and partly fears her former companions jeers and sneers. I asked her if she would not like to walk over to Sewards End, to my cottage meeting… but she made no answer to it… her Mother said they had been almost starven for wants of food of late. I have also heard so by other people but I cannot say it is positively true, but the woman professed to be a Christian, so I hope she is capable of telling the truth, I have no reason to disbelieve her myself.

she was at that time surrounded with ungodly people…she checked them in their evil course and endeavoured to keep them from the drink and by so doing they turned upon her, and turned her out of the house one night when they came home, so this young woman and her husband have taken a house in this yard… I pray God will enable her, to resist the evil set before her…

the people are very much engaged at this time of the year…. indeed all over the town and parish is much the same and will continue for about a month or six weeks.

September 1862

this person has given me a very great encouragement… lately I find many people like this woman, to have a great desire… people seem more anxious to converse with me about religion… there is scarcely a house in this neighbourhood, that I am in the habit of visiting, but what I could have a cordial reception at and read the word of God… I believe it is well known to everyone one that it is a very ignorant place as any in Walden…

October 1862

I found this poor woman very ill, I believe in a declining state… she seemed to have a great desire to be sent to the Hospital at Cambridge… she is one who has been accustomed to sit under the sound of the Gospel, I believe her mother is a religious woman, after a few minutes more conversation, she asked me to pray with her, I did so and left, the poor woman has since died.

poverty was uppermost, she evaded all my attempts by pleading distress, wishing to obtain means to get to London to her husband who is working in London, she also said she had to leave all her goods to pay the rent, at a house which she had lately left... I told her she must sell what she had got now, to go to her husband, it would be as cheap to do that as to take them, as it was very expensive to take furniture by rail. She said she had not much to sell - for she was obliged to lay her bed on the floor. I fear the principle thing she wanted to see me for, was to see if I would give her any thing to help her.

I went up into the bedroom to see the woman I found her very ill indeed, and the dark state of her mind, I could not describe to any one... I said to her, where do you think you shall go if you were to die now, she clenched her hands, and said, Hell, Hell, Hell is my portion. There are the devils waiting for me, I said devils, she rolled her eyes around and said yes, yes, multitudes of them, this is such a sight I never witnessed before...I was alone with her in the room but she seemed after this to be more at liberty and was able to speak, I said to her pray, she said I cannot pray I am gone too far, it is not for me, I said you are not gone further than the thief on the Cross... she then looked at me some-what more cheerful... I have visited her twice this day... she appeared quite another woman in her mind... I asked her if she had seen any more of those ugly things, oh no she said I shall go to heaven now when I die...

Last entry in journal

It is now over twelve months since he called me to labour, specially in his vineyard. And I can say my labours have not been in vain, to the Glory of his name.

Notes to the Chapters

Most references are gathered at the end of the relevant paragraph, beginning with primary sources, with the addition of the principal secondary texts used. All references are Saffron Walden unless otherwise stated. Saffron Walden Town Archives are currently being assigned new ERO references. Most references are given in abbreviated form here: see the bibliography for references in full. The author would be pleased to assist genuine researchers seeking further amplification of the notes.

Abbreviations

BFSS	British & Foreign Schools Society
EH	*Essex Herald*
ERO	Essex Record Office
ES	*Essex Standard*
PMM	*Primitive Methodist Magazine*
PP	Parliamentary Papers
PRO	Public Record Office
SWH	*Saffron Walden History*
SWMA	Saffron Walden Museum Archives
SWTL	Saffron Walden Town Library
TA/CA/OC	Saffron Walden Town Archives

Chapter 1: The Well-ordered Town

1   *ES*, 9 June 1832.
2   TA13, 10 January 1822; TA 599/1–8, various dates, 29 July 1830–20 September 1832; Stacey Album, vol 5 (SWTL); Rowntree, *Then and Now*, pp.36–47.
3   No meetings of Spire Committee minuted 1 May–20 September 1832; TA13; *ES*, 9 June 1832. The Reform Act was passed 4 June, Thaxted celebration 5 June, spire ceremony Wednesday 6 June.
4   *ES*, 15 September 1832.
5   Monteith thesis, p.205.
6   Census of Saffron Walden, 1831; CA10, 18 December 1837, 9 March 1838; Thomas Smyth, *Excursions Through Essex*, quoted in Player, *Sketches*, p.33.
7   TA50, 14 April 1806.
8   Pigot's *Directory* for Essex, 1823 & 1832.
9   *ES*, 13 June 1845; *Muilman*, pp.65–6; *Chelmsford Chronicle*, 8 January 1808; ERO D/DBy E33; Brown, *Essex at Work*, p.90; Maud, pp.143–5; Nurse, Pugh & Mollet, p.92.
10 SWMA 40020, 3 December 1835 report, letter 5 September 1835; Madonna, p.50.
11 SWMA 40020, letter 23 May 1836; *ES*, 5 March 1841, 14 June 1844, 7 November 1845.
12 Barker M.M., p.80; Madonna, p.50.
13 Census of Saffron Walden, 1801–61.
14 Information L.D. Barker.
15 Information L.D. Barker: TA14, 20 July 1827; CA23, 17 January 1829; Muir essay (SWTL).
16 ERO D/P 192/1/9; SWMA 40498; Barker family information from L.D. Barker; CA15/ CA 35; Census of Saffron Walden, 1831.
17 Muir essay (SWTL); Census of Saffron Walden, 1841.
18 Saffron Walden Census, 1811 (SWTL); Williams, p.25; Addison, pp.178–184.
19 SWMA 40221; Monteith thesis, p.216; Mary Whiteman, *SWH*, Spring 1986, p.145; Rowntree, *Then and Now*, pp.73, 97.
20 Barker, L.D., Castle Street study (SWTL); Monteith thesis, p.196.
21 TA9, 13 March 1807; Saffron Walden Town Mission journal, October 1862.
22 TA51,14 October 1822. See also Sessions entries for 8 August 1794, 15 July 1822, 17 October 1826, 9 January 1827, 14 July 1829, 2 May 1833, 4 July 1834.
23 TA104, 26 October 1846; TA (uncat.), General Baptist records, November 1830, 22 February 1833.
24 Quoted in Ludgate, p.35.
25 *ES* 14 July 1832, 6 October 1848.
26 ERO Q/RDc 25A, 30 June 1823, deposited 4 June 1829; TA239; Monteith thesis, pp. 208, 215, maps 20 & 214.

27 Tate, *Enclosure Movements*, pp.43, 111; Braybrooke, *Audley End*, p.237; H.C. Stacey, *SWH*, Autumn 1990, p.132.

28 Census Reports 1811/ 1831; PP 1831, XXXVI, p.196; Saffron Walden Census, 1811 (SWTL); Brown, *Essex at Work*, p.129; Brown, *Meagre Harvest*, pp.3–4.

29 SWMA 40477; ERO D/DBy 049, 12 November 1832: there are anomalies in these two surveys. Only the 1832 listing is available, discovered by the author among Audley End papers in the Essex Record Office, lacking any indication that it relates to minutes among John Player mss in SWTL. Other information L.D. Barker; Barker, Castle Street study (SWTL); 1851 Census of Saffron Walden; Muir essay (SWTL); Mills, p.67.

30 SWMA 40477, report on employment, 26 October 1832.

31 1833 Poor Law Report; CA278; Richardson, p.90; ERO D/DBy A267; Brown, *Essex People*, pp. 90–103. *SWERO—HouseForm °/cs*

32 Majendie Poor Law report, 1833, p.40; *Poor Mans Guardian*, 14 November 1835.

33 Addison, pp.185–6; Richardson, pp. 69–89 & Appendix 4.1, p.90; ERO D/DBy A267.

34 *Essex & Herts Mercury*, 24 September 1833; *Essex Chronicle*, 13 October 1837; *ES*, 23 October 1840, also 1841 report on agricultural show.

35 ERO D/Dby A272; ERO D/DBy A348 Private Account 1825–50, September & December 1838; ERO D/DBy A 273; ERO D/DBy 049, 12 November 1832; further information, L.D. Barker

36 Saffron Walden Town Mission journal, November 1861 (see chapter 12).

37 SWMA 40477, meeting 20 October 1832; ERO D/DBy 049.

38 Player omitted artisans at William Burrows' tailors, about 20 of Messrs Gibsons' artisans, shopmen at Day & Robson and Leveretts, and printers working for Youngman.

39 ERO D/DBy 049.

40 CA15, 27 March 1797; Brown *Essex at Work*, pp.3–20; Ena Wright, *SWH*, Spring 1983, p.199; Rowntree, *Then and Now*, p.1; PP 1840, XXII, pp. 127, 133,137, 195; Goose, pp.58–9.

41 Mary Whiteman, *SWH*, Spring 1986, p.144; Mary Whiteman, *SWH*, Autumn 1981, p.115; ERO D/DAd 12, various entries; ERO D/DAd 13 1823–31 (information L.D. Barker); Pigot's *Directory* of Essex, 1832, pp.705–7; Burningham's 'Memories of 50 years ago', *Saffron Walden Weekly News*, 1906; ERO D/DHt 7408/2.

42 ERO D/DBy 049; PRO HO 52 29, letter from John Player, Mayor, to Home Office, 11 May 1836; Information L.D. Barker; SWMA 41571, letter Charles Porter to John Player, 20 September 1831; Muir essay (SWTL); Booker, pp.72–3.

43 *ES*, 20 April 1833.

44 Brown, *Chartism*, p.31; Saffron Walden Census, 1811 (SWTL); Census of Saffron Walden, 1831–51; Muir essay (SWTL); H.C. Stacey, *SWH*, Spring 1982, p.130.

45 Pigot's *Directory* for Essex, 1823, 1832, 1839, 1848.

46 ERO D/DAd 12, 19 December 1810, 29 June 1819, 30 December 1816.

47 ERO T/B 495/5, 10 April 1807; ERO D/DAd 12, various entries (information L.D. Barker); Matthews & Tuke, p.174; Grieve, pp.283–6; Christy, p.7; *London Gazette*, 31 December 1825, p.2415; Preston, various pages.

48 ERO T/B 495/8, 11 November 1825; SWMA 40504, statement as at 2 January 1826; TA (uncat.), Saffron Walden General Baptist records, letter from George Smallfield to James Humphreys, 7 July 1826; see also letter 30 January 1826; SWMA 40504, letter 26 May 1826.

49 SWMA 40665; Mary Whiteman, *SWH*, Autumn 1981, p.115; Matthews & Tuke, p.174; ERO D/DAd 12–13, p.293. Catlin association with bank ceased 1831, Gibsons ran bank until 1852 when Midgley family became involved. In 1896 it became part of Barclays.

50 ERO D/CT 378A, 6 April 1842.

51 ERO D/DBy 049.

52 SWMA 40462, 1838 survey; Town Mission minutes, 1842; Municipal Boundaries Report, 1835: 990 houses, of which 683 excused rates, 280 paying rates and 27 rated with the land.

53 King, 'Gleaners', pp.116–150; *ES* October 1847; PP 1834, XXX.

Chapter 2: All the Beauty, Wealth and Intelligence of the Town

1 *ES*, 17 October 1834. The ploughing match that year took place in Town's End Field on the Little Walden Road, and the cattle show on Castle Hill; later on, it took place on the Common.

2 *ES*, 23 October 1840.

3 Rowntree, *Then and Now*, pp.36–47; *1951/ERO not on the canal* Addison, pp.141–3, 169; Shrimpton thesis, pp.27–30; ERO D/Dby A296. *Oslor 9 other a/cs*

4 Shrimpton thesis, pp. 27–30, 35; Mary Whiteman, *SWH*, Spring 1988, p.20; Wilson, p.15; Addison, pp.159–67, 170, 197; Young, *General View*, pp. 60, 237, 240.

5   *ES*, 9 November 1839; *Essex & Herts Mercury*, 24 September 1833; Addison, p.159.

6   Shrimpton thesis, p.35; Addison, pp.178–9,185–6; White thesis, p.59.

7   ERO D/DBy C35; SWMA 40020; White, *Chronological*, pp.130–32.

8   *ES*, October 1846.

9   TA (uncat.) General Baptist records, letter 17 November 1837, George Smallfield to James Humphreys.

10   Addison, p.178; Rowntree, *Then and Now*, p.9; CA188, letter 20 August 1832; TA103, 3 December 1832 and 8 March 1833; CA356; CA275.

11   *ES*, 1 June, 6 July 1838; Coronation MSS., 28 June 1838 (SWTL); SWMA 40482; Coronation posters in Saffron Walden Museum exhibition.

12   *ES*, 6 July 1838.

13   H.C. Stacey, *SWH*, February 1974, p.16; SWMA 40497; ERO D/DAd 12, 19 December 1810.

14   *ES*, October 1835; SWMA 40458, 40486, 40497, 40504; H.C. Stacey, *SWH*, June 1974; K.J. Lovatt, *SWH*, November 1976; ERO T/B 495/8, 1 August 1823.

15   SWMA 40474, 40504, 40486; *ES*, October 1835.

16   SWMA 40486, 40474; Player, *Chronicles*, January 1827.

17   SWMA 40154; CA82; SWMA 40481; Hughes thesis; Saffron Walden *Yearbook* 1853, p.22.

18   Mary Whiteman, *SWH*, Spring 1986, p.147; SWMA 40486; SWMA 41000.

19   ERO T/A 623/1–5; G. O'Leary, *SWH*, June 1974, p.28; *SWH*, Autumn 1985 and others; SWMA 40479; ERO T/A 623/1–5, 1832; SWMA 40477, *EH*, 26 September 1832; ERO T/A 623/1–5; SWMA 40163.

20   SWMA 40497.

21   SWMA 40486; *Chelmsford Chronicle*, 19 January 1836.

22   SWMA 40504, letter 27 July 1836.

23   SWMA 40504, letter 27 July 1836.

24   *ES*, 16 November 1838, 6 February 1846; CA34, 1 September 1836–1 September 1837; SWMA 40486, 5 August 1840, 28 April 1841; SWMA 40489, 10 January 1842.

25   Player, *Sketches*; SWMA 40497.

26   SWMA 40489, 10 January 1842; SWMA 40486, letter 5 August 1840.

27   SWMA 40477, statement 29 December 1830; SWMA 40500, letter 17 November 1809; SWMA 40477, letter 20 February 1833; Owen, pp.95, 98. Phrenology was the study of a person's skull, each bump supposedly reflecting certain traits.

28   *ES*, 2 & 9 March 1838; Mary Whiteman, *SWH*, Autumn 1981, p.113; CA406 (i); CA186a/b; Christine Plumb, *SWH*, Autumn 1989, p.89; H.C. Stacey, *SWH*, Autumn 1982, p.159.

29   *SWH*, Autumn 1981, p.112; in the 1835 elections, Jabez received 148 of 168 votes, Wyatt George 89; ERO G/Sw M6–8, 12 September 1862.

30   ERO T/A 284/1–2; TA 425, 30 December 1844; ERO D/DAd 12, various entries; ERO D/DAd 13; PRO MH 12/3706, 17 April 1837; Mary Whiteman, *SWH*, Autumn 1981, pp.112–17; White, *Chronological*, p.121.

31   ERO Q/SBb 467/51, 29 March 1822; TA58, November 1831, March 1833, March 1834, January 1835 & March 1836; January 1836; PRO MH/12/3706, 2 November 1836.

32   SWMA 40479; White thesis.

33   ERO D/DAd 12, various entries; H.C. Stacey, *SWH*, June 1974, p.32; SWMA 40517; CA 449, 1837.

34   ERO D/DAd 12, 24 December 1819, p.469; H.C. Stacey, *SWH*, November 1974; Gumbrell, vol 1, pp.46–7.

35   CA229; TA63; TA104, 30 October 1848; Sweet, p.149.

36   ERO D/DAd 12, 10 July 1818, 29 June 1819; TA 103, 8 March 1833, 2 June, 4 July 1834; CA208; SWMA 40478; Rowntree, *Then and Now*, p.34; TA441 (iii), 1818; TA63, 4 & 25 August 1834; *ES*, 12 July 1834, 1 January 1836, 9 November 1838.

37   TA 13, 26 March & 6 April 1821; CA106; SWMA 40369; TA104, 6 May 1839; *ES*, July & September 1846; H.C. Stacey, *SWH*, Spring 1985, p.81.

38   J. Dallaway, *SWH*, Autumn 1986, pp.152–62 & Spring 1987, pp.197–204; Pigot's *Directory*, 1832 & 1839; Gumbrell, vol 1, p.33 & vol 2, p.1; H.C. Stacey, *SWH*, Spring 1983, p.200; SWMA 40799.

39   *ES*, 15 February 1839; H.C. Stacey, *SWH*, Spring 1982, p.147; H.C. Stacey scrapbook vol 5, p.5 (SWTL); J.G. O'Leary, *SWH*, June 1974, p.28.

40   ERO D/CT 378A; further information L.D. Barker.

41   H.C. Stacey, *SWH*, November 1974, pp.17–20; Mary Whiteman, *SWH*, Spring 1986, pp.143–7; Hills thesis, p.12.

42   *ES*, 15 January, 20 May, 23 September 1836.

Chapter 3: The Formidable Clique of Gamboogers

1   *ES*, 29 March 1834.

2   SWMA 40504, letter John Player to Jabez Gibson, 27 July 1836.

3 Everett, *Civil War*; CA6 (i) & (ii); Evans, pp.71–2; E.P Thompson, pp.61, 102–3.

4 Madonna, p.53; Rowntree, *Then and Now*, pp.101–102; Wilson, p.10.

5 Information L.D. Barker: PRO WO 13/4320; Evans, p.74.

6 Hobsbawm, *Revolution*, pp.141–2; E.P. Thompson, pp.194–201.

7 *ES*, 29 April, 17 & 24 June, 8 & 29 July 1831; SWMA 40369; Evans, p.225.

8 *ES*, 8 & 15 July 1831.

9 Evans, chs. 23/24; Addison, pp.184–5; Halevy, pp.13, 40–43, 59; *ES*, 22 October 1831.

10 *ES*, 15 September 1832.

11 SWMA 40500, letter 10 December 1833; Perkin, p.313; Rowntree, *Then & Now*, p.26–7; Evans, p.401, B.ii.1; Brown, *Colchester*, p.108.

12 *ES*, 9 June 1832; Rowley, *Elections*, Illustration 4, see also portrait of C.C. Western; Brown *Colchester*, chapter 4.

13 PRO HO 52/17, letters 14 December 1832; Halevy, pp.61–2; *ES*, 13 October, 24 November 1832.

14 SWMA 40219, 20 October 1832.

15 *ES*, 15 & 29 December 1832: Tyrell (Tory) 2448 votes, Baring (Tory) 2280, Western (Liberal) 2244, Brand (Liberal) 1840.

16 *ES*, 29 December 1832.

17 Rowntree, *Then & Now*, p.69; TA103; TA 47–51.

18 Rowntree, *Then & Now*, pp.16–24; Hennock, pp.38–49; information L.D. Barker.

19 SWMA 40500, letter 10 December 1833; Hennock, p.40; Fraser, *Power and Authority*, pp.2, 6; Hills thesis, p.67.

20 TA103, 10 January 1834.

21 SWMA 40500, letter 10 December 1833; SWMA. 40486; White thesis.

22 Brown, *Colchester*, pp.42–3; *ES*, 29 March 1834.

23 PP 1835, XL & 1837, XLIV; Hennock, p40; Fraser, *Power and Authority*, pp.2, 6.

24 TA103, 17 June, 5 August 1835; PP 1835, XXVI, Pt. iv; Fraser, *Power and Authority*, p.8.

25 TA 103, 25 April, 2 June, 4 July 1834; *ES*, 12 July 1834.

26 Fraser, *Power and Authority*, p.11; Halevy, pp.217–18.

27 *ES*, 1 & 15 January 1836; Fraser, *Power and Authority*, p.149.

28 *ES*, 1 & 15 January 1836.

29 PRO HO/52/ 29, letter 9 May 1836; *ES*, 20 May 1836.

30 *ES*, 15 January 1836; H.C. Stacey, *SWH*, Autumn 1981, p.96; TA191, 2 May 1836; *EH*, 6 September 1836; White thesis; SWMA 40488, 19 November 1831; Evans, p.246.

31 CA34, 1836–7; SWMA 40499, letter from Player to Vicesimus Knox, 15 February 1838.

32 *ES*, 5 February, 23 September, 11 & 18 November 1836; SWMA. 40504, letter 27 July 1836; Hills thesis, pp.42–3.

33 *ES*, 9 March, 23 November 1838, 15 February 1839

34 TA104, 24 March 1840.

35 *ES*, 18 October 1839.

36 TA178; *ES*, 22 November 1839, 14 February 1840.

37 *ES*, 1 May & 23 October, 1840.

38 *ES*, 6 November 1840.

39 *ES*, 5 April 1844; SWMA 40363.

40 *ES*,14 January 1848; H.C. Stacey, *SWH*, Spring 1985, p.81; TA51/1; TA104, 30 October 1848; Hills thesis, pp.43, 61.

41 Brown, *Chartism*, pp.43, 98, 100,102; Perkin, p.182.

Chapter 4: A Most Unthankful Duty

1 SWMA 41570/41571, letters 20 & 26 September 1831 between Charles Porter and John Player.

2 Acknowledgements to Laurie Barker and Kate Thompson for their help with this chapter.

3 Tate, *Parish* Chest, pp.191–2; Englander, p.2.

4 See various Saffron Walden town archives; ERO D/DAd 12, July 1818; Braybrooke, *History of Audley End*, pp.173, 250; further information L.D. Barker.

5 For examples see TA21, 15 & 29 August, 24 October 1825; TA47, 24 April 1822, 13 July 1824; TA58, 12 & 15 March 1836; TA104, 1 July 1836; TA51, 27 April 1824.

6 TA64; TA58, 30 October 1820 & 12 January 1825; TA59, 3 & 24 March 1834, 30 May 1836.

7 Tate, *Parish Chest*, introduction.

8 TA103; ERO D/DAd 13, 13 June 1832; *ES*, 14 July 1832; TA51, 23 July 1832; CA29; ERO T/A 599/1–8.

9 TA15, 8 April 1831; TA6, 21 April 1794; TA13, 2 May 1823; TA50, 14 October 1801; TA15, 22 September 1829; Tate, *Parish Chest*, p.30.

10 TA58, 12 March 1816; TA11, 7 June 1816; ERO Q/SBb 467/51; TA13, 18 May & 29 June 1821; ERO T/A 261/ 3/2; ERO T/A 261/1/17–19/1–2,4; Slack, p.170.

11 Holdsworth, pp.103–107; Tate, *Parish Chest*, pp.198–203.

12 TA9, 12 October 1811; CA Poor law accounts (uncat.), July 1831, May 1834; CA23, 1837.

13 TA7; CA21, letter 1 December 1831; Sharpe in Hitchcock, King & Sharpe.

14 TA21, 20 June 1825; CA21, 1829.

15 CA22, 7 September 1825, July 1830, 1831; Landau, pp.139–59.

16 TA21, April 1833; further information L.D. Barker.

17 TA9, 20 November 1804; Tate, *Parish Chest*, p.231; information L.D. Barker.

18 TA7 & TA11, 1799,10 May 1816, 8 November 1816; Sokoll, p.291. Barker examples supplied by L.D. Barker.

19 PP 1825, XIX, pp.14–15; Majendie, Poor Law report (1833), p.40; PP 1836 XXIX; PRO MH12/3706, 16 May 1835; ERO T/A 419/12, 18 January 1822; 23 October 1829: also 12 July & 10 October 1825 & TA59, 6 January 1817; Ena Wright, *SWH*, Spring 1983, p.199.

20 TA 14; PRO MH12/3706, 3 September 1838; Ludgate, p.22; ERO D/P 333/8/1, 15 July 1760; Tate, *Parish Chest*, p.228; Brown, *Essex at Work*, p.148; H.C. Stacey, *SWH*, June 1974, p.31; Gibson, p.123.

21 TA7, 25 July 1800; TA6, 11 July 1794; TA9, 6 February 1807; TA10, 6 September, 11 October 1811; TA 21, 1833–4; Brown, *Essex at Work*, p.149.

22 TA9: 27 March 1807; TA21, Christmas 1827; CA (uncat.), workhouse provisions; CA8, 25 April 1833.

23 TA14, 23 September 1825; TA 21, 1835; CA (uncat.), 7–14 October 1831 & 17–24 July 1832; CA15, 3 April 1804 & 29 January 1831; Oxley, pp.79–119; Brown, *Colchester*, p.41.

24 TA21, March–September 1834; TA 14, 26 November 1824; TA21, 12 February 1827; CA (uncat.), workhouse records, April/July 1831; Sweet, p.167.

25 TA14, 20 May 1825; TA65, letter 31 January 1852.

26 TA 21, 4 April 1825; CA21, 1826, 1828 & 1829.

27 *ES*, 25 February 1831.

28 TA6, 21 April 1794; TA14, 30 March 1825; TA21, 2 March 1825; ERO G/Sw Z.43, 16 September 1835; TA12, 2 December 1819.

29 PRO MH/12/3710, letter 9 October 1849.

30 TA12, 24 & 31 March 1820; TA15, 17 January 1831, 13 January 1848; Pugh, p.58.

31 SWMA 40488; Evans, p.246; Brown, *Colchester*, p.47.

32 TA9, 23 & 30 January 1807.

33 TA9, 13 March 1807; Committee of Council of Education, 1846 (BFSS), p.240.

34 TA58, 19 July 1816; TA58, 27 December 1822; TA6, 3 April 1795; TA21, 15 & 29 August, 24 October 1825. TA9, 22 June 1812 (see also 22 February 1813); Tate, *Parish Chest*, p.216.

35 TA58, 2 October 1815; TA50, 24 October 1815, 17 January 1817.

36 TA14, 3 December 1824; TA21, 6 April 1827; TA14, 11 May 1827; SWMA 41456.

37 TA15, 22 September 1829; *The State of the Poor* (SWTL), 21 October, 4 & 23 November, 7 & 14 December 1829, statement 17 December 1829.

38 TA11, 27 November 1815 & TA13, 12 December 1820; tickets in SWTL mss, 25 October 1830; PRO MH 12/ 3709, letter July 1844; PRO MH 32/80, 4/ 5 July 1844; PRO MH12/3710, 1847 & 1849; Digby, 'Labour Market', pp.69–83; Digby, *Pauper Palaces*, p.116.

39 SWMA 40477, undated list; TA67, 29 December 1829.

40 PP 1843, VII; Statement re allotments, 17 December 1829 (SWTL); TA67, 17 December 1929, 16 December 1830, 2 & 22 December 1831, 20 August 1834; CA86.

41 H.C. Stacey, *Walden Charities* (SWTL); *Saffron Walden Yearbook* (1853), pp.18–21 (SWTL); Charity Commission, XI, p.816; Tate, *Parish Chest*, p.242–50.

42 TA 8, 15 December 1807; TA13, various dates, 12 December 1820–7 April 1824; TA14, 15 February 1825, 18 May 1827; TA67, 17 December 1829; TA21, 1827–35 ; Power report, p.265; Majendie report, p.40.

43 Majendie report, p.40; *ES*, 18 January 1834; SWMA 40500, letter to *EH* 18 September 1830; TA4, December 1831.

44 Majendie report, p.40; Player, *Sketches*, p.40; TA14, 16 December 1831; Power report, p.265.

45 SWMA 40477, Employment Committee, 26 October & 26 December 1832.

46 SWMA 40477, letters 30 October & 9 November 1832.

47 SWMA 40477, letter 23 January 1830; TA14, 26 December 1832; TA 15, 25 April 1834; SWMA 40493, letters 8 January, 10 & 12 February, 15 July & September 1834.

48 PP 1834, XXX–XXXIV; SWMA 40477, letter 7 March 1832.

49 SWMA 40477, letter to Ashurst Majendie from Player, February 1833; Majendie report, p.40; Power report, p.47; Baugh, p.64; Fraser, *Power and Authority*, p.6.

50 SWMA 40477, letter 23 January 1830; PRO MH12/3706, letter 23 January 1835; Baugh, pp.50–58, 63; Blaug, pp.151,178.

51 PRO MH 12/3706, 18 November 1834, statement of poor.

52 PP 1835, XXXV, p.135.

Chapter 5: Some Plums in the Pudding

1 PRO MH12/3706, letter from R.D. Thurgood to Poor Law Board, 22 December 1835.

2 ERO G/Sw M1–2A, 23 December 1835.

3 ERO G/Sw M1–2A, 15 January 1836.

4 *Essex Chronicle*, 27 January 1837 (report dated July 1836); PRO MH12/3706, 13 November 1835; ERO G/Sw M1–2A, 13 November 1835, 19 June 1840; PRO MH/9/15; Digby, *Labour Market*, p.71; Englander, pp.9–13; Halevy, pp.130–31.

5 TA58, 29 April 1835; PP 1836, XXIX, Pt. I, p.25; PRO MH12/3706, letters 18 November 1834, 24 March 1835; CA184(iii).

6 ERO G/Sw Z.43, letters 29 May, 6 August 1835; ERO G/Sw Z.1, 25 March 1836; ERO G/Sw M1–2A, 12 October 1835, 21 October 1836; SWMA 40020, letter 5 September 1835.

7 PRO MH12/3706, 16 May 1835; ERO G/Sw Z.43, letters September–December 1835.

8 TA 21, Lady Day–Midsummer 1835; ERO G/Sw M1–2A, 27 November 1835; PRO HO 52/17, 7 October 1835; *EH*, 17 March, 16 December 1835, 5 January 1836; Digby, 'Labourers' Protests', p.59 & Map 50; Edsal, p.42; Knott, pp.75, 77, 80.

9 PRO MH 12/3706, letter 22 December 1835; *ES*, 25 December 1835.

10 ERO G/Sw M1–2A, 23 December 1835; PRO MH12/3706, 23 December 1835; PRO HO 52 29, 8 July 1836; ERO G/Sw Z.43, letter 29 July 1837; Knott, p.77.

11 SWMA 40477, *EH*, 23 January 1830; PRO HO 52/29, letter and handbill, 8 July 1836; ERO FS1 11–19, letter 9 July 1836; *EH*, 29 July 1836; Edsal, pp.42–3.

12 SWMA 40504, letter from John Player to Jabez Gibson, 27 July 1836.

13 *EH*, 29 July 1836; Knott, p.81.

14 *ES*, 27 January 1837; PRO MH12/3706, 15 July 1836.

15 *ES*, 27 January 1837.

16 PRO HO 52 29, letters 17 January, 9 August & 20 August 1836, 6 November 1837; PRO HO 41, letter 24 September 1836; Elcoat, *Vicars of Thaxted*; Poor Law Report (1836), pp.250, 266.

17 Upson report; Dorothy B. Humphreys, *SWH*, November 1977, pp.94–100; ERO G/Sw M1–2A, 26 September 1848; PRO MH12/3706, letters 3, 9 & 12 September 1835.

18 PRO MH12/3706, letter 17 April 1837; Knott, p.274.

19 ERO G/Sw M1–2A, 28 October 1836; Ludgate, p.34; Archer, *Flash and a Scare*, pp.48–50.

20 PRO MH12/3706, 29 May & 29 August 1835, 13 May 1836; MH/12/3707, 3 March 1838; MH12/3708, 26 May 1840; MH 12/3709, 17 July 1843 & June 1844; ERO G/Sw M1–2A, various dates,1835–40; ERO G/Sw Z.43, letters 12 September & 11 November 1836,11 March 1837; TA15, 11 March 1838; CA (uncat.) poor law accounts; *Cambridge Chronicle*, 26 June 1835, advertisement.

21 ERO G/Sw Z.43, letter 11 March 1837.

22 ERO G/Sw Z.43, letter 27 November 1835; ERO G/Sw M1–2A, 30 October 1835, 29 January, 4 March, 27 May, 5 August, 26 August 1836, 4 January 1839; PRO MH12/3707, 8 December 1838; Worship, pp.36, 42–3; Armstrong, pp.69, 79.

23 PRO MH 12/3709, 17 October 1843.

24 ERO G/Sw M1–2A, 18 October 1839, 24 July 1840.

25 ERO G/Sw M1–2A, 29 January & 5 February 1841; MH 12/3709, letter 16 May 1843 from J. Porter of Knightsbridge, former guardian in Enniskillen, Ireland; Curtis, p.201.

26 PRO MH12/3707, 17 October 1839; MH12/3708, 22 March 1841; MH12/3710, 28 February 1850; ERO G/Sw M1–2A, 18 October 1839; Curtis, p.201.

27 ERO G/Sw Z.43, letter 9 December 1836; PRO MH12/3710, 7 May 1847.

28 PRO MH12/3710, 7 April & 11 June 1847; ERO G/Sw M1–2A, 17 March 1837; *ES*, June 1840.

29 ERO G/Sw M1–2A, 19 & 26 May 1837; PRO MH12/3710, 7 April 1847, May–June 1850.

30 PRO MH12/3706, 2 June 1837; MH12/3710, 28 April & 1 May 1848; ERO G/Sw Z.43, letter 16 September 1835; ERO G/Sw M1–2A, 12 August 1836, 9 June 1837,11 September, 4 & 18 December 1840.

31 SWMA 40440, letter from Lord Braybrooke to Board, 2 April 1838; PRO MH12/3707, 6 November 1837; *ES*, 7 April 1837; ERO G/Sw M1–2A, 1837–8; Digby, *Nineteenth Century England*, p.16.

32 CA148, 17 January 1839; CA 145; TA15, CA87 & TA24, various dates 21 April 1837–24 June 1839; *ES*, 13 July 1838; PRO MH12/3707, 19 August 1837; ERO G/Sw M1–2A, 16 February, 27 April & 13 July 1838, 24 May 1839.

33 *ES*, 6 April 1838; ERO G/Sw M1–2A, 30 March, 6 April 1838; SWMA 40429, 24 March 1838; SWMA 40486, letters 6 & 7 April 1838.

34 ERO G/Sw M1–2A, various dates, 15 January 1836–30 August 1844; ERO G/Sw Z.43, letter 29 July 1837; SWMA 40494, various dates, 8 February 1839–9 December 1844; Land, pp.26–9.

35 PRO MH/ 12/3707, 5 September 1837;
    MH12/3708, letter 20 July 1840; MH 12/
    3709, 3 November 1843; ERO G/Sw M1–
    2A, various dates, 23 February 1838–19
    April 1844.

36 ERO G/Sw M3–4, 5 & 12 January 1844;
    PRO MH12/3710, 15 February 1848.
    Number of vagrants: 28 in1846, 31 in 1847,
    62 in 1848, but only one in 1849 and 8 in
    1850.

37 *ES*, 7 April 1837.

38 PRO MH12/3707, September 1837.

39 ERO G/Sw M1–2A, various dates, 1838;
    PRO MH12/3707, letter 16 February 1838;
    Digby, *'Labourers' Protests'*, p.159;
    Brundage, pp.169–79; Englander, p.18.

40 CA75, March 1838; PRO MH12/3707, letter
    21 April 1838; ERO G/Sw M1–2A, 20 April
    1838; SWMA 40483; Poor Law Report
    (1836), p.269.

41 ERO G/Sw M1–2A, 7 & 21 December 1838;
    PRO MH 12 letter 7 December 1838.

42 Poor Law Report (1840), p.257, dated 1
    February 1839; PRO MH 32/80, letter 5
    July 1844; ERO G/Sw M1–2A, 22 February
    1839; PRO MH 12/3709, letter 13 March
    1845.

43 ERO D/P 192/1/15, 1841; ERO G/Sw
    W56; SWMA 40424, 1841 annual report;
    ERO G/Sw Z.1–4.

44 ERO G/Sw Z41; ERO G/Sw M3–4, 5 July
    1844; Curtis, p.201.

45 PRO MH 12/3709, 29 April 1843, 20
    January 1844; Englander, p.97.

46 Englander, pp.85–6; Goose, p.54; Digby,
    'Labour Market', pp.72–3.

47 PRO MH12/3710, 20 May 1847.

48 PRO MH12/3710; Population Census, 12
    April 1851; Muir essay (SWTL).

49 Goose, p.66.

50 ERO G/Sw M1–2A, 22 February 1839.

51 Brundage, p.144; Fraser, *Urban Politics*,
    pp.74–5.

Chapter 6: 'This town… infested with Gangs of Thieves and Poachers'

1   Player *Chronicles*, November 1828, January
    & February 1829 (SWTL).

2   CA17, November 1828; *EH*, 11 November
    1828.

3   TA51, 19 January 1829: William Wilson,
    John Miller and John Brewer transported;
    John Savill 12 months hard labour; William
    Atkinson died in prison; John Stacey, not
    guilty.

4   Gatrell, p.243.

5   TA 58, 1815–36 (incomplete 1820s).

6   CA362; SWMS 40494, 18 November 1840;
    Hobsbawm, p.88; Amos thesis, p.58;

7   CA15, 13 April 1836; *EH*, 19 April 1836;
    SWMA 40494, 7 October 1840.

8   SWMA 40494, 7 January 1841.

9   CA17; *Norwich Mercury* 26 October 1816;
    King thesis, p.52, table 2.8; Gyford, *Witham
    Fires*, p.11; Emsley, p.18; Addison, p.168;
    Peacock, *Bread or Blood*, p.54; Gyford thesis,
    Fig.5a; Player, *Chronicles* (SWTL); Commit-
    tee of Council on Education, minutes 1846,
    p.240.

10 *Chelmsford Chronicle*, 12 April 1833; *ES*, 17
    July 1840.

11 SWMA 40188; White, *Chronological*, pp.115–
    16; King, 'Prosecution Associations' in Hay
    & Snyder.

12 Player, *Chronicles*, April 1829 (further
    information L.D. Barker); *ES*, 19 April 1844;
    SWMA 40494, 12 April 1844.

13 SWMA 40198, gaol survey, c.1810.

14 TA50–51, 14 April 1806, 3 April 1818, 17
    October 1834; White, *Chronological*, pp. 95–7;
    Nurse, Pugh & Mollet, p.91; Grieve, p.279.

15 PRO HO 75/6, *Hue & Cry*, 20 February
    1833, p.2032.

16 TA104, 1 January, 30 March, 1 May, 4 June
    1836; SWMA 40486, letter 3 November
    1839.

17 *ES*, 3, 10 & 17 July, 30 October 1840; SWMA
    40494, 18/19 July 1840.

18 *ES*, 22 November 1839, 7 January 1853.

19 ERO J/P 8/1; TA104, 16 November, 14
    December 1840, 8 & 18 February 1841;
    CA362, 20 April 1840; CA34; *ES*, 16 May
    1845, 11 September 1846. Acknowledge-
    ments to Maureen Scollan for her assist-
    ance with this section.

20 *ES*, 28 July 1848, 9 & 16 November 1849;
    Rowntree, *Then and Now*, pp.77–9; White,
    Chronological, pp.115–18; Scollan, p.24. See
    also TA60 & TA90, CA3/4/5.

21 Player, *Chronicles*, April 1828; TA51, 15
    April 1828, 20 March 1829; SWMA 40193;
    EH, 17 March 1829.

22 TA50, 13 April 1804; letters 17/18 April
    1804.

23 *Chelmsford Chronicle*, 19 April 1833; PRO
    MH12/3709, 26 June, 20 August 1846;
    Shaw, pp.147, 150.

24 TA51, 10 & 18 January, 17 October 1834;
    CA8; *ES*, 18 January 1834.

25 TA51, 1822; PP 1824, XXXVIII; Rowntree,
    Then and Now, p.70.

26 *ES*, 28 August 1846.

27 Player, *Chronicles*, 1823–8; SWMA 40494.

28 *ES*, 20 April 1833; Gyford thesis, pp.11, 68.

29 *ES*, 2 & 9 March 1833; *Chelmsford Chronicle*,
    April, 3 May 1833; *Essex & Herts Mercury*,
    28 May 1833; CA17.

30 *Chelmsford Chronicle*, 19 April 1833.
31 CA144, 27 September 1833.
32 *ES*, 28 January 1832.
33 *EH*, 6 November 1829; CA15, 3 November 1829; SWMA 40494, 19 August 1840.
34 *ES* 6 May 1836; PRO HO 52 29, letter 9 May 1836; SWMA 40499.
35 PRO HO 52 29, letters 5 January, 2 & 11 May 1836.
36 TA51, 11 April 1836; *EH*, 19 April 1836.
37 PRO HO 52 29, letter 9 May 1836; *EH*, 31 May 1836.
38 SWMA 40499, letter 15 February 1838.
39 PRO HO 52 29, letter 25 May 1836; *EH*, 31 May, 5 July 1836; SWMA 40499; CA217, letters 23 & 25 May 1836.
40 Gatrell in F.M.L. Thompson, chapter 5.
41 CA13, 4 November 1830; TA51, 15 January & 23 April 1830; CA8.
42 TA51/1, 27/30 September & 17 October 1836, 2 January & 14 July 1837; Emsley, p.18.
43 *ES*, 9 November 1838; CA13; further information Maureen Scollan.
44 Munsche, p.66.
45 *EH*, 12 January 1836; ERO D/Dby A344, 1824–35.
46 TA21, 1834–5; CA8; SWMA 40195, letter 11 June 1829.
47 CA76; Stacey Album No 5 (SWTL), p39; Munsche, pp.28–31, 130, 115.
48 Munsche, pp.62–4.
49 CA8, 1826–7; *EH*, 28 December 1828, 20 March 1829; *EH*, 17 March 1829; Munsche, pp.66, 140–2.
50 *ES*, 31 October 1845, 7 March, 12 December 1851; Munsche, p.157.
51 *ES*, 18 January 1834.
52 CA8; Emsley, *Crime and Society*.
53 TA58, October–December 1832; PP 1846, IX, pt. 1, p.632; *ES*, 18 January 1834; TA23, 30 August 1833; Munsche, pp.60, 148, 157.
54 CA362.

Chapter 7: Tumultuously Assembled Against the Peace

1 ERO Q/SBb 502/45.
2 SWMA 40459, 12 December 1830. For possible origins of 'Swing' name, see *Cambridge Chronicle*, 17 December 1830.
3 TA (uncat.) food riots mss.; ERO D/Dby 012, including letter 27 July 1795. For various accounts see: Rowntree, *Then and Now*, pp.80–86; Addison, pp.148–51; Brown, *Meagre Harvest*, p.1; White, *Chronological*, pp.86–90; J. Dallaway, *SWH*, (Autumn 1986), pp.152–62 & (Spring 1987), pp.197–204; Wilson, pp.6–15; *Chelmsford Chronicle*, 17 April 1772.
4 Bohsted, pp.4–5.
5 TA7, October, November 1799, 26 November 1799; TA50, 21 & 27 January, 3 February 1800.
6 ERO Q/SBb 380/66/1 & 66/2; Ludgate, p.33.
7 ERO Q/SBb 380/66/3.
8 SWMA 40183; Peacock, *Bread or Blood*; Brown, *Meagre Harvest*, pp.7–9.
9 TA14, 22 September 1829.
10 Hobsbawm & Rudé, pp.152–72.
11 ERO D/Dby A266, December 1830 & December 1831; *ES*, October 1842.
12 PRO HO 52/7, letter 1 December 1830.
13 See Essex and Cambridge press, various dates, December 1830; CA173.
14 *EH*, various dates, December 1830; Amos thesis, p.99; CA173; Hobsbawm & Rudé, p.162; Brown, *Harvest*, p.10; *Cambridge Chronicle*, 31 December 1830.
15 Essex and Cambridge press, various dates, December 1830; *Cambridge Chronicle*, 17 December 1830; Hobsbawm & Rudé, appendix 3, p.349.
16 CA173; Amos thesis, p.99; *EH*, 17 December 1830.
17 Amos thesis, p.107; Grieve, p.293.
18 CA173, accounts, also correspondence 23 December 1831, 31 January & 11 October 1832.
19 Hobsbawm & Rudé, pp.258, 262; Brown, *Harvest*, p.11.
20 PRO HO 52 17, letter 27 March 1832; ERO Q/SBb 502/2, 502/3/1, 502/21, 502/45 & 502/98, January 1831; *Cambridge Chronicle*, 10 December 1830; Amos thesis, p.115.
21 PP 1834, XXX–XXXIV, question 53: 'Swing' was 'a sort of contagious infatuation' (Braintree); 'low wages and a number of men being idle to corrupt each other' (Gt Henny); 'poachers and idlers inhabiting beershops' (Lawford); 'disaffected persons from outside…evil-disposed rather than distressed peasants' (Prittlewell); 'farmers misled labourers in order to hide their own maladministration of the poor laws' (Thorpe le Soken).
22 Charlesworth, *Social Protest*, Fig.16, p.19.
23 *EH*, 21 December 1830; Charlesworth, p.31.
24 *Chelmsford Chronicle*, 19 April 1833.
25 SWMA 40477/40489, April 1831; Majendie report (1833), p.40.
26 CA173.
27 Majendie report (1833), p.40; SWMA 40178; CA12; TA 65; SWMA 40777, letter dated 20 January 1831.
28 ERO T/A 599/1–8, 27 April 1831; ERO D/Dby A266.
29 Hussey in Swash & Hussey, pp.1–11.

30 *Cambridge Chronicle*, 16 & 30 August 1816, 3 April 1830; *EH*, 7 April 1829.

31 PRO HO 52 17, letters 20 February, 27 March 1832.

32 *EH*, 26 July 1844; Archer, *Flash and Scare*, p.106; Swash & Hussey, map on pp.12–13. Minimum Essex arson figures: 3 in 1842, 2 in 1843, 21 in 1844, 19 in 1845, 6 in 1846, 9 in 1847, 9 in 1848, 17 in 1849, 8 in 1850, 16 in 1851.

33 *ES*, 26 November 1847, 18 February 1848; Archer, *Flash and a Scare*, p.22. Acknowledgements to A.F.J. Brown for allowing access to his list of fires in Essex.

34 See Essex press reports on agricultural show, 1842–50; Swash & Hussey, p.iii.

35 *ES*, 10 & 31 July 1846.

36 Fire reports in Essex press, 1851: Great Chesterford (10 January), E. Franklin of Wimbish (17 January), S Jonas of Ickleton (17 January), Tiptofts & Sadlers Farms (7 February), Pinckneys, Radwinter & Parsonage Farm, Newport (21 February); *ES*, 10 & 17 January, 7 & 21 February 1851.

37 *ES*, 1 & 14 June 1844.

38 SWMA 41522.

39 *Morning Chronicle*, 29 December 1849, quoted in Snell, *Annals*, p.126.

40 *Gentleman's Magazine*, 1800, quoted in Crouch & Ward, p.46.

41 Swash in Swash & Hussey, pp.18–20; Archer, *Flash and a Scare*, pp.56–66, 257.

Chapter 8: A Tendency to Prevent Depredations

1 *Chelmsford Chronicle*, 19 April 1833.

2 *Kent & Essex Mercury*, 24 September 1833; *EH*, 5 July 1836; Crouch & Ward, p.50; Archer, *Flash and a Scare*, p.62.

3 Riley, pp.23, 29; Crouch & Ward, pp.40, 46; Young, *An inquiry*, p.23; Young, *Annals*, quoted in Peacock, p.39.

4 Robinson, pp.44–50 (SWTL); Archer, *Flash and a Scare*, p.62; *Labourers' Friend Society* No.3 (SWMA 40477); Barnett in Jones & Mingay, pp.167, 172, 182; Crouch & Ward, p.47; PP 1843, VII, p.247, evidence by G.W. Gent, Steeple Bumpstead landowner.

5 *Quarterly Review*, vols 41 & 44, p.551; Denson, p.64; ERO D/Dby A344, p.37; SWMA 40381.

6 TA67, 11 January 1830; SWMA 40435, October 1830; Denson, p.64.

7 *Quarterly Review*, vol. 44, pp.551–2; SWMA 40380, letter from Braybrooke to Player, 18 December 1830. A linear rod, pole or perch was 5½ yards, so a square rod was just over 30 square yards.

8 SWMA 40477, 1832 correspondence & letter 23 January 1830; *EH*, 18 September 1830 (SWMA 40500).

9 TA 67, 17 & 28 December 1829, 11 January 1830.

10 TA67, 11 February & 1 March 1830; SWMA 40380, first year report, December 1830.

11 TA67, 6 & 11 March 1830; SWMA 40380, first annual report December 1830, p.8.

12 TA67, 22 February 1830, 15 March 1830.

13 TA67, 8 & 18 March 1830; SWMA 40380; SWMA 40477, letter 18 March 1830; Moselle, pp.491–2.

14 TA67, various dates, March–May 1830, April 1831, February 1834; first year report, December 1830; *ES*, 15 September 1833; CA86 (i).

15 TA67, March 1830; SWMA 40477, letter 12 April 1830; first year report, December 1830.

16 TA67, 11 September, 26 October 1830; SWMA 40477, meeting 26 October 1830.

17 SWMA 41522; Archer, *Nineteenth Century Allotment*, pp.23–4.

18 PRO HO 52/7, letter from Braybrooke to Home Office, 1 December 1830; TA 67, 29 November,1 & 9 December 1830.

19 TA67, 9 December 1830; TA34.

20 TA67, 1, 9 & 29 December 1830.

21 Majendie report (1833), p.40; SWMA 40477, letter 31 October 1831; *Essex & Herts Mercury*, 24 September 1833.

22 SWMA 40477, first year report, December 1830.

23 TA67, 29 December 1830, comparative statement by Player.

24 SWMA 40477, letters 11 January, 31 October & 21 December 1831, 7 March 1832; SWMA 40489, letter 1831; SWMA 40477, Employment Committee, 20 October 1832.

25 TA67, 10 March 1831; second-year report, 26 December 1831; Majendie report (1833), p.40; SWMA 40477, letters, various dates, 1831–3.

26 Overseers mss., 4 November 1829 (SWTL); TA21; TA67, 29 December 1830, 10 March 1831 & 1830–4 lists; SWMA 40477, letters 13 & 28 March 1832, 18 April 1833; Majendie report (1833), p.40; TA4; ERO D/DBy 049; TA23, 11 & 18 October, 13 December 1833, 19 February 1834.

27 SWMA 40383, *Quarterly Review*, 1831, pp.431–3.

28 SWMA 40380, letter 18 December 1830; SWMA 40477, letter 31 October 1831; Majendie report (1833), p.40; TA21, 1831–2.

29 SWMA 40477, letters 7 March 1832, 20 February 1833; Majendie report, (1833), p.40; TA67, 5 October 1831.

30 TA67, 29 March 1830; 237 signatures/
marks in TA67, March 1830–May 1834;
SWMA 40477, letter 31 October 1831; PP
1843, VII, p.247.

31 CA435, 1836; TA67, various dates 1830–4;
Majendie report (1833), p.40.

32 CA435; TA67, 29 August, 20 September
1831, 23 August 1832; SWMA 40477, letter
to *EH*, 12 April 1830.

33 SWMA 40477, letter 22 July 1831; TA67, 8
January, 24 February & 23 August 1832, 18
April 1833.

34 TA67/68, various dates, 1831–9; CA435;
Player, *Sketches*, p.13.

35 TA68, 18 August, 6 October 1841, 5 October
1842, 23 March 1846.

36 SWMA 40477, second-year report, letter 7
March 1832; TA24 & TA68 re rents
received; Archer, 'Nineteenth Century
Allotment', pp.35–6.

37 PP 1843 VII, p.247; Archer, 'Nineteenth
Century Allotment, pp.21–36; Burchardt,
pp.165–75.

38 SWMA 40477, second-year report, pp.11,
14–15, letter 20 February 1833.

39 Saffron Walden Horticultural Society
report, pp.4–5 (SWTL).

40 *ES*, 4 October 1844.

41 *Quarterly Review*, vol 44, p.551; PP 1843,
VII, p.247.

42 TA68: committee re-formed 1868, briefly
revived 1887, revived again 1906. In 1923,
when the Saffron Walden Horticultural
Society (which had been founded a century
earlier) decided to hold a show again, they
found there was still £140 remaining in the
old Spade Husbandry account, and used it
to pay for the event (*Herts & Essex Observer*,
10 March 1923).

43 SWMA 40477, letter 31 October 1831.

? 44, 45, 46 ?

Chapter 9: A Quality of Evil Peculiar to Themselves

1   Poor Law Report, 1834, p.361.
2   Charity Commission, XI, pp.892–4.
3   ERO D/CT 378A; SWMA 40411.
4   TA 29, 30, 31, 316, 318; Barker examples
courtesy of L.D. Barker's family research.
5   TA29, 10 August 1838.
6   TA29, 14 April 1846, 21 April 1851, 10
April 1855, 22 April 1862 and undated
loose paper.
7   TA29, 22 April 1862; Tate, *Parish Chest*,
pp.194–5.
8   Charity Commission, XI, p.894; PRO CHAR
2, correspondence April 1836; Player,
Chronicles, 30 January 1827.
9   Rowntree, *Then and Now*, pp.10, 55–63;
Charity Commission, XI, p.809.

10 Rowntree, *Then and Now*, pp.61–3; White,
Chronological, p.94; Braybrooke, *Audley End*,
pp.231–9.

11 Rowntree, *Then and Now*, p.57; 1851 Census
of Saffron Walden; Braybrooke, *Audley End*,
p.235.

12 *ES*, 31 March 1832, 7 October 1837.

13 SWMA 40486; *ES*, 7 October 1837;
Rowntree, *Then and Now*, p.59; Braybrooke,
Audley End, p.236; *ES*, 31 March 1832; 1851
Census.

14 *ES*, 23 September 1837; Charity Commission, XI, p.893.

15 Charity Commission, XI, p.820; TA32,
1852–67.

16 Charity Commission, XI, p.814; *ES*, 23
September 1837; CA76.

17 Charity Commission, XI; PRO CHAR 2.

18 Charity Commission, XI, p.893: PRO CHAR
2, letters 19 September, 3 October 1836.

19 Charity Commission, XI, p.892; PRO
CHAR2, letters 11 October 1836, 10 April, 4
May, 18 May & 15 June 1837.

20 TA 32, 33, 34, 38, 39; Charity Commission,
XI, p.820; Braybrooke, *Audley End*, p.248;
ERO D/DBy A344.

21 *ES*, 26 August, 23 September, 7 October
1836.

22 *ES*, 21 October, 2 December 1836; TA28, 34,
425.

23 CA396, 1834 annual report; Town
Missioners' journal, July 1862; Prochaska in
Thompson, *Social Agencies*, p.370.

24 CA396; SWMA 40424; *ES*, 19 November
1831.

25 SWMA 40424, annual report 1838.

26 SWMA 40424, annual reports 1834/35;
Brown, *Colchester*, p.93.

27 SWMA 40424, annual report 1831; Town
Mission journal, April 1862, p.139.

28 SWMA 40424, annual reports 1829/34;
Donajgrodski, p.17.

29 SWMA 40424 annual reports 1828/31/34/
35; minutes 16 December 1830; *ES*, 17
January 1845.

30 SWMA 40489: letter *EH*, John Player, 21
December 1831. See also the author's
unpublished thesis, *Philanthropy and Social
Control in Saffron Walden* (SWTL).

Chapter 10: Peerless Gems of Charity and Goodness

1   *ES*, October 1846.
2   SWMA 40477, letter 31 October 1831.
3   SWMA 40489, 18 April 1831; *Chelmsford
Chronicle*, 3 May 1833, *ES*, 15 September
1833; PRO MH 12/2307, letter 26 January
1838; Sweet, p.131.

4   See for instance Donajodski, p.15 and Morris, 'Voluntary Societies', p.106.
5   National Schools, Essex Society, report 1831, appendix; *ES*, 11 January 1834.
6   SWMA 40489, 8 January 1833, 1843 annual report.
7   SWMA 40489, 21 December 1831, 8 January 1833; *ES*, 17 January 1845.
8   *ES*, 11 January 1834; SWMA 40489, 10 January 1842.
9   Committee of Council on Education, 1846, p.240; Pratt, pp.59, 52, xxii; Horne, pp.380, 6, 13.
10 SWMA 40659 & 40668; ERO D/DCm Z8; *ES*, 3 January 1845; Pigot's *Directory*, 1848.
11 ERO Q/RSF5; SWMA 40394; TA6, 6 February 1795; Pratt, p.59; ERO D/DU 66/12, 23 December 1771; *Essex Chronicle*, 13 October 1837; Brown, *Essex at Work*, p.135.
12 *ES*, October 1835, 23 October 1840; Horne, p.5; Lord, pp.165–73; Glyde, p.84.
13 CA285; ERO Q/RSF6, 11 June 1832; PRO FS1/149; PP 1837, LI , p.97; Gosden, p.22, table 2; Brown, *Essex at Work*, p.135; Bohsted, p.187.
14 SWMA 40394.
15 SWMA 40394.
16 CA299, 26 February 1831.
17 CA299.
18 ERO Q/RSF6; H.C. Stacey, *SWH*, Spring 1981, p.63; TA23, 1833–5; TA21, May 1834; further information L.D. Barker.
19 *Herts & Essex Observer*, 13 July 1867; Saffron Walden Oddfellows register 1853–1964 (acknowledgements Mrs M. Day, secretary).
20 Oddfellows register. See Fisk, pp.19–21.
21 SWMA 40394, 9 September 1822.
22 Rowntree, *Then and Now*, p.101; Tholfsen, pp.288, 294–6.
23 SWMA 40389.
24 SWMA 40479.
25 CA285.
26 CA285.
27 CA285; Guildhall Museum, MS 13743, letter to Christ's Hospital, 23 January 1880.
28 Saffron Walden Town Mission journal, February/ March 1862; Gorsky, p.22; Gosden, p.210.
29 ERO D/Z 71.
30 *ES*, 7 October 1842, 20 October 1843, 24 October 1845; ERO D/DBy A344, p.103; Brown, *Chartism*, p.105; Horn, *Rural World*, p.144.
31 *ES*, 11 January 1834, 7 October 1842, 20 October 1843.
32 *ES*, 20 October 1843, 24 October 1845; SWMA 40504; Swash & Hussey, p.17; Brown, *Essex at Work*, p.33; H.C. Stacey, *SWH*, Autumn 1987.
33 *ES*, 23 October 1840; *EH*, 2 February 1836; ERO D/DBY Z79.
34 *ES*, 15 September 1833, 21 June & 17 October 1834, 11 July 1845, 11 September 1846; Horticultural Society report, pp.4–6 (SWTL).
35 *ES*, 17 October 1834, 4 November 1836, 21 October 1842.
36 *ES*, 10 October 1834, 4 November 1836, 23 October 1840, October 1841; *Essex & Herts Mercury*, 24 September 1833; *Essex Chronicle*, 13 October 1837.
37 ERO D/DBy A267–70, 305–308; *Essex Chronicle*, October 13 1837; *ES*, 10 October 1834, 7 October 1842, 5 October 1843, 25 October 1844, 31 October 1845.
38 *Essex & Herts Mercury*, 24 September 1833; *Essex Chronicle*,13 October 1837; *ES*, 1 November 1839, 23 October 1840, October 1841, 5 October 1843, 25 October 1844.
39 *Essex Chronicle*, 13 October 1837; *ES*, 4 November 1836, 28 September 1838; CA 15, 1 September 1838. William 'Rags' Barker received relief from overseers several times between 1800–17, and at his death, was said to have worked for Braybrooke over 20 years. Further information L.D. Barker.
40 ERO D/DBY Z79, 1834–6.
41 *ES*, 7 October 1842.
42 ERO D/DBY Z79, October 1847; Archer, *Flash and a Scare*, p.165; Brown, *Chartism*, p.104; Scott, p.20; Tholfson, p.124. The agricultural shows continued for many years, and this interpretation does not necessarily apply to later periods.
43 SWMA 40500, 1830 letters; Brown, *Colchester*, p.97; Brown, *Harvest*; SWMA 40477, letter 20 February 1833.

Chapter 11: A Suitable Degree of Education

1   *ES*, 20 April 1833.
2   Sanderson, p.12; F.M.L. Thompson, *Respectable Society*, p.144.
3   TA406; Rowntree, *Then and Now*, pp.1, 11; White, *Chronological*, pp.34, 84–5. Lectures by Dr A.F.J. Brown (University of Essex), and additional help from British & Foreign School Society Archives Centre are acknowledged in the preparation of this chapter, also information from L.D. Barker.
4   Census of Saffron Walden, 1841; Pigot's *Directory*, 1823–48; *Chelmsford Chronicle*, 1 January 1836; CA 1(ii), 25 August 1823; National School report, 1815, p.60; SWMA 40689; *SWH*, Spring 1983, p.231 & Autumn 1983, p.230; Benton, p.21.

5   Benton, p.21; Pigot's *Directory*,1839; Eden thesis (ERO); Committee of Council annual report, XXV, p.414; SWMA 40498; ERO D/P 28/30/18; Saffron Walden Town Mission, minutes 1 September 1842; Johnson, p.109; Brown, *Harvest*, p.31; Sanderson, p.15; McCann, p.29.

6   Rowntree, *Then and Now*, pp.67–8; Rowley, *Education*, Illustration 17.

7   TA96; ERO T/A 778/30; Braybrooke, *Audley End*, p.242; Rowntree, *Then and Now*, pp.40, 67; H.C. Stacey, *Walden Charities* (SWTL); Eden thesis (ERO); M.G. Jones, p.365; Sanderson, p.2.

8   *Chelmsford Chronicle*, 28 January 1791; Bodley, p.28; J.E. Maddams, *SWH*, October 1975, pp.9 & 11 & March 1976, p.23; ERO T/A 778/30; PRO HO/129/8/210.

9   Benton, pp.14, 19; *ES*, 11 August 1843.

10 Snell, '*Sunday School*', pp.122–68, table 2.

11 Taylor, pp.3–10: see Andrew Bell, *An experiment in education made at the Madras Asylum at Egmore, near Madras* (1797); and Joseph Lancaster, *Improvements in Education as it affects the Labouring Classes of the Community* (1803).

12 National Society, Essex branch annual report, 1812, p.49; National Society Annual Reports 1815, 1831, 1836; Digest of Parochial Returns, Select Committee on Education of the Poor, 1818, Vol. III, p.1171; leaflet issued by Rector of Mile End, Colchester, 1844 (in private custody); PP 1839, XLI, pp.1–2.

13 H.C Stacey, *Saffron Walden Weekly News*, 28 July & 4 August 1961; Stacey Album vol. 5 (SWTL); CA449, 15 April 1821, 2 April 1822, 25 March 1823; Rowntree, *Then and Now*, pp.64–7; Fell Smith, p.518; ERO T/A 778/30; TA103, 17 July 1834; *Cambridge Chronicle*, advertisement September 1821; SWMA 40689; TA88.

14 PRO CHAR2, letter 2 May 1836; SWMA 40486; TA425; TA (uncat.), admissions register, 1844–71; Charity Commission, XI, p.805; Braybrooke, *Audley End*, p.241; Gumbrell, vol. 1, pp.33–4.

15 CA449, 19 & 26 January 1841; SWMA 40689, sermon 27 July 1823; National Society annual reports, 1817, 1818, 1819; ERO D/P 28/30/18–19; *Chelmsford Chronicle*, 17 January 1817.

16 Essex National Schools Society annual reports, 1816–18, 1828, 1840; Player, *Chronicles*, 12 January 1816; ERO D/Dby A344,12 February 1824.

17 National Society, Essex reports 1817, 1828; CA449, various dates, 7 May 1817–3 November 1840; Committee of Council, 1845, XXV, p.404.

18 CA449, April 1838; Church of England Records Centre, Saffron Walden school files, letter from Rev. R. Clutton, 1845; Swash & Hussey, p.18; Committee of Council on Education,1845, XXV, p.413.

19 Clutton letter, op. cit., letter 1845; Gumbrell, vol. 1, pp.181, 216; inspector's report on 'Walden Infants School', 28 March 1850.

20 H.C. Stacey, *SWH*, Spring 1980, p.6; Committee of Council, XXV, grant applications, 1843–4.

21 SWMA 40498, November 1825.

22 Pigot's *Directory*, 1823, 1839; J.E. Maddams, *SWH*, October 1975, pp.9,11; CA449, 11 May 1837; SWMA 40477, letter from John Player to T.A. Catlin, 6 December 1825.

23 Mus. 500, 2 January 1826 (SWTL).

24 Saffron Walden Town Mission minutes, 7 April 1842; Select Committee on Education of Poor, 1818; Nurse, Pugh & Mollet, p.94.

25 CA (uncat.), workhouse records; TA8, 25 April 1806; TA11, 7 June 1816.

26 PRO MH12/3707, letters 3 & 22 March 1838; ERO D/P 18/25/1, 3 February 1836; ERO G/Sw M1–2A, 11 & 26 August, 6 October 1837; ERO G/Sw Z.43, letter 7 November 1836; Crowther, p.131; Englander, p.37. Horn, *Rural World*, p.137.

27 ERO G/Sw M1–2A, various dates, 28 June 1839–19 March 1841; TA14, 24 June 1835; PRO MH12/3708, various dates 12 March–29 September 1841.

28 PRO MH12/3710, 20 & 28 May 1847; Goose, p.58; PRO MH/12/3710, inspector's reports, 1847–50.

29 Inspector's report, 1850 (BFSS); PRO MH12/3710, 7 February 1848, 9 May 1850; ERO G/Sw M14, 9 July 1880.

30 PRO MH12/3706, 9 August 1836; ERO G/Sw M1–2A, 26 August 1836, 5 May 1837, 25 May 1838; inspector's reports, 1848 & 1850.

31 Clavering Village Guide; Committee of Council, 1846–7 reports; Guildhall Museum, Mss13743, letter 23 January 1880.

32 Guildhall Museum, op.cit.; *Herts & Essex Observer*, 17 & 24 December 1898.

33 SWMA 40498; SWMA 40689, sermon 28 July 1839; Curtis & Boultwood, p.61.

34 Brown, *Chartism*, pp.106–7; Brown, *Essex at Work*, p.139; *Essex & Suffolk Times*, 16 February & 24 August 1839; Adamson, p.132; PP 1835, XLI, p.131.

35 British & Foreign School Society Archive Centre (BFSS) Annual Reports, 1818–38.

36 BFSS reports, 1831 & 1833; Rowley, *Education*, Illustration 23.

37 Preliminary Statement (BFSS), 1846; ERO
   PH 4/140/1–4, 15 November 1838, 29 July
   1839, 1840 annual report, 28 February 1841;
   H.C Stacey, *Walden Charities*, p.22;
   Rowntree, *Boys British School*, p.3.
38 SWMA 40689; ERO PH 4/140/1–4, 10
   August 1842.
39 ERO PH 4/140/1–4, 26 July 1838.
40 ERO D/P 28/30/18–19.
41 ERO PH 4/140/1–4, 30 September & 28
   October 1839, 28 September & December
   1840; CA449, 19 November, 3 December
   1839.
42 BFSS Annual Report 1843, p.87.
43 PH 4/140/1–4, 6 December 1841, 25
   November 1844,14 June 1847; Preliminary
   statement (BFSS), 1846.
44 Fletcher Report (BFSS), 1847–8, pp.245,
   276; ERO PH 4/140/1–4, 14 & 21 June
   1847; letter from W.G. Gibson to H. Dunn
   (BFSS), 1 July 1847.
45 ERO PH 4/140/1–4, 3 April, 14 December
   1848; *ES*, 9 March 1849; CA16, 7 March
   1849.
46 ERO PH 4/140/1–4, 18 September 1848;
   inspector's report (BFSS), 26 March 1851;
   Willett testimonials (BFSS); SWMA 40689;
   Education return, 1858; CA412, inspections
   1857, 1864, 1868; Rowntree, *Boys British
   School*; Evans, pp.336, 410; Eden, p.53.
47 SWMA 40689; Pigot's *Directory*, 1848;
   inspectors' reports (BFSS), 1850/51; letter
   (BFSS) 20 November 1851; Education
   returns, 1858; Collins, p.3; Bengsten thesis.
48 SWMA 40689; Parliamentary returns, 1845;
   Jane Muir, *SWH*, Spring 1986, p.130; TA32,
   1852; Maddock thesis; Evans, p.336;
   Benton, p.22.
49 Committee of Council report, 1842, pp.404,
   411–12.
50 Committee of Council on Education, 1846,
   p.240 & 1847, p.270; Goldstrom in McCann,
   p.104; Johnson, p.100.
51 ERO D/P 333/1/5, 8, 9; ERO D/P 192/1/
   18, 1837–51; Evans, p.336. Sutherland in
   Thompson, *Social Agencies*, pp.122–5.
52 CA28, 1836, 1847.
53 TA 51/1, 1841–52 (not all found guilty).
54 Bodley, p.35; TA32, 1852–67; ERO D/P 28/
   30/18–19.
55 *ES*, 26 October 1849.
56 Saffron Walden Town Mission journal,
   November– December 1861.

Chapter 12: No Man Careth for Our Souls

1 Saffron Walden Town Mission (hereafter
   SWTM) minutes, 7 April 1842.
2 ERO Q/SBb 380/66/1.
3 Rowntree, *Then and Now*, Chapter 7;
   Bebbington, p.16. Evangelicalism (capital
   E) was an eighteenth century movement
   which influenced all denominations, its
   common characteristics being conversion,
   activism, Biblicism and crucicentrism. The
   word, evangelism (small e) denotes efforts
   to promote the Gospel, often described as
   evangelical. Ecumenical refers to churches
   working together. Nonconformists and
   Dissenters are used interchangeably. 'New'
   Dissent was Methodism, and 'Old' Dissent
   other groups of Nonconformists.
4 PRO HO/129/8/210, 30 March 1851;
   Soloway, pp.436–7, 440.
5 Mus. 434 (SWTL), p.iv; SWTM journal,
   April 1862, pp.123–4; CA 1(ii) 25 August
   1823; ERO T/A 599/1–8, 13 November
   1837, 29 October 1845; Soloway, p.443.
6 ERO T/A 284/1–2, T/A 261/1/6–7, T/A
   284/2/1, T/A 284/2/2; Rowntree, *Then
   and Now*, pp.50–51; Brown, *Prosperity*,
   pp.119–20.
7 ERO T/A 284/1–2; ERO T/A 261/ 3/2;
   ERO T/A 261/1/17–19/1–2, 4; TA58,
   November 1831, March 1833, March 1834,
   January 1835, January & March 1836.
8 ERO T/A 284/1–2; ERO T/A 284/2/2,
   p108; Mary Whiteman, *SWH*, Autumn
   1981, p.113; Madonna, p.44.
9 Rowntree, *Then and Now*, pp.49–50.
10 ERO T/B 495/8, 2 April 1819; SWMA
   40504, letter George Eachus to Nat Catlin.
11 ERO T/B 495/8, various dates; *ES*, 18
   November 1836.
12 Monkton, *Rural Mission*, p.5 (SWTL); ERO
   T/B 495/8, various dates; H.C. Stacey,
   SWH, Spring 1985, p.85.
13 ERO T/B 495/5, trust deed, 28 February
   1807; ERO T/B 495/48, 1838–1905; Brown,
   Prosperity, p.118.
14 Witard, pp.45, 64.
15 ERO RG 4/783–5, RG 785; General Baptist
   records (TA uncat.), letter George
   Smallfield to James Humphreys, 28 June
   1827; Rowntree, *Then and Now*, pp.53–4; see
   also Maddams, *Mission Unfinished*, his
   book, *Unvanquished*, articles in *SWH* and
   revised account, *Our Church's Story*.
16 General Baptist records (uncat.), correspondence, various dates; H.C. Stacey,
   SWH, Spring 1982, p.147; SWMA 40941; TA
   (uncat.) General Baptist records, correspondence 11 October 1821, 15 & 28 June
   1825.
17 Witard, pp.49, 64; SWMA 40982; White,
   Chronological, p.69; Rowntree, *Then and
   Now*, pp.52–3. Further information John
   Maddams.

18 J.E. Maddams, *SWH*, October 1975, pp.9–
    11; Mus. 500 (SWTL); SWMA 40149/ 40465,
    reports 1829/39.
19 Whitefield, p.292; John Wesley, *Journals*;
    Pollock, p.208.
20 *Methodist Recorder*, 5 March 1908, p.12; see
    also Holland Brown memoir (SWTL), also
    quoted in Rowntree, *Then and Now*.
21 *Methodist Recorder*, 5 March 1908, p.12;
    Player *Chronicles*, April 1828 (SWTL);
    SWMA 40193; H.C. Stacey, *SWH*, Novem-
    ber 1974, p.20; CA185.
22 Cooper, *Primitive Methodism* (SWTL);
    Cooper, *Primitive Methodists of Clavering*, in
    Faulkner & Finnegan (CD-ROM);
    Richardson, Chrishall booklet (SWTL); E.P.
    Thompson, p.41. 'Primitive' in this context
    meant 'prime', i.e. its adherents aimed to
    return to the traditions of early Methodists.
23 Petty, pp.431–5.
24 Petty, p.433; *PMM*, 1845, p.551; ERO Temp.
    A10222, Circuit Report, 1852.
25 Petty, p.433; ERO D/NM 3/5/1, 1860; ERO
    D/NM 3/2/1, account book, 1841–50.
26 For instance, *PMM*, 1845, pp.412, 611; 1847,
    p.561; 1851, p.368; 1853, p.453; Clavering
    chapel deeds, 1844–5; ERO Temp. 10222,
    Walden chapel members roll-books, 1846,
    1861, 1862; Obelkevich, pp.235–7, 244.
27 Spurgeon, p.87; *PMM*, 1846, p.91; ERO D/
    NM 3/5/1 1846, 1854, 1855; Petty, p.34.
28 *PMM*, 1848, pp.184–7, 750; 1851, p.373;
    Obelkevich, chapter 5.
29 ERO D/NM 3/2/1 & 3/3/1; ERO Temp.
    10222, Circuit Report, 1855.
30 SWTM journal, May 1862; *PMM* 1858,
    p.235.
31 Brown, *Prosperity*, pp.123–4; *PMM*, 1848,
    p.750; Hobsbawm & Rudé, pp.288–91;
    Newby, pp.64–6; Obelkevich, pp. 231, 245–
    6.
32 Ashby, pp.79–82; Gumbrell, vol. 1, p.199.
33 ERO T/A 599/1–8, 13 November 1837;
    Brown, *Prosperity*, pp.108–114.
34 *ES*, 1 March 1834, 16 August 1844; ERO T/
    A 599/1–8, various dates, 1820–3; CA1(2);
    ES, 2 August 1839, 20 March, 1 & 22 May,
    17 July 1840; Player, *Chronicles*, August
    1827.
35 ERO T/A 599/1–8, 5 August 1837.
36 ERO G/Sw Z.43, 29 July 1837; ERO G/Sw
    M1–2A, 25 November 1836, 26 November
    1836; Crowther, pp.128–9.
37 PRO MH/12/3706, 2 November, 2
    December 1836; G/Sw Z.43, 2 December
    1836.
38 PRO MH12/3706, letters 2 November 1836.
39 PRO MH12/3706, letters 2 & 17 April 1837;
    ERO G/Sw M1–2A, 3, 22 & 31 March 1837.
40 PRO MH 12/3706, 11 April, 15 July, 5
    August, 27 September, 6 November 1837;
    ERO G/Sw M1–2A, various dates in 1837,
    3 & 10 May, 21 June 1839; ERO G/Sw Z.43,
    29 July 1837.
41 *Kent & Essex Mercury*, 12 July 1832;
    compare *ES*, 9 June 1832 with 16 June 1837.
42 PRO HO/52/29, letter 9 May 1836; SWMA
    40479, letter 12 July 1834; Tate, *Parish
    Chest*, p.93.
43 *EH*, 12 July 1834 (SWMA 40479); *ES*, 8 & 15
    July 1831, 1 March & 24 May 1834, 15
    January 1836.
44 *ES*, 22 January & 18 November 1836, 29
    March 1839, 1 & 22 May 1840; SWMA
    40911; Evans, pp.250, 253–4; Monkton,
    Rural Mission (unpub.), pp.22–4; Tate,
    Parish Chest, pp.93, 135; Brown, *Prosperity*,
    p.113. A lot of the parish land was tithe-
    free, as it had once been owned by Walden
    Abbey.
45 Mus 499/500 (SWTL); SWMA 40504, letter
    26 May 1826; SWMA 40465.
46 *ES*, 1 April 1842, 28 March & 2 May 1845;
    ERO T/B 493/35; Monkton, *Rural Mission*.
47 SWTM, 1 February 1842; *ES*, 20 October
    1843.
48 Monkton, *Town Mission* (SWTL). Acknowl-
    edgement to David Monkton for access to
    his analysis of the Town Mission records.
49 The four missionaries over 20 years were
    Peter Johnson (1842–50), Stephen Harber
    (1850–55), William Perry (1855–61) and
    Solomon Barton (1861–3).
50 *ES*, 12 November 1847; Monkton, *Town
    Mission*, p.21.
51 SWTM minutes, 18 May 1848, 4 April 1850,
    July 1858, 5 May 1859; loose paper inside
    minute book.
52 SWTM minutes, 10 September 1861;
    journal November 1861–October 1862.
53 SWTM minutes, January 1862 & journal,
    April 1862; note inside journal.
54 SWTM journal, December 1861, June,
    August 1862.
55 SWTM journal, October 1862.
56 SWTM journal, July & September 1862.
57 SWTM minutes, 6 July 1843, 4 November
    1852, 4 October 1855.
58 SWTM journal, April, June, August &
    October 1862.
59 SWTM minutes, 1 January & 9 April 1863.
60 SWTM minutes, 2 July & 22 October 1863;
    Monkton *Rural Mission*, p.33.

Bibliography

Unless otherwise stated, all primary archives are Saffron Walden.

Saffron Walden Town Archives (CA, OC & TA)

CA u/n	Workhouse provisions, 1829–35.
CA u/n	Poor Law accounts, 1829–82.
CA1 (ii)	Alterations to Parish Church, 1820–42.
CA3	Watch Committee, 1819–44.
CA4(i)	Police Force, 1849–57.
CA5	Map of constables' beats, 1856.
CA6 (i)	Association for Suppressing Sedition, 1792.
CA6(ii)	Draft presentment, Tom Paine's *Rights of Man*, 1792.
CA8	County gaol, transportation documents, various dates.
CA12	Fire Brigade documents, 1827–1927.
CA13	Presentments, 1736–1836.
✓ CA15/16	Coroner's inquisitions, 1748–1864.
CA17	Depositions, 1828–71.
CA21	Poor Law accounts re removals, 1829–82.
CA22	Settlement examinations, 1747–1831.
CA23/24	Removal certificates, 1690–1847.
CA28	Inability to pay rates, 1837–47.
CA29	Dispute re jury room, 1832.
CA31	Increase in burgesses, 1835–54.
CA34 (i)	Treasurer's accounts, 1836–50.
CA75	Newspaper cuttings, c.1838–9.
✓ CA 76	Correspondence re Privilege Shoot, c.1858.
CA82	Literary & Scientific Institution, centenary, 1932.
CA86	Allotments, various accounts, 1830–32.
CA87	Bill of costs, Braybrooke rates appeal, 1838.
CA106	Census accounts, 1831
CA144	Overseers' accounts, 1833.
CA 145	Overseers' expenses, 1815–58.
CA148	Thurgood's bill of costs, 1839.
CA 173	Special constables' accounts to quell riots, 1830.
CA184 (iii)	Sale poster, old workhouse, 1839.
CA185	Wesleyan Chapel, Castle Hill, certificate, 1836.
CA188	Audley End fair, letter 1832.
✓ CA208	Letter re nuisance of cattle market, 1827.
CA 217	Letter re quarter sessions, 1836.
CA229	Opinion re town clerk/ mayor, 1811.
CA275	Diversion of footpath.
✓ CA278	Farm wages at Walden, 1844–84.
CA283	Booklet on Abbey Lane Congregational Church (1933).
CA285	Provident & Friendly Institute papers, est. 1838.
CA299	Poster of Friendly Society, George Inn, 1831.
CA356	Abolition of the August fair, 1871.
CA362	Correspondence of C. T. Masters, undated return.
CA388	Termination notice to Samuel Francis, gaoler, 1854.
CA396	Benevolent Society records, from 1828.
CA406 (i)	Deed of settlement, Gas Company, 1837 .
CA412(ii)	Papers relating to British School.
CA434	Papers relating to National School.
CA435	Allotments papers & notebook, 1830s.
CA447	Lying-in charity records, 1867–1949.
CA449	National School logbook, 1817–41.

OC1–3	Overseers' receipts & payments, 1835–68.
OC4–12	Surveyor of Highways' accounts, 1836–49.
OC21	Board of Surveyors minutes, 1843–52.
TA (uncat.)	Letter from F.H. Maud, 1954.
TA (uncat.)	Hill Street General Baptist records.
TA4	Surveyor's weekly accounts, 1829–33.
TA6–15	Parish Meeting books, 1793–1837.
TA16–21	Overseers' weekly payments, 1781–1835.
TA22	Overseers' casual relief payments, 1786–1810.
TA23	Vestry casual relief payments, 1833–5.
TA24	Parish receipts & payments, 1838–48 .
? ✓ TA27	Pennystone Charity accounts, 1751–1870.
TA28	Falkland's Charity, 1776–1870.
TA29	Broomfield's Charity minutes, 1836–62 .
TA30	Broomfield's Charity accounts, 1683–1871.
TA31	Suffolk & Turner's Charity, 1701–1871.
TA32	Erswell's Charity candidates, 1852–67.
TA33	Twenty Shillings money, 1848–60.
TA34	Erswell's, Turner's & Sparrow's accounts, 1824–70.
TA38	Edmund Turner's Charity accounts, 1750–1870.
TA39	Turner's, Sparrow's & Erswell's Charity accounts, 1664–1824.
TA40	Turner's Charity, 1820–70.
TA 46–51/1	Quarter Sessions minutes, 1747–1900.
TA58	Town Sessions Book, 1815–36.
TA59	Town Court Book, 1817–45.
TA60	Police Journal, 1855–7.
TA63	Elections of mayor, etc., 1818–35.
TA64	Corporation Book of Orders, 1694–1817.
TA65	Fire brigade records, 1831–1906.
— TA67–8	Spade husbandry and Allotments, 1829–1909.
TA87	Corporation of Walden, 1685–1976.
TA88	Grammar School accounts, 1802–79.
TA90	Inspectors' accounts, 1837–40.
TA 96 (340A)	Charity School minutes, 1743–1883.
TA103	Corporation minutes, 1831–5.
TA104	Borough Council minutes, 1835–56.
TA178	Poll Book, 1840–50.
TA191	Lighting borough, inspectors' minutes, 1836–54.
TA 234–6	Overseers' weekly payments, 1797–1820.
TA236/1–2	Overseers' weekly payments, 1821–36.
— TA239	Enclosure Award & Plan, 1823.
TA316	Broomfields Charity, apprenticeship vouchers, 1684–1832.
TA318	Turners Charity, apprenticeship vouchers, etc.
TA406	Licence from Abbot for teaching, 1423.
TA 425	Grammar School trustees' minutes, 1844–79.
TA (uncat.)	Grammar School admissions register, 1844–71.
TA441 (iii)	Receipt for materials, malt mill & Market Cross, 1818.

Saffron Walden Museum Archives (SWMA)

40020	Papers re railway, 1835 etc.
40143	Newscuttings, various dates.
40149	Auxiliary Bible Society, 1827–44.
40154	Book Society rules, 1814.
40163	Mental Improvement Society, 1837.
40178	Volunteer Fire Brigade papers, from 1818.
40183	Riots at Ely & Littleport, 1816; police history.
40188	Rules of Prosecution Association, 1840/1879.
40193	Royal pardon, 1828.

40195	Letter re poachers, 1829.
40198	Gaol survey, c.1810.
40219	Election addresses, 1832.
40221	Cuckingstool End Street, 1818.
40363	Election addresses, political posters, 1832, 1848, etc.
40369	Reformers' Registration Club rules, 1835.
40380 —	Allotments papers, 1830–1.
40381 —	Allotments annual reports, 1830–1.
40383	Extract from *Quarterly Review* re allotments, 1831.
40389	John Player, booklet on Provident Society, 1838.
40394	Rules of New Union Society, 1822.
40411	Charities in Saffron Walden, 1818.
40424	Benevolent Society papers, c.1828.
40429	Guardians notice, John Player, 1838.
40435	Plan to regulate employment of labouring poor, 1830.
40440	Letter from Lord Braybrooke to Guardians, 1838.
40454/8	John Player papers, various dates.
40459	Gallow Hill improvements, 1829–30.
40462	Working population of Saffron Walden, 1838.
40465	Missionary Society, 1825–33.
40474	Philosophical Society papers, 1826.
40477 ☞	Allotments and spade husbandry, 1829–44.
40478	Cattle market removal, papers 1829–32.
40479	John Player papers, 1830s, etc.
40481	Literary Institute papers, 1821–38.
40482	Queen Victoria's Coronation dinner, 1838.
40483	Poor Law papers, 1834–7
40486	John Player letters & addresses, 1835–41.
40488	Board of Health and cholera papers, 1831–2.
40489	Clothing Bank papers, 1831–45.
40493	Correspondence re emigration to Canada, 1834.
40494	John Player notebook of a magistrate, 1840–5.
40497	Account of John Player's life by Ecroyd Smith, pre-1909.
40498	Education survey, 1825; factory schools petition, 1835.
40499	Petition & notes re retention of Quarter Sessions, 1836–8.
40500/04	John Player correspondence, various subjects,1803–37.
40517	Archer family tree.
40659	Papers re Savings Bank, 1817–93.
40667	Provident & Friendly Institution, 1838.
40668	Papers re Clothing Bank.
40689	Elementary education, 1817–1910.
40799	Sale catalogue of effects of late C. Baron, undated.
40911	Braintree church rate subscriptions, 1837–8.
40941	Pamphlet on Cundill affair, 1824.
40982	Proceedings against Joseph Player, 1822.
41000	Museum catalogue, 1845.
41456	Overseers papers, Burdett dispute, 1827.
41522	Unpublished letter to *The Times*, 1830.
41570/1	Correspondence, Charles Porter & John Player, 1831.

Saffron Walden Town Library Archives (SWTL)

Barker, L.D., *Saffron Walden, Essex: personal names and locations from Rate Books 1790–1891 & Census 1841–91 in Castle Street, Museum Street, Church Street* (unpub. paper, 1999).
Bible Society Auxiliary minutes, 1812–25, and subscriptions, 1825–31 (Mus 499/500).
Bocock, N. Willett, *The Abbey Lane Congregational Church 1665–1933* (1933).
Braybrooke, Lord, *The History of Audley End* (1836).
Browne, R., Population Census, Saffron Walden, mss. (1811).
Census of Saffron Walden, 1841–61 (microfilm).

Clavering Village Guide, Clavering Parish Council (c.1976).

Collins, Gillian, *Education Matters: Excerpts from the Saffron Walden College Magazines 1899–1995.*

Cooper, Jacqueline, *Primitive Methodism in the Saffron Walden Area from 1810–1900* (Saffron Walden Local History Competition unpub. essay, 1995).

Coronation 1838: insert to blue copy of Braybrooke *History* (1838)

Holland Brown J., *Memoir of Miss Berger* (1879).

Horticultural Society report (E SAFF 635).

Hughes, Barbara, *The Saffron Walden Literary & Scientific Institute: its Place in the Cultural Life of the Town, 1832–1930* (Saffron Walden Local History Competition unpub. essay, 1993).

Maddams, J.E., *Unvanquished: a History of the Baptists of Saffron Walden and their Antecedents, 1550–1975* (1975).

Maddams, J.E., *Mission Unfinished: 1550 to 1990 Baptist Witness at Saffron Walden* (1989).

Maddams, J.E., *Our Church's Story: Saffron Walden Baptist Church* (1998).

Monkton, David, *An Ecumenical Study of Mid–nineteenth century Rural Mission in East Anglia* (unpub. essay).

Monkton, David, *Saffron Walden Town Mission: an Early Ecumenical Venture in Saffron Walden, 1842–1863* (1970).

Muilman, P., *History of Essex by a Gentleman*, vol. IV (1771).

Muir, Jane, *Saffron Walden in 1851: a study based on census data* (unpub. essay, 1985).

Player, John, *Chronicles, 1799–1826* .

Player, John, *Sketches of Saffron Walden and its Vicinity* (1845).

Redford, Rev Josiah, lectures (Mus. 434, 1838).

Richardson, Margaret, *From Upwell to Chrishall*, (c.1988).

Robinson, William, *A Brief Account of the Festival 1814* (1814).

Saffron Walden History (*SWH*: Journal of Saffron Walden Historical Society),1974–90.

Saffron Walden Town Mission minutes 1842–62 & journal 1861–2.

Saffron Walden Vestry Employment Committee papers, 1829 & 1832.

Saffron Walden Vestry, *The State of the Poor* (mss., 1829).

Saffron Walden *Yearbook* (1853).

Stacey Album, vol. 5.

Stacey, H.C. *History of the Walden Charities* (1967).

Essex Record Office Chelmsford (ERO)

* Currently available in microform at the ERO Archive Access Point, Saffron Walden Town Hall.

D/DBy A230/266–73, 296, 305–08/ 344	Audley End account books, various dates.
D/DBy C35	Letter from John Collins to Lord Braybrooke, 1842 .
D/DBy E19A/ 19E/33/ 40	Audley End estate papers, various dates.
D/DBy 049	Mechanics & labourers employed at weekly wages, 1832.
D/DBy380/66	Letter, Braybrooke to William Bullock, 1800.
D/DBy/Z79	Newscuttings book kept by 3rd Lady Braybrooke.
*D/CT 378A	Tithe Award, 1842.
*D/DAd 12/13	Chipping Walden Manor Court books 1808–22, 1823–31.
D/DCm Z8	Savings Bank records.
*D/DHt 7408/2	Gibson public houses in N.W. Essex, 1838.
D/DU 66/12	Deeds of Saffron Walden, 1771.
D/DU 66/25,27, 28	Mortgage, Butter Market, 1822.
D/NM 3/2/1 & 3/3/1	Primitive Methodist Circuit accounts, 1841–70.
D/NM 3/5/1	Primitive Methodist Circuit annual reports, from 1846.
*D/P 18/25/1	Ashdon Charities accounts, 1745–1863.
D/P 28/30/18–19	Diocesan Returns of Education, 1839.
*D/P 192/1/9	Baptism register, 1813–29.
*D/P 192/1/15	Burial register, 1840–92.
*D/P 192/1/18	Marriage register, 1837–51.
*D/P 333/1/5, 8, 9	Clavering marriage registers, 1800–1900.
D/P 333/8/1	Clavering Vestry Minutes, 1724–76.

D/Z 71	Chelmsford Provident Society, from 1818.
*G/Sw M1–14	Guardians minutes, 1835–80.
*G/Sw W56	Workhouse burial records, 1836–48.
G/Sw Z.1–4	Guardians ledgers, 1835–45.
G/Sw Z.41	Guardians cash account book, 1835–6.
G/Sw Z.43	Guardians letterbook, from 1835.
J/P 8/1	Walden Police Order Book, 1840s.
*PH 4/140/1–4	Boys' British School managers minutes, 1838–1938 .
*Q/RDc 25A	Enclosure Award, 1812.
*RG 4/783–5	General Baptists burials and births records, 1826–37.
Q/SBb 380/66/1–3	Threatening letters, 1800.
Q/RSF6	Returns of Friendly Societies to Quarter Sessions, 1810–31.
Q/SBb 467/51	Essex Quarter Sessions, appeal against poor rate, 1822.
Q/SBb 502/3/1	Essex Quarter Sessions, 'Swing' indictments, 1831.
Q/SBb 502/21	Essex Easter Sessions, 1831.
Q/SBb 502/45	Newport House of Correction, calendar, 1831.
Q/SBb 502/98	Essex Quarter Sessions, previous convictions, 1831.
Q/SPb/20	Essex Process Book, 1824–31.
*T/A 261 & 284	Society of Friends, Thaxted monthly meeting, various records.
*T/A 419/12	Quarter Sessions minutes, 1836–1900.
*T/A 599/1–8	St Mary the Virgin, vestry minutes, 1822–96.
*T/A 623/1–5	Natural History Society trustees' minutes, 1832–41.
*T/B 493/35	Auxiliary Tract Society minutes, 1829–43.
*T/B 495	Abbey Lane Independents, various records.
T/A 778/30	Archdeaconry of Essex Returns, 1810.
Temp. A10222	Primitive Methodist Circuit Roll-books, from 1851.
Poor Law Reports	1833, Ashurst Majendie; 1834, Alfred Power.

Other Repositories

(BFSS: British & Foreign Schools Society; CER: Church of England Records Centre; GM: Guildhall Museum; PRO: Public Record Office)

BFSS Annual Reports 1818–43.
BFSS Correspondence files, various dates.
BFSS Education Commission circular D, 1858.
BFSS Inspector's reports on Saffron Walden British School, 1847–8 and appendix.
BFSS Preliminary statement for Saffron Walden Boys' British School, 1846.
BFSS Committee of Council on Education reports, 1839–47.
BFSS Report on Walden parochial union schools, 4 May 1848.
CER: Saffron Walden school files.
CER: National Schools Society Annual Reports, 1815–36.
CER: National Schools Society, Essex branch annual reports 1812–31.
GM: Mss 13743, Christ's Hospital archives.

PRO CHAR 2	Piece No.87, Charity Commission, letters re Saffron Walden charities, 1818–37.
PRO FS1/149	Returns of Friendly Societies
PRO HO 52/7, 52/17, PRO 52/29	Letters from Saffron Walden to Home Office, 1830–36.
PRO HO 75/6	*Hue & Cry*, 20 February 1833.
PRO HO/129/8/210	Religious Census, 1851 (copy in ERO).
PRO MH12/3706–10	Guardians correspondence with Poor Law Commission, 1834–50.
PRO WO 13/4320	Essex Volunteer Corps 1803–5, pay lists (information L.D. Barker).

Printed Sources

Annals of Agriculture, XXXIV, 1800.
Cambridge Chronicle, 1816–35.
Chelmsford Chronicle,1772–1836.

Essex Chronicle, 1837.
Essex & Herts Mercury, 1833.
Essex & Suffolk Times, 1839.
Essex Archaeology (1998) 'Poor Law buildings — an Essex survey'.
Essex Herald (EH), 1829–44.
Essex Mercury, 1833.
Essex Standard (ES), 1831–51.
Gentleman's Magazine, 1800.
Herts & Essex Observer, 1867, 1898, 1923.
Kent & Essex Mercury, 1832–3.
London Gazette, 1825.
Methodist Recorder, 5 March 1908.
Morning Chronicle, 1849.
Norwich Mercury, 1816.
Pigot's *Directory* for Essex: 1823, 1832, 1839, 1848.
Poor Mans Guardian, 1835.
Primitive Methodist Magazine (PMM), 1845–58.
Quarterly Review, Vols 41 & 44.
Saffron Walden Weekly News, 1961.

Parliamentary Papers (PP)

1818   LII, Select Committee on Education of the Poor.
1821   XI, Abstract of Population Returns, p.107.
1821   XV, Population: enumeration & parish registers, pp.102–3.
1824   XXXVIII, Poor Law Commissioners, appendix E on vagrancy.
1825   XIX, Abstract of Returns, Labourers' wages.
1831   I, Enumeration abstract, pp.196–7.
1831   XXXVI, Accounts & Papers: returns under the Population Act.
1833   III, Accounts & Papers: Population abstract, p.105.
1833   XXXVI, Population of Great Britain, vol I.
1834   XXX–XXXIV, Poor Law Commissioners: Rural Queries.
1835   XXIII, Report of Royal Commission on Municipal Corporations.
1835   XXVI, Pt. IV, Reports from Poor Law Commissioners.
1835   XXXV, Poor Law Reports: survey of Essex, Cambs & Herts.
1835   XL, Accounts & Papers re Municipal Commission, pp.407–519.
1835   XLI, Education Enquiry Abstract, vol Vll Appendix.
1836   XXIX, Poor Law Commissioners, with appendices.
1837   XXVIII, Boundaries of certain boroughs & towns, pp.135–9.
1837   XLIV, Municipal Commission, pp.15–35.
1837   LI, Returns of Friendly Societies.
1839   XLI, Committee of Privy Council on Education, pp.1–2.
1840   XXII, Hand-loom weavers.
1841   III, Population, enumeration abstract, p.97.
1841   IV, Population, age abstract, pp.84–5.
1843   VII, Labouring Poor (Allotments of Land).
1846   IX, Select Committee, pt 1 & Criminal Returns 1835–42.
1851   I, Population tables, 1801–51, pp.7, 22.
Extracts from the reports of the Commissioners concerning charities in Essex Vol. XI (1824, 1832–34, 1837).

Journal articles & books (*local interest)

Adamson, J.W., *English Education 1789–1902* (1964).
*Addison, William, *Audley End* (1953).
Archer John E., *By A Flash and a Scare: Incendiarism, Animal Maiming and Poaching In East Anglia 1815–1870* (1990).

Archer John, 'The nineteenth century allotment: half an acre and a cow' in *Economic History Review*, vol 50, pt. 1 (1997).

Armstrong, Alan, *Farmworkers: a social and economic history 1770–1980* (1988).

Ashby, M.K., *Joseph Ashby of Tysoe, 1859–1919* (1961).

*Barker, M.M., *Ordnance Survey of England & Wales, Saffron Walden District*, 1913.

Barnett, D.C., 'Allotments and the problem of rural poverty 1780–1840', in Jones & Mingay, op.cit.

Baugh, D.A., 'The cost of poor relief in south-east England 1790–1834' in *Economic History Review*, vol 28 (1975), p.64.

Bebbington, D.W., *Evangelicalism in Modern Britain: a History from the 1730s to the 1980s* (1989).

*Benton, G.M.'The early progress of elementary education in Saffron Walden' in *Essex Review*, vol 29 (1920), p.21 (copy in SWMA 40686).

Blaug, Mark, 'The myth of the old poor law and the making of the new', in *Economic History Review* vol 23, 1963.

*Bodley, R. D.'Elementary education of the poor in the early nineteenth century', *Essex Review*, LVII, p.28.

Bohstedt, J., *Riots and Community Politics in England & Wales 1790–1810* (1983).

*Booker, John, *Essex and the Industrial Revolution* (1974).

*Braybrooke, Richard, Lord, *The History of Audley End* (1836).

*Brown, A.F.J., *Essex at Work 1700–1815* (1969).

Brown A.F.J., *Essex People 1750–1900, from their diaries, memoirs and letters* (1972).

Brown, A.F.J., *Colchester 1815–1914* (1980).

*Brown, A.F.J., *Chartism in Essex and Suffolk* (1982).

*Brown, A.F.J., *Meagre Harvest: the Essex Farmworkers' Struggle against Poverty 1750–1914* (1990).

*Brown, A.F.J., *Prosperity and Poverty: Rural Essex, 1788–1815* (1996).

Brundage, Anthony, *The Making of the New Poor Law. The Politics of Inquiry, Enactment and Implementation, 1832–39* (1978).

Burchardt, Jeremy, 'Rural social relations, 1830–50: Opposition to Allotments for Labourers' in *Agricultural History Review*, 45, pt. 2 (1997), pp.165–75.

Burn, W.L., *The Age of Equipoise* (1964).

Charlesworth, Andrew (ed.) *An Atlas of Rural Protest in England 1548–1900* (1983).

Charlesworth, Andrew, *Social Protest in a Rural Society: the Spatial Diffusion of the Captain Swing Disturbances* (1979).

*Cooper, Jacqueline, 'The Primitive Methodists of Clavering, Essex, 1841–61: factors affecting their formation, rise and decline', CD-ROM (CDR0008) in Faulkner & Finnegan, 1996.

Crompton, Frank, *Workhouse Children* (1997).

Crouch, David & Ward, Colin, *The Allotment: its Landscape and Culture* (1988).

Crowther, M.A., *The Workhouse System 1836–1929* (1981).

Curtis S.J. & Boultwood, M.E.A., *An Introductory History of English Education since 1800* (1960).

*Curtis, Gerald, *The Story of the Sampfords* (1981).

Davidoff, Leonore & Hall, Catherine, *Family Fortunes: Men and Women of the English Middle Class, 1780–1850* (1987).

*Denson, John, *A Peasant's Voice to Landowners*. (1830, reprinted 1991).

*Digby, Anne, 'The labour market and the continuity of social policy after 1834: the case of the Eastern Counties' in *Economic History Review*, vol 28, 1975.

*Digby, Anne, *Pauper Palaces* (1978).

*Digby, Anne, *The Poor Law in Nineteenth Century England and Wales* (1982).

*Digby, Anne, 'The agricultural labourers' protests in East Anglia in the 1840's', in Charlesworth, *Atlas*, op.cit. (1983).

Donajgrodski, A.P. (ed.), *Social Control in Nineteenth Century England* (1977).

Dunbabin, J.P., *Rural Discontent in Nineteenth Century Britain* (1974).

Eastwood, David, *Governing Rural England: Tradition and Transformation in Local Government 1780–1840* (1994).

*Edsal N.C., *The Anti Poor Law Movement* 1834–44 (1971).

*Elcoat, Geoffrey, *A Brief History of The Vicars of Thaxted* (1999).

Emsley, Clive, *Crime and Society in England 1750–1900* (1987).

Englander, David, *Poverty and Poor Law Reform in Britain: from Chadwick to Booth, 1834–1914* (1998).

Evans E.J., *The Forging of the Modern State: Early Industrial Britain 1783–1870* (1983).

*Everett, Martin & Newman, Howard, *Saffron Walden: a Pictorial History* (1998).

*Everett, Martyn, *Saffron Walden in the English Civil War* (1994).

*Everett, Zofia, *1 Myddylton Place* (2000).

*Faulkner, L. & Finnegan, R. (eds.), *Project reports in family and community history*, CD-ROM annual series (CDR0008, 1996), Open University.

*Fell Smith, C., *A short history of Saffron Walden School 1317–1929'* in *Victoria County History of Essex*, vol 2.

Fisk, Audrey, 'Diversity within the Friendly Society Movement 1834–1911: the Value to Community Studies, in *Family & Community History*, Vol. 3/1,May 2000.

Fowler, Simon, *Philanthropy and the Poor Law in Richmond 1834–1871*, Richmond Local History Society Special Paper No 3 (1991).

Fraser, Derek, *Urban Politics in Victorian England: the Structure of Politics in Victorian Cities* (1979).

Fraser, Derek, *Power and Authority in the Victorian City* (1979).

Gatrell, V.A.C., 'Crime, authority and the policeman-state' in Thompson, *Social agencies*, op.cit.

*Gibson, Robert, *Annals of Ashdon: No Ordinary Village* (1988).

Glyde, John, *The Moral Social and Religious Condition of Ipswich in the Middle of the Nineteenth Century* (1850, reprinted 1971).

Goldstrom, M.,'The content of education and the socialization of the working class child 1830–1860' in McCann, op.cit.

Goose, Nigel, 'Workhouse populations in the mid-nineteenth century: the case of Hertfordshire' in *Local Population Studies* No 62, Spring 1999, pp52–69.

Gorsky, Martin, 'Experiments in Poor Relief: Bristol 1816–1818 in *The Local Historian*, vol 25, No. 1 (1995).

Gosden, Peter, *The Friendly Societies in England 1815–1875* (1961).

Grieve, Hilda, *The Sleepers and the Shadows: Chelmsford: a Town, its People and its Past* Vol 2, *From Market Town to Chartered Borough 1608–1888'* (1994).

*Gumbrell, Jean, *Down Your Street*, vols 1 (1989) & 2 (1992).

Gyford, Janet, *Men of Bad Character: the Witham Fires of the 1820s* (1991).

Halevy, Elie, *A History of the English People 1830–1841* (1927).

Hammond, J.L. & Barbara, *The Village Labourer 1760–1832: a Study of the Government of England before the Reform Bill* (1911, reprint 1995).

Hay, D. & Snyder, F. (eds), *Policing and Prosecution in Britain, 1750–1850* (1989).

Hennock, E.P. 'Central/local government relations in England: an outline, 1800–1950' in *Urban History Yearbook* (1982).

Hitchcock, Tim, King, Peter & Sharpe, Pamela (eds), *Chronicling Poverty: the Voices and Strategies of the English Poor, 1640–1840* (1997).

Hobsbawm E.J., *The Age of Revolution 1789–1848* (1962).

*Hobsbawm, E.J. & Rudé, George, *Captain Swing* (1969).

Holderness, B.A. & Turner, M. (eds), *Land, Labour & Agriculture 1700–1920* (1991).

Holdsworth, W.A. *The Handy Book of Parish Law* (1859, reprinted 1995).

Hopkins, Harry, *The Long Affray: the Poaching Wars 1760–1914* (1986).

Horn, Pamela *The Rural World 1780–1850: Social Change in the English Countryside* (1980).

*Horne, H.O., *A History of Savings Banks* (1947).

Howkins, Alun, *Reshaping Rural England: a Social History 1850–1925* (1991).

*Hussey, Stephen & Swash, Laura, *Horrid Lights: Nineteenth Century Incendiarism in Essex* (1994).

Johnson, R. 'Educational Policy and Social Control', *Past & Present* (49), p.109.

Jones, E.L. & Mingay, G.E. (eds), *Land, Labour and Population in the Industrial Revolution* (1967).

Jones, David, 'Village radicalism in East Anglia 1800–50' in Dunbabin, op.cit.

Jones, M.G., *The Charity School Movement* (1938).

Kidd, A.J., 'Philanthropy and the "Social History" Paradigm' in *Social History* 21 (2), May 1996.

King, Peter, 'Gleaners, farmers and the failure of legal sanctions in England 1750–1850' in *Past & Present*, 125 (1989).

*King, Peter, 'Prosecution Associations and their importance in eighteenth century Essex' in Hay & Snyder, op.cit. (1989).

*Knott, John, *Popular Opposition to the 1834 Poor Law* (1986).

Land, Neville, *Victorian Workhouse: a Study of the Bromsgrove Union Workhouse 1836–1901* (1990).

Landau, Norma, 'Who was subjected to the Laws of Settlement? Procedure under the Settlement Laws in eighteenth century England' in *Agricultural History Review*, 43, pt. 2 (1995).

Laqueur, T.W., *Religion and Respectability: Sunday Schools and Working Class Culture 1780–1850* (1976).

Lord, Evelyn, 'The Friendly Society Movement and the Respectability of the Rural Working Class' in *Rural History*, vol. 8, No. 2 (October 1997), p. 167.

*Ludgate, E.M., *Clavering & Langley 1783–1983* (1984).

*Madonna, P. (ed.) *Saffron Walden 1286–1986* (1986).

Matthews P.W. & Tuke, A.W., *History of Barclays Bank*, 1926.

*Maud, F.H., 'Notes on an Essex Canal', *Essex Review*, LIV, pp.143–5 (1945).

McCann, Philip (ed.), *Popular Education and Socialization in the nineteenth century* (1977).

Midwinter, E., *Nineteenth Century Education*, Seminar Studies in History (1970), pp31–2.

*Miller, Christy, *'The History of Banks and Banking in Essex'* (1906).

Mills, Dennis R., 'Farm Statistics from census 1851–81' in *Agricultural History Review*, 47, pt.1 (1999).

*Monkton, David *'Saffron Walden Town Mission: an Early Ecumenical Venture in Saffron Walden 1842–1863*.

Morris, R.J. (ed.), *Class, Power & Social Structure in British Nineteenth Century Towns* (1986).

Morris, R.J., 'Voluntary Societies and British Urban Elites 1780–1850: an Analysis' in *The Historical Journal*, 26 (1), 1983, p.106.

Moselle, Boaz, 'Allotments, Enclosure and Proletarianisation in early Nineteenth Century Southern England' in *Economic History Review*, XLVIII, 3 (1995), p.491.

Munsche, P.B., *Gentlemen and Poachers: The English Game Laws 1671–1831* (1981).

Neave, David, *Mutual Aid in the Victorian Countryside: Friendly Societies in the Rural East Riding 1830–1912* (1991).

Newby, Howard, *The Deferential Worker: a Study of Farm Workers in East Anglia* (1977).

*Nurse, Bernard, Joy Pugh & Imogen Mollet (Angela Archer, ed.), *A Village in Time: the History of Newport, Essex* (1995).

Obelkevich, James, *Religion and Rural Society: South Lindsey 1825–1875* (1976).

Owen, David, *English Philanthropy 1660–1960* (1964).

Oxley, Geoffrey, *Poor Relief in England and Wales 1601–1834* (1974).

Peacock, A.J.,'Village Radicalism in East Anglia, 1800–50' in Dunbabin, op.cit.

Peacock, A.J., *Bread or Blood* (1965).

Perkin, Harold, *The Origins of Modern English Society 1780–1880* (1969).

*Petty, John, *The History of the Primitive Methodist Connexion* (1864).

*Pole, Len, *Britain in Old Photographs: Saffron Walden* (1997).

Pollock, John, *John Wesley* (1989).

*Pratt, J.T., *The History of Savings Banks* (1830).

*Preston, Harold, *'Early East Anglian Banks and Bankers* (1994).

Prochaska, Frank, 'Philanthropy' in Thompson, *Social Agencies*, op.cit. (1990).

*Pugh, Joy, 'The dreaded scourge: preventative medicine in Newport — 1772', *Newport News*, December 1988, p.58.

Reid, Andy, *Fire at the Workhouse: a Study in Cause and Motive'* (1988).

*Richardson, T.L., 'Agricultural Labourers' Wages and the Cost of Living in Essex 1790–1840' in Holderness & Turner, op.cit. (1991).

Riley, Pete, *Economic Growth: The Allotments Campaign Guide* (1979).

Rowley, Norman, SEAX Portfolio on education in Essex (1974)

Rowley , Norman, *Essex Elections and the Great Reform Bill*, SEAX Portfolio (1976).

*Rowntree C.B., *East Street Boys British School, Saffron Walden: The History of a Hundred Years* (1938).

*Rowntree, C.B. *Saffron Walden Then and Now* (1951).

Sanderson, M., *Education, Economic Change and Society in England 1780–1870* (1995).

*Scollan, Maureen, *Sworn to Serve: Police in Essex, 1840–1990* (1993).

Scott, James C., *Domination and the Arts of Resistance: Hidden Transcripts'* (1990).

Sharpe, Pamela, 'The bowels of compation: a labouring family and the law, c.1790–1834' in Hitchcock, King & Sharpe, op.cit. (1997).

Shaw, A.G.L., *Convicts and the Colonies: a Study of Penal Transportation from Great Britain & Ireland to Australia and Other Parts of the British Empire* (1966).

Slack, Paul, *The English Poor Law* (1990).

Snell K.D.M., 'The Sunday School Movement in England & Wales: Child Labour, Denominational Control & Working-Class Culture' in *Past & Present* 164 (August 1999), pp.122–68.

Snell, K.D.M., *Annals of the Labouring Poor: Social Change and Agrarian England, 1660–1900* (1985).

Sokoll, Thomas, *Household and Family among the Poor, the Case of two Essex communities in the late Eighteenth and Early Nineteenth centuries'* (1993).

Soloway, R.A., *Prelates and People, Ecclesiastical Social Thought in England 1783–1852* (1969).

Spurgeon, C.H., *Autobiography, The Early Years 1834–59*, vol 1 (1897).

Sutherland, Gillian, 'Education' in Thompson, *Social Agencies*, op.cit. (1990).

Sweet, Rosemary, *The English Town 1680–1840: Government, Society and Culture* (1999).

Tate W.E., *The Parish Chest: a Study of the Records of Parochial Administration in England* (1946, reprint 1983).

Tate, W.E., *The English Village Community and the Enclosure Movements* (1967).

Taylor, Joyce, *Joseph Lancaster: The Poor Child's Friend* (1996).

Tholfson, T.R., *Working Class Radicalism in Mid Victorian England* (1976).

Thompson, E.P., *The Making of the English Working Class* (1963).

Thompson, F.M.L. (ed.), *Social Agencies and Institutions*, Vol 3 in The Cambridge Social History of Britain, 1850–1950 (1990).

Thompson, F.M.L., *The Rise of Respectable Society* (1988).

Trainor, Richard, *Black Country Elites: the Exercise of Authority in an Industrialised Area 1830–1900* (1993).

*Upson, Anne, *A Historic Building Appraisal of Saffron Walden Workhouse, Radwinter Road, Saffron Walden, Essex*, AOC Archaeology report (1998).

Webb, Sidney & Beatrice, *English Poor Law History: Part II: the Last Hundred Years* (1963 edition).

Wells, Roger, 'The development of the English rural proletariat and social protest, 1700–1850' in *Journal of Peasant Studies*, VI (1979); & Charlesworth, A. in VIII (1980).

Wesley, John, *Journals* (ed. E.N. Curnock, 1909–16).

*White, Malcolm, *Saffron Walden's History: a Chronological Compilation* (1991).

Whitefield, George, *Journals* (repub. 1960).

*Williams, J.D., *Audley End: The Restoration of 1762–1797* (1966).

Williamson, Tom, *Polite Landscapes: Gardens and Society in Eighteenth Century England* (1995).

*Wilson, Stanley, *Saffron Crocus* (1972).

*Witard, Doris, *Bibles in Barrels: A History of Essex Baptists* (1962).

Worship, Vanessa, 'Cotton Factory or Workhouse: Poor Law Assisted Migration from Buckinghamshire to Northern England, 1835–1837' in *Family & Community History*, Vol 3/1, May 2000, pp.33–48.

Young, Arthur, *An inquiry into the propriety of applying wastes to the better maintenance and support of the poor'* (1801).

Young, Arthur, *General View of Agriculture of Essex* Vol I (1807).

Unpublished Theses

Amos, S.W., *Social Discontent and Agrarian Disturbances in Essex, 1795–1850*, (Durham, 1971).

Bengsten, Fiona, *An Inquiry into the Private Education of Females in Essex, Hertfordshire and Bedfordshire, c.1791–1861* (Cambridge, 1999).

Cooper, Jacqueline, *Philanthropy & Social Control in Saffron Walden, Essex, 1825–50* (Essex, 1997).

Eden, R.H. *An Account of the Development of Popular Education in the County of Essex during the Nineteenth Century* (Cambridge Institute of Education, 1961).

Gyford, Janet, *Men of Bad Character: Property Crime in Essex in the 1820s* (Essex, 1982).

Hills, Philip, *Division and Cohesion in the Nineteenth Century Middle Class: the Case of Ipswich 1830–1870* (Essex, 1988).

Hughes, Barbara, *The Saffron Walden Literary & Scientific Institute: its Place in the Cultural Life of the Town, 1832–1930* (Anglia, 1993).

King, Peter, 'Crime, Law and Society in Essex 1740–1820' (Cambridge, 1984).

Maddock, Alan, *State Compulsions and Children's School Attendance: Aspects of Public Elementary Education in and around Saffron Walden, c 1870–1901* (Cambridge, 1999).

Mahoney, Christine, *The History of Education... St Mary's Church of England Primary School* (North Riding College of Education, 1975).

Monteith, Dorothy, *Saffron Walden and its Environs: a Study in the Development of a Landscape* (Leicester, 1958).

Shrimpton, Colin, *The Landed Society and the Farming Community of Essex in the Late Eighteenth and Early Nineteenth Centuries* (Cambridge, 1965).

White, Malcolm, *A Nineteenth Century Empire? Parish Pump Power in Saffron Walden 1870–1902* (Essex, 1996).

Surname Index

General Index